The Encyclopaedia of Equestrian Exploration

Unabridged

Volume Three

A Study of the Geographic and Spiritual Equestrian Journey, based upon the Philosophy of Harmonious Horsemanship

by

CuChullaine O'Reilly F.R.G.S.
Founder of The Long Riders' Guild

Cover Design was conceived and created by Brian Rooney of R7 Media.

Cover Image – The cover image of Jamie Maddison appears courtesy of Matt Traver. In 2013 these exemplary British Long Riders prematurely concluded their journey across northern Kazakhstan rather than imperil the welfare of their horses.

Copy-editing by Lucy Leaf, American Long Rider.

Dedicated to
my beloved,
Basha Gypsy Moon

Table of Contents

Section Five – The Journey
Chapter 65
A Day in the Saddle

When do I wake up?

How much time should I allow to feed the horses, pack up camp, load the gear and tack up in the morning?

How should I start each day's journey?

How fast should I ride?

Do I walk, trot or canter?

Do I always stay in the saddle or should I walk sometimes?

How do I handle the pack horse?

What about lunch for me and the horses?

When do I water them?

How often do I rest the horses during a day's travel?

How many miles should I hope to travel every day?

What kind of obstacles and delays may await me?

When do I start to think about stopping for the day?

What kind of place should I look for?

How do I conclude the day's ride?

What must I never do when unsaddling at the end of the day?

Do I picket, hobble, highline, free range or stable my horse?

What should I check for before leaving my horse in a strange stable?

What do I feed the horse?

What if there is absolutely nothing to feed the horse?

Where will I sleep at night?

These aren't the kind of questions you answer from the comfort of your chair, while sitting beside the fireplace at home.

The answers to these mysteries can only be found in one place: the saddle!

Standing on the Threshold

Before setting off for Antarctica, Captain Robert Scott confided to his diary, "The worst part of an expedition was over when the preparation was finished."

Without realizing it, you've already begun your journey, for you stand on the threshold of a new way of life.

You too have laboured to improve your chances of success. Your dreams have been publicly declared. Potential difficulties have been studied. Suitable equipment has been purchased. Steady horses stand ready. The time has come to stop reading and start riding.

The four walls that previously trapped your soul will now fall away. Stars and Sun will reassert themselves into your blighted urban existence. Dawn and Dusk are no longer poetic terms seen on a page. They will become events of daily significance.

Excitement swirls and adrenalin intoxicates. The temptation is to ride away at the gallop, to surrender to the divine madness that has been calling to you during the preparation stage.

Swedish Long Rider, Countess Linde von Rosen, expressed it perfectly, when she wrote, "It is lovely this life. I feel it when I ride against the storm, and the horse rears up, his hooves dancing in the air. In that mad second, before my mount takes off in senseless fainting speed, I scream against the storm, I'm alive!"

Yet an equestrian journey is more than the outcry of our elemental passions and a gallop towards our longed for freedom.

The way we organize our daily affairs is of critical importance, as there is much to do and few enough hours in which to do them. To set off cloaked in enthusiasm is one thing. To arrive much later at our distant destination, wise and travel-stained, is a far different proposition.

Clues to how to maintain a daily and weekly routine can be found by studying the logistical strategies of the great cavalries, as the officers, veterinarians and pack masters of those organizations left records which demonstrate how to successfully accomplish each day's journey, one step at a time.

Forgotten Horses

Thanks to the onset of global equestrian amnesia, modern mankind has lost touch with how many horses recently inhabited our planet and what an impact they had on collective events. One such example was the Second World War.

History books tend to depict this global conflict as a highly mechanized war, one that depended solely upon planes, ships, tanks, trucks and jeeps for victory. Important battles are routinely cited so as to emphasize this biased view.

For example, 353 Japanese planes attacked sixteen American ships during the surprise attack on Pearl Harbor. Even larger numbers of machines took part during the savage battle of Kursk, when 2,928 German tanks fought 5,100 Soviet tanks, the result of which was 232,029 dead soldiers on both sides.

What is usually forgotten are the tremendous number of horses and mules which served all the combatants as cavalry, field artillery draft animals and in supply trains.

Italy, Hungary and Poland all relied on tens of thousands of horses for transport and cavalry purposes. France began the war with more than 500,000 horses serving in its military. But for mind-staggering numbers, one needs to look at Germany and Soviet Union.

The communist army employed 3.5 million horses in a variety of capacities. The Red cavalry remained active throughout the war, with the last Soviet cavalry action taking place in August, 1945, when communist cavalrymen rode across the Gobi Desert and invaded Peking.

If one nation epitomized the concept of mechanical efficiency in killing it was the German Third Reich. Fearsome Panzer tanks and Stuka dive-bombers convinced weaker nations that they would be destroyed if they tried to resist Hitler's blitzkrieg.

In actuality, the lethal "lightning war" was largely a deceptive myth created by German propaganda. Unlike the United States, Germany was never capable of mass-producing vehicles. Nor were there as many drivers among the general German population as there were in America.

Portraying the Nazis as ruthlessly efficient masters of millions of machines helped overcome a strong sense of American isolationism. What patriotic newspaper editors and legislators weren't eager to disclose was the German army's dependence upon horses.

Experts have estimated that the Nazi war machine employed 2,750,000 horses throughout the conflict.

But it wasn't Herr Hitler's horses that left us with an astonishing account of equestrian travel. It was Uncle Sam's mules.

5,000 Pack Mules

Even though the United States military had the highest degree of mechanization in the Second World War, that nation's military employed 56,000 horses and mules in a wide variety of combat zones.

Soon after landing in North Africa, the Americans used mules to transport supplies through the mountains of Tunisia. The invasion of Italy saw Americans relying on more than 14,000 mules to transport supplies into the rugged Apennine Mountains.

Nor were equines neglected in the Pacific theatre. The U.S. Army Veterinary Service purchased nearly 3,000 horses in Australia and shipped them to New Caledonia to work as pack animals. More than a thousand pack mules were sent from the United States to assist the marines fighting in New Guinea.

In all these cases, military commanders realized that mules and horses were able to negotiate rugged terrain that was inaccessible by vehicles.

Equine transport was also of tremendous importance in China. Like their Nazi allies, the Imperial Japanese Army relied heavily on horses and mules. Prior to the war Japan imported horses from Australia and Mongolia. Because neither nation could solve Japan's hunger for horses, after invading China the Imperial army confiscated more than half of all Chinese pack animals.

When America entered the war, Washington decided to aid its Chinese allies. A team of U.S. Army veterinarians purchased 2,000 horses in Tibet and transported the animals into China to be used as cavalry mounts.

The U.S. Army Veterinary Service also participated in what many consider to be an astonishing feat of equestrian travel, taking thousands of full-laden pack animals across nearly 1,000 miles of Burmese jungles.

In 1945 hundreds of American soldiers were brought together in Burma for a special equestrian mission. Their job was to organize, protect and accompany an enormous supply caravan being sent to China. Fifteen officers from the U.S. Army Veterinary Service were ordered to accompany the 5,397 pack mules tasked with carrying machine guns, mortars, ammunition and other supplies along the 1,154 kilometre (717 mile) long Burma Road that led to Allied military headquarters in western China.

Prior to setting off, the animals had been examined for infectious diseases and were newly shod. Twenty separate groups, consisting of between 200 and 300 pack animals, were formed. Each group then set off.

The march along the Burma Road took the mules across the Irrawaddy River and through the moist, tropical heat of the jungles, where torrential rains known as the monsoon turned the trail into a running stream of water. To help keep the mules moving, American aircraft dropped sacks of grain by parachute along the trail. But it didn't take long for the imported American pack animals to learn how to consume local banana and bamboo leaves.

When the caravan reached the mountains, temperatures plunged below freezing. At one point the terrain was so difficult that the caravan only made 3½ miles that day.

Disabilities along the way resulted from exhaustion and saddle sores. Some mules drowned while trying to cross one of the numerous rivers. Despite the difficulties the average rate of travel was 15 to 20 miles a day.

Only 142 animals, or 2.6 percent, died or were destroyed en route on account of disease. The majority of the mules and horses arrived in excellent condition.

Long Rider Lessons

What do American mules in Burma have to do with modern equestrian travel?

One of the contributing factors in the caravan's success was that the Army's wise veterinarians understood the importance of maintaining a daily schedule. By doing things carefully, in order, throughout the day, miles were gained, all the while decreasing the chances of inflicting hardship on the men or suffering on the animals.

They didn't wear khaki uniforms or carry guns, but two notable lady Long Riders understood and wrote about this enduring principle. Like the army veterinarians, they too had learned that the daily reality of equestrian travel is a great deal more physically demanding and time consuming than most people understand.

When Ella Sykes set off to ride across Persia in the late 19th century, it didn't take long for her to learn that the rigours of horse travel forced her to adhere to a strict daily schedule.

"The rule was to rise at 5 a.m., if not earlier, hastily dress and then emerge from the tent to attend to the horses. As soon as they began their morning meal, we ate our breakfast in the sharp morning air. The horses were then saddled and loaded. When everything was adjusted, and everyone ready to start, then we would walk out of camp leading our horses for nearly an hour before we began to ride. We usually marched for five hours and then halted for our lunch. We would lie by the water or in the shade of a tree if possible, as the sun by noon was very powerful. When the worst of the heat was over, we would ride for another three hours to camp. After dinner we turned in to dreamless slumbers."

At the conclusion of her 1939 ride from Cornwall to Scotland, Margaret Leigh left a similar warning for would-be Long Riders.

"In our kind of travel you have roads and maps and farms and a good climate, but you have also to do all your own animal management, packing, camping, cooking, photography, writing and surveying, as well as the mere physical activity of getting from one point to another. It is all great fun, but it takes time and effort, and the first few days will always be a trying period of experiment, delay, fatigue, and minor annoyance, in which a lively sense of humour is more valuable than the most foolproof equipment."

Margaret concluded, "Trial will show that on this kind of travel you will spend nearly as much time and effort on camp work and packing as on the march itself."

Regardless of where other Long Riders have journeyed, they have all left similar messages.

A German said, "One to one and a half hours should be allowed for getting ready to travel."

An American wrote, "I always set aside two hours every morning to feed, groom properly, pick out hooves, pack my gear and saddle up correctly."

A New Zealander advised, "No matter how far you ride, the two-hour morning routine won't get any shorter or easier."

How did these Long Riders learn to judge their time of departure against possible delays and that day's distance?

Rise and Shine – and Work

Let me give you a small hint. If you like to lie in bed, snuggled under the covers, drifting along in a warm dream – then don't sleep next to the horses.

Horses are notoriously early risers. They have no need to rely on an alarm clock, as their stomachs are calling for breakfast the moment the sun peeks up. Nor are they shy about hiding what they want. The moment they think you are awake, they'll start clamouring to be fed.

Even if you pretend to slumber, they'll stamp with impatience and shake the bells on their halters. They want their food and they want it – NOW. Eventually you'll learn that the easiest thing to do is surrender by getting up and preparing their breakfast.

Australian Long Rider Tim Cope had barely begun his journey from Mongolia to Hungary, when his horses taught him this noisy lesson.

"I was greeted at dawn by the deep neighing of the horses. Each morning as soon as there is movement in the tent they began talking to me. Sometimes it is because they are out of grass and need to be moved, but usually it just seemed like a 'good morning' gesture."

The exact time you rise will alter, depending upon the time of year. Regardless, plan on your day beginning early for two consistent reasons.

Because they go to sleep early, horses are early risers who have a demanding appetite.

Also, the horse should be allowed enough time to have comfortably finished his morning feed well before starting that day's travel.

Attending to the horse's needs is your immediate daily task. Avoiding any haste and excitement while doing so is the first order of the day

Dawn Inspection

If there are two or more of you travelling, then the first one with his boots on checks on the horses. Even if you're riding alone, this part of your routine never varies. Your brain may still be sleepy but your eyes need to automatically register the facts.

Does your horse stand alert and expectant when you approach? Is his head raised? Does he neigh when he sees you? As you approach closer, is his head up and are his eyes bright? Is there any irregularity in the way he moves? Can you see if his legs are free of wounds or swelling?

Does he act eager for his morning feed or is he lethargic, inattentive and anxious? Has he rested quietly or has he been chewing on a nearby wooden surface during the night, i.e. a stable door, tree or fence post?

Before you begin to prepare his morning feed, look for evidence that he finished all of his feed from last night's feeding. Is his manure well-formed or does he show signs of diarrhoea? Can you tell if he has drunk during the night?

Morning Feed

The morning routine depends on how many are travelling in your party. If there are at least two of you, then one person can attend to the horse's morning needs while the other Long Rider begins to prepare breakfast.

Regardless of how many are travelling, the first chore is to water the horses. They may react indifferently to being offered a drink, especially in cold weather, preferring to only take a few sips. Nevertheless, it is always water before grain, never in the opposite order.

Because Long Riders are constantly on the move, there will be mornings when the horses will have to be brought in from a nearby field. Chasing frisky horses before you're rubbed the sleep out of your eyes is never a pleasant way to start the day. An 18th century British author warned against trying to travel with a horse who had two faults, one that it took a long time to catch him in the morning and two that he wasn't worth a damn when you caught him.

A smart Long Rider foresees this problem. Prior to departure, he trains the horse to associate coming up in the morning with a quick reward of tasty grain. This is an easy task, which begins by approaching the horse in a field while carrying grain in your hat. It won't take long for a smart horse to associate the sound of the delicious grain being shaken in the hat with your approach. After you begin travelling, you can rely on the horse's memory of this grain trick to make catching him easier in the morning. It can even be used if he unexpectedly runs away, as by shaking pebbles in your hat you can imitate the sound of grain being offered.

Feeding grain to travelling horses will depend upon availability, finances and culture. Equestrian nations such as Mongolia do not grain their horses. Sometimes you may not be able to obtain it, even in a country where such practices are routine. Perhaps your pocketbook won't allow the extra expenditure.

However, if you do grain your horses then plan on splitting each day's ration into three parts; a quarter in the morning, a quarter at midday and 2 quarters given when the days work is over.

As soon as the horses have drunk, place one third of their daily grain ration in their feed bags and then allow them to quietly enjoy their morning meal.

If time allows, after the horses have finished their grain you may allow them to graze nearby while you begin clearing up camp.

During a round trip journey from Holland to Spain, Dutch Long Riders Jeannette van der Eng and Margriet Dijkstra discovered the value of allowing their horses to start each day with this peaceful routine.

"Our horses did great," Margriet wrote to the Guild. "When we started out, we wondered if they would tire of trekking to a new meadow again and again. But they didn't. Every morning they would come and greet us. Of course it helped that we had fed them before saddling."

Tacking up

Your work begins as soon as the horse starts eating his grain.

British Long Rider Donald Brown noted a special threat to loading and leaving. During his journey from the Arctic Circle to Copenhagen, he and his companion were often the guest of hospitable farmers.

"Should we have slept in a farm house; an invitation would come to us for breakfast. This caused a further hour's delay as our hosts had had time to think of more questions, and manners and gratitude forbade a hasty leaving upon the emptying of the plates."

Time is of the essence in the morning. What you eat for breakfast, and how long you spend preparing it, will affect your departure time. Better to have a light meal that is easy to arrange and then get on the road without delay.

Take care not to begin the day's activities before sunrise. Even if the idea is to avoid the onset of the sun's heat, feeding is more difficult in the dark, saddles may not be accurately adjusted and articles are often left unseen in camp.

Prior to cleaning the horses, make sure the saddles and tack are in order.

Eleventh hour repairs should only be made if they are absolutely unavoidable. Unless the problem will cause injury, the problem is better left alone at this moment and the repair done at the end of the day.

After the horses have had time to eat and digest their morning meal, they should be carefully groomed.

It's a mistake to think of horses as being non-verbal. Whereas they do not share your language, they are very vocal animals who are constantly communicating to each other via a number of intelligible sounds. Talking to your horses while you groom them in the morning will send a reassuring message and decrease the chances of you startling the horse by approaching from a blind side. Contented horses often doze while you go about brushing, grooming and talking to them.

Remove dirt and loose hair from the areas where the saddle, girth, breast collar and saddle bags will rest. Pay close attention to their hooves. If they are shod, make sure that all the nails are properly set and the shoe is sitting tightly against the hoof.

Bunched hair under the saddle can cause pain and lead to a sore back. That is why, according to ancient custom, Mongols always made sure to face their horses into the wind when saddling, so as to decrease the chance that the hair on the horse's back might be blown the wrong way.

Use the blanket to smooth the hair, moving it from the withers back to the rump twice. Then place the blanket on the back, being careful not to disturb the hair.

After the blanket is in place, don't surprise the horse by slamming the saddle onto his back. Be sure he sees you carrying and lifting the saddle into place. When the saddle is properly positioned, check to make sure it is balanced over the centre of the horse's back. Take care that the bars of the saddle tree do not rest too closely to the shoulder blades and that the saddle pad is pulled well up into the gullet of the saddle, so as to encourage the flow of cool air along the horse's back.

Care must be used when you prepare to secure the girth. Face the front of the horse. Keep your eyes on the horse, so as to not be taken by surprise if he moves suddenly. Reach under his stomach with your right arm, pull the girth towards you and secure it without delay. Be sure to keep the horse's skin smooth under the girth, as wrinkled skin may cause a girth gall.

Many horses learn to inflate their chest while the girth is being tightened. This causes inexperienced riders to routinely over-tighten the girth before mounting.

Do not secure the girth too forcefully!

It should only be snug enough to keep the saddle from moving, not so tight as to cause the horse discomfort. If properly secured, you should be able to slide two fingers between the girth and the horse's stomach. This is especially important in the morning, as you won't be mounting up and riding out of camp. You want the saddle to be in place, not screwed down tight.

If your saddle is equipped with a breast collar, be sure it is loose enough to allow the horse to graze and drink in comfort.

Not only does your life depend upon how well you go about this work, it is often difficult to find a safe spot to adjust tack once you begin that day's travel.

The cavalry had a saying which still applies to modern Long Riders.

"Safe bind, safe find."

Trust this task to no one. You must be absolutely certain in your own mind that the work has been done correctly.

When you think the horse is properly tacked up, step back and inspect your work. Is the saddle properly positioned? Is the blanket well up in the arch of the saddle? Are the bit and bridle causing any discomfort?

Right. It's time to depart.

Setting Off

Do not water your horse immediately before you begin the day's journey.

Travel only when it's light.

Do not mount up and begin riding immediately.

Start the day's march by walking alongside the horse for fifteen minutes. This allows his muscles to limber up, stimulates the circulation of blood to his hooves, and allows the horse's back muscles to become used to your weight.

Use this time to check the action of the horse's movements.

After a quarter of an hour, halt, check the adjustment of the saddle, tighten the girth and prepare to mount.

Mounting Up

No matter what country you ride in, every Long Rider begins his day with a inescapable moment of danger. Poised between the Heavens and the Earth, you are always vulnerable the instant you try to swing into the saddle.

Horses, like humans, are susceptible to excitement. They too are anxious to get underway in the morning. This may lead to confusion, with the pack horse pushing up against the road horse. Or a frisky mount may just want to express his *joie de vivre*. No matter what the cause, mounting in the morning should always be done with care and deliberation.

Mounting a horse should take less time to accomplish than it does to write about. Yet a number of things can go wrong. The horse may shy and step aside. This may cause you to lose your balance, fall backwards and hit the ground hard. In the worst case, the horse can panic and bolt. If your foot is caught in the stirrup, you can be severely injured or dragged to death.

To diminish this risk, the American cavalry equipped their saddles with leather hoods, known as tapaderos, which kept the rider's foot from slipping through the stirrup. Lacking tapaderos, most Long Riders need to concentrate on the task at hand, especially when they are mounting for the first time in the morning.

After walking alongside the horse for fifteen minutes, find a safe place to stop. Then check to make sure the saddle and tack are all in accord, as any maladjustment will usually show up during the first walk of the morning. This is especially true if you started at dawn, when the light is poor and some minor detail in saddling may have escaped your notice.

Take this opportunity to tighten the girth, leaving enough room for the horse to breathe easily and being sure not to wrinkle the skin.

When everything is in place, it's time to mount. Remember, your life is in the horse's hands, so to speak, at this moment. That is why the actions you take and the signals you send must be clear and concise.

Take the reins in your left hand. Keep the left rein shorter as this as acts a precaution in case the horse tries to step away. With the reins grasped firmly in your left hand, take hold of the saddle with your right hand.

Do not face the horse straight on. Place yourself slightly aside, so that you face to the rear. Should the horse move forward unexpectedly, this will automatically pivot you forwards and help you enter the saddle.

With your hands in place, and your body in position, place your foot in the stirrup and swing into the saddle in one smooth, graceful motion. Do not slam down into the saddle in triumph, as the impact of your body will smash into the horse's kidneys. Come to rest lightly. Quickly place your feet into the stirrups. Take up the reins and assume complete control.

One thing to keep in mind is that long distance travel often places Long Riders in peculiar situations, which may require them to mount from the off-side. Training your horse to allow you to mount from either side is of immense practical use, especially if you find yourself having to dismount along a narrow mountain trail.

Moreover, there is another distinct advantage to mounting on both sides.

Welsh Long Rider Jeremy James believes strongly that always mounting on the left places an unnecessary strain on the road horse's back. He advocates mounting from both sides.

"Strikes me as daft mounting on one side. I don't know why people insist on mounting one side anyway. What for? Why? Someone once bellowed at me for mounting on the right leg and said it was wrong. I told them to tell that to the horse. You're far more likely to damage a back like that than keeping both sides even. That's why I won't mount a horse the same side twice. You just can't afford to go pulling away at one side of the saddle, on one side of the horse's back, the whole time you're travelling with them. No, you mount one side, then the other, get off different sides. None of it's easy with all the clobber on when you're travelling but you don't get sore backs that way," Jeremy advised.

In the Saddle

Never set off until everyone is mounted and ready to depart. Once you are under way, lead out in the pre-arranged direction. Always keep one horse length away from the horse in front of you.

Few riders realize the potential trouble they inflict upon their horse by riding in a sloppy manner. If you ride the horse badly, the distance won't become shorter. If you ride well, the distance won't become longer. Careful handling ensures a longer-lasting horse. Rough handling is a sure sign of incompetence on behalf of the rider.

Learn to ride the horse correctly.

Remember to keep your upper torso and head erect, not flopping back and forth or swaying side to side. Only the lower body from the hips down should move with the animal. Do not wave your arms about. Keep them alongside your body.

Don't fret with the reins. Ride with quiet hands and never pull back and forth on the bit. Remember, it's made of iron and a horse's mouth isn't made of steel.

Always keep your eyes on the move, watching far ahead for trouble, glancing down to check on your horse, throwing a swift look back at the pack horse, then sweeping round in all directions.

Your stirrups should have been carefully adjusted before you set off. To check their length, there should be two inches of clearance above the seat of the saddle if you stand in the stirrups. If not, your stirrups are too short, which may induce a cramp in your legs.

Never punish a horse for stumbling. Leave him alone. A horse can see where to put his feet, which the man cannot.

And above all, remember, never lose your temper with a horse.

During the course of an extended journey, the road horse is probably going to take fright at an object which may appear to you to pose no threat. A prudent Long Rider is always on the alert in the saddle, with his feet firmly in the stirrups and no slack in the reins. Be prepared to instantly react, but exercise patience after the situation is under control.

If you are riding in a western saddle, resist the temptation to lean on the saddle horn for support. This selfish act on your part transfers weight and pressure down onto the sensitive withers. Sit up straight, keeping your weight over the centre of the horse's spine.

During a long day travelling, a rider will get cramped from hours in the saddle. This often causes him to twist and turn in the saddle, lean forward or quit the stirrups. This rolling in the saddle is seldom the actual cause of a horse's sore back but it gives the horse considerable inconvenience because it causes a displacement of the balance of weight to occur, resulting in more weight being carried on one side than the other.

No matter how tired you may become, never slouch in the saddle. If you feel yourself starting to slump, then the time has come to dismount.

Dismounting

Who shall decide when horsemen disagree?

After he was kidnapped while riding through Morocco, Don Roberto Cunninghame Graham found himself imprisoned in a remote castle. This enforced isolation allowed him to discuss local equestrian practices with his Muslim hosts.

After Don Roberto regained his freedom, he wrote, "The Arabs have an idea that a man should dismount as seldom as he can. They say dismounting and remounting tires the horse more than a league on the road; they therefore sit the livelong day without dismounting from their seats."

But blaming the horse for staying in the saddle didn't fool a seasoned Long Rider like Don Roberto. He rightly concluded that it was vanity, not charity, that kept the Moroccans in the saddle.

"It may be therefore that given the loose girth, short stirrup leathers, and their own flowing clothes, that personal convenience has more to do with the custom of not getting off and on, than regard for the welfare of their beast."

Too many modern Long Riders swing aboard and then mistakenly stay in the saddle during the course of a long day's travel. I myself made this mistake in my previous journeys because no one had ever alerted me to the damage caused by this fundamental equestrian error.

Dismounting helps the horse.

To test the effectiveness of this policy one need only compare the French and German cavalries.

The French cavalryman was rarely seen off his horse during the First World War. Consequently ninety percent of French equine losses in 1914 resulted from sickness or injury, and fully twenty-five percent of all of France's mobilized horses were dead by year's end.

Because the German cavalry always dismounted to spare their horses, injuries and losses were drastically reduced.

Every Long Rider should dismount and walk beside the horse for a portion of every hour, as this practice produces benefits for both horse and human.

Walking is good for the Long Rider as it offsets cramps.

It prevents the traveller from getting lazy and rolling in the saddle. It has the further advantage of bringing into play other muscles besides those exerted in riding. After a brief walk tired riding muscles will have regained their tone and the traveller can then remount.

Also, always remain flexible in terms of when you dismount and walk alongside the horse, as every bit of assistance you provide favours him in the long term. Even a few minutes walking provides significant relief to the horse as it relieves the weight on the horse's back, allows his muscles to relax and restores vital blood circulation to his skin.

Steep hills are particularly suitable places to relieve horses by dismounting and walking.

It is equally important that you do not sit on your horse when halted. Dismount at every stop, however short. The relief to the horse is immense.

When you halt for a rest, don't forget to loosen the horse's girth. He, too, is entitled to be comfortable and to breathe freely.

When dismounted it is well to look over everything once more lest something should have escaped you before starting.

The welfare of your horse is a never-ending priority. Compromising your comfort is part of travelling in an ethical manner. Mixing walking with riding should be part of your hourly routine.

Leading a Pack String

Many Long Riders travel with a pack animal.

Like the road horse, care must be taken to ensure that the pack animal has been carefully groomed and tacked up prior to departure. This is especially important with the pack horse, as unlike the live and moving weight of the rider, the dead weight of the panniers continually bears straight down on the pack animal's back.

That is why it is well to remember to never overload your pack horse. Always make it a part of your morning policy to ruthlessly reduce the load before you begin to tack up.

If your pack saddle is equipped with a breeching, be sure that it is not fitted too tightly as it can restrict the movement of the legs, quickly rub off the hair and create a raw wound. You can check if there is enough slack in the rear quarter straps, by making sure there is at least the width of one hand between the horse's hip and the breeching.

It is vitally important the panniers be carefully weighed prior to loading. The cargo must be equally distributed, as even a few pounds' difference will result in throwing the pack horse off balance during the course of a long day's travel.

A common mistake is to allow the panniers to hang too low along the sides of the pack horse. This places undue lateral pressure against the flexible portion of the rib cage, which in turn restricts breathing. Positioning the panniers correctly, by placing them higher up along the stronger section of the ribcage, helps relieve this problem.

It is never advisable to use a top pack if it can be avoided, as it has a tendency to shift during the day's travel. This can throw the pack saddle off balance and result in the quick onset of a saddle sore. If you decide to use a top pack, place it above the mid-line of the pack saddle and then secure it tightly.

Involving a pack horse in your journey also introduces an added element of concern to daily travel.

Horses, like humans, communicate constantly. If the road horse sees something of interest he may snort in alarm, stop dead in his tracks, stare incredulously at an unfamiliar object or leap sideways because of a rustle in the bushes. Maintaining your balance during such an episode requires vigilance and skill.

Trying to keep your balance while your road horse is attempting to evade a phantom becomes more complicated if you have one hand on the reins and the other holding the pack horse's lead rope.

Remember the first rule of travelling with a pack animal.

Never wrap the lead rope over your hand or loop it around the saddle horn!

If the pack horse panics and pulls back, the rope can slice off your fingers or rip off the top of your saddle. Even if you avoid losing your fingers, chances are the pack horse will yank you backwards out of the saddle. Double the rope in your hand if you need a better grip.

Monitoring the pack saddle and panniers during the day's travel is important as the constant movement, even at the walk, will loosen knots and throw the load off balance.

Opinions differ regarding wearing spurs. This is something to consider when travelling with a pack horse, as obtaining an instant response from your road horse in an emergency is important.

If circumstances require you to turn around on a steep trail, then release the lead rope and point the road horse's head out and downhill. The horse will not step off the trail if he can see what is below him while turning around.

Courtesy

Once you are under way, maintaining good manners becomes part of your day.

Do not deviate off designated trails, as the horse's hooves may damage the environment. This is especially important if the ground is wet after raining.

If you happen to meet pedestrians, remember what an imposing, large, and tall object a Long Rider on a horse can be. Stop far enough away so as not to frighten people on foot. Depending upon the circumstances be prepared to dismount if time and your safety allow.

Courtesy dictates that if two groups of mounted strangers meet on the trail, then the group travelling uphill has the right-of-way in the morning, while the group travelling downhill retains that privilege in the afternoon. If two groups of travellers meet on level ground, then the larger group has the right-of-way.

Do not frighten domestic animals if you come across them grazing. Pass by quietly

Your sense of courtesy should also extend to your horse. Pay close attention to your horse's carriage, watching his ears and offering him verbal encouragement during the day.

If you are travelling with a companion, be prepared to ride alongside and talk. Alternatively realize that there will be times when each person will want to sink into their own thoughts. Permit your friend the liberty to chat when they want or draw away as the need arises.

Being polite to others, be they animals or humans, costs nothing and increases the joy of the journey.

Rest Halts

When people fantasize about travelling across country on an extended equestrian journey, they envision bright sunlight, effortless miles and an easy day's ride. They seldom realize that they're going to be climbing in and out of the saddle all day.

It is a mistake to get into the saddle and stay perched there like an obstinate tyrant. Your horse's health, especially the sensitive nature of his back, must be of constant consideration.

To help reduce the strain placed on the road horse's back, each day's journey should include hourly halts.

The first halt should be made after travelling about 45 minutes or about two miles. This rest stop is important as it will allow the horse time to stale (urinate). Allow fifteen minutes for the horse to stale, rest, shake and grab a few mouthfuls of grass before proceeding.

Subsequently, after the first halt you should travel for 50 minutes and then allow the horse a ten minute rest every hour.

After three to four hours travel, you should allow the horses a longer rest. Time and circumstances may not allow you to off-saddle. However you should loosen the girth so as to relieve pressure on the back and to encourage circulation of the skin to be restored.

These halts are primarily done to protect the health of the horses. But discipline and common sense dictate how, when and where you rest.

Horses must never rest along the edge of the road. Always move them well away from the traffic.

Never halt on a curve, close to a railroad crossing or near the crest of a hill.

Always look for shade in summer or protection from the wind in winter.

Particular care should be taken in choosing where you take the first halt of the day, as Long Riders may wish to attend to personal matters or relieve themselves.

Once the spot has been chosen, always dismount at once.

At every ten-minute halt loosen the girth and make sure the stirrups are placed across the saddle so as to prevent a horse from catching a hind foot in the stirrup iron.

You can easily tell when the horse wants to stale, as he will stop, stretch his legs and often groan with pleasure.

Before departing after an hourly halt, sufficient time should be allowed to allow you to carefully inspect and when necessary adjust the saddles and equipment. The time spent on this minor chore is well spent, since this precaution helps prevent trouble later in the day.

The rest period made in the middle of a long day's journey is termed the noon halt. How much time you spend on this important halt depends upon local conditions, weather and the length of that day's travel. If you are going to be in the saddle longer than six hours, then you should plan on giving the horses an extended noon halt. Allow the horses at least an hour to eat and digest their midday ration of grain. If the rest is a long one, the horse will be eager to graze or may even doze after finishing his grain.

The onset of hot weather will also influence the decision about a noon halt and how long it should be. Don't be tempted to take a relaxing afternoon siesta, as unnecessarily long halts on the road should be avoided. It is always best to arrive at that night's destination as early as possible, as this will provide the horse with a far better rest.

Be careful not to automatically pull either the riding or pack saddles off the horses, as what you perceive to be an act of charity may in fact cause immediate harm to their hot and sweaty backs. Loosen the cinches on the riding and pack saddle. Remove the panniers from the pack horse.

Because you don't want to be left afoot, make sure the horses are kept secured when you stop for a rest. Even if the halt is a short ten-minute rest, hold the reins in your hand to keep the horse from pulling away. If the halt is longer than a few minutes, hobble or tie the horses so that an unexpected sound may not suddenly frighten them.

Before mounting, turn your attention to the welfare of the horses.

Should the weather be hot, it is always a small kindness to use a moist sponge to wipe away the sweat from the horse's nostrils, eyes and dock. If the weather is wet, be sure no mud has splattered onto his legs. Wipe them clean and rub them to restore the circulation.

Always check his hooves with care, being sure that no stone has become embedded in the hoof and that there is no sign of splintering along the hoof wall. If he is shod, use your hand to make sure the shoe is set firmly.

No matter how long the halt, do not mount and depart until you are confident that the horses appear well and the equipment is secure.

Occasionally, if the weather is extremely hot, or the trail takes you through mud, sand, or up a steep hill, it may be necessary for you to halt more frequently so as to provide the horses with extra relief.

By protecting their welfare and harbouring their strength, the horses will be able to respond well should the time come when you have to ask them to carry you beyond a normal day's distance. Be sure to reward them with a couple of quiet rest days, during which time they should be carefully fed and allowed to relax without inter-ruption.

Watering

It is of the utmost importance that your horses be frequently watered while travelling.

The usual practice of watering before his morning feed should of course be adhered to. But horses may be reluctant to drink in the morning, especially if the weather is cold. They are however often anxious to drink after they have set off.

No matter what the weather, travelling is a hard business.

Too infrequent watering will have a serious effect on the horse's condition.

Never pass up an opportunity to offer your horse a refreshing drink from any clean source of water you encounter.

A small quantity is far better than a copious draught and far less dangerous.

Offer the horse his first drink after you have been travelling for at least 30 minutes and it has been at least an hour since he was grained.

After that, if circumstances permit, plan on watering them on average once every two hours.

The temperature will influence the frequency with which they must be watered.

In hot, sultry weather you must keep a close eye on how much water your horse is consuming, as frequent watering is essential. It may be difficult to find an adequate water source while riding through desert country. Do not let a lack of a water source prevent you from helping your thirsty friend. In extreme cases, after removing the bit, pour some water from your canteen into your hat and allow him a few short swallows. Then use what's left to wipe off his eyes and his nostrils.

Cold weather will allow horses to travel further without watering. However, no opportunity should be missed to offer water to the horses. Even if the weather is cold, watering at least once during the day's travel is essential.

Drinking can be dangerous. Before you trot your thirsty pony up to that delicious looking stream, be sure you have dismounted and checked to make sure the footing is strong enough to hold the horse's weight. Another danger is to try and ride a horse down a steep river bank. If you suspect trouble, then secure the horses and bring them water in a bucket.

If you find a water source during the day's ride, you can permit the horse to drink with the bit in his mouth, as this does not interfere with his drinking. Then move out promptly so as to prevent chilling and possible foundering.

During a short ten-minute halt water can be given at once. If the halt is to be longer the horses must be allowed to cool off before watering.

At the end of the day, remove the bit and lead the horse to drink in his halter, as if he is very thirsty he may drag you into the water. No horse should be permitted to leave until every horse is finished drinking.

Riding over the Roof of the World

It might seem an obvious linguistic fact but a caravan is not a Long Rider. Both employ horses yet there are several important distinctions between how the two different types of equestrian travellers operate. One of these is their view on feeding the horses during the day.

Even though the weather was always variable, commercial travellers who journeyed along an established trail had prior knowledge of where they were going and what to expect. In many cases caravan travellers were walking in the footsteps of their forefathers, who had used ancient trails for thousands of years.

Long Rider Otto Schoener discovered this in the spring of 1938 when he joined a caravan of 30 horses travelling from Kashgar in western China to Srinagar in British held Kashmir. The 47 day journey took the young American traveller through the Pamirs, the Hindu-Kush, the Karakoram and Himalayan mountains.

"The borders of Russia, Afghanistan, China and India came together up there in the clouds of those high mountains," Schoener later wrote.

Horse caravans had been making their way along these dangerous paths for countless generations.

"The trails were very dangerous, as rock slides destroyed the narrow pathways high up on the mountain sides. Many of the wooden bridges we had to cross with our loaded animals were in bad need of repair. Three horses were lost on the trip because of these difficult roads."

The most perilous episode occurred when Schoener's caravan was required to cross over the infamous "roof of the world." This was the name given to the 15,450 foot high Mintaka Pass that led through the Karakoram Mountains separating China from India.

"It is difficult to describe those forty-seven days but they were filled with excitement and new experiences I never dreamt of. Just to be on horseback that long was remarkable," Schoener recalled.

Feeding during the Day

Because Schoener's caravan master knew in advance where the camp sites and water sources were located, he could accurately estimate how many miles had to be travelled that day, as well as how many hours each day's journey would take to accomplish. Caravan masters, who were motivated by commercial interests, were loath to allow their pack horses to dawdle as this delayed the arrival of merchandise to market.

One way of keeping a long string of pack horses moving was to muzzle them, so as to prevent them from grazing along the way. This ensured that the pack ponies would travel without pause to their midday halt, when they would be permitted to briefly graze. It also ensured that by the end of the day the pack horses, which were often considered expendable, were ravenously hungry.

Likewise the world's great cavalries did not condone grazing while under saddle, as their idea of disciplined marching included three guaranteed meals a day for the horses.

The lonely Long Rider is neither caravan nor cavalry. He is riding blind. Though others may have gone along that route before, the details of any previous journey are usually unknown to him. No traditional map, nor screen shot snatched from Google Earth, is going to pinpoint the location of a small succulent snack that will suddenly appear to refresh his tired horses.

That is why Long Rider tradition has long taught that when you come across clean grass, dismount and permit the horse time to graze. If this happens to coincide with the ten minute halt you and the horse enjoy at the end of every hour's ride, fine. But do not restrict the practice only to rest halts.

While permitting your horse to stop and graze is recommended, allowing him to snatch at grass while you are travelling together puts your safety at risk. A horse whose mind is occupied on grabbing a few mouthfuls may well lose his balance, trip over something, or be startled by an unexpected noise.

Do not let the horse's hunger put your combined safety at risk. If you want to let him eat, then stop, dismount and allow him to graze.

The other exception to always seeking food is to never allow your horse to feed on grass cuttings from a mown lawn. This grass, which is often moist and hot, can quickly cause severe colic.

If you are carrying grain for his noonday meal, then provide this to the horse after he has first been watered.

You should have trained your horse prior to departure by feeding him from his own nose bag. At the noon halt, the bit having been removed, the nose bag should be secured to allow the horse to reach the feed easily and prevent him tossing his head and spilling the grain. You may need to readjust the nose bag half-way through the feed.

Carrying a ration of grain can present a problem, as it is heavy and hard to balance. While serving with the Swiss cavalry, Captain Otto Schwarz was taught to carry the daily grain ration in a cylindrical canvas sack that was attached to the front of the saddle.

Give some thought to the type of grain you carry. High-energy food is preferred. Any feed that contains molasses may turn sour or attract unwanted insects such as ants, bees or wasps. Sticky feed also soils the nose bag, making it difficult to clean while travelling.

When the horse has finished his grain, you can enjoy your own noonday meal while keeping an eye on the horse, who is now allowed to graze.

Be sure to turn the nose bag inside out to dry in the sun while you have lunch. And never fail to wash it out on a regular basis, as the combination of horse saliva and grain residue soon turns the nose bag into a vile smelling object which no horse wants to put his nose in.

Whether it is the cool dew-covered grass of a night time pasture, or a refreshing meal of sunshine-warmed greenery unexpectedly found along the road, learning to recognize the rich reward of grass becomes a standard part of the Long Rider's day.

Concluding the Day's Ride

Several Long Rider authors have written about the exciting start of a day's ride but few have revealed how that journey is concluded.

When riding in very hot weather the start must be made the moment enough light makes it safe to travel.

As previously explained, you always walk the first mile to supple the horse. Likewise, you should also walk the last mile to cool him.

This was a strict rule observed by British Long Rider Roger Pocock during his solo ride from Canada to Mexico City along the sun-drenched Outlaw Trail that ran through the badlands of Utah and New Mexico.

"In order to allow the horses to cool at the end of the day, you have to allow enough time to make the last mile of the march at a walk."

As Pocock knew, when your day is coming to an end, dismount and loosen the girth.

Always check the location where you plan to dismount before leaving the saddle, to make sure there are no obstacles in your way. The standard European dismount is the safest; the rider swings one leg over and stands on one leg in the stirrup, one hand on the pommel and the other on the cantle; then lifting his weight with his arms he kicks free of the stirrups and vaults to the ground.

Bringing the horses in cool is also advantageous when it comes time to groom for the night.

Nightly Routine

One of the difficult realities of horse travel is that we want to call it quits when we reach that day's destination. Nothing would be nicer than to just crawl out of the saddle and rest our weary bones.

Sorry.

Your work starts when the horse stops. It is an inflexible rule of the road that you must always see to your horse's welfare before your own.

This devotion to the animal was a vital lesson practiced by early Muslim travellers. Saying daily prayers is one of the most important obligations of the Islamic religion. Yet tradition states that the Prophet Muhammad (PBUH) urged his fellow travellers to delay their prayers until they had first given their riding and pack animals fodder and attended to their needs.

Though it requires diligence and discipline to begin the ride soon after daybreak, this will ensure that you will have completed the journey by early afternoon. An early conclusion provides your horse with vital time to feed and rest.

You should start looking for a suitable camp in mid-afternoon, to ensure that you will have enough light to do chores, which will include negotiating with the locals, tending to your horses, feeding yourself, and if time allows maintaining your diary or updating your internet presence.

The night duties of a Long Rider call for careful preparation. The first of these tasks to understand how and when to remove the saddle.

Off Saddling

A great journey is completed without a drop of cruelty. While the majority of modern equestrian travellers would not knowingly subject their horses to any sort of unkindness, they inadvertently place the animal at grave risk when they off saddle incorrectly.

Modern culture places an emphasis on speed and efficiency. This helps explain why when the ride is over, a pleasure rider usually yanks off the saddle, gives the horse a quick swipe with the brush, bangs him into a stall, throws him some hay, remembers to say something loving and then drives off to attend to the rest of his busy life.

What this person doesn't know is that after the saddle has pressed down on the horse's body, and fluid has collected under the injured skin, the sudden onset of cold air which results when the saddle is removed helps blister the animal's back.

As cavalrymen and Long Riders all learned to their chagrin, there is a danger when the day's march is completed. By removing the saddle in haste you expose the horse's hot and sweaty back to cool air, which increases the risk of swelling and saddle sores. Therefore it is critically important that you take steps to protect the horse's back at all costs or risk inflicting a harmful saddle sore.

Saddle Sores

Even though I have devoted a special chapter to the topic of how to prevent a sore back on a horse, it won't hurt to recall the basics.

Saddle sores can be caused by a variety of reasons including requiring a road horse to wear an ill-fitting saddle or forcing a pack horse to carry an uneven pack load.

Most people are aware that in such cases saddle sores are caused when pressure or friction from the saddle bears down without mercy on the skin, tissue, muscle and bone beneath. In order to protect the body from the unrelenting pressure of the sidebars, fluid collects between the epidermis and the tissue below.

The result is a fluid-filled blister on the horse's back. Intense pain is inflicted when pressure from the saddle is applied again. Further abuse will cause the blister to swell and burst, leaving the animal gravely wounded.

What Long Riders must remember is that saddle sores can also be caused if the saddle is removed prematurely.

Knowing how and when to remove the saddle after a long day's ride has been a preoccupying problem for many generations of horsemen. Despite the fact they belonged to many cultures, all of these horsemen realized that a moment of danger occurs after the saddle has pressed down on the horse's body during a hard ride.

Pressure from the saddle caused fluid to collect under the injured skin. By removing the saddle too soon, the sudden onset of cold air helped blister the horse's back.

To diminish this menace, they had learned to change the saddle's job. At the conclusion of the ride it no longer carried the rider. It protected the horse's back from harm.

Instead of instantly removing the saddle, they loosened the girth and then left the saddle in place until there was no sign of sweat or heat under the saddle blanket.

This practice allowed the horse's back to cool, all the while blood flow was restored and the fluid gradually dissipated.

A Tradition of Patience

Various writers, travellers and Long Riders observed this practice being enacted among many equestrian cultures. Regardless of where the ride had occurred, at the end of the day's exercise or travel, the horse would be tied securely, his girth would be loosened, then he would be left to stand quietly until he had thoroughly cooled.

For example, opposing cavalry forces often fought to the death but they agreed upon this practice.

The British cavalry manual warned, "There is a time-honoured custom not to remove saddles while the backs are hot, but to loosen the girths and let the back dry with the saddle on."

Likewise the Germans were taught, "Saddles should be left on with loosened girth."

The practice was not restricted to military men. Civilian riders were also long time proponents of keeping the saddle in place until the horse's back had completely cooled.

Mexican vaqueros and most horsemen of the south agreed that the saddle should not be shifted till the horse was cool, so as to diminish the chances of getting a sore back.

The Kyrgyz never unsaddled the horse for at least an hour, believing that removing a saddle from a sweating horse inflicted great harm.

Nor did Long Riders of old fail to pass on this important warning.

The first to do so was English Long Rider George Ruxton. In September, 1846 he arrived in Vera Cruz, Mexico and began preparations for a journey to distant Santa Fe. Ruxton was immediately struck by how many local equines bore signs of severe saddle sores.

"Although hundreds of mules and horses were brought to me, there was scarcely one that was not more or less wounded by pack saddles. It was not uncommon to see mules so lacerated by the chafing of the *aparejo* that the rib bones are plainly discernible."

Ruxton was only in his mid-twenties but he had already travelled extensively in Europe and explored Africa. During his trips he had observed how the way the horse was off saddled could affect its health.

"The removal of pack saddles from heated beasts often produces troublesome wounds. But with proper care an animal may perform the longest journey under a pack without injury."

He was as good as his word, because during his journey to New Mexico Ruxton had occasion to prove how effective it was not to off saddle too quickly.

"It is astonishing what palpable errors the Mexicans commit in the care of their beasts. The consequences of their system were very manifest in our journey to Durango. My companion allowed his servants to treat his animals according to their system; whereas mine were subject to an entirely different one, from which I never permitted my servants to deviate.

On coming in from a journey of forty miles, performed for the most part under a burning sun, my companion's animals were immediately stripped of their saddles, and frequently of large portions of their skin at the same time. They were then instantly taken to water and permitted to fill themselves at discretion.

Mine, on the other hand, remained with loose girths until they were nearly cool, and were allowed to drink but little at first, although on the road they drank when water presented itself.

Before reaching Durango the advantages of the two systems were apparent.

The Spaniard lost three mules which died on the road, and all his remaining mules and horses were actually putrefying with sores.

My animals arrived at Durango fat and strong, and without a scratch, and performed the journey to Santa Fe in New Mexico, a distance of nearly two thousand miles, with ease and comfort," Ruxton recalled in his book, *Adventures in Mexico.*

He went on to ride his horse another 5,000 kilometres (3000 miles) without injury.

In his famous equestrian travel book, *The Romany Rye*, English Long Rider George Borrow wrote in 1857, "When your horse is led into the stable, after trotting and walking, don't let the saddle be whisked off at once, for if you do your horse will have such a sore back as will frighten you, but let your saddle remain on your horse's back with the girth loosened."

At the dawning of the 20th century Roger Pocock also warned, "At the end of the day, one slacks the girth, removes the bit, gives half a drink of water and some hay. An hour later when the rider returns, he comes back to a cool horse that can be unsaddled without fear of any blisters which might turn into sores."

A new century has arrived but the tradition remains.

One of the lessons Tim Cope learned from the nomads encountered along his ride from Mongolia to Hungary was not to remove the saddle too quickly.

"The Mongols never unsaddled their horses immediately after riding them, as they realized this caused saddle sores. This was especially true if the horse had been ridden in the great heat of the summer sun. They allowed the animal to stand with its saddle still on, but loosely girthed. It was only removed when the day and horse's back had both had a chance to cool. That is also when it was allowed to eat. The Kazakhs also taught me this custom, to permit the horses to stand and cool before letting them eat and drink."

Hot Backs and Cold Water

There is one other option, to use cold water to restore the blood circulation to the horse's back.

The principle of using cold water to combat the onset of saddle sores had been recognized by the American cavalry. Their manual recommended quickly placing cold wet cloths upon a horse's back if any signs of swelling or bumps were detected when the saddle was removed.

"Such an action will reduce the swelling," the book concluded.

Modern Long Riders have learned that if you have access to cool water, the second option is to remove the saddle and immediately bathe the horse's back.

British Long Rider Penny Turner lives and rides in Greece, a country which endures terrific heat and nearly continuous harsh sunlight. She explained to the Guild how she had taken the cavalry's idea of a cold wet cloth and improved upon it.

"I made the discovery when I had a riding school. There were 40 horses working, mostly with not particularly expert riders on them. Lessons are for an hour. Then the horses would be unsaddled, might have two hours off, and then have another hour lesson," Penny explained.

In between teaching riding lessons, Penny had time to make several important observations.

"When riders are tired they tend to ride much heavier, and very often any one sidedness in their own body structure will tend to mean that they stress the horses back."

Penny noticed that a combination of inexpert horsemanship, constant re-saddling and hot weather caused some of her horses to develop little nodules under the saddle. Though not painful, the horse did lose hair because of the saddle rubbing on these nodules, which in time could have led to the sore becoming a raw spot.

She wondered what had caused these small lumps to develop. One important clue was that they seemed to occur where there had been more pressure – for example under the stirrup bars, or towards the place where the marks of the rider's seat bones could be seen in the seat of the saddle.

"I asked myself why this had happened and concluded that it was probably connected to the blood returning to the compressed areas when the saddle was removed."

Maybe, she concluded, this also explained why the other areas under the saddle that had not received extra pressure reacted differently. Having reached this point in her investigation, Penny made an essential deduction.

She remembered that a common method of reducing swelling was to apply cold, because it caused the blood vessels to contract. If, she reasoned, cold could be applied to the expanded blood vessels on the horse's hot back, it might help to prevent the lumps she had seen appearing in pressure spots.

Until now Penny had followed tradition, by loosening the girth and leaving the saddle in place until the horse had cooled. This had worked in winter. But with the onset of Greece's fierce summer heat, she concluded her horses needed additional assistance.

"In hot weather with high humidity you can get prickly heat under the saddles, especially if you are riding a western saddle equipped with a wool saddle blanket."

Forty sweaty horses standing in a boiling hot Mediterranean summer provided a perfect setting for a historic equestrian experiment.

"What we did was have someone with a bucket of cold water on one side of the horse ready to chuck it over the horse's back as someone else took the saddle off on the other side. Then a second bucket was chucked over the horse from the side the saddle was removed."

Penny Turner is a Long Rider, not a scientist. Consequently she has never been able to provide a scientific explanation for what she learned. Yet like so much of the equestrian wisdom which our species has patiently gathered throughout generations of horse handling, this keen-eyed woman seems to have found a powerful and consistent solution to an age-old problem.

"I don't know if my reasoning makes physiological sense but it certainly worked in practice. In more than 20 years we never had a saddle sore or girth gall," she reported to the Guild.

Testing the Theory

Penny wasn't content to ride in circles in a ring. She set off to explore Greece on her gelding, George. During that ride she tested her theory on the road.

She dismounted half an hour before the end of the day's ride, loosened the girth and then walked George to that night's campsite. Using the folding bucket she always carried, she would off saddle, then immediately pour two buckets of refreshing cool water over the gelding's hot back.

George's healthy journey proved that the practice was a success on the road as well in the ring.

Penny's friend and fellow Long Rider, Jeremy James, is a strong advocate of this method, which he too used during extended journeys across the blazing plains of Turkey and on a hot summer's ride from Italy to England.

When questioned about the effectiveness of Penny's two-bucket theory, Jeremy did not hesitate to recommend it, saying, "I soaked the horse's back the minute the saddle came off, which stopped the heat bumps."

Jeremy supplied the following information to the Guild so as to explain how the process works.

"When you're going to stop for the day, get off, slacken the girth, then walk for the last mile. When you arrive, leave the saddle on until you have found a bucket of cold water. Take the saddle off and douse the back immediately with COLD water, then gently massage for five minutes. Also wash under the girth area with cold water, then massage. Smooth the water and sweat off with the flat of your hand.

The application of cool water reduces the swelling, bonds the skin back to the tissue, encourages the fluid to be reintroduced into the body, stimulates and flattens the hair follicles, and diminishes the likelihood of a blister forming.

Strapping, massaging and rubbing down with straw gets the blood back to the area where blood flow has been suppressed by the weight of the saddle.

But you can't remove the saddle and apply the cool water later. It has to be applied instantly. If you leave it for one minute, you'll get a bubble under the skin that fills with lymphatic fluid. That part of the skin then detaches from the subcutaneous layer. When the saddle goes back on, the agitation of the saddle will create a sore straight away," he concluded.

Using cold water to cure hot backs in a hot climate is very enjoyable for the horses, as straight away they can immediately go and roll, which is relaxing for them.

However if you decide to use Penny's method, there are several things to keep in mind.

Only use this method if the weather is warm.

It is essential to throw the water on the horses back immediately.

Using a hose does not produce the same effect, because the volume of water is not enough to cool the back. Plus, it is difficult to get the water on the horse's back without getting soaked yourself.

Off Saddling Long Rider Horses

As these examples prove, there are two options to off saddling, both of which work. Various factors, including the weather, outside temperature, the country and culture you are riding through, the availability of water, the type of saddle you choose, and the emotional temperament of your horse, will influence which method you decide to employ on your trip.

Regardless of which tactic you choose, it is essential that you bring your horse in as cool as possible. Always dismount and walk the horse during the last mile of the ride. After you stop, leave the saddle in place, but loosen the girth.

When travelling with a pack horse, loosen the girth after arriving at camp and then remove the panniers.

If you decide to use the traditional method, offer the horses a small drink before allowing them to stand quietly under saddle until they are completely cooled.

Or if circumstances and weather permit, you may decide to use Penny's two-bucket method.

In either case, always lighten the horse's load before you begin off saddling by removing the cantle roll and saddle bags.

Grooming

As previously stressed, your horse's welfare is always the number one priority. After carrying you all day, he is tired and hungry. Take care of him without delay, unless you want to continue the rest of your journey on foot.

After off saddling, always run your hand down his withers, spine and sides looking for sore spots, lumps, bruises, blisters, chafing or rubs. Pay special attention to the girth area, which might have been galled.

The hair of a horse which has become wet from perspiration must be smoothed with a brush.

Do not neglect the care of his mane, forelock and tail, which provide such crucial protection to a travelling horse.

Pay close attention to his legs at the end of the day's ride. Always remove mud to reduce the chances of mud fever and dry out wet heels. Massage his legs well, placing special emphasis on the fetlocks. Use a gentle firm method rubbing downwards.

Examine the state of the shoes at the termination of each day. Pick out his feet with care, removing any gravel and rectifying any problems without delay.

Not until the horse is thoroughly clean, has been examined to see that he is uninjured, and that his shoes are in good order, is he able to be fed.

Feeding at Night

It is a mistake to feed and water the horse too soon after you arrive.

Watering is as important as feeding, as thirst very quickly reduces the horse's ability to travel and work. But care must be taken that the horse is not watered until he has cooled off.

Loosen the girth and allow him to rest in the shade. This will not only allow his back to cool, it will encourage the blood needed to replenish his digestive system to circulate, as too many demands on his system might cause an attack of colic.

Water should always precede feeding. After the horse has cooled, he should be allowed to drink his fill. If this requires you to take the horse to a muddy stream, dry his legs and heels afterwards. This is especially important in cold weather.

Then allow him to feed on a small amount of hay while you are grooming him.

Once he is cleaned, feed the horse his nightly grain ration. Be sure to check the adjustment and fit of the nose bag when the grain is given.

Hay or other roughage helps digestion of the concentrated grain ration. Before going to bed, give the horse a generous amount of hay. This will keep him quiet and busy during the first part of the night. Giving him a hearty meal at night is also better for his digestion than allowing him to feed too heavily prior to setting off on that day's journey.

Any loss of appetite or refusal to eat is a sign of illness and a veterinarian should be consulted at once.

Saddles and Tack

When removing the saddle, cross the girth and stirrups so as to prevent them from dragging in the dirt.

Stand the saddle upright so burrs do not become attached or the underside of the saddle, which is often wet from perspiration, becomes dirty.

Dirty saddle blankets can cause sore backs. Expose the saddle blanket or pads to the sun and fresh air at the end of the day's travel. Never put it into use the next morning in a wet and filthy condition.

Be sure you lay the bridle out carefully to prevent it from becoming tangled.

Place all your equipment to aid you in easily saddling up in the morning.

End of the Evening

Even though he is larger and stronger, you can withstand hardship better than the horse can.

That is why the horses always come first. You can only attend to your own needs after they have been fed and watered.

Not only must you attend to your own dinner, and then wash up, you should also make preparations for breakfast, so as to expedite your departure in the morning.

If time allows, this is the time when you relax by the campfire.

However take care not to stay awake too late talking to your curious hosts.

Always check on the horses before you slide into your sleeping bag. Don't spend too much time around him after the end of the day's ride. Weighed down by his evening meal, and tired from carrying you all day, the horse will appreciate a rest more than anything else.

Check to make sure the hobbles are in place, the picket line is secured, the tethering rope is properly adjusted or the stall door firmly fastened. If you're using a rope, then check to make sure all the knots are secure.

Now, with the horses secure, the fire burning low, and the camp secured, your day in the saddle is about to close. If your muscles are aching, you would be well advised to take a couple of Advil to reduce the inflammation.

Then it's time to hit the sack. After all, horses wake early and there are many more days of hard travel ahead of you.

Travelling Ever Onwards

As this chapter demonstrates, a Long Rider's day is filled with important decisions and hard work. Rising early, watering, grooming, tacking up, riding for hours, often in harsh weather, all take a physical and emotional toil on the traveller.

But is it worth it?

Believe it not, the famous jazz composer Duke Ellington understood the appeal that draws us out onto the road. He understood that travel involved something more mysterious than adhering to time tables or rushing to arrive.

As far back as 1937 Ellington's song, *Caravans*, stated, "Night and stars above that shine so bright. The mystery of their fading light that shines upon our caravan. Caravans moving out into the sun. I don't know where I'm going but I'm going."

Chances are that Adam del Amor and Jeremiah Bayes, who were in their early twenties when they rode from Colorado to Arizona in 2005, had never heard Duke Ellington's magnetic song. That didn't matter. They discovered that they and their horses had become part of a timeless rhythm that rose and set with the sun.

"Our steeds accepted and anticipated the day's routine. This pattern of daily travel seemed to groove with their natural tendency to keep moving and their willingness to work. They are shining examples of true service, strength, and courage, beckoning us to rise up to the opportunity to respect and honour their bodies and souls," Adam wrote.

As Duke Ellington sang, and these Long Riders learned, while it is true that a good part of your day will involve hard work, this should never interfere with your search for contentment.

Summary

Here is a quick summary of the day's feeding and watering.

Water the horse after morning inspection.

Feed a quarter of the daily grain ration after watering.

If time permits, allow grazing while camp is cleared.

After at least an hour has passed since he was grained, and the horse has been travelling for at least 30 minutes, offer to let him drink.

Thereafter allow him to drink as circumstances permit, trying to ensure that he drinks at least once every two hours.

Never pass an opportunity to allow the horse to stop and graze on clean grass.

Feed a quarter of the grain ration at the noon halt, after he has first been watered.

Never feed and water the horse too soon after you arrive.

Water him after he has cooled.

Feed him a small amount of hay while he is being groomed.

Feed the remaining half of his grain ration.

Feed him the majority of his hay ration at the conclusion of his day.

After the American army used 5,397 mules to transport supplies along the Burma Road in 1945, the animals were donated to the Chinese National Army. One of the mules was later captured by the Communist Chinese forces. When the Korean War broke out in 1950, the mule was recaptured by American soldiers. After six years' service in three armies, the mule, known by his brand as 08K0, was returned to the United States.

When Ella Sykes set off to ride 2,000 miles across Persia, it didn't take long for her to learn that the rigours of horse travel forced her to adhere to a strict daily schedule.

Start the day's march by walking alongside the horse for fifteen minutes. This allows his muscles to limber up and stimulates the circulation of blood to his hooves. This was the method Kohei Yamakawa used during this journey across Japan in 2014.

Rest halts are important. Billy Brenchley's horse, Nali, snoozes during the journey across North Africa.

During a round trip journey from Holland to Spain in 2006, Dutch Long Riders Jeannette van der Eng and Margriet Dijkstra discovered the value of allowing their horses to start each day with a peaceful morning routine.

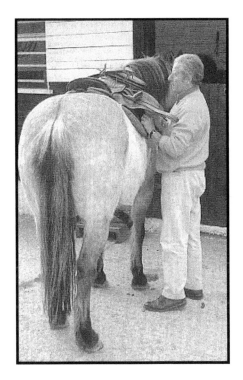

Jeremy James believes strongly that always mounting on the left places an unnecessary strain on the road horse's back. He advocates mounting from both sides.

When Otto Schoener rode from Kashgar to Kashmir in 1938, he learned that caravan masters would not permit the pack horses to graze along the way, especially along the infamous Mintaka Pass.

British Long Rider Penny Turner advocates pouring cold water on a horse's back after a day's ride. In more than 20 years her horses have never had a saddle sore or a girth gall.

During their journey from Colorado to Arizona, Adam del Amor and Jeremiah Bayes learned that the pattern of daily travel agreed with the horse's natural tendency to keep moving.

Chapter 66
Daily Distance

In 1973 three young men, Jeff Hengesbaugh, Bill Hamilton and Stephen Johnson, spent six months riding 5,000 kilometres (3000 miles) from Phoenix, Arizona to Calgary, Canada.

As expected, their journey was filled with spectacular scenery. It also revealed difficult and unforeseen lessons, one of which was how much time it took to cross a vast nation on horseback.

When the trip was complete, Jeff wrote, "Horse travel is limited travel. It is determined by destination and dependent on geography and season. Time is at the mercy of all three. There is no rule that can govern the length of a day's ride or how it will be made."

Jeff was only partially correct. There are in fact guidelines that have been used by generations of experienced equestrian travellers. These principles still hold true and can help modern Long Riders understand and estimate how far they can travel in a day.

Hidden amidst the Words

The first place to search is in literature, where accurate authors relayed important clues.

Sir Arthur Conan Doyle is usually remembered for having invented Sherlock Holmes. He also wrote best-selling books about other characters. One of the most fascinating was Brigadier Etienne Gérard, a Hussar officer who fought for Napoleon in Spain, Italy, Germany and Russia. Described as the bravest soldier, greatest swordsman and most accomplished horseman who ever served France, the Brigadier's exciting stories were published in 1894 by the Strand Magazine, the same publication that released the Sherlock Holmes stories.

Though Conan Doyle was originally a doctor, he turned his love of history into an amazing literary career. His stories were filled with forgotten equestrian details gleaned from previous ages. Brigadier Gérard was no exception.

The exploits of Napoleon's fictional officer were based upon the celebrated French cavalry officer, Baron de Marbot, who left an astonishing narrative of the man-killing horse he rode during the Napoleonic invasion of Russia in 1812. This mare, Lisette, first became infamous in France when she disembowelled her groom. Despite her savage nature, Baron de Marbot was mounted on the murderous animal at the battle of Eylau, which occurred in Prussia in February, 1807. During the conflict, Lisette killed and partially ate a Russian soldier.

During the course of his prolific career, Conan Doyle wrote many accurate things about horses. One topic which interested him was the rate of travel. Speaking via Brigadier Gérard, he wrote, "It is impossible, when you have a daily change of forage, and sometimes none at all, to move horses faster than a walk. I am aware that in the story-books the cavalry whirls past at the maddest of gallops; but for my own part, after twelve campaigns, I should be very satisfied to know that my brigade could always walk upon the march and trot in the presence of the enemy."

Such lessons in equestrian wisdom lingered after the advent of the motor age. When C.S. Lewis created his famous series, *The Chronicles of Narnia*, in the 1950s, one book in particular was of significant equestrian interest.

Published in 1954, *The Horse and his Boy* recalled how a boy named Shasta, mounted on a talking horse named Bree, set off on a long and perilous journey. Using the wise stallion as a teacher, Lewis related a proverb so that his young readers would understand the reality of how fast horses could really travel.

"'Listen,' said Bree. 'Galloping all day and all night, like they do in stories, is not possible in reality. You have to alternate walking and trotting, but fast trots and short walks. And every time we walk, you humans can get off and walk too'. And so they went on, trot and walk and trot, clickety clop, clickety clop, the smell of hot horses, smell of personal heat, blinding light, headache. All this for mile upon mile. Tashbaan, the town they had left, never seemed to get further away, even by an inch. The mountains never seemed to come any closer, even by an inch. They had the feeling that this had been going on forever, clickety clop, clickety clop, smell of hot horses, and smell of personal heat."

Turkish Truth

The dawning of this new century has seen a dramatic decrease in authors who know the difference between a mare and a mule. Those who do write about equestrian matters all too often focus on superficialities, pass along half-truths or dispense nonsense.

One of the greatest living experts is Jeremy James. Not only has he explored the distant corners of the world on horseback, Jeremy's research has uncovered major equestrian historical evidence.

One such example occurred in 2005, when he released his book, *The Byerley Turk*.

Ostensibly it told the story of the legendary Eastern sire of the English Thoroughbred. Before that Turkish stallion sired English race horses, he was ridden as a battle charger when the Ottoman army besieged Vienna in 1683. After being captured by the enemy, the Ottoman war horse saw service again. This time he rode into battle alongside the English army that invaded Ireland in 1689.

Yet *The Byerley Turk* was far more than a mounted war record. What Jeremy's book also revealed was rare information written in Turkish that had been filed away and effectively lost for generations within the Topkapi Museum in Istanbul. These Turkish papers revealed the equestrian practices of the Ottoman cavalry while on the move.

Jeremy James does more than just pass along dry historical facts. Because he is a Long Rider, he has the uncanny ability to take you inside the hearts and minds of the horses that populate his tales. His tale of Azarax, the Turkish war horse who became known as the Byerley Turk, includes details of how the massive Ottoman army made its slow way towards Vienna, all the while trying to travel with tens of thousands of horses.

As Jeremy explains, the pace of the journey was set by the horses but heavily influenced by outside factors such as topography and climate.

Accompanied by his groom, the stallion Azarax is an equine witness as the Sultan's forces began a weary march towards the distant city of Edirne.

Jeremy wrote, "One hundred miles to Edirne. As a journey on horseback, what does this mean? Until you have done it, a hundred miles is meaningless. Fifty miles is meaningless. A hundred miles has no significance. Is this fifty miles of rock? Is this a hundred miles of swamp? Is it fifty miles of forests so dense that pioneers must be sent first to clear them? Fifty miles of mud, of clay so thick it is impossible to walk in a straight line for more than the length of the body of a horse? A hundred, two hundred miles of hail and wind and rain, sleet and snow? The elements complicate distance: heat complicates it, cold complicates it, water complicates it. The effort trebles. The sweat runs, the wind chills, the soul cries out. Gender complicates travel. A mare is easy, but not when there are stallions. Stallions scream and shout and lunge and pull; they are aggressive and lash their tails, kick and squeal. They pull towards the mares, they threaten each other. The mares buck at the stallions. They exhaust their riders. The stallions are so obsessed with the mares, they do not care where they put their feet. They flounder, reins cannot be held, shoes are ripped off, horses stumble, knees are cut, fractured, broken."

He continued, "No. Distance on horseback is measured in time. A pioneer corps had set out two months earlier to clear and widen the roads, repair bridges and build pontoons to span the shifting marshes but does this make the hundred miles shorter? It might make it easier, but the hills remain: the mountains do not move. The rivers still flow: the stallions remain stallions and mares remain mares. Distance by horse is measured in time."

It took five days for the massive army to reach Edirne. To reach Vienna required months of bone-grinding effort.

Like the wise C.S. Lewis before him, Jeremy cautioned his reader, "Distance on horseback is measured in time".

This is one of the oldest rules of equestrian travel and was first recorded by the English Long Rider Fynes Moryson who explored Europe extensively in 1592. He wrote, "The miles of Switzerland are so long that they reckon the journey on horseback by the hours not by the miles."

Recognizing Reality

These authors all knew one thing to be true.

Any number of factors can delay or destroy your trip.

Francis Galton was an experienced British traveller who addressed this issue in 1855. In his how-to book for explorers entitled, *The Art of Travel*, Galton offered many crucial warnings, one of which states, "The success of the expedition depends on a chain of eventualities, each link of which must be a success; for if one link fails, at that point, there must be an end to further advance."

Long Rider Raphael Plumpelly learned this lesson the hard way. He made a perilous ride through Arizona's Apache territory in the 1860s. Then he switched his saddle for sails. Asked to go to Japan, he left San Francisco aboard a ship called the *Carrington*. Plumpelly was expecting a fast trip because the vessel had just completed the passage from Yokohama to San Francisco in the record time of 27 days.

Instead the trip became a nightmare. What was supposed to be a quick journey lasted an agonizing 87 days, during which time the ship was becalmed, its rudder broke and the water ran out.

After her ride from Cornwall to Scotland in 1939, Margaret Leigh recognized that a horse trip would also include delays.

"Riding is a slow, anachronistic mode of travel. Nothing is ready for the Long Rider, neither stabling, nor corn, nor a decent surface to ride on. He must find his own routes and make his own arrangements as he goes," she advised.

The day hasn't yet arrived when travellers can be instantly beamed to a distant location via a Star Trek style transporter. Yet millions already associate modern travel with ease and efficiency.

Our Long Rider forefathers understood that there are no guarantees in horse travel and that miles are won by great effort.

Deciphering Distance

Nowadays people can tell you how many gigabytes their mobile phone has but haven't a clue how far you can travel in a day by horse.

In fact this used to be a topic of intense international interest.

John Jervis was known as "the old Coachman," thanks to the decades he spent driving passenger stage coaches along early 19th century English roads. In 1827 Jervis' reminiscences were released in a book entitled *The Traveller's Oracle*. Therein he proclaimed with conviction, "Daily mileage will always vary because of the inherent difficulties associated with horse travel."

The majority of Jervis' wisdom could still be found nearly a hundred years later when in 1917 the British cavalry manual stated, "The rate of travel will vary according to the nature of the country and the climate."

The authors of these books realized that the distance a Long Rider may travel in the course of the day will depend on a number of factors, the most basic of which is the size, age and condition of the horse.

Another critical aspect is how much the rider weighs and how talented a rider he is.

How much gear, including saddle, bridle, saddle bags, etc., is the riding horse carrying in addition to the rider?

The time of year the trip is being taken matters too, as do the length of the days.

Weather, the climate and the amount of available daylight affect daily distance.

Progress will vary depending upon the type of terrain that is encountered; i.e. is the traveller attempting to fight his way through the swamps in Columbia's Darien Gap jungle or trying to survive crossing the sand dunes of the Gobi desert?

The condition of the route helps or hampers progress; i.e. will the Long Rider be passing along a dry flat road winding alongside the peaceful pastures of Maryland or struggling up the rattlesnake-infested switchback trails found in the Rocky Mountains?

The gradient of a steep road will always delay horses.

An increase in the number of horses will invariably reduce the overall progress, especially if pack horses are involved. The larger the force, the slower the progress.

How much the pack saddle weighs will influence the equation.

If the road horse and pack animal work well together this can have an effect on daily events.

The availability of water and grazing will aid or hamper speedy progress.

All of these points alter the daily distance.

Rate of March

Each of these reasons might influence daily events. However there is one aspect that is always present: the speed of the horse.

Cavalry officers wore different uniforms but followed the same rules of the road.

It was essential for them to understand what horses could and could not achieve at various gaits. To determine this vital information they used what was known as the "rate of march."

To achieve maximum efficiency, troopers and horses were trained to maintain standardized rates of speed for each gait.

Because horses lacked a speedometer, cavalry officers needed to invent a way to measure and maintain a horse's speed. The basis for this movable standard was the pace.

Though horses differed in size, cavalry officers were able to establish that the average pace was about 78 centimetres (31 inches). Using the pace as a basic measure, riders were taught to calculate distance by determining how many paces the horse took at any of the four gaits: walk, trot, canter and gallop.

Dr. David Dorondo, a historical expert on the German cavalry, wrote, "German horsemen could cover between 125 (walk) and 700 (extended gallop) paces per minute, a pace being about 31 inches (78 cm). In other words cavalry at the walk – the most frequent marching gait – would cover just over 100 yards (91 m) per minute or about three and a half miles per hour".

Prior to the outbreak of the Second World War, the American cavalry officers were taught that a horse proceeding at a brisk walk could cover 117 yards in one minute, a quarter of a mile in 3.45 minutes and four miles in one hour. By proceeding at the trot, the horse could cover 235 yards in one minute, a quarter of a mile in 1.52 minutes and eight miles in one hour. The canter permitted the horse to cover 293 yards in one minute, a quarter of a mile in 1.30 minutes and ten miles in one hour. A galloping horse covered 440 yards in one minute, a quarter of a mile in 1.0 minutes and 15 miles in one hour.

Other experts agreed that the speeds at which the average horse travelled were:

4 miles an hour is 1 mile in 15 minutes

5 miles an hour is 1 mile in 12 minutes

6 miles an hour is 1 mile in 10 minutes

7 miles an hour is 1 mile in 8 ½ minutes

8 miles an hour is 1 mile in 7 ½ minutes

9 miles an hour is 1 mile in 6 ½ minutes

10 miles an hour is 1 mile in 6 minutes

The fundamental gait for all cavalries was the walk.

On average cavalry would cover just over 91 metres (100 yards) per minute or about three and a half miles per hour at the walk. British cavalry averaged four miles an hour at the walk. By increasing the pace slightly, the Americans travelled at 4½ miles an hour.

Knowing that even a slow-moving pack horse walks a minimum of three miles an hour, a cavalry officer could count on covering at least 21 miles during a seven-hour day.

Even before the various cavalries began to practise these standard speeds, John Jervis, the old Coachman, had determined that pace could be used to make an accurate prediction of how fast a rider might travel, if no unexpected factors were encountered.

Jervis wrote, "To know to a nicety at what time you must start to arrive at a certain place at a certain hour, you have nothing to do but to ascertain the distance and direct the pace of travelling."

If you went looking for an "old coachman" today, you'd end up at a retirement home for Greyhound bus drivers, none of whom could shed any light on how fast you might travel on a horse. So even if we know the ideal speed, how do we achieve it?

Setting the Pace

Too many modern travellers swing into the saddle and then proceed to amble down the road at a leisurely walk. Such a slovenly style is bad for the horse.

These riders fail to understand a vital fact. The weight being carried by the horses is guaranteed to produce fatigue irrespective of the distance travelled. Thus, you are harming your horse, not doing him any favours, by travelling along at a dawdling amble, not a brisk walk. It is the lazy gait which causes the most weariness.

That is why it is a priority to bring the horse through each day's travel by subjecting it to the least number of hours under saddle, as the quicker a journey is completed the less strenuous it is to both horse and rider.

Of all the gaits, the walk is the most important for equestrian travellers, followed by the trot. Canters seldom figure into travel and galloping should be avoided.

Not all horses are brisk walkers. As explained earlier in this work, a Long Rider should always avoid purchasing a slow-walking horse, as an animal that is slow and unwilling is worse that walking on foot.

The speed of the horse's walk can be influenced by a variety of factors, including their breed, or even the type of work they do. For example, horses used by cowboys during cattle drives were found to walk slower than usual, as they learned to match the plodding progress of their bovine companions.

But Long Riders are not cowboys. Through the ages their road horses have demonstrated time and time again that a brisk walk is capable of being kept up for very long journeys.

During her ride from Stockholm to Rome, Countess Linde von Rosen made impressive mileage thanks to her horse's quick walk.

"Our pace has been mostly at the walk on a long rein, to allow the propelling power of the hind end to work freely. Castor normally covers 10 kilometers (6.25 miles) in 70 minutes. He keeps this pace up all day, every day."

What you must not overlook is the emotional excitement which horses are capable of. Trudging along at a slow pace is mentally wearisome and physically fatiguing for the horse too; whereas trotting adds to his cheerfulness.

Pack animals are not expected to trot. But if the traveller is not using a pack horse, and the road horse is not carrying too much weight, then trotting may be suitable for short periods.

The trot was originally called posting in England because it was used by the postillions who rode horses in front of carriages and coaches. It presupposes a slight bent knee and a certain amount of weight placed in the stirrups, so that the rider can clear the saddle at every second pace of the horse. This faster pace allows for a dramatic increase in miles covered.

Lt. Cornelius Smith provided such an example. Having obtained leave from his cavalry unit to attend his sister's marriage, he set off in April, 1895 from Fort Wingate, Arizona bound for Fort Sam Houston, Texas. Even though the journey was accomplished in the fast time of only twenty-eight days, Smith's mustang arrived in excellent condition.

"I have always thought myself fortunate to belong to an organization whose Captain believed in making camp early in the day. To do so, he trotted the horses, perhaps three-quarters the length of any march we ever made. This allowed men and horses to rest comfortably in camp, a rest they could not attain by loafing along the road all day. I patterned after this, and indeed did so during my entire career in the cavalry. Of the thousand miles covered during my ride to Texas, I trotted Blue for about 700 miles. I did not gallop him one step."

As Smith's journey indicates, alternating the trot and walk was a powerful way to increase daily mileage. Even large groups of trained riders could average impressive distances.

Normally, the larger the cavalry force the slower was the progress. Yet General Ingelfingen, of the German cavalry, recalled how he used the trot to great advantage.

"I directed that the force should walk for half an hour and then trot for 2¼ miles, and so on alternately; during the first day's march however I walked for a quarter of an hour and trotted for 1 1/8 mile only. In this manner I got over about 4½ miles in the hour. When the march was longer than 18 miles I used in the middle of it to trot 4½ miles at one spell instead of 2¼ , after which I walked for a short distance, and then halted for half an hour. In this manner we marched our 18 miles in four hours, while the horses and men kept quite fresh, and the former even put on flesh."

Long Riders, such as Malcolm Darling, who crossed India in 1947, would walk the horse for five minutes and then trot for ten minutes.

Darling wrote, "A fast walk, a steady comfortable trot, and sound legs are the three things most needed in a horse for a tour of this kind."

Don't be tempted to trot briskly and then stroll along at a sedate walk. A slow walk places pressure and strain on the same area all the time. To reduce the chances of damage and injury, it is always advisable to walk alongside the horse so as to lessen the strain and to bring other muscles into play. Don't forget to loosen the girth to provide relief.

Though it may seem apparent, do not gallop the road horse. Even the cavalry maintained strict rules about the use of what was termed the "urgent rate." Because it required the horse to travel at the highest possible speed, cavalry riders were instructed not to gallop their horses more than a mile.

After riding across England in 1851, Long Rider George Borrow left this stern warning about the use of that gait while travelling.

"If you trot him a mile and then walk him a quarter of a mile, his wind will not be distressed and you may go on in that way for thirty miles. But never gallop, for none but fools or highwaymen ever hurtle their horses along the road."

A la Turcoman

There is one method of travel which produces a strong daily rate of travel. It is the Central Asian method known as 'à la Turcoman', or 'à la Turkmène'.

This method is linked to mounted slave raids perpetrated by the Turcoman tribe against their neighbours, the Persians. Swiss Long Rider Henri Moser interviewed the participants of such raids.

He wrote, "The Yomud horse will travel 700 Russian versts across the desert, cross the territory of their enemies the Turkoman Tekes, with whom they are continually at war, emerge on the other side, and raid on the other side of the Atrek river into Persia, after having travelled 1200 versts (790 miles) from their tents; one verst being equal to 1.06 kilometre. The raiders capture women, tie them hand and foot, throw them across the crupper like a sack, and with this double load, plus food and water for all three, he will cover 150 versts a day until he returns home."

These Central Asian raiders were mounted on what is today known as the Akhal Teke. When not raiding, the tribal riders would cover great distances by travelling with two horses. One horse carried the rider and a minimum amount of equipment. The second horse was completely unencumbered.

The Turcomans knew that it was the weight being carried, not the act of running, that wearied the horse. They would ride one horse from dawn till noon, off saddle, then mount and ride the second horse until the end of the day.

A few Long Riders have successfully adapted the Turcoman method. They travel with two horses, both of whom have been trained to trot quickly.

The most successful traveller to use this method was the Russian Long Rider Mikhail Asseyev. He rode from Kiev, Russia to the newly-erected Eiffel Tower in Paris, France in 1889. During the journey he travelled 2,633 kilometres (1,646 miles) on his two horses, Diana and Vlaga, by using the "à la Turkmène" method.

Asseyev's method was to ride one horse in the morning and the other in the afternoon, the led horse being completely "naked" – no pack, no weight. For, as all Long Riders understand, the horse's enemy is not the kilometres but the kilograms. When Asseyev arrived with his two mares beneath the Eiffel Tower, the Society for the Protection of Animals decorated him with a special gold medal because his horses were in excellent shape after such a long journey.

Travelling à la Turcoman requires the Long Rider to carry the absolute minimum of weight. But by using this method one can travel long distances at a great pace, for a horse with no weight on his back is not easily tired

In 2012 the Lithuanian Long Rider Vaidotas Digaitis used this method with great success when he made a 1,600 kilometre (1,000 miles) journey to the Arctic Circle and back. Like Asseyev, Digaitis' two horses also returned in excellent condition.

Whether you walk, trot or go à la Turcoman, the best way to spare a horse is to set a pace that is reasonable and corresponds to the animal's strength.

So can you estimate average daily mileage?

That depends on what century you're riding in.

Answers in Greece

Ancient Greece is usually associated with the birth of democracy. It is also linked to the discovery of an overlooked facet of equestrian travel; despite the passage of nearly 2,000 years, equestrian travellers covered roughly the same daily distance when riding across the same ground.

The first to understand and write about this was Long Rider Edward Dodwell.

Dodwell is the ancestor of the celebrated modern Long Rider, Christina Dodwell. But before he became someone's long-lost uncle, Dodwell was a prisoner of war. Having been captured by the French during the Napoleonic Wars, the Irish officer was offered his freedom; on one condition.

He was granted parole, provided that he did not return to Britain to fight again. This prompted Dodwell to set off in 1801 to ride through Greece instead. He spent the next five years searching for architectural evidence of Greek's classic period.

Dodwell's book, *A Classical and Topographical Tour through Greece*, recounts how he sought out classical ruins, measured neglected temples, painted hundreds of landscapes and revelled in the beauty of the countryside.

In addition to writing about the wonders of that lost world, Dodwell also made keen equestrian observations. For example, he recalled how his pack horse fell into a stream, thereby damaging the beautiful drawings he had painstakingly made of the ancient buildings. Ever the student of architecture, Dodwell also recorded how the Greek Orthodox churches were intentionally built with doors so narrow as to allow only one person to pass through. This was designed to deter mounted warriors from the neighbouring Ottoman Empire from turning the churches into stables.

But the Irish Long Rider's most significant equestrian discovery was that despite the passage of centuries, the distances he travelled on horseback matched those made by Greek scholars who had ridden the same roads centuries before.

Two classic Greek scholars provided the academic evidence needed for Dodwell to reach this conclusion.

The geographer Strabo (64 B.C. – 29 A.D.) travelled extensively in Egypt, Kush and the Mediterranean world, then wrote a seventeen volume descriptive history which described all the people and places known at that time.

Another renowned traveller was Pausanias (110 A.D. - 180 A.D.), who was famous for his first-hand account in his ten-volume travel book *Descriptions of Greece.*

Armed with the works of these earlier travellers, Dodwell set out to explore Greece in the hoofprints of their horses. He was shocked to realize that despite the passage of nearly 2,000 years, the daily progress of equestrian travellers had remained constant.

"Distances in Greece are not regulated by measure, but computed by time. The Tartars, who travel on small and fleet horses, without any encumbrance, except their pipe and tobacco bag, pass over rocks and mountains, through forests, swamps, and trackless wilds, with a truly astonishing velocity. They accordingly use a totally different method of computation from that which is commonly adopted in Greece by those who travel with luggage horses, which are calculated to go throughout the day's journey, at the average pace of three miles an hour; but from this rate, some deductions must be made in mountainous roads."

This rough kind of calculation is more accurate than might be imagined."

After he concluded his extended equestrian trip, Dodwell wrote, "The Author, during his journey, measured all the distances by this method, and comparing the result with the Greek historian Strabo and the Greek traveller Pausanias, he had the satisfaction to find, that the difference was frequently very immaterial."

Constant Mileage

The discovery made by Dodwell demonstrated how the average daily distance travelled remained remarkably consistent for hundreds of years.

Given ideal conditions mounted travellers did cover an impressive number of miles.

For example, in 1892 Evelyn Burnaby, brother of the famous English Rider, Frederick Burnaby who had ridden across Central Asia, averaged 27 miles a day during his 2,050 kilometre (1270 miles) ride from Land's End, England to John O'Groats, Scotland.

"Dodwell's Discovery," that equestrian travel allowed for some degree of prediction, was confirmed by a Long Rider who journeyed in two centuries.

Swedish Long Rider Valdemar Langlet first rode across Russia in 1894. He concluded that journey by staying with the famous author and enthusiastic horseman, Count Leo Tolstoy. Then in the early 1930s Langlet made an extended journey across Hungary. Though the journeys had been made in the 19th and 20th centuries, they had some similarities.

After the Hungarian ride, Langlet wrote, "How many miles can one cover under a glaring summer sun? It depends entirely on the horse and his rider. If we mount at six in the morning and take some intermediate rest, we can make 15 to 20 miles by eleven o'clock, when we have to stop because of the heat. By getting up at sunrise, and profiting by the cooler hours of the afternoon too, we can easily put behind us 25 to 30 miles a day, with 30 being taken as the maximum. With the two indispensable rest days a week, we can cover about 650 miles a month. It is not a long-distance ride; some would call it making ground slowly, though I know the speed is just right."

But unforeseen circumstances were always lurking in the background, ready to slow down a traveller's progress.

Long Rider and equestrian author Roger Pocock remarked on this in 1914, when he wrote, "For the day's work, an average horse can keep up an average of five miles an hour, and this with most horses is the best speed for sustained travel.

For 1,000 miles and upwards, or a month's work, few horses can average more than 21 miles a day without breaking down in the forelimbs. For sustained work at high speeds more than one horse is needed, and the cowboy, working eight months at 50 miles a day, requires six horses, three ridden each day, with one animal in reserve."

Yet even as the 20th century progressed towards the halfway point, remnants of the previous equestrian age still allowed Long Riders to maintain a strong average daily speed.

During Malcolm Darling's ride across India in 1947 he covered 2,500 kilometres (1,500 miles), during 85 marches, averaging 16½ miles each, with 32 for the longest and 4 for the shortest. On 22 days he did not ride.

A study of previous generations of Long Riders reveals that they averaged 20 miles per day.

This mileage was however based upon physical facts and cultural features which were dependent upon the time when the ride was made.

Long Riders travelling up to 1910 routinely made rapid progress, thanks to a number of reasons. Overall, the riders were in better shape than modern travellers. They rode horses which were in better overall condition. Because so many suitable horses were available, riders could easily change animals when trouble arose. Most importantly, travellers had far more logistical support, in terms of finding food, farriers and shelter. It was thanks to this abundant supply of grain, hay and stables that they spent far less time trying to find food and shelter for themselves and their mounts.

The echoes of these ancient equestrian practices held sway until the halfway point in the 20th century. Until then Long Riders could still hope to find remnants of the previous equestrian age, any one of which helped increase their overall daily progress. Even if the stables were now closed, at least there were plenty of people still alive who had grown up around horses and understood their needs.

New Century, New Problems

Historical facts demonstrate that from Edward Dodwell's journey in 1801 until Malcolm Darling's ride in 1947, a person could make an accurate estimate based on level, trouble-free travel. Twenty miles was in fact an average daily distance.

That number was based upon there being no geographic challenges, no extremes of temperature, the roads being good, forage and shelter being routinely available, and the riders and horses both being properly conditioned.

The question then becomes, what can a modern Long Rider estimate as the average modern day's distance?

Popular belief is that under favourable conditions you can still aim for 20 miles per day as an average.

In actuality the dawning of the internet age brought an end to mankind's rapid equestrian progress.

The daily average has decreased by nearly half in the 21st century, with today's equestrian travellers averaging between 11 and 15 miles per day.

A recent example was found when Pete Langford rode across both islands in New Zealand in 2013.

"So in the last 33 days I have had 13 rest days and 20 riding days. The longest day's ride was the infamous Nokomai Station to Nevis Crossing overnighter. That lasted 19 hours and covered 60 kilometres (37 miles). The shortest day has been Omakau to Lauder, which was only 8 kilometres (5 miles). In the 20 days of actual riding I have covered 381 kilometres (236 miles) which gives me an average daily distance of 19.01 kilometres (11.8 miles). I'm happy with that. It is good steady progress without pushing the horses too hard at the beginning of the ride."

Previously, in 2011, Long Rider Colleen Hamer averaged 11 miles a day during her journey in the United States.

Two different journeys, on either side of the planet, but both demonstrate a sharp decrease in mileage.

Why?

Previous generations were most often delayed by harsh weather and bad roads.

From a purely technical point of view ghastly trails, cruel weather and challenging terrain will still delay any Long Rider's progress. The Gobi hasn't become any cooler or the Himalayas any smaller.

But in the past Long Riders travelled through a world largely devoted to the pursuit of agriculture. This meant suitable food and adequate shelter was often available and costs were minimal.

Things are different for the modern Long Rider. He has become an anomaly, an equine oddity looking for grain and hay in a motorized age.

As a result Long Riders around the world increasingly devote a large part of the afternoon searching for food and shelter. This in turn decreases the daily mileage.

Other new types of delays abound. An ever-increasing number of cities are banning horses entirely. Police routinely harass mounted travellers. Motorized traffic is a murderous menace.

And there is another reason daily progress has decreased; a radical change in the social climate.

In the past people routinely saw horses during the course of the day, as major cities were the homes of vast urban herds of equines that worked in a wide variety of occupations. Seeing a horse did not elicit surprise or draw large crowds of astonished on-lookers.

Times have changed.

The sudden appearance of a Long Rider reveals a travelling remnant from another age. Suddenly an immensely large, beautiful and mythical animal has entered into a mundane world addicted to chrome-covered machines.

Modern Long Riders have learned that their travel plans are increasingly delayed by people seeking to touch the horse, to ask questions, to take photos, to share the magic of the journey. Such interactions take time and delay progress.

Thus daily distance has decreased. Yet no matter what century a Long Rider made his journey in, he had to learn how to balance a desire for mileage against the welfare of the horses.

In this respect a modern Long Rider must realize that there are still a number of things, places and events that will affect your rate of travel.

The first is you.

Tough Riders

Experts in the 19th century believed that a man's endurance was about two and a half times that of a horse. While I have no way of gauging the accuracy of that estimation, what I can confidently predict is that it has dramatically diminished thanks to the onset of global obesity and an overall decline in human strength.

Have no doubt that neither you nor your horse will ever equal horsemen of yore or their mounts.

A brilliant example of this bygone age was Subotai, the renowned Mongolian general who led the army of Genghis Khan to so many victories. In 1239 he and his Mongol cavalry crushed the Russians. He wasted no time invading Europe. The flower of European knighthood gathered to fight the fast-riding Mongols. Subotai smashed them into dust.

Having spent his life riding fast and far, the Mongol general had little respect for the fair-weather riders he encountered in Europe.

"They are town-bred people," he is quoted as saying, "so they cannot endure fatigue."

Subotai was also an astonishing equestrian traveller.

At one point he was required to return from the edge of Europe to the heart of Central Asia as quickly as possible. He did so thanks to the ingenious and efficient mail system known as *örtöö* which Genghis Khan had instituted across his vast empire. This predecessor of the American Pony Express made use of well guarded relay stations where large numbers of horses were ready for instant service.

Riding from one *örtöö* outpost to another, sometimes tied to the saddle to ward off exhaustion, stopping only for short periods to eat, Subotai galloped 2,000 kilometres (1,200 miles) from the shore of the Caspian Sea to Samarkand in little more than a week.

The Mongols were a dim memory by 1759, when an Englishman named John Woodcock proved that tough horsemen were still in the saddle. Woodcock responded to a challenge which stated that he could ride 4,700 kilometres (2,900 miles) in twenty-nine consecutive days, using no more than one horse a day.

Woodcock set off on May 4th at 1 a.m., his route having been illuminated by lamps fixed on posts. His only crisis came on the day when his horse, Quidnunc, tired after sixty miles; he had to requisition a replacement and start again. This required him to ride a total of 160 miles in one day. He successfully completed the challenge on June 1st at six p.m.

Remarkable rides were being recorded well into the 19th century. Swiss Long Rider Henri Moser observed how the Turcomans, "were known to make long journeys of eight days of 120 miles a day, staying in the saddle for 20 hours a day."

Because modern riders aren't as robust as their forefathers, they can't hope to cover such dramatic distances.

The next major consideration is the horse.

Soft Horses

Even if the rider was as hard as nails, the horse had to be equally athletic otherwise the journey was doomed.

Previous generations understood that the ability to cover many miles depended on what condition the horse was in. That is why Mongols believed that if you had a strong horse great distance was of no concern.

This distrust of soft horses was not restricted to the East, as knowledgeable travellers, authors, and even politicians, voiced worries about the rise of pampered equines.

As early as 1836 M. G. Manwaring expressed concern in his book, *A Comparative View of the Form and Character of the English Racer and Saddle Horse during the Past and Present Centuries.*

He wrote, "The natural qualities of the horse's endurance, weight-carrying power and speed maintained over long distances, are found at their best in the animal which has been reared under natural conditions."

Across the Atlantic, American equestrian expert Colonel Theodore Dodge made a similar observation when he released his book, *Riders of Many Lands*, in 1901.

Dodge believed that civilization spoiled the horse.

"When the horse is stabled, shod, and fed on corn, his character undergoes a change. He either becomes morose, ill-tempered, hard to manage and dangerous, or he degenerates into a fat, lazy, short-winded cob only fit for a baby or an octogenarian."

He endorsed the ranch horse that worked hard and was then turned out on the prairie. Such horses were tough survivors capable of travelling great distances.

This antagonism towards preferential treatment even became government policy in some countries.

Cecil Rhodes, founder of Rhodesia, was opposed to importing English horses and breeding them to the hardy horses which lived in the Cape Colony.

He voiced his opinion against allowing large hot-blooded English horses to be bred with the smaller, resilient native horses that lived in the Colony. Imported horses, Rhodes said, were unsuitable for work and travel in Africa, as they needed greater care in housing, feeding, and grooming than the conditions of life in Africa would allow owners to bestow upon them.

"The hardships attendant upon long journeys over rough country, the extremes of heat and cold which horses must endure with insufficient shelter or none at all, must inevitably overtax the stamina which has been weakened by generations of luxurious existence in England," Rhodes warned.

Rhodes believed that no infusion of refined English Thoroughbred blood would enhance the powers of the small colonial breed. On the contrary, even if Thoroughbred blood improved the native horse's height and speed, these advantages would be obtained at the cost of such indispensable qualities as endurance and the ability to thrive on poor and scanty fare.

Horses in Condition

Modern Long Riders should pay careful heed to these arguments.

It is taken for granted that any horse used for a journey has been well-conditioned but the importance of this point must be again insisted upon. Without proper conditioning it is impossible for the animal to properly endure the fatigue and exertion involved with any prolonged effort.

History is replete with examples which demonstrate how conditioning a horse can affect the outcome of a journey. One extraordinary example occurred in 1885 when Colonel John Biddulph led the 19th Hussars into the Sudan.

British cavalry officers realized that English horses could not endure travelling under a tropical sun, all the while being required to survive on a scarcity of water and scanty desert food. It was therefore decided before leaving Cairo to mount the English regiment entirely on the Arabian stallions normally used by the Egyptian cavalry.

Three hundred and fifty of these small horses were procured. The average height was 14 hands, the average age was 8 years and the average price was £18.

It was, according to Colonel Biddulph, the best money England ever spent.

To say the horses were in good condition would be an understatement. They had already survived a brutal campaign in the Eastern Sudan, before they were marched 350 kilometres (210 miles) to meet the Hussars.

No sooner were the Hussars mounted than the column set off. It promptly marched across 580 kilometres (360 miles) of desert to Korti, covering an average of 26 kilometres (16 miles) per day, during which the horses survived on a daily ration of 6 pounds of barley and 10 pounds of chopped barley stalks.

While the main body rested at Korti, a detachment of fifty Hussars went to Gakdul, 160 kilometres (100 miles) distant, on a reconnaissance; they performed the march in sixty-three hours, had fifteen hours' rest at Gakdul, and returned in the same time. Six of the party returned more rapidly, covering the 100 miles in forty-six hours, the last 50 being covered in seven and a-half hours. During these marches the horses were ridden for eighty-three hours, the remaining fifty-eight hours of the time being absorbed by halts.

The regiment then rapidly crossed 540 kilometres (336 miles) of desert to reach Gubat. They averaged nearly 28 miles per day during this part of the trip.

The hardest day occurred when the Hussars travelled 40 miles in 11½ hours, from 4.30 a.m. to 4 p.m., the horses receiving each half a gallon of water and 4 pounds of grain. When the final advance to the Nile was made, the horses went fifty-five hours with no water at all and only 1 pound of grain.

The English Hussars were able to travel so effectively because their Arab horses were in splendid condition.

As this gruelling ride through the Sudan demonstrates, one of the preliminary requirements in preparing for any journey is to properly condition the horses. The only way horses can be hardened properly is to put them under saddle and take them on the road prior to departure.

Horses in bad condition are the mark of inefficient training. If asked to undergo hard travel in a soft state, exhaustion and sore backs will soon occur. Such accidents will delay your progress or result in your trip being cancelled.

In addition, there are many other challenges waiting to impede your progress.

Delays and detours

There are a number of consistencies in the history of equestrian travel. One of them is how Long Riders throughout the ages have struggled to move forward.

Three Americans provide evidence of this unfailing theme.

In the early 1930s Ernest Fox made an extensive equestrian exploration of Afghanistan. The trip was brutal.

"We walked and climbed and worked at the exhausting task of taking horses down into deep, hot, steep-walled ravines, and out again, and down and up and out and down and up again until we cried out to Nature for mercy."

At the beginning of the 21ˢᵗ century Stan Perdue set off to ride across the United States.

"My shortest riding day was 6 miles and the LONGEST day was 45 miles thru the desert of New Mexico. What a day!"

More recently Ed Anderson rode the length of the Pacific Crest Trail from Mexico to Canada.

"There are places and days where five miles seemed like an eternity."

You would do well to heed these travellers' warnings.

Never underestimate the day's challenges.

Expect them.

They're unaccountable, unavoidable and will test your resolve.

Weather Causes Delays

Bad weather is part of every journey.

Being caught out in a cold rain storm will slow your progress and threaten to break your spirits. Those who have done it will remember the acute discomfort; those who have not will never be able to really understand the intensity of this distress.

Riding in the rain should be avoided if possible. Yet as Sea G Rhydr discovered, rain is often inescapable.

"Within an hour it started to pour, thunder and lightning and hail. Cold and wet and the trail running like a small river. Waterfalls were cascading down the steep rock canyon walls. There were 37 river crossings on the way out and the trail was rocky and slick. After about four miles my horse, Jesse, just quit. He'd had enough and wasn't carrying me another step. I got off and walked the next five miles, leading Jesse and trusting the packhorse Finehorn to follow, which she did. Eventually the trail levelled out and Jesse came up and nudged me and let me know that I should get back on, which I gratefully did."

When halted in cold, stormy and rainy weather the horse's tail should be turned to the wind.

Extreme heat will also alter your travel plans and decrease your daily mileage.

Tim Cope endured life-threatening heat while crossing the desert of Kazakhstan.

"Because of the heat, I would rise at 3 a.m. and be on the move by 5. The sun would rise almost at the same moment that the moon set. They seemed to mirror each other for a moment before saying goodbye. At this point the day begins to heat up rapidly. By 9 a.m. you are wondering if that cool air was just a dream or not."

As Tim learned, in the hot weather it is well to start at sunrise so as to make use of the cool hours and to get your horse under cover before the sun is at its hottest. It is a great mistake to set a fast pace if one has far to go, tempting as the early morning may be. A slow steady pace should be set and kept.

Horses sustain dry heat much better than they do moist. If you must travel in very hot weather it is a good plan to make short halts under shade as a respite from the direct rays of the sun has a most refreshing effect on the horse. The rider should always dismount when halted and, in hot weather, should turn the horse's head to face the breeze.

Do not forget that riding directly towards the rising or setting sun will impede progress.

Terrain cause Delays

Attention should always be paid to the condition of the ground travelled over.

Canadian Long Rider Bonnie Folkins discovered how dangerous it can be to travel across poor ground.

"There is a devastating new problem in Mongolia brought on by over-grazing. Because of the globalization of the cashmere industry, nomads are raising huge herds of Cashmere goats that not only eat the grass but pull out the roots. As a result of overgrazing the terrain has become the home to a certain type of steppe mouse. These rodents dig enormous colonies underground, which are extremely dangerous to the rider as the horse sinks down hard and fast without warning. There were areas where we had to move at a snail's-pace for days because of these treacherous mouse colonies."

You must remain mentally flexible when you are in the saddle. If the terrain presents unexpected challenges, don't allow loyalty to a prearranged route to blind you to the safety and needs of your horse.

Muddy ground should not be covered at a fast pace. If you run into stony ground, be alert to the clicking sound of a loose shoe.

Obstacles Cause Delays

Never take your daily distance for granted. This was a lesson learned by Long Rider Lewis Freeman, who set off in 1920 to explore the remote Selkirk Mountains of British Columbia.

Freeman was no novice. He had spent the years between 1899 and 1912 travelling in Asia, Africa, America and the Pacific Islands. During those journeys he rode horses, pedalled bicycles, paddled canoes, flew in early aircraft and sailed for 22,500 kilometres (14,000 miles).

But even this veteran rover ran into trouble on the Horse Thief Trail.

According to the map the trail ran through the mountains to the headwaters of the Columbia River. Yet as every Long Rider knows, maps are flat-faced liars. The reality was that Freeman encountered a dictionary full of horse-stopping obstacles.

In his book, *Down the Columbia*, he recalled how he and a handful of companions encountered "a beastly stretch of trail."

At first the path took the Long Rider far up the side of a nameless mountain, while a raging stream filled the gorge below with white water. After traversing the dangerous precipice, the trail dropped down and levelled out. That's when Freeman's path was blocked by fallen trees for twelve miles. Having eventually sawed and chopped their way free, the weary travellers encountered a new nightmare.

"The going for the horses was hard at all times, but worst perhaps where the dam of a slide had checked the natural drainage and formed a bottomless bog too large for the trail to avoid. Here the hard-blown animals floundered belly deep in mud and rotten wood, as did also their riders when they had to slide from the saddles to give their mounts a chance to reach a solid footing."

As Freeman proves, trying to travel on a rigid schedule with horses is virtually impossible, as there will be many unpredictable obstacles including heavy snow and forest fires.

If you are riding though timber country then you should expect to encounter downed trees. Ed Anderson had to cut through more than 60 downed trees during his 4,200 kilometre (2,600 miles) ride along the Pacific Crest Trail. Depending upon the size of the fallen timber, this unwelcome task can take minutes or hours to accomplish.

Regardless of the cause, equestrian travellers have to find a way past, around or over obstacles that would cause little delay to a hiker.

Having overcome these sorts of obstacles, Ed cautioned, "Being able to take your time is safest and more fun."

Bad Roads Cause Delays

Previous generations of humans took a dim view of efficient transportation. To them roads meant conquest, exploitation, disinheritance and death. One way people protected themselves from invasion was by making it nearly impossible to travel within the country. The result was villainous horse-killing trails.

Austrian Long Rider Joseph Rock spent two decades exploring remote portions of China. During his travels he routinely eluded murderous bandits and travelled through decidedly dangerous country.

One such trip happened in 1925 when Rock was forced to ride along a "road" that took him through a notorious defile known as the Min-chow Ho.

"We pass over a terrible trail built on props, logs are placed horizontally, one end placed into holes in the cliff, the other supported by props; the whole is covered with twigs and earth and rocks. There are many holes and one can see the river through the trail."

Even if the journey doesn't require you to ride over the tops of logs, roads vary wildly from one nation to the next. In many countries a road is only good for a year and bad for ten.

Care should also be taken even if your journey occurs in a nation blessed with an efficient modern road system. Daily progress is determined by the pace, which in turn is affected by the condition of the road.

Riding a horse at an accelerated pace along a hard road can provoke lameness.

Soft, loose, uneven ground on the roadside often causes injuries to tendons and ligaments. Muddy ground dramatically increases casualties to the lower limbs and induces exhaustion.

During his ride to all 48 American states in 1925, Frank Heath was on the road 231 days, of which he has spent 182 in the saddle, making an average of 22 miles a day.

He warned, "Anyone who has given the matter any thought knows that nature created the horse untold centuries before pavements were ever dreamed of. He is largely a prairie animal. To take him from that to an inflexible surface is like taking the spring from under your automobile, it would not last. The springs within himself are very limited, not nearly enough to absorb the shock of striking a solid pavement. The strain on my horse was not because of the number of miles but because of the hard footing."

Heath also noted, "One mile of pavement takes more out of a horse than two miles of good dirt road. And one mile of dense city traffic reduces a horse as much as three miles of good dirt road in the country. Remember a horse has his limits. In the long run he is a self-repairing machine. His repair shop can work only so fast. Whether he can come back depends largely upon whether he has become merely fatigued or is ruined. The fact that some inexperienced or unthinking person has decreed that a horse must cover so many miles does not qualify him to do it."

Amateur travellers fail to realize that even a perfectly level road has its drawbacks, as interminable straight roads are oppressive to the spirit.

Bad Directions Cause Delays

There is an old proverb in Swedish, "*genvägar är senvägar*," meaning that trying to take a shortcut often makes you late instead of saving time.

When J.R.R. Tolkien completed his book, *Lord of the Rings* in 1954 he included that ancient adage.

"Short cuts make for long delays," Peregrin "Pippin" Took warned his fellow Hobbits.

No matter who first said it, Long Riders know it's still true.

Robin and Louella Hanbury-Tenison had already made equestrian journeys across Spain, France, New Zealand and China. But during their ride through the mountains of Albania, the weary Long Riders made the mistake of thinking they could save some time by cutting cross country.

In his book, *Land of Eagles*, Robin recalled how a short cut nearly led them into disaster.

"We should hit the road in about five minutes, I declared confidently to Louella. We didn't. It was very frustrating, as I knew that the village of Arren lay no more than three kilometres at the most on our left. But thick forest and steep ground lay between us. We couldn't face going back, so we decided to cut across country on a compass bearing. A bad decision. The wood was full of tracks, which petered out and disappeared. Sheer slopes confronted us and we found ourselves pushing through dense undergrowth and encountering jumbles of jagged rocks. It was limestone country and we were in an area of sinkholes, which are about the worst places to take a horse. It was surprising that neither of us were hurt. We were beginning to wonder if we would have to spend the night out, and our nerves were wearing thin, when we hit a proper path and, soon after, the road we had been seeking for two hours."

Robin concluded, "There were few opportunities for short cuts, which in any case often proved more arduous than sticking to the road and going the long way round."

Obtaining accurate directions is another common cause for delay.

Nowadays locals seldom walk or ride great distances. If they do venture far from home they usually rely on some type of motorized transport. This cultural disconnect can have dire consequences for a Long Rider.

A diminished sense of distance means that locals often provide wildly optimistic estimates of how long it will take a Long Rider to reach an outlying destination. Urbanized humans fail to realize that what might take five minutes to achieve in a car could represent many difficult hours in the saddle.

Another problem is that when directions are sought, locals tend to automatically direct a traveller along the same heavily travelled roads used by motorists. They fail to recognize that equestrian safety is more often found along small back streets rather than on a busy dual carriageway.

There is one aspect of equestrian travel which is seldom recognized: how distances can feel endless.

Crossing a vast landscape on a tired horse is certain to test the resolve of even the most dedicated Long Rider.

That was a rough lesson English author and Long Rider Somerset Maugham learned during what seemed to be an endless ride through the desolate mountains of Spain.

"I came at last to the end of the trees and found then that a mighty wind had risen, which blew straight in my teeth. It was hard work to ride against it, but I saw a white town in the distance, on a hill; and made for it, rejoicing in the prospect for I was growing very hungry," Maugham wrote.

"I went on for several hours, battling against the wind, bent down in order to expose myself as little as possible, over a huge expanse of pasture land, a desert of green. I reached the crest of the hill, but there was still no sign of Marchena, unless that was a tower which I saw very far away, its summit just rising above the horizon.

By now I was ravenous. My saddle-bags contained spaces for a bottle and for food; and I cursed my folly in stuffing them with such useless refinements of civilization as hair-brushes and soap. It is possible that one could allay the pangs of hunger with soap; but under no imaginable circumstances with hair-brushes.

At last, there was a tower in the distance, but it seemed to grow neither nearer nor larger; the wind blew without pity, and miserably Aguador tramped on until, the Saints be praised, I found a real bridle-path, signs of civilization, ploughed fields, and I came in sight of Marchena perched on a hill-top, surrounded by its walls."

Humans Cause Delays

Whereas delays such as bad roads or fallen timber are physical, as mentioned earlier in this chapter, interacting with curious human beings increasingly takes time away from a Long Rider's daily progress.

Unlike the vast majority of previous generations, a growing segment of modern humanity is disconnected from Nature. Perpetually confined within four walls, they harbour a hunger to interact with animals, especially horses. Moreover, there is an intense emotional appeal about seeing a free-roaming Long Rider making his way down the road. The dreariness of urban life, with its monthly bills and domestic drudgery, is suddenly held at bay.

The most astonishing example of this type of delay was encountered when South African Long Riders Christy Henchie and Billy Brenchley arrived in Uganda in 2011. Because horses had largely disappeared from the country since 1966, the unexpected appearance of the equestrian travellers caused pandemonium. Crowds of nearly a thousand children poured out of schools and followed Billy and Christy for miles.

In a special report to the Guild, Christy reported, "Eight hundred children of all ages come charging towards the horses which they must have viewed as strange magical creatures. The noise level was tremendous! Cantering didn't faze them. They merely ran after us. When we finally stopped for the evening, the children surrounded us in excitement and began asking questions. Is that a kangaroo? Does it eat people? Is it faster than a bus? Does it speak Arabic?"

It is hard to imagine seeing a horse for the first time. But the sudden re-appearance of travelling horses into any local culture has a dramatic effect.

Daily life is put on hold as eager children rush to inspect, and cautiously touch, these strange animals. Work comes to a halt, as fascinated adults strike up conversations with the Long Rider.

Such encounters will slow your daily progress.

In 1952 Messanie Wilkins remarked, "It wasn't a question of a delay here and there, but of one delay after the other, and all of the delays were based on kindness because people would gather and ask me questions. You can eat up an hour pretty fast that way."

This calls for a delicate balance because as Messanie rightly noted, "Miles are miles and can't be delayed."

Yet you should recognize the fact that you cannot rush the miles or ignore the rich living fabric of the people you ride among.

Making your way down the road on horseback allows you the opportunity to connect with people and to explore the corners of your own soul, one hoof print at a time.

The Horse's Welfare Causes Delays

Minor delays will occur every hour because you will always put the horse's welfare before any obedience to the clock.

Whenever a stop is made the rider should try to reduce the thirst and hunger of his horse.

On the march the horses must be offered water to drink as often as possible, even if they may not drink much; the warmer the weather the more frequent the watering.

Because you cannot be sure of the next opportunity, grazing should be allowed at every opportunity, as even small quantities are of value and yield surprising results.

Decreasing Delays

To reduce delays, you should ask yourself these questions every morning.

Are the horses fit?
Have all the shoes been checked?
Is the riding and pack saddle in proper order?
What is the designated start time?
How many miles will be travelled?
Has sufficient time been allotted?
Is the state of the road known?
Are there any rivers or bridges to cross?
What are the weather conditions?
Is there sufficient water on the route?
Are the locations for the first, hourly, and noon halts known?

Start Slow

I have previously warned about the need to begin the day's ride slowly.

There is however also a need to realize that the journey itself must begin with care.

As previously explained, the first hour and the last hour of each day's travel should be marched at a slower rate than the intervening hours. This allows the horse to warm up and loosen its muscles before any increase in the pace is required.

It is also especially important not to push forward too thoughtlessly at the outset of a long journey.

The great British Long Rider, Captain Frederick Burnaby, cautioned, "Nobody but a fool would start off rapidly on a long journey. It is always wise to make a short journey on the first day, in order to see how the saddles fit, and if the luggage has been well adjusted."

Do not hurry your horses at the start of the journey. The first day's journey should not exceed 7 to 8 miles. The second day can be extended 10 to 12 miles; and the third day can settle in to 14 to 16 miles without trouble. After three or four days of careful travel, the horses are usually ready for extended travelling.

Give yourself and the horses time to become acclimatised, make the road your home, and avoid unnecessary hardships. When some months have passed by, you will look back with surprise on the distance travelled over.

Grinding Hard Miles

Before you carry on reading, ask yourself this question.

How many miles do you think you have travelled in a car during the course of your life? Ten thousand? Half a million? Enough to circle the globe several times?

Were any of those miles hard won?

Did you sweat to achieve them?

Did you think a mere mile would never end?

If not, then you, like the majority of modern humanity, have been protected from the reality of riding one bone-shaking mile after another on a horse.

Distances are deceptive when you're on horseback. There are moments when time seems to stand still. At one point in his journey through the Andes, Aimé Tschiffely was the victim of this strange type of mileage mirage.

He wrote, "I was very glad when I sighted the mountain of Potosi, but although it appeared to be very near, I had to ride for two long days before I saw the town."

Robin Hanbury-Tenison also experienced the dreariness which can turn a day's ride into a mental struggle. While riding along the Great Wall of China he and Louella, "suffered from heat, boredom and hard sweaty saddles."

"We thought the afternoon would never end as we dragged ourselves and our tired horses towards Miyun. Our bones ached and there was little to relieve the monotony or take our minds off the discomfort," he wrote. "The very speed which seems so pleasant when all is pleasurable may become frustrating when hunger or the desire for a bath and bed grow strong and the distance ahead must still take some hours yet could be accomplished in minutes in a car."

Travelling at Night

Prior to the onset of the motorized age when millions of cars and irate drivers transformed roads into lethal equine nightmares, American and European cavalries would occasionally travel by night.

For example Britain's vast empire required that nation's far flung cavalry to sometimes undertake a night march so as to avoid riding during the heat of the day. This was a tactic used with success in the Sudan.

Modern Long Riders who are forced to ride across a harsh landscape, where scanty amounts of shade may result in lethal exposure to the hot sun, might be tempted to think that riding in the cool night air will provide an acceptable solution.

Such inexperienced travellers fail to realize that riding at night presents an alarming number of potential dangers to the horse and tactical problems to the rider.

Let's start by asking you to acknowledge how poor your night vision is.

Your ancestors lacked the constant bright light which you take for granted. Lighting was either expensive, i.e. wax candles, or labour intensive, i.e. cutting fire wood. That is why the majority of humanity used every available scrap of sunlight, so as to illuminate vitally important tasks before nightfall.

The majority of urbanized humanity is now constantly exposed to bright lights. As a result their night vision is dramatically diminished. Moreover, they have forgotten what "black night" well and truly means.

The Scottish Long Rider and author, Robert Louis Stevenson didn't devote all his time to creating fictional tales like *Treasure Island*. He also made a memorable equine-assisted journey across France in 1879.

During that trip Stevenson found himself struggling to put one foot in front of the other during a lightless night.

"I have been abroad in many a dark night but never in a blacker. A glimmer of rocks, a glimmer of the track where it was well beaten, a certain fleecy density, or night within night, for a tree, this was all that I could discriminate. The sky was simply darkness overhead; even the flying clouds pursued their way invisibly to human eyesight. I could not distinguish my hand at arm's length from the track, from the meadow or the sky," he wrote.

There are many reasons not to be tempted to ride after dark. One of the primary ones is that a life under bright lights has weakened your night vision and made you forget how truly dark it can become.

But there are plenty of other equally alarming reasons to consider.

Breaking camp is difficult and time consuming. Valuable objects are easily overlooked and often left behind.

Special care must be taken when saddling.

Darkness increases the difficulties of finding and following unknown roads, which in turn slows the journey.

Unless the road is well known the journey may be lengthened by an error in direction.

Because you are riding more slowly, you spend a longer time on the horse's back, which in turn makes night travel more fatiguing than in the day.

English Long Rider Mary Bosanquet warned, "In the day the wilderness has shape and slides past one obediently. But in the darkness it hangs suspended, till one seems to be walking on a treadmill, stationary in time and space."

Therefore, given the many dangers lurking in the darkness, don't travel at night unless you are faced with extraordinary circumstances!

If you absolutely must travel after dark, then never ride on a moonless night. Plan to take advantage of every minute of moonlight.

Whenever possible use a local guide who has knowledge of the road ahead.

Only travel over good roads.

If travelling near motor traffic, affix a light on your pack saddle or around your leg, so as to warn drivers. Wear bright, reflective clothing.

Allow extra time to complete the journey.

If there is any ray of hope in terms of night riding, it is that horses have a very good memory; in the darkest nights they will find their way homeward, if they have but once passed over the same road.

Time and Distance

There is a final hidden danger when considering daily distance: mankind's obsession with time.

Few people recall that the horse once served as an early method of time detection. According to one historian, "When the ancient Egyptians wanted to calculate the diameter of the sun, they galloped a horse along the horizon for the duration of a sunrise, and measured how far it had travelled. Based on the two courageous assumptions that the sun was a) situated on the horizon and b) circumnavigated the earth at roughly the same speed as a horse, the pharaoh's scientists concluded that the golden orb was just over a mile wide."

Telling time has progressed since then. One company proudly advertises a watch which is accurate to within 1/100th of a second.

In the intervening years since the pharaoh raced his chariot, man's liberty has been constantly threatened by a growing addiction to time. It wasn't Gutenberg's famous printing press that transformed the majority of medieval lives. The lives of peasants were radically altered by the invention of the town clock, which turned them into hourly labours. Labour-loving Puritans in Massachusetts so despised idleness that they passed a law in 1663 making it a crime to waste time. "No person shall spend his time idly or unprofitably under pain of such punishment as the court shall inflict."

The result of this century's long obsession can be seen in modern man. One of the cultural ramifications of new technology is that people live in an environment where there is no down time anymore. They have labour-saving devices but their lives are split into fractions of a second.

A wise Long Rider knows not to let time dominate the journey. There are two reasons for this; to protect the horse and to enrich your life. Let's start with you.

During her ride across the Ottoman Empire, British Long Rider Louisa Jebb wrote this reflective thought.

"Ignore Time and he is at once your servant. Treat him with respect and he at once becomes your master."

Katie Cooper did not encounter any deadly dangers during her ride across the American Southwest. Neverthe-less she had an important epiphany.

"It's hard to describe the feeling of having successfully travelled from one state, across another, into a third. It was an unexpected euphoria. Unexpected because I have not consciously thought of the ride as a goal to be achieved, measured in distances. It's more of a pilgrimage through an eternal now."

Long Riders past and present come to realize that it is not the hours on your watch that matter. The journey is measured instead by the availability of a day's grass and the passing of the seasons.

This brings me to the horses.

Don't let Time influence you into pushing your horse too fast.

In 1964 Bill Holt set off at the age of 66 to ride thousands of miles across Europe. A veteran of the First World War, the easy-going Holt had nothing to prove. After spending nearly three years constantly travelling with his beloved horse, Trigger, Holt succinctly explained why his journey had been a logistical success.

"He who travels slowly goes far."

What Bill proved was that horses that advance at a brisk walk will attain their goal by a slow and steady pace.

Fifty years later, young Katrina Littlechild followed Bill onto the road when she set off to ride from Cornwall to Scotland. Like Holt, Katrina realized that her journey was designed not to be rushed.

"My ride has been fantastic, more so now that Cognac and I have settled into a routine that is comfortable and enjoyable for us both. I knew it would have to happen, but I found it hard to slow to his pace initially, but now we have a great bond and understanding that eight years of conventional horse ownership had failed to achieve. The miles mean less now too. When I started I could tell you exactly how many miles I had done in a day. Now I don't keep count as it is not the mileage: it's the going, the weather, the number of gates and what time we set off in the morning and how we feel that determines how hard a day's ride is."

Remember, you are on a journey, not riding for the Pony Express. You are supposed to take your time, enjoy the scenery and not rush. On top of that, trying to push the pace will result in mistakes and injuries.

Tim Cope learned this lesson the hard way.

"On the Betpaqdala plain in Kazakhstan, racing to make up for delays, I went five days without a break in minus 31 degree Fahrenheit temperatures. There was one dot on the map, the village of Akbakai, and I was seduced by the thought of getting there fast. In the rush I lost some gear, my sleeping bag froze, one of my horses developed an abscess in his hoof, and the only shelter I could find was with two alcoholics of rather difficult character. I ended up being stuck in Akbakai for almost three months."

There is a delicate balance between being brisk and being brutal in the saddle.

Lost time must not be recovered by an accelerated pace over a short distance, as rapid riding may result in injuries. But it is equally inexcusable to travel too slowly.

Let Jeremy James have the last word on time, which he prefers to ignore.

"When you have travelled for one week, two weeks, ten weeks, a magical moment arrives; we have covered five hundred miles. A threshold has been crossed, a barrier broken. When five hundred miles is complete, a thousand is as nothing. It is three months away. But once that figure is known: even though it is meaningless, then all else becomes just a matter of time. Then the end of today is the blue horizon way over there, where the edge of the plain meets the rim of the mountains."

No Cruelty

No discussion on daily distance would be complete without acknowledging how mankind has on occasion treated the horse with incredible cruelty.

Animals, like humans, differ greatly. The horse, for example, is unlike the dog.

The dog, the faithful companion who never forsakes his master, when over-fatigued will lie down on the wayside, leaving his friend to proceed alone; no entreaty can urge the canine to exert himself unto death.

Not so the faithful horse. No matter how fatigued or ill he may be, the devoted horse plods on his weary way till death kindly relieves him. What other animal does this?

History has provided dramatic examples of horses accomplishing astonishing tasks. When Harry de Windt visited St. Petersburg, he wasn't impressed by the Czar's jewels or palaces. It was the strength of Russia's horses which put Harry's pen to work.

"I shall not attempt to describe the famous Hermitage with its valuable paintings and exquisite art-treasures; nor the Imperial Treasury and its crown jewels, for details of these may be found in any guide-book. I may mention, however, one object which attracted my attention: the colossal bronze statue of Peter the Great, and especially its pedestal, an enormous block of granite which, weighing over 15,000 tons, was dragged from the marsh where it was unearthed, five miles away, by primitive machinery and 80,000 horses," de Windt wrote.

The equestrian statue which so impressed Harry had been commissioned by Catherine the Great. It required twelve years, from 1770 to 1782, to create the bronze horseman, including pedestal, horse and rider. The statue's pedestal is the enormous Thunder Stone, claimed to be the largest stone ever moved by man (1,250 tons). In its original state the stone weighed 1,500 tonnes.

I cannot advise you on how to harness the power of 80,000 horses so as to pull an enormous rock out of a bog. However, I can say that the success of your journey depends in large measure on the treatment of your equine companion.

Constant hard days on the road will push the horse too hard. If high mileage is demanded for several days it will adversely affect the health of the horse.

Have a care! Exhausted horses can be a danger to themselves and the rider. A horse ridden too hard is more prone to stumble, step off the trail or make mental mistakes. If abused, a horse can be ridden to death.

Stress must be laid on the fact that the horse is the Long Rider's best friend who will carry you through thick and thin.

Upon completing his ride from the Arctic Circle to Copenhagen in 1953, British Long Rider Donald Brown wrote, "Careless horsemanship would have weakened the horses; and there was the pleasure far greater than any miles per hour of finishing 1,500 miles with horses as well filled out and in far harder condition than at the start five months before."

No journey may be counted a success unless you have taken more care of the horse than yourself. To help you do so, it is but right and reasonable to remember the words of *The Horse's Prayer* (author unknown).

> Oh master
> Don't think that I'm your conquest;
> I'm your comrade.
> Speak to me: I will try to understand.
> Lead me: I know how to obey.
> Trust me: I'm loyal.
> Ride, travel with me: I'm strong.
> Do not make me a minion, but your friend.
> You will find none better.

Summary

Carry these ideas with you.

Distance is measured in time not miles.

Count no mile until it is ridden.

The length of each day's journey and pace must be adapted to the condition of the horse, the state of the road and the season of the year.

Every mile travelled is a mile survived.

One day done; many more to come.

He who goes gently goes safely; he who goes safely goes far.

After riding from Arizona to Canada in 1973, Jeff Hengesbaugh discovered that equestrian travel is influenced by a variety of factors, including geography and season.

Authors like C.S. Lewis, Sir Arthur Conan Doyle and Jeremy James have warned that galloping all day and all night is not possible in reality.

In 1895 Lieutenant Cornelius Smith rode from Fort Wingate, Arizona to Fort Sam Houston, Texas in twenty-eight days thanks to the brisk trot of his mustang, Blue.

Russian Long Rider Mikhail Asseyev rode from Kiev, Russia to Paris, France in 1889. During the journey he travelled on his two mares, Diana and Vlaga, by using the "à la Turkmène" method.

Despite the passage of nearly 2,000 years, Edward Dodwell's ride through Greece in 1801 proved that the daily progress of equestrian travellers had remained constant for centuries.

During Swedish Long Rider Valdemar Langlet's rides in the 19th and 20th centuries, he averaged between 20 and 30 miles per day.

Long Riders in the 21st century, such as Pete Langford who rode across New Zealand, have seen their average distance drop to between 11 and 15 miles per day.

During his ride through Central Asia, Swiss Long Rider Henri Moser met Turcomans who routinely made long journeys of eight days of 120 miles a day, staying in the saddle for 20 hours a day.

Knowing they needed horses in excellent condition, British Hussars used Arab stallions to fight in the Sudan in 1885.

During his ride into the Selkirk Mountains of British Columbia, Lewis Freeman's journey was blocked by twelve miles of fallen timber.

Austrian Long Rider Joseph Rock spent the 1920s and 30s exploring remote portions of China.

In 1925 Rock was forced to ride along the notorious the Min-chow Ho trail, which consisted of logs placed horizontally, one end placed into holes in the cliff, the other supported by props, the surface being covered with twigs and earth and rocks.

During her ride across Turkey, French Long Rider Magali Pavin learned that maps can be deceptive and local people often give bad directions.

Interacting with curious people causes a delay in daily progress. These Ugandan school children look in awe upon that strange and rare creature – the horse – ridden by Billy Brenchley.

As a rule the French cavalry did not dismount, which inflicted saddle sores on their mounts.

During her ride across Britain, Katrina Littlechild learned that equestrian travel is about being liberated from time, not being enslaved to it.

After completing their ride from Amsterdam to St. Petersburg, Dutch Long Rider Michel Jacobs and his mare, Lista, stand in front of the statue of Peter the Great, which 80,000 horses pulled into place.

Chapter 67
Hospitality or Hostility?

The history of mankind would be very different if the Chinese communist leader, Mao Tse-tung, had not understood the strategic importance of hospitality.

In October, 1935 Mao and his Communist army were threatened by imminent annihilation from hostile government forces. Realizing that a pitched battle meant defeat for his cause, the ragtag group's leader ordered the Communist troops to undertake one of the greatest strategic retreats in history

Determined to avoid capture and delay any conflict until his army had grown stronger, Mao and his troops set off on a journey across China's most hostile terrain. During the next 368 days they were forced to cross 24 rivers, 18 mountain ranges and dozens of swamps, all the while struggling to keep the troops and their host of animal allies fed, watered and sheltered.

Only 4,000 survivors completed the 6,000 mile journey which has become known as the "Long March." As a result of the incredible hardship and sacrifice suffered during the trip, what might have been an ignoble retreat has entered into China's modern realm of legend as a demonstration of that people's tenacious will to survive at all costs.

While the political implications of Mao's survival are well known, what has not been recognized is that the most enduring bit of wisdom attributed to the Chinese leader has immediate implications for all Long Riders.

"The guerrilla must move amongst the people as a fish swims in the sea," the Chinese guerrilla leader wrote.

Equestrian travel history demonstrates that, like Mao's guerrillas, the success of any Long Ride depends upon the traveller's ability to pass through the countryside peacefully.

Unfortunately, while that is an admirable goal, Long Riders have often found themselves forced to cope with hostility, suspicion and danger.

Ride or Die

It doesn't matter if you are studying a ride across ancient Rome or contemplating a journey through modern Romania, there are certain fundamental rules connected to the practice of equestrian travel which apply in any age and in every country. One of these principles states that if hospitality is withheld the traveller and his horse will surely suffer and perhaps die.

American Long Rider Ernest Fox nearly lost his life as a result of hospitality being withheld. He was making his way through the remote mountains of central Afghanistan in 1937 when his guide deserted him.

"I turned west, keeping a sharp lookout, dejected, disappointed and lonely. Later in the afternoon clouds gathered behind me. The temperature dropped sharply. The western horizon darkened and the wind bore rain in a heavy squall."

It didn't take long before Fox was thoroughly wet and stiff with cold. Frost soon formed on his horse. The freezing duo were relieved when they came over a ridge and spotted the dwelling of an Afghan family. The sight of the home gave Fox and his horse fresh courage. They galloped forward believing rescue was imminent. Instead of a warm welcome, the freezing travellers were rudely rebuffed.

"When I dismounted and shouted for help, a young man told me to be on my way."

The rain turned to heavy, sticky snow as Fox continued his search.

"Soon the wind increased, tearing at us with icy claws; the snow came mixed with sleet driven in swirling sheets; and then the blizzard smothered everything with howling snow and darkness. With nothing left now save my horse and empty saddle, I dismounted to keep from freezing and continued stumbling westward."

Near evening, the half-frozen Long Rider discovered an encampment of Kochi nomads. The migratory Kochis were even more detached from the outside world than most Afghans.

"They are ignorant of all things outside their little pasture, are stubborn, suspicious, unfriendly, and sometimes hostile even to other factions of their own clan," Fox recalled in his book, *Travels in Afghanistan.*

Yet when Fox approached the tent, one of these wanderers rushed out barefoot into the snow to assist the stricken traveller.

"He helped me to dismount, for I had ridden the last mile or so and was then solid in an armour of frozen snow and too stiff with cold and damp to leave my horse."

As this example proves, Long Riders quickly learn that you never take hospitality for granted.

In the case of Fox, the rootless nomads who rescued him maintained an ancient custom of extending hospitality to travellers. But not all nations favour the unexpected appearance of a mounted stranger.

Different Views on Hospitality

The concept of hospitality differs greatly among nations and the citizens of every country. Some nations enjoy a reputation for kindness. Others will let you die on the doorstep.

Russia historically maintained a deep suspicion of travellers. Under the stern government of the Czar, Russians were required to obtain permission from their local police chief before they were allowed to depart from their village or town. Foreign travellers were seldom authorized to enter the country. The result was a nation-wide antagonism against both domestic and foreign travellers.

When American Long Rider Thomas Stevens rode across that country in 1890 he learned that the Russians suspected a traveller on principle, treating him with brusque inhospitality and a spirit of hostility.

"So uneventful is the life of these people that the appearance of a stranger on horseback dressed differently from themselves is an event of portentous possibilities. To some I was a mysterious stranger spying out the country, to others I was an agent of the secret police. In either case I had sinister designs on the people. I received not so much as a solitary glass of milk, from one end of Russia to the other, without buying it."

Primal hospitality is not the readiness to receive into your house a gentleman who has made a favorable impression on you at a social gathering. It is the willingness to host the passing stranger, in need of assistance, whom you never saw before, and never expect to see again. This is the test that is applicable to a country where distances are great and the traveller liable to find himself fatigued or benighted where public accommodation is not to be found.

More than a century after Stevenson rode across Russia; Basha O'Reilly found that a deep-rooted suspicion of strangers had lingered over the years. During her entire journey across that country, she was only invited to a meal once.

Time after time Long Riders learned that a mounted traveller is never his own master. His fate is dependent upon the actions of strangers. That is why even in a nation such as Mongolia, which has always enjoyed a reputation for hospitality; individual reactions to an equestrian traveller could never be taken for granted.

During the winter of 1892 the Japanese Long Rider, Baron Fukushima, tried to negotiate to sleep inside a Mongol's yurt. The suspicious owner refused.

"That night was spent on the cold dirt behind the yurt," the Baron wrote.

The Roots of Suspicion

As these examples demonstrate, the concept of hospitality is a two-edged sword. It is vitally important to the success of your journey but receiving it depends upon the acceptance, trust, tolerance, assistance, patience and generosity of strangers.

In the past, culture, race, geography and tradition all too often separated us from our neighbours. These differences lay at the heart of many ancient feuds. Modern tourism has helped decrease some of these tensions by encouraging the belief that humanity is interconnected.

But tourists are not Long Riders. Their journey is about avoiding difficulties. They fly there. They pay for services. Their needs and desires are obtained in exchange for money. They do not have a large, hungry, tired animal to tend to. They jet home, tanned but untouched. Unlike you, they have never really entered into the heart of the country.

Tourists reside in the climate-controlled environment of a hotel. That is not like the intimacy which a Long Rider experiences when staying with a host. A Long Rider wakes up in the home of his host like a strange bird in a nest. For a short time both your lives have become entwined thanks to the magic of the horse. The ancient tradition of hospitality is at the heart of this generosity.

Brotherhood

Hospitality laws were real in Dark Ages society. A host and guest were not allowed to harm each other even if they were enemies. By violating that law, the phrase is, they "condemn themselves for all time."

Many countries still respect this sacred code. One sterling example is tiny Albania, Europe's only primarily Muslim country, where a code of honour known as *besa* treats hospitality as a sacred obligation.

Though their journeys were separated by a century, two Long Riders enjoyed the benefits of *besa* in Albania.

The English poet Lord Byron was the first Long Rider to write about this country's hospitality. During his equestrian travels through Albania in 1809, Byron was deeply impressed with "the Albanian's instinctive hospitality and kindness." He contrasted it with "the absence of these qualities in more civilized societies."

Byron had noted how the hardy Albanian mountaineers had extended the "hand of welcome" and treated him with unexpected kindness.

Time marches on. Governments come and go. But *besa* has survived in Albania, as Robin and Louella Hanbury-Tenison discovered when they rode through the same country Byron had previously explored.

The mountain village of Shkoder was isolated much of the year due to heavy snowfall, making it difficult for supplies to be brought in. A lack of amenities was not enough to break the code of *besa*. When the weary Long Riders reached Shkoder, the village school master rushed to comfort the strangers.

"They had almost nothing. Yet they willingly offered it all."

Why, Robin wondered? As he prepared to leave, the school master hugged the Long Rider and said, "We would sacrifice our sons for our guests."

A Sacred Trust

Though Long Riders are required to spend a great deal of time alone in the saddle, theirs is not a lonely endeavour. Circumstances demand they become socially involved with the people whose country they are riding through.

The weary Long Rider appears in search of the legendary requirements of all equestrian travellers: food, fire, shelter, grass and water. In exchange for providing these necessities the host receives an emotional return from the traveller. For at night the walls of his home are enlivened with stories from afar.

Thus is established the sacred bond of trust between a Long Rider and his hosts.

But seeking hospitality makes us emotionally vulnerable. We must summon the courage to approach a stranger and ask for help. The host in turn is suddenly asked to stop the flow of his well-ordered existence, to unlock his door, to throw open his heart so as to tend to the needs of a stranger.

This type of exchange has been happening between "people with walls" and "people with saddles" since the days when Kikkuli the Mitanni horse master undertook an equestrian journey in 1400 B.C. Kikkuli's journey demonstrates that Long Riders have been riding into villages and people's lives for at least 3,500 years.

Thus your trip represents more than just an individual journey. It represents a tradition of trust that reaches back to the Bronze Age roots of the Long Rider movement.

Long Rider Legacy

We would expect that travellers who display an attitude of emotional hostility and physical aggression against the natives will leave a residue of evil behind them. Yet it is more subtle than that.

In the year 1873 English Long Rider Andrew Wilson travelled through one of the most inhospitable but beautiful mountain ranges in the world, the mighty Himalayas. For six months Wilson made his way through these unforgiving mountains, struggling against the elements, desperate to buy provisions from a suspicious native populace, and always trying to fight off the unrelenting cold.

A veteran correspondent, he noted, "Some men will travel through a country without being guilty of any act of violence, or even of uttering an angry word, and yet they leave behind a feeling of bitter hatred not only towards themselves but also towards the race and government to which they belong."

Wilson was right. The impression you create leaves an equestrian echo which will affect the destiny of other travellers who follow in the hoofprints of your horse.

This principle was demonstrated in 2013 when Sea G Rhydr rode into the tiny town of Flora, Mississippi. Sea's "ocean to ocean" journey had required her to interact with a multitude of strangers. But that day in April she was surprised to see a man walking purposefully towards her.

Leslie Childress, the mayor of Flora, was determined to meet Sea. He was motivated by a similar chance encounter that had occurred in 1976. That was the year that 14-year-old Leslie Childress had met Lucy Leaf, another Long Rider who had ridden into Flora on her own journey across America. Lucy had planted a seed which took 37 years to bloom.

During the intervening years Mayor Childress had told many people about Lucy's trip and how it had inspired him throughout his life to have met a person who had the courage to follow her dream. It took nearly forty years before the boy, who had grown up to become the town mayor, invited Sea to become the second Long Rider guest at his family home.

Back in 1940 an astute English Long Rider named James Wentworth Day put his finger on why the event in Flora, Mississippi had taken place.

"No matter where you ride," he said, "I found the sound of a horse's hooves to act as an open sesame to a stranger's heart."

During her ride across America in 2013, Katie Russell made this important observation.

"One lady said to me, 'Just remember, you are riding for all of us!' That meant a lot to me. Sometimes I feel like a symbol to people, a symbol of the freedom so many people desire but are unable to realize. I hope at least one person is inspired to live their dreams because of us!"

Sundowners

As these examples demonstrate, from Albania to Mississippi many cultures look upon hospitality as the first task of civilized man. What is seldom reported is the guest's equal responsibility to behave in an ethical manner to his hosts.

Unfortunately there are those who have realized that the horse can be turned into an accomplice to crime.

A special breed of loafer was found in Australia in the late 19th century. Known as "sundowners," these roamers knew how to exploit the charity and kindness of others.

In the days of the Old West American cowboys were often required to ride from ranch to ranch in search of honest work. Long Riders were also able to find food and shelter amidst these far flung homes.

Frank Heath set off in 1925, determined to ride to all 48 American states. During the course of his gruelling 18,000 kilometre (11,000 miles) trip he and his mare, Gypsy Queen, were the guests of some remarkable people.

"This is a strange life. One night I curl up in an empty stall, the next I am being entertained like a prince. In Utah I was invited to spend the night with a Ute Indian. You come my house, you put your horse my barn. Him sit down. You come my house. You sit down, he said, eyeing me critically. I looked him straight in the eye, nodded, and said not a word. He was satisfied. He knew I was a traveller, not a renegade. This was the custom of the country. Even if a man is broke, he is not sent away from the ranch, unless he shows signs of being a professional bum."

"Down Under" in Australia another type of person also made the rounds between ranches. Known as "sundowners," these individuals would wander from one ranch to the next. They were not looking for employment; in fact they were intent on avoiding it. Their loyalty was to their stomachs.

Sundowners gained their name because they timed their arrival at a ranch to coincide with sundown, by which time there was no possibility of having to work for supper. Such individuals gained a bad reputation across the country.

Fast forward into the 21st century and a new type of mounted exploiter has emerged to prey upon the public. Having learned the truth in the old Long Rider saying, "The horse is the key to the village," various types of rogues, deceivers, crooks, liars and cheats have used the horse to exploit the trust of the public and to beguile the press.

These travelling con artists often claim they are motivated by patriotism or religion. They are quick to accept donations for a charity that doesn't exist. They grasp the Bible in one hand and pick the pockets of the unwary with the other. They wave the flag and steal people blind. They exploit the kindness of their hosts in order to gain money, shelter, supplies and services.

Such modern Sundowners are not restricted to Australia, though glaring examples have been found there.

One such woman in Australia ran up an extraordinary long-distance telephone bill in the home of the elderly lady she was staying with. In the wake of the 9-11 tragedy, one mounted American conman used his ride to "Ground Zero" to fleece unsuspecting shop owners into supplying him with valuable supplies which he never paid for. One bold bandit spent the night as the guest of a mounted police force and stole equestrian gear from their tack room during the night. Others have moved in on their hosts like hungry locusts and were nearly impossible to dislodge afterwards.

A French traveller even published hints on how to take advantage of potential hosts.

"Steal milk from goats grazing in unwatched pastures. At sunset, give children candy or a ride on the horse in the hopes that their grateful parents will invite you to supper, stay with the peasants being sure you leave before dawn, after quietly stealing grain and fresh eggs. When about to be presented with a bill for your lodging and you see the proprietor about to tell you the price, warmly thank him for his gracious hospitality. Taken aback, he will not dare present the bill. If he does demand the money, either burst into tears or turn out your pockets smiling. He will be angry and despise you, but tell you to leave without paying."

These are the ones who poison the metaphorical watering hole for all those unlucky Long Riders who follow in their wake by jeopardizing the future goodwill of the people.

The sacred law of hospitality to the stranger cannot be underestimated.

Local Suspicions

Our potential hosts aren't stupid. Rumours linger long after a mounted charlatan has ridden on.

A prospective host makes a decision based upon available information. Unfortunately it isn't always accurate. When locals distrust travellers, it is the Long Rider and his horses who suffer.

Plus, we are constantly reminded that we live in highly insecure times.

People fear what they do not know or understand. They long for a feeling of safety. They struggle with the desire to help a stranger versus the need to protect their family. History proves that sometimes they keep the door locked and deny hospitality to avoid risk.

The term "long rider" once had a very different meaning. It was associated with the infamous American bandit, Jesse James. Willard Glazier encountered such intense misgivings during his "ocean to ocean" journey across North America in 1875 because of this reason.

"Upon leaving La Salle at three o'clock in the afternoon, I was told that I would have no difficulty in securing accommodations for myself and horse at Hollowayville. So with the assurance of finding everything lovely there, I jogged along over the intervening twelve miles at my leisure. My feelings can better be imagined than described when, on my arrival at the little hamlet, I was looked upon with suspicion. The simple-minded inhabitants hinted that I might possibly be a "highwayman" or a "horse thief," or, for aught they knew, one of the Jesse James gang. These desperadoes were then exciting the people on both sides of the Mississippi and my equipment, set off with high top boots and gauntlets, with the peculiar trappings of my horse, only made matters worse. Finding it impossible to secure lodging in the village, I rode on into the country, stopping at a farm house which looked inviting."

Suspicion is not sexist. It falls upon female travellers just as quickly as it does on men.

Mary Bosanquet was denied hospitality during her ride across Canada in 1939.

"I chose a large and prosperous looking house, deciding that here they would hardly fail to have room for me. I knocked. After some time a middle-aged lady – grey hair, grey eyes, grey dress and straight as a pine – lifted the latch and looked at me through the screen door. What did I want, she inquired? Diffidently I asked whether the pony and I might stay the night. She regarded us. 'No,' she said finally, 'I have men in for the haying. I hardly think I can keep you for the night.' I wilted. Had she any friends who might keep us, I wondered? She continued to hold me with her unwavering eyes. There was an emphatic silence. Finally she gave judgment. 'Yes, said the steel-grey lady. 'I have a great many friends around here. But I don't think any of them would want to have you.' I retreated with my pennant in the dust."

Jeremy James made an insightful comment about another reason a potential host might deny hospitality to a traveller.

"I met people with many times their resources yet who were unprepared to share even the shadows that were cast in their garden. They exemplified something I have found from my journeys with horses. The poorer the people the more likely they are to help and the poorer the country the kinder the people. Maybe it's because our television sets have replaced our neighbours and we don't need to know them since we get all the information we think we need over the air."

This sense of isolation has been enhanced because of the onset of motorized transport and the dominion of the internet. An increasing number of urban humans lead a largely private experience of life. They ride alone in their car, sit alone in their office, and often live alone in their homes. They are emotionally unprepared for the sudden intrusion of a mounted stranger.

Long Rider Catherine Thompson observed this during her journeys. Whereas she had never been denied a night's rest while riding through the ranch lands of western Canada, the closer she rode to urban areas the more likely it became that a welcome would be refused.

"Thinking of the kind hospitality I have met, it got me thinking of how that changes, how a sort of fear and distrust can develop as one gets closer to more urbanised areas. I think that it is true enough even though I have witnessed the opposite as well. Suddenly there seems to be more wealth, more stuff, more cars and more locked doors."

Cultural Distinctions

Richard Barnes is one of the great poetic Long Riders of the last century. He once wrote, "If only the cynical and the disillusioned knew what it is like to leave the confines of what is generally accepted to be normal life, to make their home by a stream."

The majority of humanity will never participate in that Arcadian event.

Whereas it is true that certain individuals are discourteous and lack the gene of generosity, another element may come into play in terms of being denied hospitality; namely a long-running dislike which settled people harbour against mounted travellers.

Genghis Khan worshipped the blue sky and rode upon the great sea of grass that runs across the Equestrian Equator. He was only restricted, in a geographic sense, by the limits he placed upon his own courage. The world was there, waiting to be explored, if he could summon the bravery to do so.

But the villager, whether he lived in the Middle Ages or resides in the Internet Age, survives in a vastly different world. His physical surroundings don't encourage him to wander away from the security of the village. His nuclear family, his peers, his work mates, his government and his priests actively conspire to crush the spirit of exploration which may dwell in his breast. He lives in a world full of geographical, cultural, spiritual and equestrian restrictions.

And the roads which the villager is encouraged to follow represent the standard of rigid taboos by which his universe is ruled. The road represents the restrictions laid down by the forces of government, the authority of religion, the servitude to money and the ties of domestic duty.

Which brings me to mention the horse; that liberator of humanity.

What the Long Rider represents is another type of brain wave activity, one who isn't restricted by restrictions of the village or even the rules of gravity. Whereas the villager spends his life in some sort of feudalism, be it the slavery of the peasants in the past, or the soul-crushing credit card debt of today's modern urban serfs, nevertheless these people lead lives of quiet drudgery. It's not that they can't just uproot themselves physically, as much as they can't break away emotionally from the system in which they were born, which they know in their soul is destroying them and nevertheless to which they will die in obedience.

Go on your journey, finish your trip and return to the theoretical village we are discussing and what will you find; the same ox-eyed man who rose and ate and slept from year's end to year's end in a narrow, stagnant circle of existence.

By mounting their horse and leaving all that behind, nomadic humans went where they wanted, when they wanted, alongside whom they wanted, as and when they chose. That is why some people may resent you, and deny you hospitality because you violated the lifetime they have spent abiding by the rules, and tending a road that leads only to the grave.

Expect Rejection

It seems obvious, but most fledgling Long Riders do not allow enough time to find nightly accommodations. So long as the sun is shining they push their luck and diminish their chances of locating a safe spot for the night.

Starting as early as possible in the morning allows you to make good mileage, allows your horse to rest at midday and then have time to locate a good night's lodging. If all goes well, you should try to be off the road by 3 p.m., as this will provide your horse time to relax, eat and rest.

But finding such a rarity as a nightly host is not an easy task. Straight away you should not always expect to find anyone at home in every house you see.

If they are home, you have to expect opposition and be ready for rejection.

One Long Rider accurately summed up the search for a host when he wrote, "Some couldn't. Some wouldn't."

Mungo Park is remembered for having made an astonishing equestrian journey through Senegal in 1796. He suffered extreme privation and starvation among the hard-hearted natives. One native chief in particular made a point of denying hospitality to the famished Long Rider.

"With this foreboding, I left my poor horse, and with great reluctance followed my guide on foot, along the bank of the river, until about noon; when we reached Kea, which I found to be nothing more than a small fishing village. The chief, a surly old man, who was sitting by the gate, received me very coolly; and when I informed him of my situation, and begged his protection, told me, with great indifference, that he paid very little attention to fine speeches, and that I should not enter his house. My guide remonstrated in my favour, but to no purpose; for the chief remained inflexible in his determination, I knew not where to rest my wearied limbs."

Learning how to put people's fears to rest is an important part of making your journey a success.

Overcoming Our Own Apprehension

Poor Mungo Park was later captured and held captive for months. He escaped with nothing but his horse and compass.

Luckily modern Long Riders don't have to negotiate with sceptical tribal chiefs.

But just like Mungo, it's your job to overcome local suspicions and your own apprehensions. And this isn't easy. The courage to be emotionally vulnerable is a precondition for a Long Rider.

Jeremy James wrote, "The morning rides were easy because you were relaxed, it was cool, the horse was going well, and there was a prospect of a nice picnic lunch somewhere."

But Jeremy learned that the worry of where he was going to stay always took the thrill out of the afternoon ride.

"It was always a difficult time of day. At your most tired, most hungry, anxious about your night's lodging, food for the horse and a stable, you have also to be at your most charming. It's not easy. Four in the afternoon is quite late to start looking for a night's lodging. I found that if you weren't settled by five, you were not likely to be settled by dark."

The horses don't care about your inner turmoil. They just want to be fed.

Finding food and shelter is a time-consuming daily task. You don't start looking and asking at sundown. You have to expect rejection. You have to allow enough time to move on.

You increase your chances of success by giving a thought to how you look.

Your Appearance

You may be tempted to think that when you are travelling no one worries about the look of your clothes or the dirt under your fingernails.

Appearances can be deceiving. Your travel-stained face and unclean garments may work against you.

It is well known that the horse is exceedingly strong in odour. The overpowering smell of his sweat clings to your hands, soaks your clothes and makes the hot saddle blankets a stinking offence.

When British Long Rider Frederick Burnaby was making his way across Russia in the 1870s his appearance was held against him. Having arrived at a small town, the tired and dirty traveller went to the only hotel.

"On inquiring if I could have a room the suspicious manager informed me that there would be no room vacant for several days. However he gave me the name of an individual who kept a sort of rough lodging house.

It is very dirty but I dare say you don't mind that.

Do you know of anywhere else?

No, and with these words he slammed the door in my face."

As Burnaby discovered, first impressions influence your chances of obtaining food and lodging.

The further he travels the more likely it is that a Long Rider will become increasingly dirty. Unfortunately the chance to bathe is often infrequent. The ability to wash clothes is often restricted to a dunk in the river or a drenching under a water tap.

A noted Swedish traveller once wrote, "Living on the road requires its own tricks. You need to recognize the psychological angle of being clean. It makes you feel more confident when you meet strangers. To be invited out of courtesy as being to someone worthy of respect is quite a different thing from being invited out of mercy."

Many Long Riders have learned to never pass up an opportunity to stay clean and combed. They take every chance to deal with dirty laundry. If need be, they use a bar of soap to wash their clothes when the occasion arises.

That one feels healthier with a change of clean clothes is no secret. To stop for a day's rest without having to occupy oneself with having to wash clothes makes for more freedom and rest.

Give a thought to your appearance. If you look like you ride with Jesse James, don't expect a sceptical hostess to open her door.

Riding to the Door Protocol

Because this book is designed to apply to a vast number of cultures and nations, it is impossible to provide you with an exact formula as to how you approach a dwelling.

Riding up to the door of a ranch house in Mexico will require different social skills than approaching a yurt on the Mongolian steppe. Each country has a different social protocol.

Charles Thurlow Craig learned this during his journey through Paraguay's Chaco jungle.

"Shortly before sundown we pulled up in front of a little ranch that seemed as if it should be able to satisfy our needs. Formalities differ in different countries. In Spanish America, the custom is to ride up and yell, "*Ave Maria*." The owner of the house would then come out and reply in a good hearty yodel "*sin pecado concebida*," which means "conceived without sin," to indicate that no dirty work was intended on either side. It broke the ice, and then you rode in and unsaddled.

But in Brazil the procedure is slightly different. There, on approaching a strange house, it is etiquette to heave to about sixty or more yards off and yell out, "*Da licenca*?" until someone comes out. If he considers you are a safe person he will tell you to get down, and you dismount and approach on foot, leading your horse, If, on the other hand, he does not like the look of you, he will either ask you in an uncompromising voice what you want, or else tell you that he has the smallpox in the family, and return to the house."

No matter where you ride the tradition in most countries is that a stranger never gets off his horse until he is invited to do so.

How and when you dismount depends upon several factors.

Safety in the Saddle

Travelling with horses places us in close physical proximity to strangers. Thus there are issues of personal safety involved every time you dismount.

A keen-eyed Long Rider always looks the scene over carefully as he approaches a potential night's shelter. He knows that more than just social custom require him to stay in the saddle until he is certain all is well.

Many nations keep savage dogs. Ernest Fox was attacked by such beasts in Afghanistan.

"The noisy dogs attempted to make prey of me, holding me mounted, until their masters came to my rescue."

As the day reaches its climax many Long Riders are inclined to look for a potential host among people who happen to already be outside their homes.

The watering of a horse affords an excuse for entering a village or starting a conversation with a stranger. That initial question may in turn lead to a discussion about the availability of grazing, the possibility of obtaining grain or the advisability of the next day's route.

All the while these questions are under way it is the Long Rider who is making his own careful judgment of the prospective host and the safety of the physical surroundings.

Australian Tim Cope's journey from Mongolia to Hungary required him to interact with some potentially dangerous hosts. He developed a careful strategy which he used before dismounting.

"This was part of my plan to drop my guard cautiously, layer by layer, in case I could not trust my hosts. It became a protocol that I would adhere to religiously. The first step was to trust the stranger enough to get out of the saddle. If I felt comfortable after getting out of the saddle I would risk unloading the animals and enter the home. Only over a cup of tea would I explain who I was and where I was headed. The ultimate shedding of defence was unsaddling the horses."

Explain Your Needs

Once you have decided it is safe to dismount, articulate your needs. If you are carrying a firman (official letter of introduction) this is the time to show it.

Newspaper stories also help establish your credibility.

Always explain how briefly you plan to stay and that you will be sure to clean up any manure left by your horse.

Articulate your basic requirements; grass and water for your horse, a corner where you might sleep. Of course modern amenities like a meal and a shower wouldn't go amiss.

Be quick to offer to pay for anything you need, stressing that you're a Long Rider not a saddle bum.

Human Nature

Long Riders are not like mountain climbers or sailors, who interact with the elements and not the people.

Wariness of a mounted stranger is often quickly dispensed with. Curiosity about your journey will turn a frosty sceptic into a potential friend. Once the host laughs, any constraint or reserve shown at first disappears, leaving a feeling of friendliness followed by offers of hospitality.

Once scepticism is laid to rest, curiosity is sure to follow.

People retain many basic characteristics through the ages, one of which is their desire to talk to travellers. In 1795 a Long Rider named Hezekiah Prince made a remarkable 2,000 kilometres (1,200 miles) journey across the newly formed United States. During the course of this singular journey, Hezekiah met President George Washington, whom he noted "was a fine rider on horseback." Hezekiah also observed the White House being built. He was bound for Philadelphia when he made this interesting comment about the locals he encountered en route.

"Their curiosity was boundless. Often have I been stopped abruptly by them, even in solitary parts of the road; and, without any further preface, have been asked where I came from, if I was acquainted with any news, where I was bound to and what was my name?"

Nowadays humans are bombarded by a constant stream of global news.

Yet there is an additional element at play in this ancient give and take between Long Rider and host.

Noted travel author Ed Byrne wrote, "Travellers make many more friends than people who stay put. You get to know someone only for a short while and you show only your best side to each other. Then you part and these new people remain your friends forever. People confide their inmost thoughts. Preliminaries are dispensed with because you're coming from nowhere, going nowhere and you'll probably never see them again."

Byrne was right.

During his journey from Canada to Mexico, Allen Russell, one of the wisest of Long Riders, arrived at a remarkable understanding of why an initially sceptical person suddenly becomes a warm and hospitable host.

Lone Ranger Syndrome

In a special message to the Guild, Allen wrote, "I have never heard a Long Rider say, 'the reason I want to make my Long Ride is to meet people.' In fact, some, I am sure, are more motivated to get away from people. Yet I also have not met a Long Rider who was not deeply moved and inspired by the fascinating people they met and the intense relationships that were formed along the trail. I know this has been so true for me.

It seemed over and over I have ended up in situations where very short-term situations resulted in extremely close kinships. It seemed people were so willing, almost needy, to open up to me. They told me things of the most intimate nature. Sometimes they explained that they had never told anyone these things before or that they had not even realized these things about themselves before Kono (my horse) and I rode into their lives.

Certainly, having a lone horseman on an adventuresome and romantic cross country journey ride into their lives inspired people to draw upon their dreams. Additionally, hearing travel tales of adventure and fulfilment first hand made their own fantasies seem so much more obtainable. I'm sure they also thought that in me they had found an ally who would understand their eccentric yearnings.

Still, I was baffled by the intensity of my experiences and maybe even a little full of myself for having this power, even though, what it was, I had no idea.

Then one day as I rode out of town after such an encounter, it suddenly hit me. It was the Lone Ranger Syndrome. I remembered my favourite (and first) TV show as a child. The mysterious masked man would ride into town, immediately become immersed in people's lives and then ride out of town with a mighty 'Hi Ho Silver Away.'

It all became clear. Sure, having a mysterious horseman ride into their lives, a real life example of living your dreams, rather than talking about them, stimulated the relationships. But, what gave rise to people going to such depths and letting loose thoughts they had never before voiced is not that I rode into town. It was, much more important, that I was going to ride out of town. The reason people opened up and showed me a side of themselves they don't even share with their best friend or spouse was because I was soon going to be gone, out of their lives, never to judge them and their dreams. Hi Ho Kono Away."

As Allen learned, to a settled person the Long Rider appears to be living a dream rooted in personal freedom. Such an idea can be very appealing to those caught up in the daily drudgery of a predictable life.

Unfortunately it's not all wine and roses out there. The human race is an amazingly diverse species. Some people will act like saints. Others will display cruelty and rudeness.

The Antagonism of Settled People

Being adrift and alone makes a Long Rider emotionally vulnerable. Needing to find food and shelter on a daily basis is a daunting task. As might be expected, some individuals take a dim view of a roving rider.

Margaret Leigh was making her way from Cornwall to Scotland when she entered a bad stretch where the farms were large and far apart, making camping very difficult. With night fast approaching, and the weather bad, she approached a farm in search of shelter.

"'Clear out of here,' the farmer yelled, and then plunged into a diatribe against the nasty habits of nomadic people," Margaret later wrote.

Other Long Riders have detected a strong sense of hostility when they enter certain towns and villages.

During his journey through Central America, Orion Kraus was often showered with tremendous outpourings of warmth, affection and generosity; but not always.

"I've mentioned at some point about the feeling one gets when entering a particular town. I know almost immediately when a town has had troubles or is safe. In a troubled area, women peer out their windows cautiously. Kids look at you instead of smiling and laughing. People don't say hello and courtesy and hospitality are in short supply. In safe places, however, the opposite is the case. You can close your eyes and pick any house, and almost be rest assured that they will give you a hand or direct you to someone who can."

Luckily for Long Riders more often than not the people you meet will be friendly, not hostile.

Riding through the dark Canadian night, Mary Bosanquet was in desperate need of help.

"Four houses turned us down. Feeling small and negligible as a leaf in the wind, I wandered on into the gathering dusk, wishing I were either child enough to cry or adult enough not to want to."

But it wasn't always bad. A few miles may spell all the difference. Later in her trip Mary was the recipient of one of the most dramatic examples of hospitality ever recorded.

"Out of the car climbed a fair-haired young cowboy whom I had met some time before in the course of my travels. He pushed his hat back, looked at me with sky-blue eyes and said, 'Come back and marry me girl. I'll give you all the Thoroughbreds you can ride.' He accepted my kind refusal with fortitude."

As Mary learned, the discovery of so many surprising people brings a deep emotional richness into a Long Rider's life.

The Need for Companionship

Don't confuse travelling alone with being alone. Long Riders need human companionship, not just from a practical point of view but on a deeply emotional level as well.

In many respects a Long Rider travelling across the landscape is a small island of isolation.

There are intense periods of dire loneliness; great gulfs of gut-wrenching boredom. The further you ride from home, the greater will grow the sense of remoteness from others.

What few would-be equestrian travellers recognize is that seeking hospitality is connected with more than a search for hay and sleeping quarters. The human interaction is more than just a meal. It is the longing of our starving souls for companionship.

The good news is that new friendships are made every day. Strangers become allies. And by journey's end your emotional life has been deeply enriched.

Repaying Hospitality

One of the consistent threads that runs through the history of equestrian travel is how kind-hearted hosts refuse to accept offers of payment.

Malcolm Darling made a remarkable journey in 1947, when he rode from Peshawar more than a thousand miles across India, to Jubbulpore. Even though the villages he visited were in the grip of poverty, the generous locals were offended if Darling offered payment in exchange for their kindness.

"Any offer of money for their very useful services is invariably refused. But we are guests of the people and have to at least endeavour to give him a full wage for his time and trouble and to pay him direct".

Having made five equestrian journeys on various continents, Robin Hanbury-Tenison has also faced this problem repeatedly. He advises, "Repaying hospitality and spontaneous generosity is always difficult, especially in a country where both are regarded as obligatory and money, apart from payment for grain and hay, would be an insult."

Knowing in advance that this problem will arise, Robin dispenses small gifts which he brings along for this specific purpose.

"These were a brilliant choice and always went down well."

Another option is to follow the example of author Robert Louis Stevenson, who made a journey with a donkey across France in 1878. His offers to pay were also repeatedly rejected. Finally, he hit upon a unique way to reimburse the kind people among whom he travelled.

"I felt I was in some one's debt for all this liberal entertainment. And so it pleased me to leave pieces of money on the turf as I went along, until I had left enough for my night's lodging."

There is a one thing you can always do to repay your host's hospitality. You can treat them with the respect and loyalty they deserve.

Acknowledge their generosity on your blog. Praise them by name to the local press. Keep your word. Let them know you finished your journey. Mention them in your book.

The Ultimate Guest

Let us conclude this talk about hosts and guests by recalling one of history's most revered travellers, a legendary figure who knew a great deal about wandering the land in search of hospitality.

According to tradition Jesus led his Apostles on a journey across Palestine. He walked across the land, always deemed a stranger, a vagabond, a wanderer, a road fellow, the chance guest led by dusk to a stranger's door. Those who journeyed with Jesus were a tired company, weary, hungry, thirsty, footsore and covered with the dust of the road.

Traditionally the only time Jesus is shown mounted he is always represented on a donkey because of his humble status in the world. But one artist dared to be different. He alone painted Jesus as a wandering horseman.

In the Cathedral of St. Etienne, in the city of Auxerre, in Burgundy, France, is a wall painting which depicts Jesus riding a white horse, which usually stands for majesty. His right hand holds a staff. His left hand is kept in a high position in a waving gesture or to hold the invisible reins. There are no stirrups, which conform to the situation of that time.

Whether Jesus rode or walked is beside the point. He is credited with leaving a message which still resonates with every Long Rider, regardless of where he travels.

One of the important messages which Jesus taught his disciples was the need to recognize your neighbour as your unknown self made visible.

Your host is a mirror wherein you shall behold your countenance. What you project is reflected in what you receive. If you reflect happiness, trust and serenity, chances are the stranger before you will become your host.

When one begins to understand this concept the fog clears. With understanding, all walls fall down.

Jesus is credited with saying, "Peace be to this house and to those who dwell in it."

Reflecting peace is the proper way to travel.

Summary

You arrived covered with the dust of the ancient road, simple, alone, weary, uncertain, in need, the enemy of no man and no race. Your normal shyness is pushed aside by the urgent need to care for your horses.

You and your hosts are brought together for a night. For a mere moment you share a common bond.

Their hospitality enfolds you like a warm garment on a cold night. They fed you, quenched your thirst, soothed your fears, shared their roof, called you their own till the sun rose and you rode on.

Thanks to that stream of human kindness, you met as strangers but parted as brothers.

The true span of your visit may take years or even generations to realize. Decades may pass but they shall utter your name and honour your memory.

A common tongue is not vital to understanding that civility is a language understood all over the world.

Do not dishonour the laws of hospitality.

Do not profane the trust of your hosts.

Be a blessing, not a burden. Always leave the situation better than when you found it.

Pete Langford summed it up best when he said, "Expect nothing. Appreciate everything."

Chinese communist leader Mao Tse-tung understood the strategic importance of hospitality. "The guerrilla must move amongst the people as a fish swims in the sea," he wrote.

Time after time Long Riders learned that the fate of a mounted traveller is dependent upon the actions of strangers. During the winter of 1892 the Japanese Long Rider, Baron Fukushima, was forced to sleep on the cold dirt outside a Mongol's yurt.

Lucy Leaf (left) rode across the USA in 1976. She planted a seed of friendship which bloomed 37 years later when Sea G Rhydr was a guest of the same family which had originally hosted Lucy in Flora, Mississippi.

Whereas it is true that certain individuals are discourteous and lack the gene of generosity, another element may come into play in terms of being denied hospitality: a long-running dislike which settled people harbour against mounted travellers. The sign reads "Nomads Prohibited."

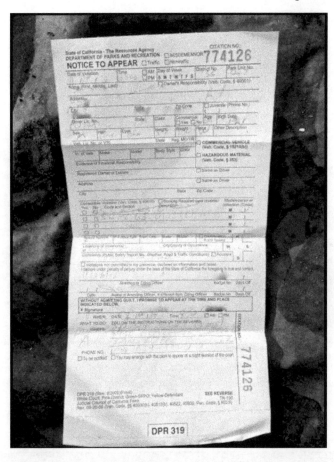

Another increasing problem for Long Riders is the fear of being harassed by the law. State parks are increasingly denying access to equestrian travellers. Famous national trails prohibit horses. One equestrian traveller in California was issued with this ticket, which resulted in a fine of $485, because he was found guilty of sleeping alongside the road without permission.

Not all cultures exhibit a tradition of hospitality. During his ride across Brazil, Filipe Leite encountered large parts of the country reserved for Native Americans. Access or entry is denied to Long Riders.

The Cathedral of St. Etienne, in Auxerre, France has the only known painting which depicts Jesus riding a horse. Jesus taught that what you project is reflected in what you receive. If you reflect happiness, trust and serenity, chances are the stranger before you will become your host.

Chapter 68
Surviving Local Accommodations

You have to realize it's not going to be a bed of roses.

Hippisley Cunliffe Marsh spoke for many exhausted Long Riders when he referred to his ride across Persia in 1877.

"The place we slept at that night was the essence of disgust and only fatigue enabled me to get any sleep."

Ask any equestrian traveller and they will regale you with tales of where they chanced to find a few hours of fitful repose.

During my travels in Pakistan, for example, I was required by circumstances to sleep on the judge's table in a courtroom, under the only tree growing along the bleak Malakand Pass, on the floor of a sugar cane factory and in an abandoned Raj rest house which had not seen a visitor in nearly a decade.

Adjusting your Expectations

The life of an equestrian traveller is in stark contrast to the sedentary and civilized world where we have tended to try and dictate that the natural world fit in with our needs and lifestyle.

A look at Long Rider history demonstrates how a common thread weaves its way through equestrian events. You have to expect to rough it.

Before he became known as the father of evolution, Charles Darwin was an enthusiastic young Long Rider. In 1834 he was riding across the pampas of Chile when night found him approaching a rich ranch house.

"At night I was exceedingly exhausted but had the uncommon luck of obtaining some clean straw for my bed. I was amused afterwards by reflecting how truly comparative all comfort is. If I had been in England, clean straw and stinking horse blankets would have been thought a very miserable bed."

Things hadn't improved much with the dawning of the 20th century. Joseph Smeaton Chase set out in 1910 to ride from Mexico to Oregon. After spending weeks sleeping outdoors he made a note of how relieved he was to reach a small California town.

"I exchanged the vague discomforts of the road for the concrete misery of a typical country hotel. Passed a night enlivened with dogs, fleas, and mosquitoes, but with a conspicuous absence of sleep."

Fame and money are no guarantee of personal comfort, as famous Long Rider author Graham Greene discovered during his ride across Mexico in 1938.

"I think the hut had once been a stable; now it seemed to be divided by thin partitions into three. In one division we slept, in another small children cried all night, and behind my head, in the third, I could hear the slow movements and the regular coughing of cows. I slept very badly in my clothes."

Where you spend the night is as varied as the geography across which you pass and all Long Riders will find themselves in need of hospitality at one time or another.

Caravanserai

In the not-too-distant past many Long Riders sought safety, shelter and food within the walls of a caravanserai. Part hotel, part fortress, the caravanserai was built in the shape of an immense square. Its high walls and single gate made it easy to defend and difficult for thieves to enter.

Within its open courtyard caravans could safely unload the large numbers of horses and camels which carried precious goods. Large numbers of stalls were built along the inside walls of the enclosure to house and feed the animals. Chambers were also provided to accommodate the travellers, merchants and servants who sought shelter.

Swiss Long Rider Ella Maillart was one of the last to spend the night in a caravanserai before they disappeared with the onset of modernity. During her solo journey across Chinese Turkestan in 1932 she remarked on the quality of such local accommodations.

"We were now in Kuntigmas, meaning 'the place which the sun cannot reach' and our halting place changed considerably for the worse; indeed, the animals were relatively better housed than the human beings. We rode into a small yard, two sides of which were given up to the ponies, while only dark rooms lit by a hole in the roof were interspersed for travellers. The ceilings were unplastered. There was no furniture of any kind. Nor was it easy to sleep, as my room was merely wattle-and-daub, so I could hear every movement of the animals on the other side, as they munched their fodder, fidgeted and now and again screamed and kicked at each other."

Dak Bungalows

Another time-honoured shelter for travellers which passed away more recently was the dak bungalow.

Dak is the Hindi word for mail. During the days of the British Raj an overland system of trails and roads allowed mail to reach the furthermost corners of England's Indian colony. These well-built buildings were roughly twenty miles distant from each other and there the needy traveller could find fodder at reasonable prices. The upkeep of the dak bungalow was maintained by a guard known as a chowkidar, who resided in the nearest village.

Because the dak bungalows were government-owned and controlled, they were not open to random travellers. It was essential to obtain written permission in advance from the recognized authority to use these restricted residences. Though there was usually no charge, it was an accepted courtesy to reward the chowkidar.

After the partition of India and Pakistan in 1947, the dak bungalow system fell into disuse. Yet having been built by Queen Victoria's sturdy Victorian colonists, the small buildings were too robust to simply blow away with the winds of time.

During my last journey in Pakistan I chanced upon a forgotten dak bungalow. Horses like mine had once travelled the ancient caravan trail that made its way between the towns of Gilgit and Chilas. But owing to the recently-constructed roadway, autos, trucks and buses now sped through that bleak part of Pakistan's northern region.

These hectic motorists had no time to notice tiny Jalupar.

Though in plain sight, the hamlet slumbered undisturbed off the side of the road as the rest of the world rushed by. After having completed a hard day's ride from Gilgit, I ventured into Jalupar in search of grass for my horse and food for me. I never suspected that hidden beneath the tall and ancient trees which screened the village I would find a remnant of the Raj.

There were but eight families living in this village nestled up next to the river that ran close by. A small intact dak bungalow was also there to greet me. Sturdy, weathered, intact, peaceful, and locked, it stood like an old soldier still on guard, waiting for travellers who came no more.

The key to the door was eventually found. Inside was the guest register which held names dating back many decades. Mine was the first signature to be placed upon the page in seven years.

Inns and Hotels

Modern man has come to accept a certain amount of refinement as his established right: clean sheets, gallons of hot water, refreshing food, and a door that locks. These are recent innovations which are automatically assumed to be part of any standard hotel.

Such amenities were not always taken for granted. Throughout most of Long Rider history cleanliness was only a word in the dictionary.

Most equestrian travellers spent their nights sleeping in barns, livery stables or underneath the stars. On the odd occasion when they could afford to sleep in a local hotel or an inn there were a number of singular problems waiting to tax their patience.

After having survived a particularly horrible part of the trail, Aimé Tschiffely was overjoyed to learn that rest and relaxation might be just ahead.

"We came to a little village where I actually found what they called a hotel. Alas, it was merely a mud hut and the room had no other ventilation but the door, for windows did not exist."

Cheerless accommodations and tasteless food were not restricted to exotic locations.

Evelyn Burnaby made his ride from Land's End, Cornwall to John O'Groats, Scotland in 1892. A man of robust appetite, Evelyn was disappointed with what he found along the way.

"Our experience at Bathgate was very droll. The hotel, if so it may be called, was very cheerless. No good food was to be obtained, and a boiled egg, which might have been laid weeks before, and so-called tea, with a fluid declared to be milk, but which had no resemblance to the produce of the cow, had to satisfy a craving and weary frame. Alas, it was too late to move on."

So, you must be saying, what does it matter what happened back then or over there?

Modern Long Riders have stories aplenty that match the tales of old.

During their ride from South Africa to Kenya, Austrian Long Riders Esther Stein and Horst Hausleitner endured gruelling conditions in the bush. Finally, after months of dirt and deprivation, they reached a so-called "hotel" in Tanzania. Hoping for the best, it didn't take long for them to be disappointed.

Esther wrote, "This hotel is ten times as expensive as a normal local guesthouse. This means the price of a room costs a third of the average monthly wage in Tanzania. For our money we have our own bathroom, which has a hole in the ground from which cockroaches emerge as soon as it gets dark. But the bathroom has a door, which is a luxury. Inside is a bathtub where you can obtain a bucket full of either milky-white or muddy-brown water. The plug in the bath didn't work. The sink leaked. The mosquito net had big holes in it. But we did get what is termed a continental breakfast. This consisted of two pieces of bread, with just enough butter for one piece, hot water and instant coffee. No milk, jam or tea. One becomes modest in Africa."

Other modern Long Riders have also learned to be grateful for what little bit of comfort they could find.

After having survived an exhausting journey across Bolivia, French Long Riders Marie-Emmanuelle Tugler and Marc Witz eventually arrived at San Jose, Bolivia.

"We stopped at this old missionary town to rest in the hotel. It wasn't very luxurious but in our 48 hours there we must have spent 36 hours asleep and two in the shower!"

The final word on hotels goes to Robin Hanbury-Tenison. While riding with his wife Louella along the length of China's great wall, the tired travellers came to a small country hotel.

"Do you have hot water," Robin asked in eager anticipation?

"Of course," replied the proprietor.

But when Robin ran the bath only cold water came gushing from the tap.

The hot water, in this case, referred to what was kept in the thermos for making tea.

Local Residences

As might be expected, Long Riders are forced by circumstances to spend the night in a host of housing as diverse as the human race. They have slept in leafy huts in the jungles of New Guinea, under the eves of log cabins in Siberia, been the guests of royalty and taken refuge in a ditch.

A list of where Long Riders have resided for the night brings forth some strange tales. What is surprising is that though the wayfarer lingered but a night, their hosts viewed nothing amiss.

George Whitfield Ray set off in 1889 to find a lost tribe of sun-worshipping natives who resided in the unexplored forests of Paraguay.

Ray's journey was so brutal that it defies belief. The horses were repeatedly attacked by vampire bats. The traveller and his horses were reduced to sucking dew off leaves to survive. His clothes were in rags held together by horse hair thread. He lost two toes to blood-sucking insects whose bites also caused much of the flesh on his feet to rot off.

But even a daredevil like Ray learned early on that a Long Rider has to take it as he finds it.

"The hot sun had ruthlessly shone on me all day as I waded through the long arrow grass that reached up to my saddle. The scorching rays, pitiless in their intensity, seemed to take the energy from everything living. All animate creation was paralyzed. The relentless ball of fire in the heavens, pouring down like molten brass, appeared to be trying to set the world on fire; and I lay utterly exhausted on my horse's neck, half expecting to see all kindled in one mighty blaze!

I had drunk the hot, putrid water of the hollows, which did not seem to quench my thirst any, but perhaps did help to keep me from drying up and blowing away. My tongue was parched and my lips dried together. Fortunately, I had a very quiet horse, and when I could no longer bear the sun's burning rays I got down for a few moments and crept under him. Shelter there was none. The copious draughts of evil-smelling water I had drunk in my raging thirst brought on nausea, and it was only by force of will that I kept myself from falling, when on an eminence I joyfully sighted an estancia. Hope then revived in me.

My knowing horse had seen the house before me, and without any guidance made straight towards it at a quicker pace. Well he knew that houses in those desolate wastes were too far apart to be passed unheeded by, and I thoroughly concurred in his wisdom. As I drew up before the lonely place my tongue refused to shout "*Ave Maria*," but I clapped my perspiring hands, and soon had the satisfaction of hearing footsteps within. Visions of shade and of meat and drink and rest floated before my eyes when I saw the door opened.

A face peeped out, which, in a cracked, broken voice, I addressed, asking the privilege to dismount. Horror of horrors, I had not even been answered ere the door was shut again in my face! Get down without permission I dare not."

For more than thirty minutes Ray sat in the saddle, boiling in the blazing sun, all the while the suspicious home owner debated whether to offer any hospitality.

"Were the inmates fiends that they let me sit there, knowing well that there was no other habitation within miles? As the minutes slowly lengthened out, and the door remained closed, my spirits sank lower and lower."

Then the man reappeared, satisfied it seemed that the exhausted traveller presented no threat.

"Conducting me to a shack built of canes and mud, he told me that I could sleep on a pile of sheepskins. So I lay down on the hides in the shade of the wall, and, utterly tired out, with visions of banquets floating before my eyes, I dropped off to sleep. Fatigued as I was, I passed a wretched night, for dozens of huge rats ran over my body, bit my hands, and scratched my face, the whole night long. Morning at last dawned, and, with the first streaks of coming day, I saddled my horse, and, shaking the dust of the estancia off my feet, resumed my journey."

Modern Long Riders likewise must remain alert to the need to be ready to constantly adapt to what is on offer in terms of local hospitality. During his ride from Mongolia to Hungary Tim Cope stayed with 70 local families, all of whom shared various levels of comfort with him.

Unorthodox Quarters

What marks a man? What scores his soul? What glimmer of a passing experience can affect us these many long years later?

After the journey is ended, where we spent the night often leaves a mark upon our memory.

Long Riders have slept in jail cells, school rooms, grain silos, airplane hangars, hospitals, abandoned buildings, and barns. They have pitched their tents in cemeteries, behind gas stations, atop baseball fields, on golf courses. They have slept in stalls, thrown their sleeping bag down behind rodeo arenas and gone to rest amidst the crops, beneath the trees and under the stars.

No matter where they manage to find a few hours' rest, they have learned that sooner or later they are going to be required to endure hard times, rough circumstances and the company of uncouth company.

Long Rider Hezekiah Prince learned that tough lesson in the winter of 1793, when the young scholar made a ride across the newly-formed United States. During the course of this singular journey, Hezekiah dined with a descendant of Pocahontas, paid homage at the grave of recently deceased Benjamin Franklin and kept a detailed diary during his journey.

But it wasn't all pleasant.

South of the fledgling city of Washington, Prince complained about bad roads and how he had to ride through "a miserable God-forsaken region of humanity" near the village of Sheepsgut.

Respecting the Locals

It might seem obvious but be courteous. Don't impose.

British Long Rider Christina Dodwell has had many adventures in various tribal societies. She recommends, "When you stay overnight in a village it is a good idea to go and greet the headman or chief, otherwise he may feel snubbed. Shake hands with everyone and smile a lot. Shaking hands is a useful gesture of goodwill. It can take away tension and makes people well disposed toward you."

With the demise of the stables and inns which routinely catered to equestrian travellers, finding accommodation for one traveller and a horse will present a tactical problem in an urbanized setting. Most potential hosts are not equipped to offer shelter to more than two travellers.

An even number is far better than an odd one in terms of obtaining shelter and help for horses and riders.

Mongolian Manners

In the West the round felt residence is commonly known as a yurt. But the Mongols correctly refer to this mobile house as a ger. No matter what you call it, there are strict rules in how you act inside and around it.

Bonnie Folkins has travelled and ridden with the Mongols and their nomadic kinsmen the Kazakhs on many occasions. She made a note of the special customs which are deemed good manners in and around the ger.

If you step on the threshold of a ger you will insult the owner.

If you trip at the threshold it will drive away happiness.

If you enter with a sigh, it is disrespectful.

You must move inside the ger in a clockwise direction.

Do not cross the path of an elderly person as this is considered disrespectful.

Do not whistle in a ger as it will bring bad luck.

If you step on a hat it will insult the owner.

If you step on a lasso it will bring bad luck to the owner.

Touching the rim of a cup with your fingers is considered a bad omen.

Make sure your sleeves are rolled down.

It is disrespectful to turn your back to the altar or to sit in front of it.

Do not put anything into the fire.

Most importantly, do not lie with your feet pointing toward the fire as this will drive out the household gods.

When you are outdoors near the ger, do not use an axe near fire as it threatens the god of fire. Never stamp out the fire with your feet. It is sacred. If you step on ashes, it will bring the spirit of the dead into the ashes.

Summary

One thing which often surprises would-be Long Riders is how inexpensive it is to travel on horseback. Thanks to the generosity and kindness of hosts, expenses are often kept manageable.

It would be a mistake then to think that great sums of money are required to cover the costs of sheltering you and your horse. For example one inexperienced person who wanted to ride across England mistakenly thought she needed to raise $33,000, including $17,000 for lodging and livery.

What she didn't know was that when you sleep in your cloak there's no lodging to pay, that you will be grateful when you are offered the softest boards on the floor for a bed and that a tired body is the softest mattress.

No one had taught her that a Long Rider learns to never complain about hunger and hardship. Neither man nor horse must be particular about quarters, and he who looks for a stable, or perhaps even a lavatory, in villages and small towns might just as well seek Atlantis.

Above all, the traveller must not be delicate. He must be satisfied with any kind of protection and remember that when his stomach is empty, he can always feed later on a dish of horizon and tomorrow.

Throughout the centuries Long Riders routinely sought rest, safety, food and fodder in a caravanserai.

During their ride through the Karakorum Mountains, Noor Mohammad Khan and the author spent the night in the abandoned dak bungalow near the village of Pingal, Pakistan.

Long Riders learn to make do. While riding across Albania, Robin and Louella Hanbury-Tenison sheltered in an abandoned building. Once a hospital, it was now without doors or windows and full of animal and human excrement. Cold and wet, they broke up the last remaining window ledges and made a fire in one of the abandoned rooms to keep Louella warm.

During the course of his journey across the newly-formed United States, Hezekiah Prince complained about how he had to ride through "a miserable God-forsaken region of humanity" near the village of Sheepsgut.

During the blazing hot summers, Kazakhs sleep outside on flat wooden beds. As many Long Riders have found, a tired body is the softest mattress, even when sleeping on boards.

Modern Long Riders must be ready to constantly adapt to what is on offer in terms of local hospitality. During their ride in South America French Long Riders Marie-Emmanuelle Tugler and Marc Witz spent the night in this unorthodox dwelling while riding through the Mato Grosso du Sud in Brazil.

Chapter 69
Adapting to New Cultures

Should you perchance plan to ride within the borders of your own country, amongst those who speak your language and share your values, then there will be a diminished need to delve into the wondrous and mysterious diversity of humanity, for a domestic journey, while apt to supply adventures, will not normally provide the emotional, religious and culinary challenges which await the Long Rider who ventures far from home.

It would be easy to reduce my task by rushing through this topic. I could do so by muttering all the time-worn phrases, such as urging anyone undertaking a foreign journey to leave their prejudices at home, to travel with an open mind and to adapt in terms of tolerating differences in diet, faith etc. But placing words on the page does not provide an explanation of why cultural differences play so deep a role in affecting the possible success of equestrian journeys which occur overseas.

What is more, for too many years the public has been misled into believing the saccharine sweet view of the world peddled by Walt Disney that, "It's a small world after all…."

Like many another Hollywood fiction, that too is a shallow and harmful inaccuracy.

New research indicates that we humans are far more intellectually and culturally diverse than was previously believed, that we don't all get along, that our differences are deeply rooted, firmly held, and that we Long Riders cannot afford to ignore the deadly differences which set us apart as a species.

Thus, whereas it may seem obvious to warn a vegetarian Long Rider from Los Angeles that she may well be expected to dine on roast horse in Kazakhstan, this chapter opens the door to other obscure areas of human thought and behaviour, all of which may affect your health, your safety and ultimately the success of your journey.

Many Humans – Many Views

When the Guild launched its website at the beginning of the 21st century, it bore the words, "New Ideas for a New Millennium." New ideas are rare; so is the realignment of those beliefs held sacred by science. One such example was released while I was working on this book.

A shift in conventional wisdom occurred in late 2013 when two psychologists named Joseph Henrich and Steven Heine called upon the scientific community to re-evaluate many commonly-held beliefs.

In an innovative report Henrich and Heine provided strong evidence indicating that previous academic studies were based upon flawed assumptions.

They presented data suggesting that scientists routinely publish broad claims about human psychology, cognition and behaviour based solely on samples drawn entirely from highly-educated segments of Western, educated, industrialized, rich, and democratic societies.

The make-up of these studies reflected the country of residence of the authors, as 73% of the authors were at American universities, and 99% were at universities in Western countries. This means that 96% of psychological samples come from countries with only 12% of the world's population.

The term "Western" referred to those countries clustered in the north-west of Europe (Great Britain, Scandinavia, France, Germany, Switzerland, the Netherlands, etc.), and the United States, Canada, New Zealand, and Australia.

Henrich and Heine dared to ask just how justified researchers were in assuming findings for the entire human species based on findings from such a narrow portion of the human population.

"It is not just our Western habits and cultural preferences that are different from the rest of the world it appears," they wrote. "The very way we think about ourselves and others, and even the way we perceive reality, makes us distinct from other humans on the planet, not to mention from the vast majority of our ancestors."

This underscores the prevalent assumption that the study of one human sample is much the same as the next. But new data gathered from across the behavioural sciences suggests there is substantial variability among different populations.

Growing evidence indicates that invisible cultural perceptions influence human actions and choices. Even the concept of perceiving colours differs widely.

As might be expected, the way our brains operate is affected by our geographic and cultural background. Such divisions in thought have been detected between nomadic people and subsistence farmers, as well as Eastern and Western nations.

Research suggested that the mind's capacity to adapt itself to cultural and environmental settings was far greater than had been assumed. Americans, for example, gaze at focal objects longer than East Asians, who in turn gaze at the background more than Americans.

Some cultures regard the self as independent from others; others see the self as interdependent.

"Whether you think of yourself as interdependent or independent may depend on whether your distant ancestors farmed rice (which required a great deal of shared labour and group cooperation) or herded animals (which rewarded individualism and aggression)."

Thus, the long-held assumption that under the skin everyone is the same has been severely undermined.

"The most interesting thing about cultures may not be in the observable things they do—the rituals, eating preferences, codes of behaviour, and the like—but in the way they affect our most fundamental conscious and unconscious thinking and perception."

A broader, richer and better-grounded understanding of our species is now under way.

No thin slice of humanity has all the answers or represents a monopoly on the truth.

Knowing that your own beliefs and practices are not sacrosanct is the first step in realizing how much you still have to learn about other people and cultures.

New Rules

Humans, as we commonly recognize them today, first appeared in the fossil record 195,000 years ago. Hundreds of generations had to pass before mankind was able to create the societies which now exist. For most of that time people did not interact with large numbers of strangers. They found safety amongst the members of their extended family and the village which was the focus of their daily life.

As late as 1947 the English Long Rider Malcolm Darling recorded two remarkable incidents which demonstrated how this long sense of isolation still lingered. During Darling's ride across India he had occasion to meet an elderly villager who recalled how he had never seen an orange until the First World War. Another small hamlet retained a communal story of how people would walk from miles around so as to come and stare at the first man who had earned a hundred rupees.

It isn't a sense of nostalgia which leads me to say that these Indian villagers had no refrigerator, microwave, computer, television or automobile. But look at what they did have: a tremendous sense of community, friends with whom they shared love and loss, the knowledge that they were part of the natural world, the give and take of life.

In contrast much of modern urban life is linked to a sense of unease. People are urged to adapt a homogeneous set of global values which range from provocative to repulsive. They publish the minor details of their lives on the internet for the entire world to see. As voluntary residents in an increasingly electronic environment, they measure their self-worth by the number of "friends" whose pictures they gather like sad tokens of self-esteem.

People whose lives embrace these sorts of social realities do not readily adapt to the cultural challenges waiting to ambush their preconceived notions of personal and national supremacy. The rest of the world, they soon learn, doesn't think you're important, doesn't doff its cap in respect to your ingrained sense of cultural superiority, isn't willing to accommodate your desires, accede to your demands, agree with your religious views, tolerate your dietary preferences or even treat you with anything but cool disdain.

Who you were, what you drove, how much you made at home, means nothing once you are in the saddle and far from home. The rules have changed and it is you who had better learn quickly or perish.

Let us take one small but obvious example: the concept of efficiency. Forget it. Being quick and efficient may be the norm in New York but not in many other parts of the world.

Jeremy James is an easy-going fellow with many countries, countless adventures and thousands of miles under his saddle. Yet even a weathered traveller like Jeremy learned he had to adapt or suffer in a country other than his own.

He wrote, "The maddening thing about France was that everything was always shut. I kept running out of money and whenever I went into a town it was either Monday and shut, or Saturday and shut because it shouldn't be open, or Sunday and shut because it should be. On Tuesdays everything was abandoned, and on Wednesdays you couldn't buy anything because no one had been around on Tuesday. On Thursdays if you were lucky enough to find a *boulangerie* open, the fellow would just be selling the last morsel of food to his friend, and on Fridays I gave up. It drove me completely berserk, and I spent days without any food at all."

Don't fool yourself. If you break the local rules, you will pay the price.

And learning the local rules will test you in ways you never imagined.

Inner Exploration

As Jeremy's search for a bank and a baguette proves, learning the rules is a matter of survival. Break the rules, go hungry, or worse.

But there is more to it than just memorizing the opening hours of the local bakery. A Long Rider must throw down the walls erected by years of enforced cultural practice. He must make a conscious effort to view things from the perspective of his host nation. He must be seen to respect local customs.

As Jeremy mentioned France, so shall I, for it was Napoleon who wisely said, "Conform to the customs of the country; never run down anything; find everything splendid; and don't say, 'We do this better in Paris.'"

Australian Long Rider Tim Cope had to face his fair share of extreme cultural tests. Several years after his epic journey was over, he looked back and penned this thought on the need to adapt a policy of cultural sensitivity.

"For me, adventures are a vehicle for travelling deep into the fabric of society, coming to know the environmental conditions that shape people's lives, and viewing the present in the context of history. It's about letting go of western-orientated preconceptions, and even awareness of one's own difficulties, and viewing the world through the eyes of others. Ultimately, it's a sense of camaraderie and friendship with local people that is core to my journeys. Overwhelmingly the people were hospitable, but to survive and learn required changing my mindset somewhat, and not taking things too personally. There are many ways of looking at the world and forging your life, and the evidence can be found in the many rich and diverse cultures of our planet."

This isn't to say that everyone is going to welcome you with open arms. In fact chances are that you're going to be treated rudely, be asked to consume some gut-wrenching meals and have your sense of privacy routinely violated.

Another Long Rider who has spent much time in Mongolia, Bonnie Folkins, issued this warning on the topic.

"Physical and emotional stress finds its way into one's character in many ways. I certainly have had rude circumstances and have been pushed to the limit in trying to understand the people who are like aliens to our own culture. But isn't part of exploring about the chance to turn a difficult personal situation into an opportunity to gain a better understanding of human behaviour? Shouldn't we strive to accept adversity and turn it into revelation?"

Personal Tolerance

Legendary Long Rider George Patterson risked his life to go to Tibet in 1946, so as to share his Christian beliefs with the Khampa tribesmen. A quiet, scholarly, spiritual and dignified man, George's life was a reflection of the love which so many people have associated with Christianity throughout the ages.

Despite his reputation for tolerance, George was no fool. It was George who warned, "Beware the man who prays on his knees on Sunday and preys on his neighbours the rest of the week."

Long Riders have been long-time practitioners of various religions. By and large they are curious, adaptable, open minded and polite regarding this subject. But exceptions do exist.

Whereas we are free to share our personal spiritual beliefs, expounding rigid religious philosophies from the saddle isn't apt to open many doors.

One notable exception was the evangelical American who billed himself as a "circuit riding preacher" and used his ride to export a severe view of Christianity.

He greeted strangers by asking, "Are you wearing Jesus' brand every day?

If you love Jesus you'll help us round up the strays."

For those who declined to adhere to his view of Christianity, he warned, "Don't be lukewarm or Jesus will spit you out of his mouth."

When in Rome

Acting like you have all the answers isn't the way to go about making friends. Learning how to recognize the subtle, invisible rules upon which different societies and families operate is a skill that must be developed with time and practice.

"There is a saying, When in Rome, do as the Romans do," Sea G Rhydr wrote. But she went on to pose the question, "But of course one must first determine what it is that the Romans are doing."

Having been a guest in so many homes, Sea expressed a deep-seated concern which most Long Riders encounter. How do you behave? How do you avoid committing an embarrassing social blunder?

Time after time Long Riders have learned the futility of trying to keep their comfort zone intact while riding.

One such unique episode occurred when Messanie Wilkins was making her cross-country ride from Maine to California in 1952.

Riding along solo through the backwoods of Arkansas, Messanie was suddenly confronted with a giant 7 foot tall man, who walked into the middle of the road, held up his hand and ordered the little Long Rider to halt.

"Mom wants to meet you. Come," he ordered, and pointed to a nearby farm house.

After tying up her horse, Messanie entered the old house with a sense of trepidation. Awaiting her was "Mom," an older woman who was nearly as tall as her gruff son.

"When I went into the house to meet her, she seemed to be very unfriendly. She just stared at me for a minute and, then pointed to a chair at the kitchen table. After I sat down, she brought a long loaf of bread to the table. Then she poured some salt on a piece of paper and sat down opposite me.

While I watched, Mom tore off a hunk of bread, sprinkled salt on it, and started eating. Without saying a word, I did the same. I figured that was the right thing to do, and it was. Back in Maine, when I was in the homes of strangers, I always did as they did.

We sat there about five minutes, each taking a turn at the bread, until we'd eaten the whole loaf. After that, Mom smiled and said, "You stay here tonight."

Humour and Good Manners

Many invisible traits make up a successful Long Rider. Having a sense of humour is one of them.

Don't take yourself too seriously. A smile has opened more doors than money. Never underestimate how important humour is. But be aware that in its sense of humour, before everything else, every country is alone.

Also, recall that many nations view the arrival of a guest as a special occasion.

Sir Ahmed Mohammed Hassanein was the Egyptian Long Rider who made a tremendous ride deep into the heart of the Libyan Desert. Being an Islamic scholar, as well as a diplomat, Hassanein knew that on those rare occasions when he would be a guest of local dignitaries, custom dictated that he provide them warning of his forthcoming arrival.

"I sent a man ahead with a letter to the Sayid at the oasis to inform him of my approach. In the desert one does not rush upon a friend or a dignitary headlong and unannounced. There should be time for both to put on fresh clothing and go with dignity to the meeting as becomes gentlemen of breeding."

Taking it easy

If you're in a hurry, buy a car. If you want to live surrounded by efficiency, move to Switzerland.

As for most of the rest of the world, they've adapted a policy of taking things easy.

Sam Southey made such a cultural discovery during her ride in Mongolia.

"The Spanish have *mañana*, the Mongolian's маргааш (pronounced Margaash). It means tomorrow and rather than signify laziness it really signifies that Mongolians like to take things slowly. Another word we find our-selves using a lot is байх (pronounced bekh). As with most Mongolian words it has a large number of meanings but one can add it to the end of a sentence to signify uncertainty."

Strange local beliefs

You can always count on certain guarantees, for example the fact that people everywhere care deeply about their families. Yet riding slowly across any nation will expose you to an on-going set of incredible practices and beliefs.

Learn to have an open mind. Listen, don't talk. Don't be judgmental. If you don't understand, ask politely for an explanation.

That's what Danish Long Rider Ole Olufsen did when he ventured deep into the Pamir Mountains in1896. He came across a tribe of nomadic Kyrgyz tribesmen living next to the remote and beautiful Lake Yashilkul.

One of the most astonishing equestrian conversations ever recorded by a Long Rider occurred when Olufsen fell into a conversation with the Kyrgyz chief. When the Dane made a chance remark about how strong and hardy the tribe's horses were, the chief expressed no surprise at so obvious a fact.

"The lake, he told me, was inhabited by seahorses, which come out at night to graze. They then breed with the local horses, which produces a superior animal."

Examples of Culture

Seahorses grazing under the moonlight might seem to be an extreme example. But the delicacies of how easily you can upset local customs are far more often connected with everyday practices.

For example, according to ancient tradition, the charpoy or string bedstead binds India together as few other things do. One or more are to be found in almost every house. However there are rules as to its use. Who sits on it, or even if it is offered, carries secret signals. According to custom, a tenant cannot sit on the same charpoy as his landlord. If a stranger appears at the home, and he is not given a charpoy to sit upon by himself, it is a sure sign he is not welcome to spend the night.

Different Views on Hygiene

Cleanliness may be next to Godliness, but cultural definitions on sanitation and personal hygiene are tremendously varied. Rules and habits range from the mildly eccentric to the widely offensive.

According to an old Turkish superstition, it is considered ill-mannered to place a piece of soap into the hands of another. It must instead be placed on the washstand or the ground, as to give the soap into another's hands will wash away love.

One Long Rider who had reached Khiva remarked on how an immense crowd gathered to watch him visit the barber. Whereas the local men kept their heads shaved and grew luxurious beards, the English traveller shocked local sensibilities by having his chin shaved and not his head.

Another traveller, who recently rode in China, was disgusted when he observed how the local inhabitants constantly spit on the floor in front of his feet. The Chinese in turn couldn't hide their revulsion when the Englishman blew his nose into a pocket handkerchief.

Household health is another matter of interpretation.

A Scottish Long Rider was offered the hospitality of a small hut in the Himalayas. His gratitude soon turned to horror when he realized that he was sharing a roof with more than just the hardy mountaineers.

"I had noticed several cockroaches running about as I had sat drinking tea, but since these are part of the domestic scenery all over Tibet I had paid little attention to them. If their activities had been limited to attacks upon my food I might have been constrained to concede some of it for the sake of general socialistic principles, but they had not only attacked my food and drink but proceeded to crawl over me and inside my shirt as well. This was communism with a vengeance, and I immediately leaped into a struggle of class distinction and mass extinction, hitting out right and left with a will. The struggle was doomed to failure. There were too many of them. The floor swarmed with them, from the very small quarter-inch to the large inch kind, they ran hither and yon with their loathsome lurch. All this was to be seen in the circle of firelight. As I looked up at the roof and around the walls and saw the light reflected from thousands of moving scaly bodies, I shuddered to think of the night."

As these brief episodes illustrate, there are no universal standards of behaviour or belief when it comes to health and hygiene. Luckily, not every traveller encounters an offensive situation.

Yet after their journey is concluded, many a Long Rider can relate to what Kate Marsden said after surviving her epic ride through the Siberian taiga.

"I think the sufferings of that journey added twenty years to my age."

Lack of Privacy

First-time travellers from Occidental countries are often deeply disturbed by how other cultures have an utter disregard for the concept of privacy.

Many are the stories of a lady Long Rider finding herself surrounded by a crowd of curious natives, who have come to stare at the traveller while she attempts to attend to her bodily functions in a quiet manner behind some convenient bush.

Being gawked at like a monkey in a zoo, at the very moment they are most in need of seclusion, has caused many a Long Rider of both sexes to snap under the stress of finding themselves in this situation. Shouting at the curious locals to leave you in peace at this delicate moment generally elicits peals of laughter from the crowd and a general wonder why the stranger is so shy about such a natural function.

This book lists the names of many Long Riders, yet Ida Pfeiffer was one of the most remarkable, if least known. A prolific writer, she recorded an event when her privacy became the target of village curiosity and local gossip.

Ida was born in Vienna, Austria, in 1797 and, thanks to an indulgent father, was encouraged to follow her tomboyish tendencies. This instilling of courageous behaviour at such a young age led to Ida becoming a determined, brave and outspoken young woman. After the death of her father, Ida reluctantly married a man several years older than she was. Yet though they had two sons, Ida laboured under the constraints placed upon her by conventional society. Therefore, after her husband died, and as soon as her sons had homes of their own, the still-young Ida set off from home anxious to fulfil one desire: to explore the world at last!

Ida travelled to many exotic parts of the planet, including Scandinavia, South America, the South Pacific, China, India, Persia, Asia Minor, Europe and North Africa.

By 1856 Ida's travel books had been translated into seven languages, she had seen a great deal of the world and survived a host of dangerous adventures. With those qualifications in mind, the diminutive Long Rider ventured to London. Her goal was to meet England's most celebrated explorer, Sir Richard Francis Burton and convince him to allow her to accompany him on his forthcoming journey to find the source of the Nile River. Despite having entered into Mecca in disguise, the flamboyant Burton wasn't able to evade the persistent Pfeiffer, who methodically peppered him with requests.

Despite her excellent travel qualifications, and disregarding her documented courage, the normally unorthodox Burton sided with the patriarchal forces of conventional society. As history later revealed, this was one of the most remarkable "what if?" moments in exploration history. What if these two incredible Historical Long Riders had defied custom and ignored the allure of patriotism by creating an International Expedition to explore the Nile?

When her hopes were dashed by Burton, Pfeiffer responded in her usual resolute manner by announcing that if Captain Burton would not allow her to accompany him into the interior of the Dark Continent, then she would venture into another area of the world alone.

A hardened traveller, Ida had learned to bite her tongue and endure local customs. But the desperate need for a bath taxed her patience to the limit. While riding across Persia, she found herself in Ravandus, "one of the most miserable towns I ever saw."

Upon asking where she might find lodgings, the headman took her to a house, the courtyard of which was small and completely filled with rubbish. Near the doorway four women sat on a dirty rug playing with some small children.

"I was obliged to sit down with them, and undergo the usual curious examination and staring. For some time I put up with it, but then left this charming society, and looked about for a place where I could arrange my toilette a little. I had not changed my clothes for six days, having been exposed, at the same time, to great heat. I found a dirty and smutty room, which, in addition to the disgust it excited, made me fear the presence of vermin and scorpions; of the latter I had a particular dread."

Ida had scarcely gone into the beggarly room, when one woman after the other came in; the women were followed by the children, and then by several neighbours, who had heard of the arrival of a foreign woman.

"At last, one of the women luckily thought of offering me a bath, and I accepted the proposal with great joy. Hot water was prepared, and they made a sign for me to follow them, which I did, and found myself in the sheep-stall, which had not been cleaned for years. In this place they pushed two stones together, upon which I was to stand, and in the presence of the whole company, who followed me like my shadow, allowed myself to be bathed with water. I made signs to them to go out, as I wished to perform this office myself; they did indeed leave me, but as misfortune had it, the stall had no door, and they were all able to look in just the same."

During her lifetime Ida was awarded membership into the geographical societies of both Germany and France. Sadly, the Royal Geographical Society of England denied her that honour due to her sex. Today Ida's legacy lives on by providing us with the memory of a woman of matchless intrepidity, surprising energy and heroic fixity of purpose.

Learning to do Without

Not all the world is a "land of plenty." Food is often scarce. Clean water is a luxury. Adjusting your expectations includes realizing that what other cultures consider a cornucopia may not match your expectations.

During an extremely long day's ride in the Karakoram Mountains, I found myself starving in the saddle. I had by chance spent the previous night as the guest of a miserly man. As soon as the sun was up my host gave me a single piece of bread, a small cup of tea for breakfast and then hastened me on my way with the assurance that the nearby village was rich in food and refreshment.

Being a naïve young fool, I saddled up and rode off thinking about the large late breakfast I would soon feast upon. Time for brunch came and went. Likewise lunch sank behind me all the while I made my way through bleak and foodless mountains. My hunger became increasingly desperate. By late afternoon I met a local walking along the road. In great anxiety I asked if the longed-for village was nearby and did it truly have supplies for sale.

"It has everything," he told me with complete confidence.

I hurried my horse on. And as I sit here now I still remember the excitement I felt when I saw that village at last. It took but a moment to tie Pasha to a tree and walk towards the building which I took to be the local shop. Along the way I passed a small boy who was standing next to a rickety wooden table placed alongside the side of the road. Atop the table were placed various small items. These included old packets of cheap cigarettes, small boxes of wooden matches and a few cheap ball-point pens. Everything was covered in the dust thrown up by the road. I didn't give the table, its contents, or the boy more than a passing thought, dreaming instead of the hot meal I was about to enjoy indoors.

Imagine my surprise when I reached the door of the building only to be brusquely informed that I had burst into a private dwelling. The "shop" I had ridden all day to find was out there in the street behind me.

When I returned to the wooden table which served as the village market, I found that the boy had two boxes of stale banana-flavoured cookies for sale. That was the extent of the food on offer at the store which had "everything."

Sadder, but wiser, I sat in the dust and shared my cookies with my horse. During my absence he had stripped the bark off the tree he was tethered to and eaten it in similar desperate hunger.

Before leaving that town I had to cut a new hole in my sword belt, as my already lean frame had reached such diminished proportions that my pistol and sword threatened to slide down past my hips.

I then swung back into the saddle and rode on in search of more food and a night's lodging.

Hunger

As my tale demonstrates, food takes on a special meaning to a Long Rider.

Brushing big horses, breaking camp, loading up equipment, lifting heavy saddles, riding all day and enduring harsh weather gives you the appetite of a ravenous lion. The problem is that your stomach is a rascal. It doesn't remember how well you treated it yesterday. It will cry out for more tomorrow.

Hunger has an insistent voice. When it pinches, you have little inclination to admire the beauties of nature. The landscape is robbed of her charm when all you can think about is your next meal.

No one is immune to this pain. After riding through a barren stretch of wilderness Frederick Burnaby remarked, "After a hard ride the traveller soon loses every other feeling in the absorbing one of hunger, and at that time I think I could have eaten my great-grandfather if he had been properly roasted for the occasion."

Supper is never as good as when you have ridden all day to get it. The problem is what's to be found at day's end?

After starving in the saddle all day while riding across a remote part of the Ottoman Empire, Louisa Jebb had a unique conversation with a local inn keeper.

"What will you have for supper?

What can we have?

What you wish.

Get a chicken.

There is not one left here.

Eggs then?

No chicken, no eggs.

Well we will have what there is.

There is nothing."

No chicken or eggs? Then no problem, as other Long Riders have learned the truth in the old saying that a hungry stomach is easily satisfied.

One memorable roadside recipe stated, "Take a piece of sheep, and with an axe cut it into chunks, regardless of bones and gristle; take a chunk and throw it on to the red hot charcoal in a brazier; when there is a distinct smell of burning and the hissing has nearly ceased, turn it over on the other side. When it resembles a piece of burnt charcoal, remove it and serve at once; swallow whole, as if you try to bite it your teeth will remind you of it for a considerable time."

Mind you, modern Long Riders tend not to exhibit the culinary bravery of their forebears. A remarkable example of such dietary daintiness was noted recently during a high profile equestrian journey that would have put a Maharaja's kitchen to shame.

Realism versus Romance

When the original international meeting of the Long Riders Guild was held there were but a handful of brave equestrian explorers still in the saddle in a few distant corners of the globe. One expedition was starving in the Chaco jungle, while another was making its way from the frozen corner of Patagonia to the distant top of Alaska.

Yet as the 21st century advanced and as the Guild made a bonanza of equestrian travel advice free to the public, a growing number of eager amateurs sought to appease their appetite for equestrian adventure.

Many dreamed. Only a few dared take to the saddle. As more and more were caught up in the excitement they undertook rides which were increasingly disconnected with the reality of equestrian travel.

One high profile trip was undertaken in California, a land often noted for its love of style over substance. A group of dashing debutantes announced plans to ride to the old Spanish missions that stretched from Santa Cruz to San Diego; albeit in a culinary fashion undreamed of in olden days.

Such a journey had been made in 1910 by Joseph Smeaton Chase. In his book *California Coast Trails* he described how he rode from Mexico to Oregon. The amateur scientist recorded a treasure trove of observations, including the architecture of the Spanish Missions, the hospitality of the people, and the beauties of a fabled countryside in the last days of its pristine natural glory.

Smeaton Chase had also written about the gratitude he felt when local Mexican families invited him to step down from the saddle and enjoy a humble meal of corn tortillas and frijoles (beans).

But diets change with the times.

When the modern group of eleven mounted tourists decided to dine their way south from Santa Cruz to San Diego their menu left little to be desired.

The team leader wrote, "Our film crew will be following the ride in a vehicle that will carry film equipment, a first aid kit, and other items, including supplies for campsite meals as needed along the way."

Buying food for eleven riders and crew, she wrote, was no easy task, so basic ingredients had included "granola, dried fruits, nuts, onions and potatoes, garlic, tortillas, beans, rice, spices, a planter for fresh herbs and tablets of cinnamon chocolate."

Having planned the route so as to arrive at historic Spanish missions, each rendezvous was designed to incorporate a particular local delight.

"In Sonoma, we'll take advantage of the region's fantastic olive groves to stock up on local olive oil, in San Juan Bautista we'll savour artichokes cut from their stalks just before cooking and in Carmel we'll dine on grilled sardines fresh from the bay of Monterey."

While this may seem to be an ideal example of living off the gourmet land, the ride organizer sought the advice of a California chef who suggested a menu which has made its own unusual mark in Long Rider history.

"I emailed the Assistant Curator of Mission Dolores, whom I'd interviewed a few months ago. He kindly suggested some menu ideas. He noted that one traditional dish, acorn mush, would probably be too challenging to make on the trail ride. But here are his suggestions for a workable campsite meal. An appetizer of pine nuts, fresh oysters and grilled seaweed, followed by a main course consisting of roasted venison, fried abalone and greens, concluding with a dessert of acorn bread with blackberries and local honey."

The excited gourmet rider concluded, "Wow! This certainly got creative juices flowing. But where to find acorn bread and how to prepare the dishes?"

No matter what society you come from, we all have our favourite dishes and our beloved cultural recipes. Our mouths water at the memory of some exceptional dish our mother prepared for us on some special emotional occasion in our childhood.

Savour those memories, and remember them when you are nearly fainting from hunger on the trail, for unlike the pampered California mission riders, the majority of Long Riders, both past and present, soon learn that appeasing their raging appetites is a matter of reality not romance.

Gabriel Bonvalot was the French Long Rider who rode across Tibet during the winter of 1889. Accompanying him were a hardy band of Siberians whom he had hired as servants. The winter was so harsh that the Siberians begged Bonvalot to let them return home, rather than face another minute in the frozen world he had led them into.

Bonvalot told them to stop snivelling, act like men – and get on with making dinner.

"Our circumstances leave much to be desired. In the first place the food is such that appetite soon wearies of it. Our bill of fare is always the same: meat boiled in mutton fat, tea that never really boils on account of our altitude, and made with water that is sometimes brackish and always dirty, which we get by melting ice that is full of impurities. The frozen meat, too, which we have to chop with an axe, is always tough, and never cooked through, while, when we try vegetables or rice, we find it impossible to soften them, and they crackle between our teeth. The dust, mud, and sand that we have swallowed, and the numerous hairs from our furs and beasts which we find in our food, are things to which we have long ceased to pay any attention, for here we have no longer any pretensions of cleanliness, and we have come to consider even a washing of the hands as a thing of the past."

Before you accuse me of reciting old tales which have no bearing on a progressive age, let me share one of the numerous stories which modern Long Riders have sent to the Guild about the fare they have been forced to endure.

Honour before Disgrace

Two French Long Riders who recently rode through South America recalled how the issue of finding food was a matter of life and death to the people they met. They shared a tale about people who were barely able to feed their children but shared their scant rations with the two hungry travellers.

"We have been in Bolivia for a month and learned that the people are extremely kind. We have never been refused any hospitality, quite the reverse. But fruit, vegetables, meat and even eggs are hard to find. There is little cheese because the undernourished cattle are giving so little milk. As a result, the women bring up their five to seven children on only one meal a day of some tea and a piece of bread."

The Long Riders noted how the lack of food caused the local men to go out hunting morning and evening. They augmented the family diet with caimans, deer, armadillos and rodents.

"We have tasted them all."

One episode in particular made a deep impression upon the travellers. They had been invited to become the guests of a family who endured deep poverty but were determined to honour their unexpected guests.

"They have had to sell their refrigerator, horse, cart, cows and work on another estancia in order to survive. Yet in spite of all this, they welcomed us very cheerfully. However they were embarrassed because there was neither meat nor eggs in the village. So they killed one of their few remaining chickens for our dinner. That evening they invited us to sleep indoors on a mattress. We were very touched by the generosity of these people who have nothing left."

The Commissary

When you're sitting in the comfort and safety of your home, planning the exciting equestrian journey you're anxious to make, you probably focus your attention on things such as horses, saddles and a route. Chances are you don't give much thought to what the cavalry used to call the "commissary department."

Cowboys were able to undertake a long cattle drive across vast and desolate parts of the American west thanks to the supplies which accompanied them in the chuck wagon.

But even if you're planning to take along a pack animal, your ability to carry food and supplies is going to be severely limited. That is why careful planning for this part of your trip is of great importance. There are a variety of factors which will affect your diet. The state of your finances first has to be considered. How many mouths will you have to feed? How far will you travel? Is the land bleak or plentiful in terms of availability of food? Will you be able to replenish supplies along the way?

After a few weeks on the trail, most Long Riders judge food by its quantity rather than by any standard of taste.

Three lady Long Riders, all from different countries, learned how to simplify their diet and subsist on wholesome local food.

In 1929 Countess Linde von Rosen rode from Stockholm to Rome, where she had a private audience with the Pope. The meeting might have been glamorous but Linde's diet along the way was anything but.

"My meals I divide into: breakfast with coffee, egg, bread and butter at eight a.m., followed by a cup of chocolate between five and six p.m. After I arrive at my destination, I normally have my dinner at eight p.m. It consists of an omelette and bread, plus some fruit."

Jane Dotchin has been making equestrian journeys across Great Britain for many years. She is one of the few remaining English Long Riders who remembered how it was once possible to ride from village to village, finding food and shelter along the way.

"In the early days I could easily pick up supplies along the way, because every village had a grocery store, a chemist and a post office. But there are very few village shops left, so I have to carry much more in the way of supplies with me."

Carrying her provisions in home-made saddlebags, Jane's daily diet tends to consist of bread, cheese and porridge, cooked up on a small Primus stove.

Over in Canada, Catherine Thompson has made a number of journeys across the prairies and into the Rocky Mountains. Experience has taught her to supplement her diet by dining on local foodstuffs.

"I ate simply, twice a day, just breakfast and supper. I would carry eggs with me for breakfast and canned wild salmon which I would use as a base to make stews and curries. Most of the greens that I ate I picked in the wild; stinging nettles, lamb's quarters, dandelions and mint for the most part. I managed to find a couple of great patches of raspberries. I carried nuts and dried fruit. I also dried my own meat before I left, making jerky and pemmican."

Catherine isn't the first to learn one of the unavoidable side-effects of making an extended equestrian journey.

"A few friends have suggested I write a book called *The Long Riders Weight Loss Program*. Though an effective weight loss program it would be, it would unfortunately be a pretty short book and so not a viable income generator – 'Go on a long ride, lose weight', that just about covers it."

Dietary Customs

Few things separate us like food.

Somerset Maugham made an interesting observation on this subject during his ride across Spain.

"Food is even more an affair of birth than religion, since a man may change his faith, but hardly his manner of eating: the stomach used to roast meat and Yorkshire pudding rebels against Eastern cookery, and a Christian may sooner become a Buddhist than a beef-eater a guzzler of tofu."

Culinary preferences and dietary customs have a way of influencing daily events.

Many nomadic cultures consider bread and salt sacred. Not eating or trying the bread shows a grave disrespect for the host.

It is often customary in Islamic countries to forego the use of cutlery, with the diners using their right hands to eat from a common bowl or platter.

Another tradition is that all talk ceases lest it insult the quality of the food.

One Long Rider crossing North Africa noted, "In the primitive surroundings of an oasis, there is nothing to be had in the way of pleasure except eating. It is the spirit that counts in these matters and not the intrinsic value of the offering."

No matter what was served during his journey across Spain, Washington Irving took the view that "I endeavour to take things as they come with cheerfulness."

Hippophagy

Food is an essential part of life. That is why, given the right circumstances, the gnawing power of hunger can make one eat almost anything.

An extreme example of this philosophy was enacted by British Long Rider John Talbot Clifton, a compulsive traveller who explored Canada, Siberia, Burma, Malaya, Indonesia, Africa and South America. He once dined on mammoth recovered frozen from the Arctic permafrost.

One of the most challenging taboos which Long Riders from the Occident will encounter is the way other cultures enjoy eating horse meat.

The practice of eating horse meat, known as hippophagy, is connected to cultural and religious practices. Countries such as the USA, UK and Australia largely view horses as companion animals that should not be consumed. This taboo has its roots in a religious edict passed in 732 A.D. when Pope Gregory III forbade Christians to consume horse meat, because it was widely viewed as being closely associated with the pagan practices of the Norse.

Other European nations view horse meat as a tasty national tradition. Austria, Belgium, France, Germany, Hungary, Italy, Netherlands, Serbia and Switzerland are just some of the countries which partake of this particular type of protein. An estimated 90% of all horses bred in Poland are destined for the dinner table.

In other parts of the world, where you go will determine if you are faced with the possibility of being served this type of meat. It is considered taboo to eat horse meat in Argentina but next door in Chile horse meat is used to make a local dish known as *charqui*. Mexico is the second largest producer of horse meat in the world but you can't buy it in Venezuela. Values even differ within countries. You can buy horse steak in French-speaking Quebec but not out west in Victoria.

Some countries, such as the Mongols, eat horses in the winter. Other nations, such as Kazakhstan, eat them all year.

Many Long Riders who have journeyed across these two countries have been confronted with a meal of horse meat. Consuming it is as normal to the inhabitants of those nations as enjoying a hamburger is to an American.

There are many personal, religious, cultural and dietary factors which will influence your individual decision to avoid or eat this type of meat.

What you should be aware of is that the majority of the world does not adhere to the Anglo prohibition of not consuming horses. So having researched the dietary practices of the country where you plan to travel, you should not be taken unaware if the choice is presented to you.

The Dangers of Drinking

Mankind doesn't change much despite the passage of time. When Ernest Fox ventured out to Afghanistan in 1937, he first stopped at Kabul. There he met the small handful of foreigners who had been employed by the Afghan king to oversee various engineering and scholastic projects.

Like many lonely men stationed far from home, this handful of Europeans and Americans sought to ease the strain of their lonely exile by gathering together at night for talk and a drink. Their favourite was a stout cocktail known as the "Khyber Passout," which according to Fox was so strong that it laid a grown man out cold.

Drinking and long riding often bring about dangerous or unfortunate events.

Thomas Stevens remarked on how he saw the devastating results of massive alcoholism as he rode across Czarist Russia in 1870.

"Vodka drinking is at the root of half the misery one sees in Russia. The evil is enormous."

Consumption of vodka in Russia is still a major social problem, where the average Russian consumes nearly 16 litres of vodka per year, twice the average intake of most countries. The high prevalence of alcohol consumption means that an equestrian traveller is likely to encounter intoxicated and aggressive men who have participated in binge drinking.

Alcohol can also turn a friendly encounter with a local into an episode linked to theft and robbery.

One English Long Rider was taken by surprise while riding in Romania. Having met what seemed like a friendly fellow, the traveller sat down in the shade of a tree to enjoy a drink of beer on a hot summer's day. Things seemed sociable until the local man pulled a knife on the Long Rider and robbed him of several hundred dollars.

"I felt such an arse. I watched him run off through the trees and I was sweating. Probably it was the beer and the fright of a smiling face suddenly turned ugly and my weakness in failing to overpower him, but the shock was immense. I couldn't say if he'd have driven that knife into me, but he looked bitter and twisted enough to do it."

Another problem connected to alcohol is the theft of horses and equipment.

Mongolia has long had a reputation for aggressive alcohol abuse. *Kumis*, a drink made of fermented mare's milk, is the drink of the Mongols. The addiction to *kumis* is so strongly rooted in the culture that Genghis Khan denounced the drunkenness which was a part of the steppe culture.

"What could be better," Genghis is reported to have said, "than that a man should not drink at all."

Soon after the death of Genghis Khan, Friar Giovanni Carpini became one of the first Europeans to journey to the distant capital of the Mongol empire.

Carpini warned other travellers to be aware of the widespread drunkenness among the Mongols. Genghis Khan's son and heir, Ögedei Khan, died as a result of alcoholism. It was his death which prompted the Mongol army to halt its invasion of Europe and return to their homeland.

Centuries have passed but fear of drunken Mongols still stalks many a Long Rider. Travellers have had their horses and equipment stolen by locals drunk on *kumis* and vodka. However physical attacks and thefts are heightened during the summer months, which coincide with the peak production of mare's milk and the fermenting of *kumis*.

One other problem associated with alcohol is the possibility that you might be arrested for riding your horse while intoxicated. Various American states enforce statutes which make it a crime to ride if you are under the influence of alcohol.

The Colorado legislation, for example, states, "It is unlawful for any person who is under the influence of alcohol or of any controlled substance... or of any stupefying drug to walk or be upon that portion of any highway normally used by moving motor vehicle traffic. This section applying to pedestrians shall also be applicable to riders of animals."

Disregarding the social implications of being arrested, there is another serious safety concern connected to drinking and then riding in a country such as America.

In Mongolia the onset of warm weather means the making of *kumis*, which means that the intoxicated Mongol swings into the saddle and rides back home to his distant yurt. As there is no traffic, and the horse knows the way home, no harm done.

But in the traffic-heavy American environment, there is the potential for terrible injuries and deaths.

Unlike automobiles, horses don't dent, they die.

Beware of Courtesy

Take note that the concept of courtesy has different shades of meaning, depending upon the country in which you ride.

The Afghans are friendly, but one is expected to use discretion in accepting that which is paraded in the garb of hospitality.

If a village chief invites a stranger to spend the night in his village, the courteous thing is to accept, for the invitation may involve the safety of the chief as well as the men invited. But if an official invites you to ride his prized stallion you may well be expected to smile sweetly and thank him profusely, but stay off the horse.

Taboos

While there has been much talk about how the internet age has rapidly altered our world, a large portion of humanity remains unconnected and immune. In much of the world the old prevails, the new intrudes, and the people remain unchanged.

One portion of the human existence which resists alteration is tribal taboos.

No society is immune from adhering to some level of taboo. They touch on the topics which challenge a society's comfortable beliefs. Death, sex, family, food and religion; these are just some of the issues which expose our collective beliefs. Agreeing on what actions and topics are forbidden helps people create a sense of collective identity and define themselves in opposition to others.

There are various reasons why people adhere to these prohibitions. Many are religious. Some are regional. Most are cultural. They can be of recent origin, though most have been passed down for generations. Some are out of date. All of them are dangerous.

Taboos vary widely from one country to the next. They are psychologically powerful and can be extremely hazardous. It's not your job to diagnose or comment on taboos. It's your responsibility to avoid breaking them.

Many of the cultural taboos which held sway for thousands of years, especially those connected to sexuality and bigotry, have undergone recent changes. But adherents of traditional beliefs are left feeling angry and bewildered when their beliefs are undermined.

One notable example of breaking a tribal taboo occurred in Tibet in the summer of 1949. The American Long Rider Leonard Clark was returning from an extremely perilous journey to a mysterious mountain rumoured to be higher than Mount Everest.

Clark's route took him through the land of the notorious Torgut tribesmen, mounted warriors who detested outsiders. Upon approaching a large lake, believed by the Torguts to be sacred, Clark found the bodies of two young French explorers. The travellers had been warned by the Torguts to stay out of the sacred lake. They had paid no heed and gone swimming. Their bullet-riddled bodies were evidence of the price they paid for breaking this tribal taboo.

Films and Photographs

The idea of having our personal space invaded by paparazzi photographers has taken on new significance since the death of Princess Diana in 1997. Intruding upon others, and capturing their images, is not a recent innovation.

When Napoleon invaded Egypt in 1789, he took 167 scientists, including mathematicians, naturalists, chemists and artists, with him to record the antiquities found there. The French emperor employed the artist Rigo to make drawings of the Nubians in their native costumes. As soon as they saw their drawings on canvas, the Nubians took fright.

"He's taken my head. He's taken my arm," they shouted and fled.

Long Riders have broken the taboo of taking images without permission.

Clyde Kluckhohn eventually became one of America's leading anthropologists, thanks to the specialized work he did among the Navajo. But he began his studies among the Native Americans by making an extended ride through the American Southwest. It was during that 1920s ride that the naïve young traveller let his enthusiasm overrule his common sense.

"I had ridden to the Taos Pueblo to see a sacred dance. In the excess of my enthusiasm for the snake dance I became guilty of a breach of etiquette. Fearing lest it would soon be too dark, I took out my camera and took a snap shot of the dancers. This produced a jarring note among the Indians, who began shouting in English, Spanish and Taos. I was in danger of being mobbed, when I was confronted by the governor of the pueblo. He threatened to put me in jail but then let me off with a fine."

Bringing out a camera changes the chemistry of a social situation. Unless it is done with care, filming and photography make many people uncomfortable, nervous and even dangerous.

Friendship Book

One custom which some Long Riders have used with great success is to carry a "Friendship Book" in their saddlebag. It may seem like a small indulgence in terms of weight, but it serves as a way of involving all of the people you meet along the way. Placing their names alongside those who have hosted you reinforces their sense of involvement in the concepts of brotherhood, hospitality and humanity which are so crucially important to any equestrian journey.

One World – Many Views

Who decides what is good or bad? Travel for any length at all and you will soon learn that one society's besetting sin is another society's honourable tradition.

Before his death, DC Vision, one of the Founders of the Guild, wrote, "We most certainly are not all one. We are individuals with unique personal experiences that have shaped our beliefs. We are all essentially looking at the same view, just interpreting it in our own particular and peculiar ways. Debate presupposes that the other person is wrong, and that you are right. Dialogue accepts that the other person's awareness is appropriate to all of their experiences and inheritances. No one person is right or wrong. There is just the difference of how much truth is being experienced by either.

I have seen many people with the desire to find the flaws in other people's beliefs. They will offer very little but borrowed words, and will not attempt to see or hear the other person they are trying in desperation to correct. Were they capable of turning off their reactions to the words, they might discover that the other person speaks of the same truth as they do, but in a language unique to their experience (much like two people witnessing the same accident, but giving different reports of it).

In dialogue, however, by accepting that the other person's perceptions are supposed to be different from my own, since they've had a history different than I have, it has always been my experience that both of our eyes and ears tended to be more open."

Summary

No matter what strange or exotic customs you encounter along the way, what must be remembered is that we are all making a journey in the same direction. Along the way we meet people who enrich our lives, some for a few hours, some for a few days, some for a lifetime. The true riches of your journey are not the accumulation of mere miles but the discovery of the richness of the human experience which they can share with you.

When Danish Long Rider Ole Olufsen encountered a tribe of Kyrgyz tribesmen living beside a lake in the Pamir Mountains, he was surprised to learn they believed the lake was inhabited by seahorses which came out at night to graze in the moonlight.

Ida Pfeiffer was the heroic Austrian Long Rider who travelled to all parts of the world but was denied membership in the Royal Geographical Society due to her sex.

A Long Rider learns to do without. This wooden cabinet served as a shop in one of the remote villages visited by the author during his ride through northern Pakistan.

Having a friendly drink along the way has its appeal. Arthur Elliott is seen enjoying a pint of beer during his ride across England in 1952. But care must be taken not to let alcohol endanger the Long Rider, his horse or equipment.

In 2013 this equestrian traveller was arrested in Boulder, Colorado for riding drunk during his journey to Utah.

Chapter 70
Stables and Shelter

A Russian proverb states, "The wagon rests in winter, the sleigh in summer, the horse never."

Nothing wears out a horse faster on a journey more than the want of sleep. It is vitally important that every effort be made to provide the horse with the best quarters circumstances permit and to then allow him every opportunity to enjoy a night's sleep.

Adjusting to Change

Dr. John Dolittle was the fictional 19th century naturalist who had the unique ability to speak to animals. Sadly, we Long Riders do not possess the capacity to explain our travel tactics to our horses. Our plans are made. The horse is led out and tacked up. We swing into the saddle and, without understanding what is about to occur, the horse walks away from all he knows.

Margaret Leigh remarked upon this lack of communication as she and a companion rode from Cornwall to Scotland.

"I always pitied the horses for their ignorance. They never knew where they were being taken or whether we planned to keep them trekking for the rest of their lives."

Whereas we can wish that we might communicate our plans with our equine companions, it would be a mistake to attribute a strong sense of nostalgia or homesickness to the horse. They are not like cows, who find comfort staying behind the confines of a well-ordered fence. Before mankind began incarcerating them in small stalls or enclosing them within restricted pastures, wild horses roamed as and where they willed. They often covered great distances in search of grazing, water or merely in quest of a new place to visit.

Like humans, horses develop a taste for travel.

There is an initial period of a few days when the horses realize they are moving beyond the emotional and geographic boundaries of their previously known world.

In Argentina the gauchos use the word *querencia* to denote the place which the horse feels is his emotional home. During the first few days of a journey, a horse often flees back towards his *querencia*. There are stories told on the pampas of horses which responded to this deep homing instinct. In some cases horses have travelled tremendous distances, swum rivers, traversed deserts or climbed mountains so as to return to the place they viewed as the centre of their lives.

But many a Long Rider has remarked upon the fact that at some point after the journey begins, the horse passes an invisible line whereupon he realizes that all he knew lies behind him. The *querencia* and the members of his former herd become a dimmer and dimmer memory. Unlike humans, who are capable of planning ahead, the horse resides in the present. In terms of travel, he learns to adjust his emotional needs to fit these new circumstances.

In his remarkable book, *A Tale of Two Horses*, Aimé Tschiffely recounted the story of his ride from Buenos Aires to New York from the point of view of his Criollo companions, Mancha and Gato.

In that tale, Gato made this unique observation.

"After the first few days travelling, one day was like another. We knew that we were in a strange land where we had no friends."

As the miles passed and the various countries fell behind them, later in the journey Gato remarked, "By this time we were so used to travelling that I often felt as if I had done nothing else all my life. My home seemed like a strange dream. As I jogged along, I only wondered where and when I would get my next drink of water or something to eat."

Two Hearts – One Journey

In an age when motorized transport has become the norm, it is increasingly likely that you might meet a person who holds the mistaken view that travelling with a horse is inappropriate or even cruel. While well-meaning, this is an indication of a person who does not understand the many benefits which a horse derives from making a journey.

From a purely physical point of view, the combination of daily exercise, delicious sunlight, pure air, good food, clean water and emotional satisfaction results in a road or pack horse becoming a superb athlete. These facts were common knowledge among those nations which boasted of hosting celebrated horsemen and great travellers.

British Long Rider Harry de Windt made an important observation related to this topic while riding across Russia. He noted that the horses ridden by the Czar's Cossacks were kept in the pink of condition and were lavished with food, grooming and exercise.

"I could cite many instances of when, in the deserts of Central Asia, Cossacks have given their last drop of water and mouthful of bread to sustain the life of an equine friend while they themselves have perished."

Harry reported that, "The Cossack loves his horse as dearly as his wife and children; in fact, it is practically regarded as a member of the family. Because of this superb handling, the Cossack horses were able to cover fifty miles a day, for a month on end, without showing signs of distress."

Cossacks were not mounted on mere workaday drudges. Like modern Long Riders, Cossacks knew that travelling horses respond in a different way than stabled horses. Thus, never believe the person who says horses do not comprehend love and loyalty, for the road horse soon learns that the Long Rider represents the one constant element of emotional stability in an ever-changing world.

During the day the horse carries us on and on into the unknown, trusting us at sunset to feed, water and protect him in return for his service. Therein springs a sense of mutual respect that many have experienced but few can adequately articulate.

Trigger was such an equine example. In terms of breeding, he was nothing special, just an old white cart horse which Bill Holt had bought from an English tinker. Despite his humble origins, Trigger's loyalty to Bill became a legend. They journeyed for many thousands of miles across various countries in Western Europe. No matter how bad the weather, Bill always chose to sleep outside on the grass close to his beloved horse. Trigger in turn would lie down next to his trusted companion.

Soon after they first set out, Bill wrote about how Trigger began the habit of sleeping next to him.

"That night after I had let him loose on grass at the edge of a wood Trigger again watched me intently. He saw me turn his saddle upside down for a pillow, unroll my blanket over my ground-sheet, and then, to his astonishment, lie down to sleep. As if he could not believe this really to be true he grazed slowly and thoughtfully, moving round me in smaller and smaller circles, watching me out of the corner of eye in the growing darkness, his ears turned towards me. Finally he came to a halt and stood over me, his forefeet at the edge of my ground-sheet, his head high, silhouetted among the stars. In the morning when I awoke he was lying by my side."

Tschiffely made a similar historic observation about his horses, Mancha and Gato.

"In order to appreciate fully the friendship of a horse, a man has to live out in the open with him for some time, and as soon as the animal comes to a region that is strange to him he will never go away from his master but will look for his company and in case of danger seek his protection. By this time both my horses were so fond of me that I have never had to tie them again, and even if I slept in some lonely hut I simply turned them loose at night, well knowing that they would never go more than a few yards away and that they would be waiting for me at the door in the early morning, when they always greeted me with a friendly nicker."

There is ample evidence therefore indicating that the horses develop a remarkable emotional bond for the Long Rider. But emotions aside, what must be remembered is that, like you, horses too need to sleep.

To Sleep, Perchance to Dream

Wild horses spend their time travelling across the land looking for grazing and water. Their need to protect their lives at a moment's notice means that no matter how weary, they must be ready to instantly run away. Wild horses normally never lie down as cows and camels do to rest, unless they are confident as to their safety. They sleep while standing, with three and a half hours often being sufficient to refresh a horse.

Frank Heath was one of the most remarkable, albeit forgotten, Long Riders of the last century. Mounted on his mare, Gypsy Queen, he rode more than 18,000 kilometres (11,000 miles) to all 48 American states. Because he was determined to complete the entire journey on his mare, Heath kept meticulous notes during the trip about what he fed his horse, how the further she travelled the stronger she became, and how many hours of sleep she averaged during the trip.

Other Long Riders have noted a few observations about when their horses rested, but Heath's account of his horse's sleep records are, I believe, unique in Long Rider history.

Heath realized that the type of bed, and the subsequent sense of security she felt in regards to her surroundings, would affect Gypsy Queen's decision to either sleep or merely slumber.

"I've found her sleeping soundly at 10 p.m. when she had a good bed and she would lie stretched out until about 5:30 a.m. Then again, when there was not a good bed she often does not lie down at all and sleeps little if any. I've known this to continue three nights when we were in the wilds. But that was rather long for a horse to remain on its feet. The more we have of such a life the longer the rests we require when we get a chance."

Frank Heath was a retired U.S. cavalry man, not a scientist. But thanks to his keen-eyed observations of Gypsy Queen he made many an accurate observation. His belief, for example, that the mare eventually had to lie down in order to achieve a deeper sleep pattern has since been proved accurate.

One study reported, "Recent studies into sleep patterns have shown how horses cannot usually experience REM sleep unless they are sleeping in the prone position. This restive state is essential for all mammals including ourselves."

Frank also noted, "Midnight is when a horse usually sleeps soundly, if undisturbed. But it is generally believed, and I concede, that a horse sleeps best, generally, early in the morning."

Another important observation was that Gypsy Queen would use the afternoon lunch break to rest and recover. Experts use the term "rebound sleep" or "power nap" to describe how a weary human uses a few minutes to re-charge his physical and emotional batteries. Frank's mare was a marvel at adapting this technique to keep up her strength.

"Queen seems to be refreshed by a four hour rest at midday. But she does not sleep. She is drowsy but not sleeping."

No matter if your horse is dozing in the sun during a lunch break or sleeping deeply in a safe stall for the night, your challenge is to find a place where you tired companion can rest at the end of the day.

Changing Times

One hundred years ago, in 1914, a Long Rider named Jay Ransom made a vital discovery. After having ridden more than 15,000 miles to more than forty states in America, he had at last left behind the busy East Coast and the Deep South. In his diary he wrote about the sense of intense emotional relief he felt to once again find himself "out West" in the land of wide-open spaces and mounted men.

"These are horse people, cattle people, out of doors people. They are on their own and they know damn well we are on our own, and are not craving sympathy. We can't buy a bed or a meal in this part of the country. It's all give and no take. They just want to talk horses and gear and pump us for yarns about our trip. We don't have to tell them about our hardships on the trail; they know all about rough going in a raw new country like this," Jay confided in his diary.

Ransom was one of the first to realize that the equestrian age which mankind had taken for granted for so many millennia was disappearing before his eyes. Frank Heath followed Ransom out across America a mere ten years later, departing in early 1925, but in the short space of a single decade the landscape had already been denuded of equestrian accommodations and foodstuffs.

"I expected to stay at a barn where I had put up three years previously," Heath wrote soon after he began his journey. "Imagine my disappointment at finding the barn dark and deserted. As I made my way across the country, I found the barns were now full of automobiles. There was no bedding for my horse. And when I asked where I could get some feed for my horse, they didn't know. Many a night the only feed I could find for my horse was a package of oatmeal for table use."

The world was changing, being mechanized, and this meant that all of the traditional services connected to horses and equestrian travel were becoming extinct.

Welsh Long Rider Thurlow Craig had left home at an early age to take up work as a cowboy on the vast estancias of South America. After many years away from home he returned to Great Britain before the outbreak of the Second World War to find that the horse-related services of his childhood were but a memory.

"The horse was never so well understood or tended as in the few short years of the seventh Edward's reign. There used to be many ostlers, grooms, vets, saddlers and seven blacksmiths inside a three-mile circle of my village. Nowadays things are completely different. How many of us can afford a groom? How far off is our nearest vet, and he doesn't want to be a city vet who specializes in small pets. How far is the blacksmith, and he doesn't want to only do a cold-shoe with his heart in his mouth. Where is the small town saddler, who can stuff and repair a saddle? Where is the nearest bed and breakfast inn that still caters to Long Rider and Road Horse? The entire face of horsemanship has changed. Prices of everything to do with horses have rocketed right off the graph. Most of what was done for the rider and his horse we have to do for ourselves today."

This isn't to say that people's hearts had hardened, only that the towns no longer employed people who understood horses and could offer them basic services. In their place a new type of urban human had come upon the scene. Though they were generous, they were unaware of a Long Rider's needs.

Soon after Bill Holt set off across England, bound for the ferry that would take him and Trigger across the Channel to France, he rode up to the edge of this new type of metropolitan hazard.

"The sun was setting as we rode towards Wolverhampton. A car drew up and a man and woman got out. They invited me to their home in Wolverhampton. You can have a bed, bath and breakfast. It was embarrassing. People who don't ride horses don't understand. They did not say where Trigger could sleep. Their home was ten miles away. A mile is a mile for a horse. I did not want them to be embarrassed so I made some excuse and rode on. As I went on I saw less and less grass but more and more houses."

As Bill learned, not only do the people fail to understand what you need, but even if they did, they couldn't supply it.

Things have only got worse since then. That is why it is important to know what to look for when it comes time to stable or shelter your horse for the night.

Sheltering the Horses

Though patriotism was often the cause of national conflicts among them, German, British and American cavalry officers shared a common understanding of the basic requirements needed to safeguard a horse for the night. Like modern Long Riders, the cavalry officer's decision on where he rested his horse for the night was frequently a matter of necessity rather than choice.

Yet thankfully much of that wisdom has been retained and can be shared.

In bad weather, even the worst shelter is preferable to having the horses standing exposed to the elements. But circumstances often dictate that a traveller must make a decision as to where he can safely place his horse outside for the night. That is why the provision of a good place for your horse to bed down is an important detail in keeping your animal happy and healthy.

The selection of where the horses will be placed depends upon the length of stay and the time of year.

Regardless of the country, pure air, good light, dry ground and good water are the essentials sought at day's end when a suitable spot is needed to picket horses. That is why the prospective night's lodging must be considered carefully.

First, assess the potential site in regard to access to a good water supply, availability of fodder and protection against wet and cold. Be sure the area is large enough to provide adequate space for each horse to move comfortably.

The state of the ground is of great importance. Avoid placing your horse on a steep hillside. Try to choose flat level ground for the horses to stand on.

Horses can obtain a considerable amount of rest standing, and in fact there are some which rarely lie down; but the more rest they can be induced to take, the longer their legs will probably last, and the more likely are they to keep in good condition. That is why it is important that the site should be cleared of stones and any other objects which might interfere with the horses lying down comfortably.

Ideally the ground should have good drainage to carry away storm water. Marshy ground should always be avoided as dampness causes hoof rot. Avoid river bottoms which may flood.

When travelling in hot climates, providing protection from the sun is essential and in this case any light structure or trees may be employed as shelter during the day.

Horses are almost indifferent to the greatest extremes of dry cold, yet, if exposed to wind, they lose weight rapidly, and are intensely susceptible to draughts. Always try to choose a spot which acts as a wind break and offers some degree of natural protection from the prevailing wind.

Choose an area free from briars and poisonous plants.

Whenever possible, always chose a spot as close as possible to where you will be camping.

Off Saddling

Because we are studying the topic of ending a day's travelling, it bears repeating that while you are preparing a campsite, or perhaps negotiating for a night's stabling, you should be careful not to rush to remove the saddle or pack saddle from your horse, as exposing the horse's hot sweaty back to a blast of cold air is a recipe for saddle sores.

Baron Fukushima, the great Japanese Long Rider, held a historic conversation with the Emperor of Japan about the need to remove the saddle slowly and with great care. The Meiji Emperor was an avid horseman who was extremely interested in horses, so he quizzed Fukushima on how he had managed to bring his horses all the way across Siberia to Tokyo in such excellent health.

Fukushima explained that every day upon arriving at the rest area he followed a very careful routine. When he arrived at that night's lodging, he would remove the saddle slowly, taking two to four hours, depending upon the conditions and the weather. He was confident that this slow approach had been effective in preventing saddle sores. In addition, while his horses ate, he would massage their legs, wash and clean their hooves, and finally carefully check their horseshoes.

"These horses were the saviours of my life," the Baron explained to the Emperor. "Taking good care of them was never a bothersome task or a problem, but instead a pleasure. My love for the horses grew every day. After travelling for months together, they became friends that I talked to all the time."

The exception to this rule of unsaddling slowly is if the horses have sweated during the day, and if it is not too cold or too near sundown, to wash their backs down with fresh water where the saddle has rested, also underneath and behind the elbows where the girth has pressed.

The Drawbacks of Using Rugs

When considering protecting your horse one point needs to be taken into consideration: the increasingly popular belief that a horse must be covered with a warm blanket or rug.

Straight away the weight of a heavy horse blanket or rug normally prohibits a Long Rider from carrying such a piece of equipment. However there are other concerns connected with its use.

Nature equipped the horse to adapt to extremes of both hot and cold weather. In extremely hot temperatures the horse can, through muscular action, dilate blood vessels near the surface of its skin to cool off. Additionally, it can raise the hairs and even point them in the direction of a breeze to cool down.

The remarkable horses of the Yakut region of Siberia, which routinely thrive in temperatures ranging as low as minus sixty degrees Fahrenheit, are an example of how a horse can raise the hairs on its skin to create a thermal blanket to protect itself.

By covering a horse with blanket or rug for any length of time, the horse's natural defences against cold begin to atrophy over time, making it impossible for the horse to raise or lower the hair on its skin. This diminishes its capacity to warm itself and in turn reduces its core body temperature. Extended use of a blanket or rug effectively robs a horse of its natural, vital, efficient thermoregulatory system.

Additionally, a blanket or rug is inefficient in that it leaves the belly and upper legs still exposed to the cold.

Instead of covering the horse with a blanket, when travelling the goal should be to provide the horse with a shelter that provides a dry, well-ventilated, comfortable haven that is free from draughts.

Fever Nests

Stables used to be a standard feature across the landscape of many nations. Nowadays they are increasingly rare.

What is seldom recalled is that they were often described as "fever nests."

The worst equestrian epidemic in the 19th century history took place in 1872. Known as the "Great Epizootic," it was an equine tragedy so deadly that one wave of the infection swept south like a Biblical plague from its origin in Toronto, Canada, down the Atlantic Seaboard to Havana, Cuba, leaving everything in its path in ruins in weeks, while another branch simultaneously raced west to the Pacific.

One of the contributing factors connected to the rapid spread of the disease was the fact that so many horses were sheltered in close proximity to each other in massive urban stables. The stables used to house the horses which pulled the city trams, for example, often held more than a thousand horses. One famous four-storey facility in Germany was a veritable apartment block full of horses.

Communicable diseases spread like wildfire in such confined environments.

Additionally, the science of veterinary medicine was in its infancy, so medical practices were extremely primitive. The result was that when the Great Epizootic broke out, millions of horses and mules sickened or died in the space of a few weeks.

Medicine has made remarkable progress since then, but a Long Rider must still view a stable as a potential place where his horse might come in contact with strange animals which may be suffering from contagious respiratory ailments or other illnesses.

As medical science progressed during the remainder of the 19th century, several vital discoveries were made. One notable discovery occurred in 1854 when Dr. John Snow was the first to prove that the deadly disease of cholera was linked to contaminated public water supplies.

The growth of tremendous 19th century cities required millions of horses to reside either within the city limits or close by. Well-meaning sympathetic public appeals often raised funds to construct public watering troughs for these hot and hard-working horses. It took some time before veterinarians realized that these public troughs were often the source of contagious equestrian diseases.

Once this medical threat became common knowledge in the 1920s, US Cavalry officers were issued orders not to use public watering troughs so as to limit the chances of valuable military mounts becoming infected.

Safe Stables

Travelling horses soon learn to associate the setting sun with journey's end and food. Should the chance present itself, and you are invited to let your horse spend the night in a strange stable, be quick to express your thanks and then inspect the premises in as diplomatic a manner as possible.

If the horse is to be placed within a stall, spend the time to look for unknown dangers in advance. Be sure to run your hand along the edges of the manger to make sure there are no sharp edges. Pay careful attention to examining the walls for sharp objects that can cause injury. Otherwise your mount will suffer the moment you turn your back. Exposed nails in stalls are especially dangerous as they can be a source of the deadly tetanus virus.

Before you even enter into the stall, be absolutely certain that the door operates properly and can be opened quickly in case of an emergency. The stable should be a refuge not a prison cell. The stall should ideally be at least 10 by 12 feet, be well-ventilated and allow plenty of light.

Providing comfortable, clean and warm bedding encourages horses to lie down and thus rest their legs. Various nations use an assortment of materials as bedding including sand, peat moss, bracken, leaves, sawdust, wood shavings and straw.

Because you will be a guest for the night, you must use your wits and exercise your diplomatic talents if your host offers to place your horse into a stall covered in old straw or thick dung, as both can harbour bacteria. Your horse doesn't need a soft bed as much as he needs a dry, level, clean surface where he can rest quietly.

As any horseman knows, the problem of urine is always connected to stabling horses indoors. Urine-saturated bedding will rot the horn of the foot. Male horses are reluctant to foul their stall and bespatter themselves with urine. So choosing a possible stall for the night should take into account if urine can drain away or be absorbed by adequate bedding.

There are other practical preparations involved in safe stabling, including determining a safe place to tie or secure your horse. Never rope your horse to dangerous and moveable objects such as doors, heavy equipment or wagon wheels. Once you have established that the stall is safe, lead the horse in and remove the halter. Leaving a halter on overnight might result in the animal getting caught and then going into a panic.

Horses, like humans, have the ability to sense the peace and quiet which comes over a stable where horses have dwelt for many years. But don't let the looks of a place put you off your guard.

Hierarchy is important to horses. Quarrels, biting, kicking and screaming can result when strange horses are introduced into a stable for the night. It is not uncommon for a Long Rider to go into the stable in the morning and find that his horse has suffered injuries during the night.

Take care not to place your horse too close to others. Also, make sure that your horse's food cannot be stolen by a greedy neighbour reaching over the stall wall.

The Danger of Fire

There is another element connected with placing your horse in a strange stable for the night: safety.

From a practical point of view, you should try to sleep as close as possible to the stable. This helps deter the theft of your horse, saddle and equipment.

Yet the worst possible scenario involves a stable fire.

There have been cases in the past when the massive loss of so many horses' lives is hard for modern minds to grasp.

The most horrendous stable fire in modern history occurred on the night of May 27, 1887, when more than a thousand horses died in an inferno.

According to the New York Times, "The greatest fire that has taken place in this city for many years broke out at 1.30 o'clock this morning in the stables of the Belt Line Horse Railroad. The stables occupied the whole front of the west side of Tenth Avenue and extended down Fifty-Third and Fifty-Fourth Avenues, half way to Eleventh Avenue. The building was three storeys high. The fire was discovered in the cellar in the extreme western end of the stables.

When the fire broke out, the entire stock of horses owned by the company, nearly 1500 in all, were in their stalls on the second and third floors of the building. The watchmen ran up the runway, and in the first few minutes they managed to release forty of the frightened animals and rush them out into the street.

Then the flames leapt from floor to ceiling and wall to wall, and within six minutes had obtained a start that nothing could check. The fire ate its way through every opening, simultaneously bursting out the windows. A brisk wind was blowing and what impetus the flames lacked they got from the outside element. Despite desperate efforts to release the other horses, the rapid spread of the flames prevented the employees from saving the remaining animals.

When the firemen arrived the whole building was in flames, and the heat was so intense that the firemen could not approach close enough to be of any service to save the premises from destruction.

The helpless horses made their horrible situation known by agonising cries. Long before the flames enveloped the great building, more than 1400 horses perished in the flames."

Fires still destroy barns and stables with alarming frequency. Between 2002 and 2005 more than a thousand barn fires were reported by the U.S. National Fire Protection Agency. This means that every time you place your horse within a barn or stable you expose it to the risk of fire. That is why at every rest stop care must be taken in reducing the danger of fire.

Heat lamps used to heat the stable are a common cause of fires. Faulty electrical outlets often spark and ignite a flame. Heating coils used to warm icy water during winter are sometimes left on by accident. Smoking and matches are of course obvious dangers and should not be permitted near the stables.

Here again, it is your job to cast a careful eye over the stable, looking for possible obvious causes of concern. If you have any doubts about the safety of the building, then don't risk your horse's life by placing him inside a potential firetrap.

Should you awake to find the barn or stable is on fire, do not enter the building if it is already engulfed in flames. In their desire to save their horses, many people have perished by becoming trapped inside a burning barn that collapsed on them.

If you believe you can enter the building with some degree of safety, concentrate on evacuating the horses closest to the doors. Do not think that you can simply open the stall door and drive the horse outside towards safety. Horses are particularly terrified by fire and if freed from their stall have been known to rush into the burning building, not away from it.

Immediately place a halter or bridle on the horse. Then blindfold the horse with any convenient cloth that is close to hand. When horses see or smell fire, they often obstinately refuse to walk towards safety. If he declines to move forward, back him out of the burning building.

Once the horse is outside, do not let him run loose as he may return to the burning building. Tie him or place him within a secure fenced area away from the flames.

Pastures

Long Riders are often forced by circumstances to accept whatever accommodations are on offer for their horses. This frequently means that they will be required to place their animals in a strange pasture for the night.

While the idea of allowing your horse to graze peacefully in the moonlight might seem like a romantic notion, wise equestrians from earlier centuries knew otherwise.

Soon after the sun came up, farmers went to the barn to harness their horses and prepare them for a full day's work pulling a plough, hauling a hay wagon, etc. Likewise horses who resided in urban centres had to be fully rested if they were to tow heavy passenger trams, deliver tons of coal, haul goods from the dockyards to distant warehouses, etc.

What these early horsemen knew was that placing a horse in a pasture or a field for the night did not automatically guarantee that the animal would receive a full night's rest; far from it. Horses are gregarious and mischievous. If left to their own devices, they will spend part of the night grazing. Once their initial hunger pangs are salved, they often begin to misbehave. They will chase each other, bully smaller animals, and expend valuable energy which will be needed for the next day's work or travel.

If you have been travelling with your own horses for a long time or across a great distance, then placing them alone in a pasture for the night may not result in any loss of rest or energy, as most road and pack horses are wise enough to recognize the need to eat as much as possible and rest for as long as they can.

But placing your horses in a pasture populated by strange horses exposes them to the danger of being chased, bitten and kicked. So have a care before you put your valuable equine friends inside a pasture and walk away thinking that all is well.

Pasture Patrol

There will be many times when you won't have a choice. The only option on offer will be a pasture. Express your gratitude and agree to accept the offer of placing your horses there for the night. But under no circumstances should you ever put your horses into a field or pasture without having first patrolled it for potential problems.

Being a Long Rider requires you to develop a certain level of diplomacy. It doesn't especially matter what you tell your potential host, so long as he understands that you would feel safer if he lets you take a casual stroll about the field. Perhaps, you might explain, your horses are apt to try and wander back from the direction you've been travelling. Thus you'd feel more at ease walking along the fence line to ensure that the wire is intact, the fence posts are all in place and the gate can be properly secured.

Your greatest concern is barbed wire, which presents a number of different types of dangers to horses. The sharp points can rip open a horse's hide, leaving a nasty wound that bleeds all night. Loose strands of barbed wire left lying on the ground can entangle a horse's hooves, causing it to trip. Should something cause a horse to panic during the night, and he runs through the barbed wire fence, the razor sharp edges may enwrap his body and slice him to bits. Another danger may be found if other horses are placed in an adjacent pasture that is separated by a barbed wire fence. Fights and bickering may occur over the barbed wire fence, leading to cuts and injuries.

No matter what excuse you use to inspect the field, do so. And it's not just stray pieces of barbed wire you have to be worried about. Be on the lookout for broken glass or any sharp objects which might also cause an injury in your absence.

During her many years exploring all parts of the United States, American Long Rider Janine Wilder was forced to place her horses in many strange places for the night. It was while camping in the wilderness that she made an important observation, which no other Long Rider had previously noted.

"When over-nighting, scope out your tether areas for animal dens, tunnels or other signs of activity. You don't need your horse falling into a hole or upsetting the local badger or porcupine."

The last major worry connected to fields and pastures is the possible presence of poisonous plants. Long Riders crossing many nations will be hard pressed to know what local trees, bushes and plants may harm or kill their horses. So the first thing to do is to ask the owner of the field if there is anything poisonous for horses on the property.

If you are on your own and encounter plants in a pasture that appear at all suspicious, pull or dig them up.

Remember, what you think of as an innocent plant or tree may be fatal to your horse. An excellent example is the avocado tree. Every part of this tree, including the leaves, bark, skin and stone, are poisonous to horses. It is dangerous to even allow a horse to graze in a field where avocado trees have been grown, as the leaves contain deadly levels of toxin.

Other fields in other countries can also host a deadly tree or plant. Leaves from the English Yew have been known to kill a horse within 24 hours. The oleander plant, which is widely grown all over Australia, is so deadly that eating a handful of leaves can rapidly kill a horse.

At the end of a long day in the saddle, you will want nothing more than to sit and rest. But never neglect to put your horse's safety before your own comfort. Whether it be checking the stable or patrolling the pasture, it's a job that must always be done.

Unorthodox Accommodations

Prior to reviewing my notes on this part of the chapter, I had thought to explain how various Long Riders had been forced by circumstances to seek a night's shelter for their horses amidst some peculiar places.

However, the list of episodes was so extensive, as was the number of Long Riders, that I decided to summarize this part of my work so as to give you a strong dose of the oddities and dangers that await you.

Keith Clark recalled, "I camped right next to a large and noisy pig slaughterhouse. At least it got the horses used to strange sounds."

Mikhaïl Asseyev tells us, "I was obsessed with what was waiting for me at the end of each day, all the way to Paris. We spent one night in a small, filthy and humid shed, full of stinking rags. It was so narrow that I had to put my mares in one standing behind the other."

One Long Rider went to sleep on the beach, only to be awakened in the middle of the night by the incoming tide. He and his horse were trapped between the raging waves and a looming concrete seawall. They barely survived being swept out to sea.

After weeks in the saddle, Basha O'Reilly was looking forward to reaching the so-called "Olympic Stables" in Minsk. There was nothing remotely Olympian about them, just a couple of scruffy huts.

During his first "ocean to ocean" ride across the United States Howard Wooldridge and his mare, Misty, camped behind a billboard, on a baseball ground, in a city park, beneath a football stadium, at a deserted rodeo ground, by a county fair grounds and under the tree on the right side of the Dairy King restaurant in Last Chance, Colorado.

But the award for staying in the most unusual refuge goes to Jeremy James' famous Criollo, Gonzo.

"One night while riding across France, I stayed in a zoo at Maison Blanche. When the owner led Gonzo past the exotic animals housed there, he pulled a set of faces I've never seen before. Gonzo refused to believe in elephants. He eyed the apes and ant-eaters with suspicion. Giraffes proved to be the most horrible creatures that he had ever heard of and much to my surprise he and the zebras scared the living daylights out of each other. Gonzo was given a stable between the camels and the wallabies, both of which he eyed suspiciously as he ate his dinner."

Thus one of the unusual side-effects of travelling with horses is that you must be prepared for the unexpected.

As one Long Rider wrote, "After months on the road you will wake up and take several moments trying to remember what state you are in, let alone what town. That night's lodgings, however weird they might have appeared to you when you began your journey, will have become just another aspect of the new life you are leading."

Emotional Dependence

Living with horses changes humans. The longer you're with them, the more emotionally attuned they become to you.

Sea G Rhydr wrote, "We think of them as our travelling companions and co-adventurers, with all of the responsibility and autonomy that that implies. We trust them with our lives and vice versa. When we turn them loose for the night in a pasture of several hundred acres we don't worry about being able to find them in the morning; they're right there waiting for us."

This emotional symbiosis served as part of the inspiration for one of the world's most famous travel books.

After making an equestrian journey across Ireland in 1726, Irish author and Long Rider Jonathan Swift wrote his famous travel tale, *Gulliver's Travels*. During one of his fictional voyages, Gulliver visited the land of the Houyhnhnms, an astonishing race of talking horses whose wisdom surpassed that of humanity. The barbaric humans who dwelt among that land were known as Yahoos. A link between that long-ago tale and a modern equestrian traveller in Greece demonstrated how wise Swift had been when he attributed such noble sentiments to horses.

British Long Rider Penny Turner made many journeys across her adopted homeland of Greece, always in the company of her faithful gelding, George. Pity the person who doesn't realize that a horse can sense and sympathize with the grief of its human companion.

"I was just suffering from the effects of a new kind of road rage – a state of shock, despair and exhaustion which is caused by constantly seeing unbearably sad things as you go along a road. I trudged to the place well outside the village, 'with water and grazing', where they sent me. When the bit about grazing turned out to be an exaggeration, and the bit about water an outright lie, it was the last straw. I hardly knew how to find the strength to walk back to the nearest house with my bucket. The man there was so kind that when I tried to thank him, I disconcerted him and myself by bursting into tears. I was still snivelling and gulping as I gave George water and apologised to him for the poor grazing. When a mare wants to calm a foal she puts her muzzle on its neck, just above the withers, quite firmly, and steadies it. That's what George did to me; he demonstrated compassion for me, a mere yahoo, from that noblest of beings, my own dear Houyhnhnm."

Nor is this emotional dependence restricted to humans. A horse is a sociable animal. He craves companionship. As the journey lengthens, horses which travel together form intense emotional bonds amongst each other.

As Robin Hanbury-Tenison wisely noted, "The magic begins to work. They became inseparable, standing or lying side by side at all times."

He summarized his two brave Camargues as being "hardy, resilient, coping with difficult and dangerous terrain, nice natured, sensible, lively, agile, brave, possessing great stamina, able to withstand long fasts and endure bad weather."

The journey creates such an intense emotional link between the horses that if you separate the horses from each other, they will scream, pull away and try to rejoin their companions.

Protect Your Horse

If you remember one single thing from this book, remember this.

Trust no one with the welfare of your horse! Ever!

The moment you take your eye off your horse he is in peril of damage or death.

Robert Louis Stevenson understood this, when he wrote, "Now a horse, delicate in eating and of tender health, is too valuable to be left alone, so you are chained to him as to a fellow galley-slave."

No matter how many miles you've ridden together, regardless of how many adventures you have mutually survived, the moment you delegate his safety to another you imperil the life and health of your friend.

History proves that I am not exaggerating. One Long Rider set out to ride from the Arctic Circle to the Equator. He had reached Guatemala, where a family of American missionaries invited the hungry traveller to come in and celebrate a Thanksgiving dinner with them. His stomach overruled his common sense.

The Long Rider hesitated, knowing he should attend to his horse's needs first. But when a local Guatemalan promised to feed the traveller's horse, the hungry American stepped away from his responsibilities. That turkey dinner cost him his horse. Though the circumstances were never completely established, the native had inadvertently fed the American Quarter Horse some sort of inappropriate food. The animal was dead before sunrise.

During his ride from Patagonia to Alaska, Louis Bruhnke left his horse in a pasture which he had not thoroughly checked in advance. When he returned two days later, he discovered the horse had become entangled in loose wire that had lain hidden in the grass. One hoof was irreparably damaged and the horse died from complications of the injury.

Tim Cope had to renew his visa while riding through Kazakhstan, so he left the horses with people who assured him they would be treated with the greatest kindness. When he returned, however, the horses had vanished.

"When I eventually found them, it turned out that they had been prepared for a race – and the local means of getting horses ready for a race is to starve them and rug them up warmly! I arrived just in time to rescue them – literally with only hours to spare."

Nor is overt cruelty the only thing that must concern you. Well-meaning strangers have perpetrated cruel tricks on Long Riders and their horses. One of the worst episodes happened to Richard Barnes during his ride across Great Britain in the 1970s.

The sun was setting, and Richard was beginning to worry about where he and his Cob, Remus, might camp for the night, when fate intervened. A local gentry, of the old-fashioned fox-hunting set, invited Richard to spend the night on his land.

"A man on the roadside drew me into a conversation with such phrases as 'one horseman to another.' He offered stabling for the night. I was grateful and within a few minutes we were off the road, Remus in a stable, while I pitched my tent in the field. As this little scene developed I wondered what I had ridden into. The man had the best of intentions but as soon as Remus was on his land he took command of the situation."

Having been assured that Remus was safe, the host urged Richard to visit the nearby pub to enjoy a drink and a chat with the friendly local lads. When Richard returned he discovered to his horror that his host had cut two feet off Remus' long tail which had hung nearly to the ground.

"Can't have him crossing the country looking like he was," the arrogant man proudly announced.

Struggling for self-control, Richard counted to ten and said nothing.

"I have never been so English, decent and reserved. I did not clout the man, nor did I say how far he had overstepped the mark with his scissors and ridiculous notions. No wonder people make fun of "horsy types" when they conform to archetype and confuse their animal with status, social life and the shallow world of prestige and appearance. I went to sleep feeling compromised, repressed and angry. When I awoke my first thought was how to escape this well-intentioned do-gooder before it was too late."

Remember your horses are not special to anyone else but you. The journey means nothing to outsiders.

And the temptation is that upon reaching what appears to be a point of physical and emotional safety, you may relinquish your responsibility to a stranger. That's when your journey fails.

Don't trust their welfare to strangers, no matter how well meaning they appear. Don't drop your guard, when it looks like the coast is clear. As equestrian travel history proves, it's when things look safe that your horses will be killed by strangers or misguided kindness.

Moreover, you may lend your last dollar to a friend, but never lend him your horse.

There is one final point connected to the topic of protecting your horses. Never allow anyone to mistreat your comrades. See that his punishment is more severe than that which he gave to the horse.

Such an occasion arose when Aimé Tschiffely found two local toughs abusing his horses, Mancha and Gato.

"The horses were lodged in a public corral and when I went to feed them I found two young men in the corral, one of them chasing the horses around the enclosure by hitting them with his walking stick. I introduced myself in language that suited the occasion, whereupon one told me that he had merely wished to see if the horses had a good gallop. I recommended both of them to go to a certain hot place. One protested and added that he considered these horses to be public property and that he could do as he liked in his town, and then he turned and hit one of the frightened animals once more. I gave him a sound beating and rolled him in the filth of the corral," the norm-ally mild-mannered Swiss Long Rider recalled.

Night Guard

As these stories illustrate, you must remain alert.

If you are camping, keep your horses as close as possible to your tent. As I have written before, placing bells on their halters not only lets you hear them during the night, but should they stray the sound of the bells provides you with a valuable clue about which direction in which they fled.

Remember that the horse's senses are much more highly developed than yours. They can see very well in the dark, can hear subtle noises, smell strange odours and detect vibrations through the ground made by other animal's footsteps.

Horses are liable to panic and may stampede for what appear to be very trivial causes. But there is, almost without exception, a good reason for it. Therefore, do not punish a horse for getting scared.

Learn to listen to the horses during the night. So long as they are grazing peacefully or standing quietly, then your own rest may be assured.

At the first hint of trouble, you should be up and alert.

If you have a flashlight/torch, use it sparingly around the horses as the bright white light will blind them at a time when it is critically important that they be able to see.

Jeff Hengesbaugh rode from Phoenix, Arizona, to Banff, Canada in the 1970s. In his book, *Head West and Turn Right*, he recalled how during the night one of his horses slipped its hobbles and escaped. In the morning Jeff discovered the horse had wandered onto a road and been killed by a large truck.

Times have changed since then.

New Zealand, for example, enforces its strict *Animal Law Reform Act* which states that if an animal strays onto the highway there are several key factors which must, by statute, be considered when determining whether or not the owner of the animal is liable for the damage caused by their animal.

Horses are Destructive

It would be a sentimental mistake to underestimate the power and strength of these animals. The way to get killed around horses is to take things for granted.

You must also realize that horses can create a great deal of destruction in a very short amount of time.

Sanitation is a primary consideration. The average horse produces several quarts of urine every four hours, totalling nearly two gallons (4½ litres) a day. Horse urine has a strong smell and many home owners are going to be unhappy with large pools of yellow urine staining their lovely well-manicured lawns.

Horse manure is another fact of life for a Long Rider. Horses excrete manure on average every four hours. They create an average of between 30 to 50 pounds (about 18 kilos) of manure a day, depending upon the size of the animal. Dealing with manure is a daily problem for a Long Rider.

Many cities are increasingly unwilling to allow horse travellers to let their animals foul the streets. You may be stopped, fined or arrested, depending upon how vigorous the local law views the issue of your horse pooping on a clean city street or near a busy sidewalk.

During his journey across Japan in 2014, Kohei Yamakawa crossed many cities. The law required Kohei to stop and sweep up any manure left by his horses. He placed the manure in two special boxes which were strapped to the top of the pack saddle.

Even if you are staying on private property, when morning arises you are going to be faced with a large pile of manure. How you deal with it deals upon where your horse spent the night. If he was in a stall, offer to muck it out and leave it tidy. If the horse spent the night in a pasture, take the time to clean up after your horse. Kicking the piles of horse poop helps it to disperse and disintegrate. This type of considerate behaviour impresses home-owners and demonstrates that you're making an effort to respect their property.

Another serious consideration is the destruction which horses can have on a farmer's valuable crops. From a strictly health point of view, a horse who wanders into a field and spends all night eating may end up being affected by colic, which in turn can result in injury or death. Plus, farmers in poor nations must exert incredible amounts of labour to grow the food needed to keep their families alive. A careless mistake on your part may let your horse damage food which a poor family desperately needs.

There is another type of agricultural damage which I have never seen reported anywhere else: the chances of a hungry horse stripping the bark off valuable trees. Never tie horses to trees, especially those in an orchard, as they may cause extensive damage in a very short time.

One other destructive habit horses have is their ability to turn the ground into a grassless, muddy, manure-riddled wreck by sunrise. When you place a horse on a picket pin, he may pace or run about during the night. In the morning what was originally a green lawn looks like a helicopter landing pad.

Pay attention to the ground where you place your horses. If the earth is soft, marshy or muddy to begin with, chances are it is going look like hell come sunrise.

Finally, remember how clumsy and powerful your four-footed friend can be. Because he lacks your ability to respect the home of your host, your horse may inadvertently cause damage that puts you in trouble or forces you to pay for repairs.

Even in a place as remote as the Afghanistan's Wakhan Corridor, people view their homes with pride. Ian Robinson learned that lesson the hard way.

"The next morning I was up at five. I took my reluctant horse, Doldol, out of the garden through a doorway in the wall just big enough for him to slip through without his saddle. I tied him to the door post while I went back for his saddle and saddlebags. At first he stood there quietly while I loaded him. But he was looking wistfully back at the grass he hadn't had time to eat. When I turned away for a moment to pick something up, Doldol took this as his cue to return to the garden and finish the delicious clover. Unfortunately, he was now too large to fit through the doorway. I tried to stop him but halfway through he took fright and plunged on. He ripped out the door frame, taking it with him, and collapsed half the mud-brick wall."

Paying for the repairs put a sizeable dent in Ian's already diminished budget.

Rest and Relaxation

Rest makes a new horse.

Some Long Riders ride for five days, then allow their horses two days off to rest and recover. Others never go more than four days without giving the horses a full day's rest.

If you are travelling on an extremely long journey, which may last a year or more, then you should plan to stop after two or three months on the road, depending upon the climate, terrain, and conditions you have encountered, and allow the horses at least a week to rest in absolute peace and quiet.

During this rest period, ride them at a quiet walk for at least half an hour every day so as to keep their muscles firm.

One thing which most Long Riders overlook in terms of their horse's well-being is their emotional happiness.

It was Mary Bosanquet, who made this brilliant observation about the happiness of a road horse.

"One of the factors which make a long-distance ride very hard on a horse is the fact that he has so little fun. On a long distance trip he cannot do these things. He finds that it does not pay to waste his energy pawing in the valley. He must buckle down to the road and go steadily from the moment he starts out, if he does not want to be dead tired by the evening. That is why I have always tried to make my longer stays at places where the horses could not only have rest but recreation. It does a horse good to run out, to roll, buck round and feel for a little while that he is a free horse, and nobody in the world can gallop faster than he."

Remember, the strength of your horse must be protected and maintained with the greatest of care. Never let your desire for haste put his health at risk. Instead of pushing him to cover 25 miles today, better to travel a little slower and arrive with a hardy and healthy horse. In this way when an emergency arises, and trust me it will, your horse will be able to call upon that reserve of energy which the two of you have so wisely saved for just such an crisis.

Summary

After riding across Tibet all day back in 1946, Leonard Clark wrote, "Saddle leather creaked, horses mouthed bits, iron stirrups clanged against boots, spurs jingled. These were the sounds of my life. Grass was our life blood."

Look after your horse first, last and at all times, for when one's horses are well cared for the rider's mind and conscience are at rest.

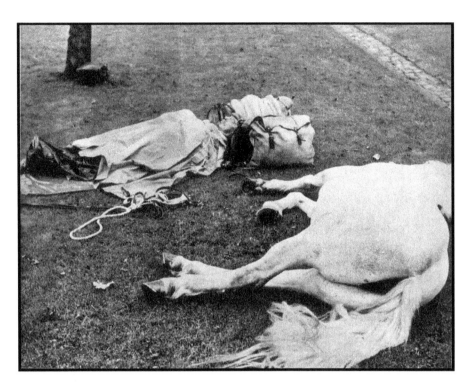

The loyalty and devotion which existed between Bill Holt and his horse, Trigger, was so strong that no matter how bad the weather, the Long Rider always chose to sleep outside on the grass close to his beloved horse.

Wild horses normally sleep while standing, with three and a half hours often being sufficient to refresh a horse. Like many travelling horses, Rahaal and Chami, who accompanied Billy Brenchley and Christine Henchie across Africa, learned to lie down and sleep whenever they could. They can be seen sleeping here in the Egyptian desert.

Johan Koch was in charge of the 1912 Danish expedition across Greenland. He led a party of four men and sixteen horses across the frozen interior of that nation.

Unlike other polar explorers, Koch did not let his horses stand out in the cold wind. He and his men would dig a hole down into the snow just large enough to allow the horses to stand close together for warmth. A tarpaulin would then be placed overhead and secured in place. In this way the animal's body heat was retained within their little underground igloo.

By the end of the 19ᵗʰ century, massive multi-floored stables had been built to house the millions of horses which provided vital services to industrialized cities. Though it appears large by today's standards, this German stable was nothing to compare to the gigantic establishments which could house and feed 1500 horses.

Communicable diseases spread like wildfire within giant urban stables, which became known as fever nests. Public watering troughs were also the source of contagious equestrian diseases. This particular watering trough was created by using an inverted bell.

Horses die in spectacular blaze

Several horses were burned to death and a number of others had to be destroyed on Tuesday afternoon when fire levelled a barn at a boarding stable on 14th Avenue east of the 10th Concession near Cedar Grove. The stable, operated by Mrs. Rhiar Miller, housed 32 horses. When the fire broke out the handler and operator were away, and only one stable boy was on duty. He was able to release a number of the horses but it was impossible for him to handle all of them.

According to Markham Township Police, nine or ten animals were lost. Others were injured. Cause of the fire is unknown. The Fire Department is investigating.

The most horrendous stable fire in modern history occurred in New York on the night of May 27, 1887, when more than 1400 horses died in an inferno. Fires still destroy barns and stables with alarming frequency. Between 2002 and 2005 more than a thousand barn fires were reported by the U.S. National Fire Protection Agency.

Never put your horse into a strange pasture without checking to make sure there are no poisonous or dangerous plants nearby. When Orion Kraus checked his horse, Aztlan, in the morning he found the animal covered with thousands of burrs and thorns.

Under no circumstances should you ever put your horses into a field or pasture without having first patrolled it for potential problems. This horse had to be extracted from an abandoned well.

Long Riders and their horses must learn to expect to spend the night in unorthodox accommodations. During the author's solo ride across Pakistan's North West Frontier Province, his Palomino mare, Shavon, rested in everything ranging from a comfortable stall at an army camp to this patch of waste ground outside a shack.

Your horses are not special to anyone but you. The journey means nothing to outsiders. Never trust the welfare of your horse to anyone else! This image shows the author grooming his horses during his subsequent journey at one of the few remaining stables that still existed in northern Pakistan between the small towns of Chitral and Gilgit.

Many cities are increasingly unwilling to allow horse travellers to let their animals foul the streets. This traveller was stopped in San Diego, California after his mules befouled the clean city street. (Photo courtesy John McDonald.)

Japanese law required Kohei Yamakawa to sweep up and carry away any manure left by his horses.

Chapter 71
Finding Fodder

Earlier in this book I devoted an entire chapter to the idea of "Feeding Your Horse." Therein was information about the horse's digestive system, the various types of food which he might consume, how often he needed grain to maintain his strength, etc.

Discussing digestion is one thing. Finding anything to feed your horse in an often bleak landscape is something very different.

That poet of the saddle, Jeremy James, once remarked upon the remarkable emotional symbiosis which eventually develops between horse and human during an extended journey.

"A thousand miles with a horse and the original goal of the journey is lost to the mind. Everything is noticed: the trees, the peasants working in the fields, the animals drawing carts, the churches and villages. Somewhere a dog barks. Strangers stop to talk. Every dimple in the ground, every hollow, every rut is noticed as the horseman passes by. A sense of comradeship builds among the travellers and their horses. The man stands close to the horse at the end of the day and the horse moves close to him in the morning. He is the known point amongst all the unknown things around him. No other comradeship with a horse is so fine as to travel with one for a thousand miles."

What Jeremy, like so many Long Riders before him, knew was that as the sun begins to dip down towards the horizon, the horse often begins to show subtle signs of emotional agitation. He has carried you all day, and now he wants his reward.

Living in the Moment

Let's be brutally honest with each other. Aimé Tschiffely didn't walk out to the pasture and hold a conversation with Mancha and Gato about how he planned to ride them for more than 10,000 miles across some of the most inhospitable places on Earth.

"See here fellows, I've got this plan to ride you over the Andes Mountains, through the jungles of Central America, and across this rather tricky bit known as the "Horse Killer" Desert. But when we reach this distant place called New York, which is full of people, cars and concrete, we'll all be famous."

If they had been able to understand him, those wise old Criollos would have snorted with derision.

"What? Go all that way. Endure all that hardship? When there's plenty of delicious grass right here in our own pasture! No thank you and goodbye," Gato, always the polite one, would have said.

"Crazy gringo," Mancha would have muttered rudely and turned back to the serious business of living in the moment, which meant eating the best bits of grass before Gato saw them. Mancha's life plan didn't include participating in a historical quest, because horses don't look ahead to the future. They can't anticipate the thrill of discovery. They don't give a hoot about fame.

What they can and do understand is a full stomach and a sense of safety. That is why food becomes so important to a travelling horse. First, it provides the raw power that allows the journey to continue. But on a deeper level it affords a potent emotional reward, which because it always comes from the loving hand of the Long Rider, becomes a source of constant daily happiness.

Food is therefore more than mere fuel. It is a reassuring comfort in a world full of strange terrors. Because of this it does more than just nourish the horse's body. It strengthens his soul.

The trick is where to find it.

The Need for Food

Before he became a Long Rider, Donald Brown had ridden with a cavalry unit in South Africa during the Second World War. Thanks to his intense knowledge of horses, their care and feeding, Donald realized that one of the tribulations he was going to face during his ride from the Arctic Circle to Copenhagen in 1952 would be to find grazing amidst the wild forests of Scandinavia.

"One of our greatest problems was to keep the horses fit on the irregular feeding that was their lot. A horse will lose condition more quickly than a man on meagre food and with more serious results. He must travel every yard by his own energy where his rider may relax in his saddle and make smaller demands upon his flesh. Since the horse has a small stomach he cannot carry a reserve of food, hence the horse master's rule for feeding is 'little and often'."

Donald, that wise old cavalry man, did indeed know a thing or two. Sitting up there on the saddle means that a man's work is usually about one-fifth that of the horse. He also understood that horses cannot maintain their condition and continue to travel unless they are provided with sufficient amounts of bulk food/fodder, in addition to some sort of grain ration to produce vital extra energy.

In a word: no food, no travel. The horse must have plenty of calories and he is entitled to the best forage available.

Do the Maths

Saying, "Feed the horse a lot of nice food" is a bit simplistic, isn't it?

You don't have to be a rocket scientist to understand how the labour of the horse is affected by what he does, how fast he travels, even how steep the ground is. All these things influence how much and how often the horse eats.

First, let's consider the simple fact that a horse breathes 142 cubic feet of air per hour, so just keeping him breathing, running and acting frisky requires plenty of raw fuel.

Next, adding even the smallest amount of weight to his back will reduce the horse's ability to proceed. The heavier the weight he carries, the more nutrients he will require to replace the energy expended during travel.

Back in the days when the health of horses was of national importance, an American professor named Frank Barron Morrison devoted several years to studying the equine diet and how it might be improved. In his book, *Feeds and Feeding*, published in 1915, he presented a summary of how speed, weight and food were all inter-related.

"The horse is par excellence the creature of motion. It will be noted that 26 per cent more net nutrients are required when the horse walks a mile at the speed of 3.5 mph than 2.5 mph. When his gait is hastened to a trot, nearly twice as much food is required per mile of travel, as at the slower walk. Among the reasons why rapid labour consumes more power than slow motion, even when the distance travelled and the actual work done are the same, are the following: When a horse is walking at a rapid speed the work of the heart is greatly increased. In trotting or galloping a smaller part of the energy is available for onward movement. The temperature also rises, and much heat is lost by the evaporation of water through the skin and lungs. The proportion of food producing heat is thus increased, while that appearing as work is diminishing. A horse walking 12.5 miles a day was kept in condition on a daily allowance of 19.4 lbs of hay per day, while a ration of 24 pounds was insufficient when the same distance was covered at a trot".

That wasn't the only observation Professor Morrison made. In that age when teams of horses were required to pull tremendous loaded wagons up sharp hills, the equine academic also noted how the steepness of the hill affected the amount of calories consumed.

In his warning, Morrison wrote, "In climbing a hill the horse does much more work than when going on a level course, for besides propelling his body, he must raise it against the force of gravity. In ascending a grade at 3 mph, a horse will expend more than 3 times the energy as in walking the same distance on the level. In raising his body 200 feet in going up a grade, he would use almost as much feed as in travelling a mile horizontally."

It's often said that academics make simple things sound complex, but not Professor Morrison. He summed it all up when he wrote, "The more severe the labour which the horse performs, the larger must be the supply of net nutrients".

So there you have it.

If you want to travel on a horse, you had better be ready to spend lots of time searching the countryside for suitable food.

And how difficult is that?

A Military Priority

Think of all the movies you've ever seen about the First World War. It won't be hard for you to recall the images of the brave British soldiers, all decked out in their new khaki uniforms, packs on their backs, and rifles on their shoulders marching up the gangway onto the ship about to carry them off to the deadly fields of Flanders. Meanwhile, crowds of patriotic parents, weeping wives and confused children all milled about on the dock below, waving little Union Jack flags, trying to hold back their tears, as their beloved sons, brothers, uncles, husbands and fathers sailed away to what had been erroneously called the "Great War."

Experts believe that more than 22,477,500 soldiers from all sides were killed, wounded or went missing during the ensuing global bloodbath.

But while Hollywood prefers to focus its cameras on the ships carrying officers and soldiers off to war, little thought has been given to the dirty job of shipping the hundreds of thousands of English horses – and the tons of fodder they required – to France.

Luckily another equine professor, this time a modern one named David Dorondo, has made a study of how the German army used horses in the First and Second World War. In his book, *Riders of the Apocalypse*, Dorondo noted how the provisioning of military horses was considered a supreme military necessity by combatants on both sides during that bloody conflict. It was while he was documenting the German war effort that Dorondo recorded a fascinating fact about the magnitude of the British endeavour to feed their horses.

"Such huge numbers of troops had to be supplied by logistics trains. An indication of horses' continued necessity reveals itself in the following statistic: the single largest category of cargo unloaded in the French ports for the British army throughout the entire period of 1914-18 was horse fodder. As British preparations entered their final stages in the late spring of 1916, fully 100,000 horses crowded behind the British front lines; all of them had to be provided with shelter, feed and fodder, an enormous undertaking."

Of course unloading millions of pounds of hay and grain onto a French dock isn't going to magically transport it to the hungry horses out at the front.

That is why even though tons of fodder were being shipped into France to supply English army horses, British cavalry officers were reminded that one of their primary orders was to instil in every mounted man the need to realize that providing sufficient rations was never guaranteed.

Every cavalryman, no matter which side he fought and rode on, was taught to take every opportunity to maintain the strength of his horse by paying special attention to finding fodder, and allowing his horse to graze, whenever the chance arose.

Like the cavalryman of old, every Long Rider must learn to keep a sharp eye out for every chance to find grazing, locate grain and do everything possible to add to the overall strength of his mount.

Going to Remarkable Lengths

You might think that's just a silly old wives' tale about going to great lengths to keep your horse alive, if you didn't know the story of Private Melet. He was a Dragoon in Napoleon's Imperial Guard. Along with his horse,

Cadet, they had served together from 1806 until 1814, during which time they fought in Austria, France, Prussia, Poland, Saxony and Russia.

During the course of twelve great battles and thirty minor ones Melet had always placed the welfare of his mount before his own survival. That philosophy was put to its greatest test during the disastrous winter of 1812.

When the Emperor Napoleon decided to begin his retreat from Russia, he departed with more than 150,000 horses but less than a week's fodder. The freezing weather soon reduced the French horses to trying to survive by eating bark off trees.

Melet may have only held the rank of private but he was wiser than many a well-mounted general.

"If I save my horse, he in turn will save me," Melet is credited with saying.

Donning the coat and helmet of a Russian dragoon he had killed in battle, Melet would slip past the enemy pickets. Once inside the camp, he would stealthily load up enough hay and oats for a few days' rations and then ride Cadet back to the safety of the French lines. Using this unusual tactic, the daring Dragoon was able to return to France with Cadet.

Sadly, this remarkable relationship came to an end when Melet was wounded and Cadet was killed at the battle of Waterloo.

A Daily Obsession

You may not have to don the uniform of an enemy soldier and sneak behind enemy lines to find an armful of hay, but the day will come when you look back upon your journey. When that moment arrives a flood of memories may come rushing back. I guarantee that one of them will be connected to how the search for horse food became such an unexpected dominant factor in your daily life.

One weary Long Rider making his way across Europe scribbled in his diary, "When you're cold and lonely, and all you've got is a tired horse who is looking for you to provide his supper, you have to go and find it. It can't wait. You can't rest until your horse has got all he needs."

Meanwhile, on the far side of the world another Long Rider wrote something similar when he said, "The biggest challenge is finding grass and water and keeping the horses in good condition. One gets used to thinking 24/7 about grass. Paradise is sinking into sleep at night listening to the horses munching through thick pasture. Hell is going to bed at night to silence, knowing that the horses have gone hungry and have nothing to chew on."

A third summed it all up when he wrote in his diary, "I dream about finding hay."

Never Pass Grazing

Anyone who has seen horses in a pasture can recall how much time they spend with their heads down, grazing their way through as much grass as they can. Even if he's not working or travelling, to maintain his strength without grain a horse needs at least eight hours of good foraging a day.

There are two points about letting your horse graze during the course of the day.

The utilization of every opportunity to graze must be used so as to aid in maintaining his basic health. To put it bluntly: never pass up a chance to let your horse forage. Giving him every occasion to graze helps maintain his physical strength.

Also, the horse may not care about riding all the way to New York but he will walk forward with eagerness if he thinks he is moving in search of the next patch of succulent forage.

It must become second nature to let your horses stop and graze when the opportunity occurs.

The Lack of Grass

In all my years answering questions from would-be Long Riders, no one ever wrote to ask me, "Where do I find grass?"

Like air and water, it seems to be something which they take for granted, especially those who reside in urban environments. But the days when great swathes of our planet were covered in a rich carpet of tall grass are a thing of the past.

Grass, any grass, is important to an equestrian traveller, as it translates into calories which in turn become miles.

But true grassland is increasingly rare. Canadian Long Rider Catherine Thompson made a journey in 2012 across one of the last surviving prairies which once swept across that nation for hundreds of miles. In the early part of her ride across western Canada, Catherine saw many abandoned homesteads. These were places where "families had tried to eke out a living on a small parcel of sometimes-harsh land."

The pioneer farmsteads were gone, replaced by giant establishments, "where I would find myself travelling through ranches of 100,000 acres, all growing mono crops of massive proportions."

Finally, after long riding through remote country, Catherine found her way to those "rare and special spots" where the last remnants of the wild Canadian grass still grew.

"True native grass, the old growth of the prairies, is a rare and extremely endangered ecosystem all through North America. I was deeply aware of this as I rode along."

As she made her way through, Catherine knew that she and her horses were passing over "a rare patch of earth struggling to survive."

Grass, as Catherine, had learned, is a precious commodity.

Hereditary Grazing

Negley Farson was a survivor. He walked away from plane crashes during his days as a pilot during the First World War. He took part in the Bolshevik Revolution. He spent a year living in a remote cabin in the Canadian wilderness. He was also an esteemed international journalist who had a keen nose for a good story.

That's why he became a Long Rider by accident. In the spring of 1929 Farson managed to convince the revolutionaries in Moscow that the European and American press weren't presenting an accurate picture of the improvements the Communists had achieved since seizing power from the Czar. A horseback trip among the simple working people, he said, would give him the information to set the record straight.

Negley's plan was simple. He wasn't going to trot from one state-operated farm to another, always under the watchful eye of a Red Commissar delegated to guard him. Farson was determined to explore the remote and beautiful Caucasus Mountains. Despite having no prior equestrian travel experience, he set off to discover the realities of life amidst the Chechens, Avars and Dagestanis, some of the last people yet untouched by the Soviet experiences.

He was lashed by hailstorms, threatened by sceptical political commissars, denied shelter by suspicious natives, and spent night after night in rain-soaked misery. A personal chronicle of an already-exciting life, *Caucasian Journey* tells how Farson also discovered the seldom-seen splendours of this mountainous region with its alpine snowfields painted gold by the sun, picturesque villages forgotten by the outer world, and magnificent horsemen who were practically born in the saddle.

But what Farson also did was to make an important historical observation.

There may have been plenty of grass growing in the beautiful Alpine mountain valleys, but you risked your life if you allowed your hungry horse to graze upon it.

"Grazing lands in the mountains have a complicated ownership," he wrote. "In a sense of the word they belong to no one at all, but it is the unwritten law that those lands adjacent to a village are sacred to its own horses and cattle, so much so that a stranger coming into a village is not supposed to graze his own horse even on the outskirts. And the mountain lands are, whenever they are occupied, the hereditary grazing rights of the particular village."

In parts of the world where the growing season is short and the winters are long, growing and harvesting enough hay or grass to feed a family's animals during the winter may mean the difference between life and death.

English Long Rider Thomas Bartz recently rode across Kyrgyzstan. In the intervening years since Negley Farson made his ride, the Communist regime which Negley had witnessed being born had passed away. But the tradition of who owned the local grass had outlasted Lenin.

Thomas wrote, "For the horses, food and grass is readily available everywhere. Although, as always, you must be careful not to graze the horses near other herds, and should always ask for permission if it looks like it's on someone's private property."

Not only must you be on your guard when you deal with nomadic people whose animals depend upon local grass, you must also keep in mind that the land round encampments, gers, and villages is often overgrazed. It is very disheartening to ride all day, see some sign of habitation on the skyline, reach it at last, only to realize that the local animals have left little grazing for your tired and hungry horses.

Times Change

It's not just politics that have altered, so has the land itself. The grass which had covered the land for centuries may now be no more than a memory.

Prior to making his long journey through Chile, Keith Clark contacted the British Long Rider Rosie Swale Pope. She had made a difficult solo ride through that country and was glad to share her wisdom with the younger traveller.

What Rosie didn't realize was how much Chile had changed during the ten years since she had been there. What had once been pampas had been ploughed under and turned into profitable fruit orchards.

"If you've never suffered from stress, try finding food for two hungry horses in Chile," Keith wrote. "I never thought that feeding my horses would be such a problem but Chile must have changed a great deal since Rosie rode through here. There is very little land put down to grass or alfalfa where I am at the moment. In fact it's an apple desert: nothing but apples for miles around."

Eventually Keith rode into a part of the country where livestock was more plentiful. In theory he should have been able to procure hay and grain from local farmers. But once again he was in for a shock.

"After a long day I descended from the mountains down into a valley and went through the usual routine of looking for hay. I walked along for four hours asking at each farm without success. People had their backyards full of hay but no one would sell any to me. Finally it got dark and I had to make camp at an abandoned farm where there was water. I was forced to feed the horses leaves off an old grape vine and gave them oats but they were still hungry. They have a massive appetite for roughage."

Grazing the Long Acre

As Keith and many other Long Riders have learned, good grass is a precious commodity. Relying on finding a lush pasture owned by a kindly farmer as the sun sets is a fairytale believed by children.

If you see grass, stop and let your animals enjoy it.

The Irish have an apt expression for this practice. It is known as "grazing the long acre," and refers to the once-common habit of allowing a local cow, donkey or horse to graze the lush grass that grew alongside the government roadside near the village. In those days, when neighbours lived in peaceful proximity to each other, it was not uncommon to see a farmer's milk cow enjoying the free grass that would have otherwise gone to waste before making her way home at the end of the day.

There were, in theory, regulations in place which prohibited animals from grazing on the side of an Irish public road. And in rare cases an owner could be summoned to court and fined for allowing his animal to wander onto a public thoroughfare. Yet Ireland was a poor country, and the law often turned a blind eye to a bit of casual grazing.

Other countries, most notably Russia, took the exact opposite view of the roadside grass. When Thomas Stevens rode across Czarist Russia, as an American he simply took it for granted that he could just stop as and where he wanted to let his horse graze on the lush grass growing alongside both sides of the road leading from Moscow.

How wrong he was.

"Our horses walked through clover the whole distance from Moscow, but we could not permit them to take a mouthful for every blade had been paid for by villagers who could ill afford to give away even a bite of grass. All the grass along the roadside had been rented out by the government to the closest village, who in turn guarded it jealously and used it to make hay for the winter."

Being inconvenienced by a local custom is one thing. Almost getting killed over an argument about a bit of grass is quite another matter.

Ana Beker was travelling in the inhospitable Andes Mountains when she chanced upon a bit of good grazing. Her hungry horses didn't ask permission. They simply began gorging themselves on the luscious and much-needed forage. Regrettably, Beker had allowed her horses to graze on valuable grass owned by the local Aymara Indians.

When she observed the stranger's horses eating the precious grass, an Aymara woman ran up and began yelling at Beker in a fearful rage.

"With all the haste she could muster the woman began tearing the grass out of the mouths of the horses. But the animals, hungry as they always were on such occasions, ate so fast that her interference did not succeed in depriving them of their meal."

In a fury, the woman picked up a stick and began beating the horses. In defence of her horses, Ana pulled out her revolver, at which point the Indian woman ran to the nearby village in search of reinforcements.

"The woman's attitude changed in a flash. She spun round and tore off as fast as her legs would carry her till she was out of sight. I had been quietly watching the grazing horses for some time when I heard some deafening yells; some fifty people, men, women and children, were running up the road towards me, screaming at the tops of their voices. Next moment a shower of stones rained down on the animals and me. One of these missiles caught me such a hard blow on the knee that I could not bend it for quite a while. Two pretty big stones hit the mare's head and brought her to her knees, though she stood up again directly afterwards. There was obviously no time to lose; I drew my revolver, sprang onto Luchador and galloped full tilt at the Indians, firing two shots in the air as I did so. This had the effect I had anticipated. The whole crowd scattered, each one running as if the devil were after him," Beker wrote.

Despite being hit in the head by a stone, taking pot shots at local people defending their own grass is not a diplomatic solution to the problem of keeping your horse fed.

Plus, there are other issues to contend with. The margins of country roads are often strewn with litter, which might include dangerous broken glass. Noxious weeds may lurk amidst what looks likes good grass. Even worse, roadside grass is often sprayed with pesticides. So care must be taken about where you stop.

In addition, Ireland and Great Britain have changed their once-benign view of allowing horses to stroll along and snatch a meal along the roadway. Local council governments take a dim view of what is now known as "fly grazing," a practice whereby unethical horse owners allow their animals to roam free over common land at night in search of what scanty pasturage might be found. These animals often wander onto roads, causing major accidents.

Nor is such government hostility restricted to one side of the Atlantic.

In 2013 an equestrian traveller named Bryan Brant was fined $160 in Brown County, Indiana because he stopped in a state park and allowed his animals to graze.

As you can see, not all grass is free. Nor can you just take it for granted that it's there waiting for your horses to enjoy. Serious social and legal rules are connected to the growing and protection of it.

But, because a travelling horse needs energy, lots of it, you must never pass up an opportunity to allow him to graze as and where he can.

Expecting Opposition

It was Keith Clark who wisely said, "Any shyness that I may have had has long disappeared."

Now that you realize that the world isn't a lush pasture just waiting for your horse's arrival, you may have realized that in order to feed your animals you are going to need to develop an unexpected set of skills which includes patience, strategy, determination and sheer stubbornness.

First, if you're lazy by nature and like to lie abed, then stay home and don't become a Long Rider. You must be on the road early, and then off it in plenty of time so as to allow you to locate and negotiate for a night's pasture, food or grain.

Refused Hospitality

And did I mention opposition, indifference, hostility or suspicion? You'll find plenty of that too at the end of a hard day in the saddle.

Tex Cashner was only a seventeen-year-old boy when he set off in the summer of 1951 to ride from Ohio to Texas. He grew up fast on that tough trip.

"It began raining hard, so I stopped at a farm and knocked on the door. I asked if I could go into the barn and wait until the storm eased off a bit. All the man said was, 'We have no room for you,' and closed the door in my face."

Long Riders have heard so many excuses about why they can't be permitted to spend the night, that I can't list them all. But one of the most common claims is that permission can't be granted because the person in authority is absent.

While riding across Sussex, Jane Dotchin encountered that recurring problem.

"I couldn't find a farmer willing to allow me to set up camp. They all said the same thing: that they were tenants and there was a clause in their leases forbidding them from allowing camping on their land."

Time after time, night after night, you are going to be faced with the difficult task of negotiating for permission to stay on someone else's land. Determining who is capable of making the decision to let you stay often takes a bit of nerve.

Mefo Phillips and her sister, Susie Gray, ran into that dilemma in Spain.

After a blazing hot day's ride across Spain, they arrived at a local village where the hostess of the local hostel was indifferent to the plight of the tired travellers and their hungry horses. There was a bit of land close by where the horses could have theoretically stayed. Nevertheless the hostess obstinately refused to discuss helping Mefo and Susie.

"The Señora is less than obliging. She just says no. We gather that the *refugio* owns no land at all and what's around it is private. But then the Señora says its communal land and we need to speak to the mayor. But there is no mayor. Well, we must ask the people. What people? Finally, she admits that the roped-off square of ground opposite the *refugio* is owned by the bar next door. Why didn't she say so in the first place? Susie goes in, armed with her best bad Spanish sob-story and the owner of the bar beams beatifically at her. Campo? Si! he exclaims and thus it is all arranged. The Campo's tiny but at least it's full of grass."

Never leave this vital negotiation until the end of the day. Remember, you need the best pasture you can find and locating the person who can grant you permission takes time and patience.

Hay - A Precious Commodity

Let us say, for the sake of argument, that you've arrived at some small village and been granted permission to place your horses within a stable.

Now what?

Every day on the road will be different. Nevertheless, every night will be the same.

No matter how tired, dirty or discouraged you may have become by the challenges of that day's ride, duty requires you to set aside your own worries so as to undertake one final difficult and often humiliating task. The time has come for you to set off to search a strange landscape so as to locate the twin treasures of your horse's life; a full belly and a safe bed.

There are a variety of reasons why locating hay for your horses may prove to be challenging.

First there is the logistical problem of what to do with the horses during your absence. As one Long Rider wrote, "I needed hay and food for myself but have you ever tried going shopping with two horses in tow?"

Aimé Tschiffely arrived at a clever solution when confronted with this problem.

"I left them at the police station and after a lengthy search, purchased a bale of hay and carted it on my back to the corral."

Next, there is the issue of finding hay. If you think the world is a land of plenty, then think again.

Time after time an equestrian traveller has arrived at an isolated village only to be told there is no hay or grass to spare.

After Basha O'Reilly rode through Russia, she wrote, "You can't buy hay because there is nothing to buy. They keep it for themselves and their animals."

The journey Janja Kovačič made through the Andes Mountains in Bolivia taught her the same lesson. She wrote, "It is very hard to find food for the horses. Grass doesn't exist and we have to buy whatever there is."

Another lady Long Rider and another country, but the same hard rule of the road, happened to Penny Turner in Greece. "People in the mountains are very hospitable. In fact they are the kindest sweetest people that you could ever hope to meet. But they do not have anything extra. This means it is often hard to get fodder for the horse."

I too encountered this problem while riding in the remote regions of northern Pakistan. Only one farmer in the tiny mountain village of Gupis was willing to sell me hay. Not only was the price exorbitant, I had to make a two hour round-trip walk to the distant alpine pasture, where the grass had to be cut by hand, then hauled back in the dark using my turban as a rope to carry the precious fodder on my back.

In cases such as the one I found in Gupis, the farmer generally only has just enough hay to see his animals through the winter. Thus, the idea of selling hay for a profit is either not considered or not appealing. Therefore instead of being viewed as an unexpected source of potential profit, the sudden appearance of mounted strangers is often considered a nuisance. A common ploy is to urge the Long Rider to travel on to the next village, which is falsely described as being rich in fodder and a legendary centre of hospitality.

Maintaining Strength

If you took a moment to think about all of the ways in which horses traditionally worked you might think of those millions of hard-working animals that pulled stagecoaches full of fat passengers between cities, hauled delivery wagons carrying hundreds of pounds of coal door to door, towed heavy barges along the English canals or dragged a plough across the muddy fields in all kinds of weather.

It wouldn't surprise you to learn that those equine athletes required special dietary supplements to keep up their strength. That's exactly what Dr. James Law told the U.S. Department of Agriculture's Bureau of Animal Industry in 1916. In his study entitled *Special Report on Diseases of the Horse*, Law warned that a horse could not be kept healthy unless its natural diet of grass was supplemented with some sort of grain ration.

"Grass is the natural food of horses. It is composed of a great variety of plants, differing widely as to the amount of nourishment contained, some being almost entirely without value and only eaten when nothing else is obtainable, while others are positively injurious, or even poisonous. None of the grasses are sufficient to keep the horse in condition for work. Horses thus fed are 'soft,' sweat easily, purge, and soon tire on the road or when at hard work."

Many amateur travellers make two mistakes. They fail to realize that travelling is hard work just like pulling a stagecoach; i.e. the more miles you travel the greater are the chances that his health will eventually begin to deteriorate. Also, many first-time travellers make the error of thinking their horses can survive only on a diet of grass or hay. The average horse needs from 10 to 12 pounds of good hay a day. But if his diet does not include a grain ration, the animal will become potbellied, fall in flesh and lose vitality.

Of course you don't have to take my word for it; just look at history if you want to see how important grain is in terms of maintaining a horse's health.

Hitler's Horses

In one of the greatest propaganda coups in history, Hitler managed to convince the world that his "blitzkrieg" was an invincible steel war machine equipped with limitless Stuka dive bombers and an armada of Panzer tanks. In fact the Nazis were totally reliant upon horses in a way which is only now being finally studied and understood.

According to Professor David Dorondo, between 1939 and 1945 approximately seven million horses saw active duty in the armed forces of European countries directly involved in the Second World War. On the German side alone the number of horses and mules employed by the Wehrmacht, Luftwaffe and Navy totalled nearly three million animals.

The Nazi need for horses was so intense that Professor Dorondo's research revealed that the total number of horses purchased or requisitioned by the Germans from all private sources through 1944 reached an amazing 1,645,000. The Germans required that many horses because they were losing an estimated 30,000 animals a month. Reports compiled after the war estimate that the Wehrmacht lost 1,558,508 horses during the conflict.

Why should a Long Rider in the 21st century care about "Hitler's horses"? Because the German Wehrmacht employed some of the most intelligent and experienced equine veterinarians, blacksmiths and saddlers alive in the mid-twentieth century.

These men knew that their lives depended upon the health of their horses. That's why, with typical German attention to detail, they determined that the German horses' standard daily ration in 1941 consisted of 11 pounds (5 kilos) of oats for cavalry mounts and light draught horses, 14 pounds (6.5 kilos) for heavy draught horses and nearly 18 pounds (8 kilos) for heavy draught horses such as Belgians and Percherons. This didn't include the daily hay ration each horse received, which varied between 8 and 11 pounds (4 or 5 kilos) depending upon availability.

The German cavalry wasn't motivated by sentimentality. These masters of equitation science knew their horses would lose strength if the food supply wasn't adequate.

Long Riders from the last century were also aware of the need to supply grain to their horses at the end of a long day's travelling.

An Excellent Example

Some Long Riders continue to pop up in this book. That's because they either wrote or did the right thing on many occasions. One such excellent example was Sweden's legendary Countess Linde von Rosen. She made many journeys across various parts of Europe during the 1920s and 30s, always on her renowned Palomino gelding, Castor.

Later in life, Linde made this careful note of the care she took in terms of how she groomed and fed Castor at the end of the day's travels.

"The care of the horse has been as follows: When the day's destination is reached around 4 to 5 p.m., sometimes earlier, sometimes later, I try to obtain the best stable possible. I prefer those where privately owned cows and horses are kept as opposed to public livery stables. (Cows and horses don't have the same illnesses.) If the horse is to be boarded in an open stall, it should be roomy and well bedded with clean straw. Better yet is to stable the horse in a box stall, where the horse is able to rest properly. Regardless, my first task is to wash out that night's manger with hot saline water.

After that I request ten kilos (22 pounds) of oats, which I carefully weigh in a bag.

Next, I wash first the hooves and legs, then the saddle area, of the horse with cold water. Then I wrap the legs with wet linen wraps (they stay on until dry) and the horse is blanketed. You have to rub him with straw if he appears too cold.

After this he is allowed to drink as much water as he wants.

I then give him 3 kilos (6.6 pounds) of oats and as much hay as he will eat, usually around 5 kilos (11 pounds). Many horses will not eat until they have had water and as the main objective is to have the horse consume as much feed as possible, I have always given him water first and never noticed any adverse effects.

When everything in the barn is done, I go to the hotel and change from top to toe and have a bath, if one is available. At 9 p.m., after my own dinner, I return to the stable, give a light grooming but let the blanket stay on over night and feed another 4 kilos (9 pounds) of oats and let the water bucket stay in the box.

Between 5 and 6 a.m. the remaining 3 kilos (6.6 pounds) of oats are fed, followed by a thorough grooming and application of hoof conditioner."

By following this careful and disciplined routine, Linde and Castor travelled thousands of miles all over Europe without accident or incident.

Finding Grain

While I don't wish to add to your worries, if you think finding hay or pasturage is tough, then wait till you set off in search for grain.

Nowadays petrol stations can be found alongside every major road. You must cast your memory back to an earlier age to realize that not too long ago it was grain, not gasoline, that provided the power to move people and goods. That is why the invention of "feed stores" was considered to be a newsworthy event back in 1857, when a Pittsburgh journalist named George Thurston wrote, "the sales of hay, corn and chopped stuff for horses, consequent upon the great number of wagons here, has given rise to a number of establishments called feed stores."

But the days of plenty did not last. As early as 1927, when Frank Heath was making his journey across the United States, he was already finding that the equestrian landscape was being changed by the advent of automobiles.

"Up in New England feed is scarce. To part with it is like parting with a tooth. I found oats in only one place, after calling at several farms. The oats belonged to a farmer, who was reserving them for his own use. He would not let me have a single grain, even though my horse might starve," a discouraged Heath wrote in his diary.

Gone are the days when there was a farm to be found along every road. The ranches which were once a ready source of grain are a distant memory. In a world covered with concrete, there are no more feed stores in every town which stock grain for a hungry horse.

Lack of Understanding

You don't have to travel too far back in history to learn how hard it can be to find grain and understanding.

In 1982 Jean-Claude Cazade and Pascale Franconie rode their Arab stallions from France to Saudi Arabia and back. They too found it difficult to feed their starving horses.

"We found deep hostility in communist Yugoslavia. The peasants often refused to sell us grain. Pascale and I could stand hunger but the horses couldn't. So we begged and bought any food we could and gave it to the hungry animals. We often slept in field-side ditches, dirty and starving and praying we'd find food the next day," Jean-Claude wrote.

Since then, it's got worse. Nowadays people find it hard to comprehend why you would even want to ride a horse across country. Such an attitude might be expected in an urbanized environment such as Hong Kong, but even countries which have always been associated with centuries of equestrian travel have now changed for the worse.

One of the most shocking examples of this shift in cultural attitudes occurred when French Long Rider Louis Meunier and Afghan Long Rider Hadji Shamsuddin made their perilous ride across the interior of war-torn Afghanistan in 2005. In a special message to the Guild, Louis sent a warning to future Long Riders who might be considering riding in that country.

"One thing I noticed which might be of importance to other Long Riders is that except for Herat the entire area we have been through since Bamiyan has very little horse culture left intact. Indeed, horses have almost disappeared from the countryside as they were stolen during the fighting. Then, about four years ago at the end of the Taliban war, motorbikes were imported into the country. They have now largely replaced our equine friends. When we go back to Turkistan, the northern part of Afghanistan, we will again find people with great horse knowledge. But it is weird to be a horse traveller here in this new century and I always face the same questions. 'Why do you go by horse? Do you travel by horse to sell them? What do you have in your saddle bags?' While many people have travelled across this country out of necessity because of the fighting and wars, it is still considered very strange to be a Long Rider here."

Stock Up and Think Ahead

During the 19th century, before the invention of so many types of highly nutritious equine dietary supplements, oats were the preferred choice of all grains as a feed for horses, as the ingredients necessary for the complete nutrition of the body exist in them in the best proportions. Also important is the fact that oats are more easily digested and a larger proportion absorbed and converted into the various tissues of the body. A hard-working horse usually received a daily ration of 12 quarts/litres of good oats.

Because very few Long Riders grew up on farms or are familiar with oats, it bears mentioning that care must be taken in selecting oats. Oats that have sprouted or fermented are injurious and should never be fed. New oats are indigestible. The best oats are one year old, plump, short, hard, clean, bright, and sweet. The oats should be given whole or crushed – whole in the majority of instances; crushed to old horses and those having defective teeth.

If you are riding in countries like the United States, Canada, Western Europe, Australia or New Zealand, then chances are that local tack or feed stores will be able to offer you a wide variety of premixed, commercially created and highly-nutritious grain-based supplements to help augment your horses' diet. As you are travelling you will also find that local riding clubs, horse-breeders, farmers and ranchers may be able to help you in terms of finding grain.

No matter where you ride, remember the old British cavalry adage which stated, "Nosebags should be kept full, no matter what the contents, so long as they are eatable."

Monday Morning Sickness

The need to feed oats or grain to your horse cannot be denied. However, horsemen of old knew that when there are several consecutive days of rest the grain ration should be reduced and the hay ration increased.

French Long Rider Jean-François Ballereau was one of the most knowledgeable 20th century equestrian travellers. He understood this threat and wrote, "The day before a rest day, grain should be seriously reduced. If you don't, it will put energy into the horse's muscles, which he can't use. And the animal risks Monday Morning Sickness."

Exotic Diets

Because we are discussing the topic of finding food during a journey, it must be recalled that travelling horses learn to consume an astonishing number of things which would not normally be considered part of the equine diet. An obvious example is that crops of all descriptions often provide excellent fodder and should not be passed without careful consideration. Fresh green corn stalks, for example, are often sold in Pakistan to supplement the diets of local horses and water buffaloes.

Trust No One

You must never forget that the horse is your primary concern. Your needs always come secondary to his. Even if he is stabled in the best of barns, never leave his care to anyone else. It is your responsibility to attend to the smallest details, down to every strap, buckle and horse shoe.

Always exercise care before feeding hay to your horse. Many countries view strangers as walking bank accounts ready to be fleeced and taken advantage of. When purchasing hay in public markets it is a common trick to try and pass off the mouldiest and most utterly worthless hay to a traveller. Inspect it carefully and be sure it is weighed accurately.

Pay careful attention to the feeding of your horse in a public stable. A common trick is to pay for the grain, to see it placed in your horse's manger, and then, after you've wandered off in search of your own dinner, to have the grain removed before your return. You never eat until you're sure the horse is fully fed. It is always safer to stay with your horse until he has completed his meal before you seek your own.

Paying the Price

After making a ride across England in 1937, Edward Percy Stebbing decried how the advent of the automobile had resulted in "an extraordinary ignorance amongst stables as to the correct charge to make for a night's stabling with forage per horse."

The British were sticklers about paying the proper price for a night's stable and rations. During the days of the Raj, the British government insisted that local inn keepers maintain a *nerrik*, which was an official list of prices which the traveller should pay for services and supplies.

Nowadays you will have to offer to pay what you think is a fair price. But don't hesitate to thank the person who has been generous enough to help feed your horse.

Summary

During her ride across Canada in 1939, Mary Bosanquet wrote, "On a journey like this a traveller does not posses his horses; they posses him, body and soul. The warmest house and the most delicious dinner have no charms whatever until one has been released by the sight of the horses contentedly feeding."

Finding fodder can be stressful, as it will require you to be part diplomat and part wily trader in order to obtain the food and shelter your horse needs.

This is why you must always start your ride early, so as to allow sufficient time towards the end of the day to undertake this vital part of your work.

The last word on the difficulty of finding fodder goes to Keith Clark

"I spend so much of my time and energy looking for it, that I have dreams about finding hay. A good title for a book about my ride would be "Can I Please Buy a Bale of Hay?"

The single largest category of cargo unloaded in the French ports for the British army throughout the entire period of 1914-18 was horse fodder. It was needed to feed the more than 100,000 horses behind the British front lines.

True grassland is increasingly rare. Canadian Long Rider Catherine Thompson made a journey in 2012 across one of the last surviving prairies which once swept across that nation for hundreds of miles.

Because a travelling horse needs lots of energy, you must never pass up an opportunity to allow him to graze as and where he can. French Long Rider Magali Pavin's animals can be seen grazing near a Turkish mosque.

Kazakh Long Riders Nurbek Dalaikhan (left) and Dalaikhan Boshai know that finding fodder is a time-consuming job and many local people will refuse to sell you hay and grain. They are negotiating with a local farmer for horse food. Never leave this vital negotiation until the end of the day. In order to feed your animals you are going to need to develop an unexpected set of skills which includes patience, strategy and determination.

Many equestrian travellers have arrived at an isolated village only to be told the farmer has just enough hay to see his animals through the winter. The author encountered this problem while riding in the remote regions of northern Pakistan. Only one farmer in the tiny mountain village of Gupis was willing to sell him hay. Not only was the price exorbitant, he had to make a two hour round-trip to walk to the distant alpine pasture, where the grass had to be cut by hand, then hauled back in the dark using his turban as a rope to carry the precious fodder on his back.

During his journey from Canada to Brazil Long Rider Filipe Leite learned that no matter how tired he was after a long day in the saddle, providing food for his horses, Frenchie, Bruiser and Dude, was his number one priority.

Christie Henchie and Nali carry a load of lucerne back to camp at the end of a long day riding across Egypt.

Long Riders must be aware of the need to supply grain to their horses at the end of a long day's travelling. Countess Linde von Rosen, who made many journeys across various parts of Europe on her gelding, Castor, fed her horse ten kilos (22 pounds) of oats a day to keep up his strength.

Travelling horses learn to consume an astonishing number of things which would not normally be considered part of the equine diet. The Icelandic horses used by Captain Johan Koch to cross Greenland not only regularly consumed a special pemmican style power-ration, they also eagerly ate polar bear fat, frozen horsemeat, including bones and gristle, butter, biscuits, hard bread, blood pudding, lemon-bonbons, sugar, oat porridge and sausages.

Chapter 72
Camping

Wilfred Noyce was a renowned mountaineer who was a member of the 1953 British Expedition that made the first ascent of Mount Everest. After having spent decades camping, travelling and climbing, in 1958 he penned a remarkable study of exploration entitled *The Springs of Adventure*.

In this book Noyce recalled how one night alone in the wilderness, he pondered about, "the bigger curiosity which comes to a man under the stars and makes him wonder what is the purpose of doing all this. I would watch them in their courses over the Heavens and think of what they are and what they represent and try to realise the place which we men hold in the universe stretched out before me."

This noteworthy scholar and explorer died at an early age, falling to his death during a climbing accident in 1962. But even before his untimely demise he had remarked on "the ever diminishing number of blank spaces on the map," and how the men who risked their lives to discover knowledge were increasingly "now considered trite."

Noyce could not have foreseen a world where a computer-user can sit at home and stare at any remote corner of the planet via the safety of using Google mapping technology.

But seeing a photo of a distant land is no more similar to real life than leering at a pornographic image is akin to experiencing the magic of an actual sexual experience.

The elementary things which drew Noyce into the wilderness still resonate in the souls of so many of us: the comforting feel of the campfire's warmth on our cold hands after a freezing day in the saddle, the taste of crisp clean water after riding across the desert, the bracing clean air which brings our blood back to life when we breathe deeply, the comforting embrace of the earth as we lay our weary bodies down to rest upon our ancient mother.

In a life increasingly dominated by a never-ending electronic outpouring of constant news, scandal and sex, in a world where the sky is polluted by the glare of artificial lights and our every movement is monitored via intrusive government cameras, some part of our spirit sickens and longs for a song our heart no longer knows how to sing.

What We Have Lost

That is one of the reasons many people become Long Riders, so as to reconnect with Mother Nature.

This is neither a new longing nor a previously unrecorded experience. And some of the most unlikely of people have written about it.

John Beard wasn't what most people would describe as a "romantic." He became a Presbyterian minister at an early age. When the United States entered the First World War, Beard immediately enlisted. He was appointed chaplain and shipped to the front, where he repeatedly risked his life ministering to the wounded in some of the most dangerous places. Known as 'the fighting chaplain," Beard became a captain, and received the French Croix de Guerre and the Silver Star for bravery.

After the war, Beard returned to the United States, married his childhood sweetheart, became a father, continued his work as a minister – and harboured a secret dream.

Amongst all the strange tales known amidst the Long Riders' Guild, Beard is the only horseback traveller whose journey can be directly linked to the influence of the famous Buffalo Bill Cody. This came about because Beard determined as a child that he wanted to see the Wild West from the back of a horse after having seen a performance of Cody's legendary Wild West show.

Yet it was to be more than sixty years after seeing the flamboyant American showman before Beard and his wife Lulu finally mounted their dreams. Setting off on a matched pair of horses, Black Diamond and Black Fairy, the Beards left to discover the long cherished equestrian quest of the author's youth. Their mission in 1948 was to ride the length of the Old Oregon Trail. What followed was a 4,000 kilometres (2,500 miles) odyssey from Oregon to Missouri through a vast sea of weariness, thirst, hunger, hardship, and danger as the aged equestrians rode down the trail of their pioneer forefathers.

You might be excused for thinking that a man who had won medals for bravery might have only kept a rough diary or scribbled down a note or two. But Beard's moving book, *Saddles East*, reveals a man in love with Nature. As they made their way across America, the Beards were able to find ruts left by the wagon wheels of the original pioneers who had blazed the Oregon Trail. They met and dined with the grandchildren of those who had settled along the famous trail.

And they camped out nearly every evening, happy to be with each other, their horses, and surrounded by the mystery of the natural world.

On one such night the "fighting chaplain" penned these simple but stirring words.

"We sat by our wee fire that night. When the brilliant stars came close we reached up and stole a double handful and hid them away in our hearts."

Beard never forgot the night the moon floated above his camp like a pearl.

Unfortunately, millions of people will never see the stars, because they live trapped in concrete-covered lives.

It was Margaret Leigh, who remarked during her ride from Cornwall to Scotland in 1939 that, "most of us never get the maximum of enjoyment out of the common amenities of civilized life, because we are never forced to do without them, and cannot imagine what life would be like in their absence. To be really appreciated, they must be welcomed like long lost friends whom we did not expect to see again"

Reconnecting with Nature

Riding a horse across the landscape creates an astonishing link between you and Nature.

"The horse," Jeremy James once wrote, "connects us to our surroundings in a way no other form of travel can. At once it shrinks a landscape – the way of the horse is not the way of the road. On the other hand it expands it – the world is a big place by hoof. A horse exposes us to it, directly. Every frisson in the air is felt: its funny little currents, wafts and vapours. Every aroma scented. All sounds are heard, birdsong, cicadas ring in the head. The essence of a place is felt long before arrival.

The horse's instinctive reaction to his surroundings stretches our minds. We, like him, become ultra-sensitive. Shapes in the twilight take on phantasmal form created by the horse. He veers away, snorting, ears pricked, watching, every sinew taut. He is a creature of fancy, a being of flight, we do not fight him, we believe him, keep away from this menace in the dark. We shy from monsters he sees hiding beneath stumps, apparitions lurking behind trees.

On horseback we experience the world in the unprotected raw. We cross countries on tiny paths, ride across mountains, ford rivers and streams, we are not bound by any path. We see beetles scurrying beneath the hooves, mice and snakes slip through the grass, lizards and birds linger close by, wild boar and wolves run through the woods, we become alarmed by elemental energies, sense peculiar atmospheres, are rained upon, are smarted by wind, are roasted in the heat of the sun.

His senses are acute: more acute than our own. His ears prick at sounds we cannot hear, his nostrils widen at scents we do not know, his eyes see far more and much further than our own. We are upon the back of a master of life. His world is wider than ours.

Then you will know you are in the company of something, some creation so attached to the earth and yet so far beyond your own sensibilities that his magnificence becomes fully apparent. In that moment, you perceive some ancient thing, some mystical thing."

Enduring

What Jeremy said was true. The horse is going to carry you far deeper into the natural world that any type of motorized transport can, as you won't be travelling sealed inside a steel cocoon. And, unlike a bicycle, a horse requires you to interact with the landscape as you search for grass and water. As for airplanes, the less said the better.

Any type of novelty has a certain amount of appeal, be it a new fashion, a new religious interpretation, a new political practice or even setting off on a longed for equestrian adventure.

But, as always, this book is about dividing the romantic notion, which many have about equestrian travel, from the harsh reality of how to actually achieve such a deed.

Two contrasting examples spring to mind.

During the early part of the 20th century Joseph Rock was one of the most celebrated Long Riders. A self-taught botanist and anthropologist, the Austrian Long Rider rode into some of the most remote mountainous regions of China, where he repeatedly risked his life to obtain photographs of obscure tribal people, discover rare plants and document strange cultural practices.

From 1922 until 1949 Rock was usually found in the saddle, amongst the natives and taking chances. However, he cherished a bit of comfort. That's why Rock routinely employed trusted locals to guide him during the day and help him create a contented camp at night. After a hard day in the saddle, he enjoyed a good soak in the Abercrombie and Fitch canvas bathtub which his servants had filled with hot water. Dinner was served on a table which was laid with fine plates and silverware.

Sounds nice, doesn't it. Bet you can't wait to saddle up and ride off on a similar adventure.

Here's the reality.

Keith Clark's experience in Chile is far more likely to match anything you will experience.

Keith wrote, "From Lago Posada I followed a dirt road to Los Antigous, where I spent the night at an estancia. One of the gauchos gave me directions to my next day's destination. He assured me that if I left at 8 a.m., even if I rode slowly, I'd reach my destination by four in the afternoon."

Thinking his next day was going to be short and easy, a contented Keith slipped into his sleeping bag, never realizing how wrong things would go the next day.

"We were a bit late in setting off, 8.30 a.m. but it wasn't the extra half an hour that mattered."

The trail started at 300 metres (1,000 feet) and then took Keith and his horses over a 1,800 metre (6,000 foot) high pass the gaucho had forgotten to mention, before it descended down to 500 metres (1,650 feet).

"All the time rain was pouring down and gale force winds were blowing. The pass was especially cold with horizontal sleet in our faces. To make matters worse, my horse, Calafate, freaks out if I wear my poncho, and as my jacket leaks like a sieve, this meant that I was cold and wet."

That "easy" day's ride didn't end until Keith and his exhausted horses struggled into the longed-for estancia at 9 p.m. On paper, they had covered "41 kilometres as the crow flies but I think we must have done nearer to 60."

Wet, cold, exhausted and starving, Keith still had to arrange with the estancia owner to let him and his horses spend the night.

"I found a bit of grass, put the horses out, made camp, had something to eat and collapsed. The horses and I were shattered. But there had been no place to stop for the last 20 kilometres."

The Limits of Advice

The world of equestrian travel is so vast, the countries which may be visited so numerous, the type of topography so diverse, the climatic conditions so extremely variable that it would be impossible to create a "one size fits all" study on the topic of how camping influences the outcome of every equestrian journey.

Some Long Riders may never spend a night under canvas, preferring to sleep in the relative comfort of the horse box/trailer that accompanies them. Many move along a stream of hospitality which includes family homes, riding schools, and accommodating barns. The majority find themselves face to face with the elements. Like their mounted ancestors, they must contend with rain, cold, wind, sun and every other nuisance or menace which Mother Nature can throw at mounted man.

Upon reflection, I realized that whereas I can attempt to provide valuable eye-witness information gathered directly from Long Riders who have survived incredible journeys, it is the responsibility of the reader to take the knowledge on offer in this chapter and then use it as a basic guide whereby the reader can create a list of equipment which fits his individual needs and the challenges of the terrain and climate where he will be riding.

The Long Riders' Guild is not a commercial enterprise. We don't sell wisdom or make a commission on what equipment an equestrian traveller ultimately decides to purchase and use.

This is therefore an attempt to explain what equipment most Long Riders have found to be the most useful. Just as importantly, it includes warnings regarding items which could not withstand the rigours of horse travel.

Camping, like equine health, requires careful study. Testing your camping skills is a vital part of your preparation. Making sure that all your equipment works properly is of supreme importance.

With that in mind, here are the ideas and items which Long Riders around the world have found to be the most useful.

The Tent

There are many reasons to take a tent.

The most obvious is that it provides a source of protection from the elements, a vital point which we shall consider.

But the tent provides other vital services as well. It grants you independence because it permits you to sleep where you like. It makes economic sense, because it frees you from paying for a night's lodging. It provides you with a degree of privacy from the prying eyes of strangers. Lastly, it offers a sense of safety in a world swirling with insecurity.

Swedish Long Rider Mikael Strandberg has spent years travelling to all parts of the world. During those journeys he has endured everything from the minus sixty degree winters of Siberia to the scorching sun of Kenya. Having lived so much of his life on the road, he has this wise observation to make about camping and tents.

"Why do so many people fail in their hope to reach the goal they've set? Out of 100 expeditions, 90 per cent of all first-timers fail to reach their goal. Half of them don't make it more than three months. The main reasons are these. The two most important things on an expedition are to sleep and eat well. Therefore, before leaving on an expedition, adventure, or travel, you need to spend a lot of time learning to live outdoors in a tent. This is your home. Your life goes on inside these walls. When you are tired, your tent is where you recuperate. When things go wrong, it is your fortress against worries and the place of peace. Before you leave home, make it comfortable. Then spend lots of time sleeping outdoors, until the day arrives when you sleep well and feel secure."

You may have considered not taking a tent at all, thinking the cost as being too prohibitive and the added weight as a burden to your pack animal. What must be recalled is that when things go bad, be it with the weather or the locals, it is the tent which is going to provide you with physical and emotional protection. So consider carefully before deciding to jettison this option.

Cheap tents are no bargain. Equestrian travel tests every type of equipment to its absolute limits. An inexpensive tent will be poorly made. An ineffective design, bad workmanship and shoddy materials may work for a weekend camper but not for a Long Rider spending months or years on the road. Never scrimp on buying your tent. Purchase the best you can afford.

Mankind has been sleeping under tents for centuries. That is why they come in so many bewildering sizes and shapes. Each has its advantages.

Stan Walchuk is the Canadian Long Rider who made an extraordinary solo ride through the Cordillera Mountains. He then organized a special school to teach horse packing to would-be travellers. This seasoned wilderness expert summed it up quite nicely when he said, "Match your tent with the job you want it to do."

In Stan's case, if he is leading a group of mounted tourists on a week-long ride through the scenic Rocky Mountains, he shelters them in large canvas wall tents, which are capable of sleeping several people and hold a wood-burning stove. But such tents are far too heavy and labour intensive for Long Riders.

The first thing to consider is size and shape. Because the tent is your home, office, kitchen, bedroom and storage space, it needs to provide you with enough room to move about in with comfort. Small backpacker tents are not suitable. Not only must you have space to live, sit, cook and sleep, but you must also recall that you will have a large amount of valuable equestrian equipment that must be protected and kept close at hand.

This question of how big a tent to choose made one equestrian traveller recall, "I was going to buy the two-man tent but decided to treat myself by buying the four-man tent instead. Now I wish I had bought the eight-man tent."

During the course of any horse trip you will have to move about, dress, repair equipment, cook and seek shelter from bad weather inside your tent. That is why many Long Riders prefer to use a tent that allows them to stand up.

Long Riders experience a great deal of bad weather, ranging from howling winds, lashing hail storms and every degree of pouring rain. The design and construction of the tent are therefore of immense importance.

Before you purchase the tent, study the tent when it is pitched.

The material should be your first concern. Is it highly water repellent, lightweight, strong and fire retardant?

Now imagine yourself alone on a dark, wet night trying to pitch the tent in a strong wind. How easy is it to set up? This is especially important when foul weather hits you out in the open.

Next, can it stand up to the elements? Is it tight? Are all of the stress points reinforced, the seams carefully stitched and the pole fittings well made?

One thing which many Long Riders overlook is the colour of the tent. Where you ride often decides on the level of danger you may encounter. It is important that your tent blend in with the colours of the natural landscape, not stick out like an advertisement for horse thieves or bandits looking for loot.

Another essential task of the tent is to provide protection against insects. Be sure your tent has strong zippers and proper vents.

A North American Long Rider travelling through a mosquito-infested area recalled, "Without our insect-proof tent, we would have found life almost unliveable."

Don't forget to think about condensation. The same waterproof material which keeps the rain out often causes intense condensation from your breath to form inside the tent. The result is that many Long Riders have awakened inside a tent which is dripping wet and has caused their sleeping bag, clothes and saddle to become wet during the night.

Before setting off on your journey, take the time to decrease the chance of leaks by placing sealer along all the seams.

The question of having a floor inside a Long Rider tent depends upon the weather and terrain you expect to encounter. Riding, walking and working round horses is a dirty business, so it is inevitable that a certain amount of dirt, mud and manure is going to be brought into the tent on the bottom of your boots.

Keeping a tent floor clean is a challenging task. If the floor is attached to the tent, then you may want to carry a small brush to sweep up and dump out the filth. Also, Long Riders routinely carry sharp objects which can quickly punch a hole in a tent floor, thereby requiring a speedy repair.

For these reasons, many Long Riders prefer to lay down a canvas tarp or plastic groundsheet to serve as a floor. This type of flooring can be arranged so that your camp stove rests on bare ground, thus reducing the chances of burning a hole in the tent floor. Plus, come morning, a tarp can be taken outside and shaken clean.

Even though many would-be travellers study the design of the tent, they often overlook the necessity of remembering how critically important the tent pegs are. Research and then purchase the most indestructible tent pegs money can buy.

The last thing to consider is how easy will it be to dismantle the tent and how much weight will it cause your horse to carry?

As early as 1855, when Francis Galton published his famous book for explorers entitled, *The Art of Travel*, he warned, "It is amazing how much heavier the tent is after it is transferred from the showroom to the field."

Don't purchase a tent until you've studied how it packs up. Are you looking at a rolled cylinder? Then where will you carry it and how will it be secured? Will it fold flat so that it might be placed atop the panniers in a top-pack? Practise setting up and breaking down your camp, and then loading your tent and gear, before you set off on the journey.

Before he became a Long Rider, Howard Saether had travelled by dogsled in the Arctic Circle and made many deep-water voyages round the world. A tough and seasoned traveller, when it came time for the Norwegian to make his ride from Uruguay to Bolivia, Howard knew he needed a tent that would stand up to blazing sun, tropical downpours and hordes of insects.

"One of the basics for a trip like ours is a very good tent. We had big faith in finding what we wanted while we spent time in the USA before our trip, but that turned out to be difficult. We finally bought a Coleman tent and brought it with us to Uruguay. It was a disaster. On our first test trip we got rain. Not only outside the tent, but inside as well.

I have spent hundreds of nights in tents in Norway during both winter and summer, so I contacted my family in Norway, and had them send my old well-proven Helsport Dovrefjell mountaineering tent. It is probably between 15 and 20 years old, but we are very pleased with it. It still stands up to tropical rain showers with heavy wind, and it takes us less than five minutes to put it up. It has three rooms. The main room is double, and where we sleep. On one side is a small room that is exactly big enough for our riding and pack-saddles. On the other side we have room for some equipment, and we also cook there if the weather is too bad. It weighs about 3.5 kilos (8 pounds)."

Under the Stars

Not everyone agrees that the tent is a necessity. In fact some Long Riders refused to carry or sleep in a tent, no matter how bad the weather.

Roger Pocock is the only person known to have ridden the Outlaw Trail from its origin in Canada to its conclusion in Mexico. Along the way the British Long Rider rode in to Butch Cassidy's "Hole-in-the-Wall" hideout unarmed and met the notorious bandit chieftain.

Originally from England, Pocock had learned frontier lore during his days as an officer of the Canadian Mounted Police. Pocock was one of those who believed that men who slept in tents put themselves in several types of disadvantage.

Because of the dangers encountered along the frontier, Pocock warned, "Men living in tents sleep heavily, hear and see nothing, and, if aroused suddenly, are embarrassed by the darkness, at the mercy of marauders or enemies, their exact locations being known."

Just such an episode occurred in 1855 when the explorer, Richard Burton, and three companions, were attacked in the night by a large group of Somali warriors. Awakening to the noise of their camp being invaded, the Englishmen were hampered in defending themselves by their tents. Lieutenant William Stroyan was speared and died inside his tent. Lieutenant John Speke managed to get outside, but was captured and wounded in eleven places before he managed to escape. Burton also fought his way free of the enveloping canvas walls, only to be severely wounded when a javelin impaled him, the point entering one cheek and exiting the other.

Even if you don't plan to go camping amidst the Somalis, there are still things to remember should you decide to sleep under the stars.

Francis Galton, who travelled extensively in Africa in the mid-19th century, was, like Pocock, another proponent of not using a tent. He wrote, "Men who sleep habitually in the open, breathe fresher air and are far more imbued with the spirit of wild life, than those who pass the night within the stuffy enclosures of a tent. It is an endless pleasure to lie awake watching the stars above, and to hear on all sides the stirrings of animal life. And later in the night, when the fire is low, and servants and horses are asleep, and there is no sound but the wind and an occasional plaintive cry of wild animals, the traveller finds himself in that close communion with nature which is the true charm of wild travel."

Even if you have a tent, you're under no obligation to always use it. You may find that awakening with a little dew on your sleeping bag is a small price to pay for having had the chance to watch the stars dance over your head all night.

Should bad weather force you to sleep outdoors without the aid of a tent, then much depends upon where you choose to sleep.

Staying warm relies upon avoiding being exposed to a cold wind. Amateur travellers often choose a tree to camp under. But even though the tree spreads out into the sky above, the only shelter it offers the traveller is that of the trunk below. Thus the tree is a roof but not a wall.

A Long Rider lying on the ground is so small that a low screen will guard him from the wind more effectively than a tree. A thick hedge protects from the wind on the leeward side a distance of up to ten to fifteen times the height of the hedge.

If a hedge can't be found, then a pile consisting of the saddle and any other equipment can be constructed as a screen against the wind. Such a screen need not be much higher than 18 inches to guard the traveller against the wind.

Long Riders travelling in Tibet learned that the natives of that country had discovered another way of staying warm without a tent. A common practice in that freezing-cold land was to encamp close to a large rock. After absorbing heat all day from the sun, the rock became a reservoir of warmth and parted with it slowly during the night.

Another well-known trick is to avoid sleeping on the ground in slight hollows during clear still nights, as a stream of cold air pours down into these depressions. That is why, as the night sets in, horses always move up to the higher grounds which rise like islands above the mist.

The Sleeping Bag

There are several items whose importance cannot be stressed enough. The sleeping bag is high on that list.

Equestrian travel is hard work and many a Long Rider has crawled into his sleeping bag after an exhausting day and longed to rest – only to discover that the cheap bag they purchased is leaving them shivering on the cold ground.

A good night's sleep will ensure that you feel emotionally rested in the morning. During the course of your journey, you will spend many hours in your sleeping bag, resting, reading, writing and sleeping. That is why you should exercise great care when you purchase your sleeping bag.

English Long Rider Elizabeth Barrett has spent years exploring every corner of Great Britain. Even though she wasn't sleeping in the freezing Himalayan Mountains, Elizabeth arrived at a common sense way of determining how to determine the type of sleeping bag you will require.

She wrote, "Grading is by 1- 4 seasons. For example, summer is 1. The average person needs a 1-season bag in a typical UK summer June-August, when overnight temperatures are at their highest. A 2-season bag is for late spring through to early summer use in the UK. A 3-season bag is for use in all but winter conditions, when quite heavy frosts are occurring overnight. A 4-season bag is for harsh winter. A 5-season is for high altitude use. When you're buying a sleeping bag it is recommended that you purchase one that is graded for one more season than you will likely need. For example, even if you plan to ride in summer, buy a 2-season bag."

A cheap sleeping bag will make you miserable. Yet a well-constructed one will keep you warm even if arctic weather is howling outside your tent. Several Long Riders have travelled and slept comfortably in temperatures as low as minus 30 degrees Fahrenheit, thanks to the down mountaineering sleeping bags they had purchased.

Inexperienced travellers think that buying a good sleeping bag solves the problem of staying warm at night. They don't realize that a person has an under as well as an upper side to keep warm.

The cold attacks one from below as well, with 3 a.m. generally being the coldest part of any night. If the ground is at all wet or snow covered, the damp will penetrate through a sleeping bag when the human body is at its lowest ebb.

It will therefore be understood why a light-weight mattress is of importance. This is not a luxury designed to provide you with a soft bed. It is a vital protection that will provide a critically-important layer of warmth against the bitter cold which is waiting to attack you from below.

Not many modern Long Riders have experienced the polar conditions which Tim Cope endured during his ride from Mongolia to Hungary. Caught out on the steppes of Kazakhstan during the winter, Tim learned that staying warm meant staying alive. He shared a vital piece of advice learned during that journey.

"Mountaineering sleeping bags are light, well made, not bulky and usually have a breathable water resistant outer shell. Be sure to use a thermal liner. Very important to remember is that even in extreme cold, it's better to strip down to thermals when inside the bag. If you don't, the sleeping bag will more quickly and easily absorb your sweat which freezes and you are left with a frozen useless bag. When riding for long periods in the wild it is better to sleep inside a vapour barrier (a big plastic bag) to stop your sweat from building up in the sleeping bag. Not comfortable but keeps you warm in the long run."

Even if you're not planning to ride in subzero temperatures, it is highly likely that you may encounter rainy weather. That is why many Long Riders not only keep their sleeping bags inside the stuff-sack which is normally supplied to carry the bag; in addition they place the sleeping bag inside a second waterproof bag as insurance that they won't be forced to slide into a soppy, wet, cold bag at night.

While we're on the subject of sleeping bags, never miss an opportunity to turn your sleeping bag inside out so as to let it air out on a dry sunny day.

Equipment

It was Colonel John Blashford-Snell, Founder of the Scientific Exploration Society, who has led so many expeditions across jungles, over mountains and through countless hazards, who wisely warned, "Any fool can be uncomfortable. It is often the small and simple things that help towards comfort."

Consider the simple matter of lighting your camp, for example.

George Younghusband was serving as a Subaltern in the British army stationed in India, when he was granted his first extended leave. Rather than return "home" to England, the young officer decided instead to explore the jungles of Burma on horseback.

In his book, *1800 Miles on a Burmese Pony*, the author learned a lesson that, even though it was written in 1888, applies to any modern Long Rider today.

Cheap equipment is utterly useless, as horse travel knocks everything about in a fearful manner. Invest in the best equipment you can afford. In Younghusband's case, he soon found himself in the jungle in the dark because of defective equipment.

"Our lantern broke very soon after we started, so that, if we could not get our evening meal by daylight, we had to eat it by the dim, evil-smelling, and smoky light afforded by a rag dipped in pig's fat and hung over the edge of a saucer."

Nowadays most equestrian travellers use a Petzel headlamp, so their hands are free to handle the horses in the dark. But having a second, sturdy lantern for use inside the tent is also of importance.

The list of what Long Riders deem to be "necessary" equipment changes dramatically, according to the era, terrain, climate and personality of the traveller.

Take for example Lady Florence Dixie, the first European woman to explore Patagonia on horseback in 1878.

She was the earliest British journalist to report from a war zone, covering the Zulu Wars in South Africa. She championed women's rights, defended animal welfare, survived an assassination attempt by Irish rebels and was friends with her fellow Long Rider author, Charles Darwin.

It was said of Florence Dixie, "She is made of the heroic stuff that knows not what defeat means."

Being a woman of courage and resource, Florence made a note in her diary of the equipment she took on that journey into the unexplored Andes Mountains.

"We limited ourselves to such things as were absolutely necessary: tent, hatchet, frying pan, coffee, tea and two kegs of whisky."

You may decide to leave the whisky at home.

But other items have been found to be of universal effectiveness.

Most people think of the United States as being a country of wide open spaces. In fact the nation is criss-crossed with wire fences. Long Riders in that country often carry a pair of wire cutters. This is not to enable them to cut a fence and trespass, but to equip them in case of an emergency situation when their horse becomes dangerously entangled with wire.

Don't be tempted to rely on a GPS. If you want to take one along, fine. But this is a high tech solution to a low tech problem. GPS technology relies on batteries. If they run out, you may find yourself far from any source which can replace them.

Always carry a reliable, small, light-weight compass, which you keep in your pocket.

In the chapter on Long Rider Health, I wrote about the critical need to be able to keep yourself healthy under extreme conditions. A first-aid kid, for you and your horses, is one piece of equipment which requires careful thought and advance study.

Opinions vary on what to place in the first aid kit, depending upon the climate, variety of insect threats and even the sex of the rider. But common items which are most often cited include Imodium, aspirin, Ibuprofen, an antibiotic, iodine, insect repellent, multi-vitamins and a strong sunscreen.

After riding "ocean to ocean" across the United States, in both directions, American Long Rider Howard Wooldridge made a startling suggestion for an item which equestrian travellers should consider to be a part of their basic equipment list.

He wrote, "A 4 ounce roll of duct tape (often called gaffer's tape in the UK and Australia) should be part of every Long Rider's equipment list. It has medical uses. It can be used as a banding material if one breaks a rib or two, is effective as a bandage (won't sweat off easily), along with elevation can be used to restrict (not stop) blood flow and can be used to secure a splint to a broken limb. Plus, it has non-medical uses as well. It can be used as an adhesive which will help keep a horseshoe on for a short distance. And if a horseshoe is lost, you can wad up paper into the hoof and secure it with it in place with duct tape as a short distance measure."

When it comes to horse travel, every ounce you place on your horse represents an expenditure of equine energy. You are therefore confronted with a challenge. You must choose the best equipment, all the while being continually reminded of the need to reduce weight at every opportunity.

This is a lesson that every Long Rider learns.

Before Tracy Paine and DC Vision set off on their 22,500 kilometre (14,000 miles) ride across the United States, they had no idea what they would require. It didn't take them long to find out, though.

"Once a week we lightened the load and disposed of unneeded items such as my curling iron and DC's silk shirts," Tracy wrote.

Being around horses means you will be handling rope. For that reason, and many others beside, you will need to carry a knife.

Knives

Knives are like religions. Opinions differ. Everyone has a story. Most people think what works for them is best. It's your task to keep an open mind and make your own decision.

The majority of Long Riders find that nearly all chores can be handled by a folding knife equipped with a 4 to 6 inch long blade. It should be strongly made, keep a good edge, and, most importantly, the blade should lock into place.

Australian Long Rider Steve Nott warned, "The best knife is the one you have with you. So a knife in the bottom of the pannier, no matter how sharp, is no good to the horseman in trouble."

Your folding knife can be carried unobtrusively in a small case on your belt, and will be ready for instant use in case a horse gets tangled in a rope and must be cut free in an emergency.

But a wide variety of other problems and occasions routinely arise during an equestrian journey which requires more than just a sharp blade. This may range from using pliers to carefully pull the nails out of a loose horse shoe, using tweezers to remove a splinter from your finger, or using a scissor to cut cloth. Long Riders have long found that the multi-functional Swiss Army knife serves many of these purposes. In addition, the multi-tool known as the Leatherman is small, light-weight, has a number of valuable uses, and can be carried on your belt.

Then there is the question of carrying a larger blade to assist in camp chores.

Captain Otto Schwarz rode 48,000 kilometres on five continents during the course of his long equestrian travel career. When travelling in mountains, woodlands or on the pampas he found that a machete was a useful tool. Though not as efficient as an axe at chopping wood, it can cut grass, brush and even be used to dig a hole.

Finally, there is the question of carrying edged weapons for the purpose of self-defence. During my last journey through the North West Frontier Province, I was issued a special weapons license by the Pakistani federal government. Across the border in neighbouring Afghanistan, the Afghan mujahadeen were engaged in a bloody war against the invading forces of the Soviet Union. An unexpected repercussion of this conflict was that the Pakistani border was populated by armed men equipped with deadly firearms.

Every type of gun, ranging from old British army Webley revolvers to state-of-the-art American Stinger anti-aircraft missiles were for sale, being smuggled, or available in the hotbed of murder and intrigue which existed in that troubled borderland.

Having already been kidnapped at gunpoint during a previous journey in the NWFP, I had learned that to appear defenceless was to invite trouble. With the government's permission, I carried a double-barrelled sawn-off shotgun in a scabbard on my saddle. Around my waist I wore a large belt. On one hip rested a seven-shot heavy-calibre semi-automatic pistol based on the American Colt .45. On my other hip I carried a specially designed scimitar known as the "Asadullah Sword." A short matching dagger hung on a thong under my shirt, ready for instant use should I be attacked or kidnapped. A third, larger dagger, I kept in my saddle bag.

The circumstances in Pakistan were extreme, and though Long Riders have been carrying swords on horseback for centuries, I may be the last one to do so for the foreseeable future.

Rope

If you've been raised in North America, Australia, Europe, or other parts of the world with easy access to plentiful supplies, then you probably just take high-quality rope for granted. In industrialized nations rope is always available at a nearby building supply store. Moreover, it's not only plentiful, it's cheap.

Not so when you ride in distant parts.

There it is a precious commodity, seldom seen, always useful and forever being stolen.

Some countries, especially Mongolia, have a reputation for stealing this valuable tool, which is of such practical daily use to people who own large herds of horses and other animals.

Other nations may have rope available, but you will find to your dismay that it is of inferior quality. This not only renders it inflexible but makes it very difficult to tie knots.

Before travelling to foreign parts, wise Long Riders purchase high quality alpinist rope. Tim Cope, for example, had three 15 metre (50 foot) ropes which he took to Mongolia. He used them for a variety of tasks, including to tether the horses at night and to lash the panniers securely to the pack saddle during the day.

The Axe and the Saw

There are two points to consider when the topic turns to carrying an axe. The first is what a practical tool it is. The second is that in certain parts of the United States you are required by law to carry an axe if you travel through the wooded mountains with horses. For example, the Montana state law requires all pack strings to have an axe, a shovel and a bucket.

Leaving aside the law for a moment, let's recall that an axe is a useful tool if you are going to build a fire or remove a tree that may have fallen across the trail and prevents your progress.

A traditional felling axe is used to chop down trees using both hands and a hard heavy swing. The famous Hudson Bay Company axe, for example, had a 2½ pound head mounted on a 26 inch long hickory handle. Most Long Riders do not encounter the type of problems, or timber, which require the inclusion of such a tool. Plus, because of their sharp blade and heavy weight, an axe can cause serious injuries to the user or others nearby, unless it is used with extreme care.

A hatchet is a small, light axe designed to be used in one hand. Not only can it be used to cut firewood for the camp, the flattened rear portion of the head, known as the butt, makes it perfect for driving in tent pegs or picket pins.

The Hultafors Company has been making axes in Sweden since 1697. Their hatchet, known as the "Classic Hunting Axe," is light-weight, extremely tough, and enjoys a reputation for reliability.

Like your knife, take the time to sharpen your axe. When not in use, it should always be covered in a leather sheath.

Another piece of equipment which is often required for Long Riders is a small saw.

The Pacific Crest Trail, which runs 4,286 kilometres (2,663 miles) from the Mexican border to Canada, is infamous for the number of fallen trees which routinely block this popular hiking and riding trail. While hikers can walk around or climb over a fallen tree, Long Riders like Ed Anderson, who rode the PCT solo, found they are often required to cut through a fallen tree or clear timber off the trail.

Ed recommended, "Bring a small saw capable of cutting through at least a 15" tree. I brought along a Silky brand folding saw with a 14.5" blade. The model is called the 'Big Boy' and I used it to cut and remove many trees on my ride."

Like your axe, be sure your saw also has a guard over the cutting edge of the saw. A piece of plastic PVC pipe, which has been split down one side, can be used for this purpose.

If you suspect you will be travelling through wooded country where you might encounter deadfalls or dangerous limbs, pack your axe, hatchet or saw where it can be reached with ease.

The Camp Fire

A camp fire is a complex thing which serves a number of purposes.

First, it protects you against the cold. There are few experiences more agonizing than to lie shivering in your sleeping bag as the cold night air increases its attack in the hours before dawn. With your blood running thin, you will have plenty of time to reproach yourself for not having had the foresight and energy to lay in a large enough supply of firewood to keep you warm till dawn.

Nor should we forget to mention the deep emotional comfort which radiates from a campfire. Sitting there, listening to the wood crackle, smelling the fragrant smoke, seeing the threatening dark held at bay, feeling the reassuring warmth of the embers, you will recall those generations of Long Riders who huddled by their fires long ago, and yet, like you, found consolation in the night.

And of course, one can cook over an open fire.

One Long Rider noted how it didn't take much of a flame to satisfy his simple needs.

"A little hole about twelve inches square and six inches deep was scraped out for the fire. Over this the wire grill was placed, the coffee pot was superimposed, and our dinner was on the way. The smaller the fire, the better for cooking."

Of course, there are drawbacks, some of which you might not expect.

Long Riders who rode into high mountains, above the timberline, made it a practice to cut and carry firewood with them.

Some countries do not have an abundance of firewood. In fact, they have none to speak of.

When Leonard Clark rode across Tibet in 1949, he noted the lack of firewood to be found in the high Himalayas. Luckily, his native companions relied on the local practice of burning animal dung as fuel.

Clark made a point of explaining, "We used only the driest dung. Actually, if this dung is too dry it contains no great heat. If too green it will not burn at high elevations. Mule and horse dung is second best as it burns too fast. Yak dung is best."

The Kyrgyz still make use of this practice when travelling with their herds in the Pamir Mountains. They use the word *kisiak* to describe the dried horse or cow dung they use as fuel for their campfires.

Dung burns well and provides a reliable amount of heat. But it has drawbacks. It has to have been turned over, so as to allow it to dry thoroughly on both sides, before being burned. Also, unlike the smell of sweet-smelling wood, burning dung emits an acrid odour which permeates one's clothes and tent.

Regardless of what fuel you are forced to use, the use of a campfire means that you must be constantly aware of the prevailing wind, as flying sparks may burn holes in your tent. That is why it is wise not to place your tent too close to the campfire.

Though our ancestors have relied upon campfires for eons, because of the threat of forest fires countries like the United States have passed an increasing number of legal restrictions making it illegal to have an open camp fire except in established campsites.

Of course many of these campsites are located in state or national parks, which restrict or prohibit horse travellers.

So what's the alternative?

The Stove

The majority of Long Riders carry some sort of portable cooking stove.

There are two major factors to consider before making this purchase. Where you are going to be travelling and how many people you will be cooking for.

Portable stoves operate on different fuels, including white gas, kerosene, propane, butane, alcohol, paraffin, diesel and petrol.

It is very important that you determine what fuel is most easily obtainable in the country where you will be riding, as replenishing your fuel will be of strategic importance. Long Riders have complained that kerosene, for example, was difficult to locate in Great Britain and non-existent in rural France. Locating butane and/or propane cylinders often proves to be impossible in remote regions.

So the more versatile and adaptable your stove the better your chances will be of having a warm meal.

Tim Cope had luck with one type of efficient portable stove.

He wrote, "I have used the MSR XGK stove on two long trips well and have found it to be quite reliable. It can operate on petrol, diesel, kerosene or pure fuel. Pure fuel is best, or the cleanest petrol you can find. In

Kazakhstan, Mongolia, and former Soviet countries A-93 is the petrol to look for. Diesel requires more priming and the stove will have to be cleaned more often."

Another important consideration is if you purchase a stove with one or two burners. A two-ring stove will provide you with the convenience of cooking dinner at the same time you are warming up a hot drink.

Food

Finding grass for the horses may prove to be easier than finding food for you.

Most Long Riders try always to carry enough food for at least two days' meals on the road.

Yet supplies disappear at an alarming rate. Replenishing them will be influenced by the country where you are riding. If you're journeying "ocean to ocean" across the United States you won't have to look hard for food.

But other countries will challenge your ingenuity and require you to tighten your belt.

After he had completed his famous ride from Buenos Aires to New York, Aimé Tschiffely returned to Argentina. In one of his lesser-known trips, he made an extensive exploration of the Patagonian wilderness. In addition to beautiful mountains, he found few people and even less food.

"Throughout Patagonia," he wrote, "huts where travellers can spend the night are known as *boliches*. Some of these are to be found in very remote places where one would think no one ever passed. I have seen such places far away in semi-deserts, or on barren cold and windswept plains, where no one would expect a human being to pass, excepting an inquisitive roamer like myself."

These *boliches* are an example of the type of out-of-the-way store, shop or shack found in other countries where many a Long Rider has gratefully arrived in search of badly-needed food.

The things you can buy in such isolated establishments are very limited. They may supply simple articles of clothing, commonly-needed tools, alcoholic drinks, and a minimum amount and type of food stuffs. What you shouldn't expect is a wide variety of culinary options. What you will find is that, owing to the cost and the difficulty of transport, prices are very high.

Prior to your departure you should stock up on dried foods that can be carried and cooked with ease. Non-perishable options such as rice, pasta, instant noodles and dried potatoes can be served in a variety of ways. Instant oatmeal, along with a hot cup of coffee or tea, has served many a Long Rider as an easy breakfast. What you need is food that is simple to prepare, provides a warm and comforting meal, and is easy to clean up afterwards.

But be prepared to tests the limits of your culinary courage.

During the winter of 2014 Canadian Long Rider Bonnie Folkins accompanied a large band of Kazakh nomads who were moving their flocks to a distant pasture.

"Kazakh families move in units called *awils* and the head of such an *awil* is led by an *awil bastiq,* or leader, who decides when and where to move," Bonnie wrote.

There were sixteen members of the Kazakh family which Bonnie rode with.

"In earlier times there might have been twenty families moving as many as 5000 sheep, 800 horses, 100 cattle and as many as 200 camels."

The migration which Bonnie joined may have been smaller but the traditional Kazakh nomad diet had stayed remarkably consistent across the centuries. Bonnie observed a giant bag of fried dough being tied to one camel pack and to another, sacks of dried meat on the bone. Having ridden with the Kazakhs on many occasions, Bonnie wasn't surprised when dinner was served.

"The nomad diet is not varied, so an offering of boiled meat was not a surprise. Such a dish is called 'five fingers' because it is eaten with the hands. In an effort to increase their herds in earlier times, poorer Kazakhs lived on cereals. Today, vegetables are rarely incorporated into the diet, with the exception of dough made from wheat products, root vegetables, wild onions or garlic."

You probably won't be required to tie a bag of dried meat to your baggage camel, but before you pack your own food supplies you should give a thought to how you can reduce every extra ounce of weight from your supplies.

Don't pack food which contains water, which is heavy. Use dried food instead, so as to eliminate the unnecessary weight of the water.

Many products come in cardboard boxes which are filled with air. Repack such food into strong Ziploc bags, being sure to cut off any cooking directions from alongside the box and place it into the bag.

Avoid carrying glass bottles. Not only can they break during travel, and thereby ruin everything in your pannier, broken glass is a hazard.

If you decide to carry your food in boxes, be sure that you label the bottom of the box, as well as the top; because when two of them have been opened at the same time, it often happens that the tops run a risk of being changed.

One final word about food: always keep your food and fuel packed in separate panniers.

Cooking

Times can be tough out on the road. One Long Rider recalled a meal eaten alongside the road in Jordan that consisted of "a meagre stew of cold beans in colder mutton fat."

Opinions vary as to what type of minimum cooking equipment to carry. Common items include a frying pan, coffee pot or tea kettle, a four or six quart pot, cutlery, plates, bowls, cups, can-opener and cork screw.

Camping stores offer cooking pots that nest inside themselves. Aluminium is the most common and inexpensive, but it can be hard to clean and dents easily.

Another consideration is the choice of your dinner ware. Metal plates are hot to hold and metal cups may burn your lips. Hard plastic plates, bowls and cups work well.

You should practise cooking your meals using your stove and cooking gear before setting off, as keeping your strength up with the help of tasty, nutritious meals is vital to your success.

The Bucket

As Tracy Paine wisely suggested, you might want to leave your curling iron at home. But it can be difficult to decide what is truly necessary and what is frivolous.

Having a heavy-duty folding bucket is one such necessity.

In the past buckets were often made of heavy canvas and came equipped with a rope handle. Times have moved on.

Many European trail riders carry a small, light-weight collapsible plastic bucket that can be quickly unfolded and filled so as to provide a thirsty horse with a drink.

But a Long Rider lives on the road, often for long periods of time. This translates into a bucket being used for a variety of purposes, both on a daily basis, and during rest days when special chores must be done.

The Ortlieb Company makes a strong rectangular folding bucket which can serve many purposes. The sizes include 5, 10 and 20 litres. Most Long Riders find the 10 litre (2.6 gallons) size works well.

Obviously the bucket can be used to supply a thirsty horse with a drink. But in addition, it can be used to wash and prepare food prior to a meal. Afterwards it serves as a sink to wash the dishes in.

On rest days it can be turned into a tub to wash clothes in or it can be used to collect water from a river for a bucket shower.

Finally, thanks to its two stout handles, it can be used as a handy general carry-all which can be quickly employed to carry vegetables or other items encountered during your day's travel.

When not in use, it folds up into a small triangle that weighs less than 10 ounces (260 grams).

The Weather

One matter which will greatly concern you is the weather.

Whereas it's true that we have no control over it, a Long Rider needs to learn to detect the tiny hints which Nature provides.

In the days before satellite technology provided advance warning about on-coming storms, a large body of folk-wisdom helped farmers and travellers make accurate assessments of the day's possible weather.

There were a number of well-known signs which indicated that it was about to rain; these included sounds being heard clearly, birds flying low, smoke hanging low, hills being seen very clearly, salt becoming damp, frogs holding concerts, flies becoming lazy and fish jumping.

Bad weather was predicted if there was a red sky at sunrise, sea-birds flying low towards shore and a halo observed round the moon.

A red sky at sunset and a clear moon were believed to indicate fine weather the next day.

There are two quick points I want to mention about Long Riders camping in the rain, both before and after a downpour.

If a storm is expected, tent ropes should be slackened at the approach of rain as they contract with wet and are apt to pull the pegs out of the sodden ground. Also, a drain should be cut round the tent to carry off the water, as otherwise the water will find its way into the tent.

Finally, to break camp in the wet is always a miserable business. You will find that you will want to pack much of your equipment inside the tent and then load the pack horse with care.

Selecting the Camp Site

At one point during his extended journey through Europe, an old woman invited William Holt and his horse, Trigger, to spend the night in her beautiful garden.

"May I ask to whom I am indebted for this very kind hospitality?" he asked.

"Your horse," she replied.

Many foresee the need to camp. Few ever give any thought to where they should spend the night, not realizing that the comfort and safety of you and the horses is connected to this fundamental daily decision. What happens between sunset and sunrise may be a pleasant experience or the basis for a terrible memory.

Because you are travelling with horses, you should always begin looking for a suitable camp site well before dark.

Even before you arrive, you should have decided if you're looking for a one night stopover just to sleep before moving on in the morning? Or are you planning to spend a few days resting? The amount of time you plan on spending at the site will influence your decision to stay or ride on.

When you arrive at a place which you believe may be suitable, do not ride directly into what you think may be the actual campsite. Halt your horse, sit in the saddle and study the site from a distance. This allows your road and pack horse to relieve themselves at a distance from what will soon be your living and cooking areas.

There are requisites and criteria which will make a campsite happy or hellish.

The first consideration will be the horses. Several times Long Riders have found beautiful places to camp but rode on in favour of what would better suit the needs of their horse. Does the campsite have abundant grass and clean water?

Next, what about your own requirements? Is firewood available? Should you feel the need, can you purchase grain, food and supplies close by?

The safety of you and the horses comes after that.

Are you far enough away from any busy roads? You don't want your horse to get loose in the night and wander into the path of an on-coming truck with its headlights blazing.

Now think ahead about the local weather and the next day's travel.

It is always preferable to set up camp on the far side of a stream or river, as a flood during the night may delay your next day's travel.

Never place your tent too close to a stream or river. Always camp on higher ground so that you will not get caught in a flash flood caused by a thunderstorm. Be especially careful of camping in dry river beds, which may flood without warning.

In case it does look like rain, is the site sufficiently high to let the water drain off downhill? If cold wind or snow looks likely, are there woods to help break the prevailing wind?

If a storm seems probable, avoid camping near large tall trees, which may attract lightning, blow over in a strong wind, or drop a large branch on your tent during the night.

Avoid camping in tall, dry grass, which may be a fire hazard and can harbour snakes.

Remember that insects will torment your horses if given the chance. Avoid swampy ground, which is a natural breeding ground for mosquitoes, gnats and flies.

After you've studied the possible site from a distance considering these various factors, ride your horses to the area where you tie or picket them while you continue your inspection of the campsite on foot. Make sure your horses are safely secure and loosen their cinches.

Then walk back and inspect the camp site.

Clear or carry off any vegetation, leaves or brush that may harbour dangerous reptiles or insects.

Consider where you are going to pitch your tent. Is the spot level? If not you may roll downhill in your sleeping bag during the night.

Have you faced the tent toward the south-east, so as to enjoy the morning sun?

Not Exactly Ideal

You may think it's going to be green grass and shining stars, but you better be prepared to lower your expectations.

During her travels through Greece, Penny Turner learned a valuable trick.

"Very often, if I have to stop near a village, I camp near the graveyard. There are very good reasons for this: There is almost always water, because people need it for looking after graves. There is normally a lot of grass as shepherds and others don't feel comfortable in the environs of the graveyard, but the main reason is that no one at all feels comfortable there after dark."

Other Long Riders would have welcomed the comfort of a graveyard.

While riding across Spain, Mefo Phillips and her horse were presented with an unsavoury option.

"The lady assures us there is accommodation for horses down the road, and she's right. It's the bullring. Or to be precise, it's under the bullring. It's the strangest billet yet. A man with a key arrives and to judge by the number of old horse craps, there've been plenty of horses here before ours. Everything is here that's guaranteed to trip or maim a horse: broken bottles, guttering, lumps of concrete, machinery bristling with shafts and spikes, and lengths of chain. It's too heavy to move, too much to fence off even if we could force the posts into the iron ground. All we can do is to point out every hazard to our horses and tell them not to get tangled up in it."

A problem associated with old camping sites and abandoned villages is that they harbour insect pests for a long time.

But in terms of picking unlikely campsites, Billy Brenchley encountered a unique problem when he and Christine Henchie were riding across the war zone of Southern Sudan in 2010.

Billy recalled, "There have been major battles fought in this area and unexploded ordinance and mines are everywhere. We can only go off the road at settlements or well-worn tracks because when the villagers find unexploded mines they throw them in the bush."

Yet a villager assured Billy and Christy not to worry.

"The mines have expired now and the best way to remove them is by hoe! And to test that it's expired, you can jump on it like this!"

At which point, the villager jumped on a mine in front of the startled travellers.

Where to Place the Horses

One of the most important decisions connected to choosing a campsite is where to picket, tether, tie or pasture the horses.

Once you have scouted your camp, take your horses directly to the area where they will spend the night. Make sure it is far enough away from your tent and cooking area so that manure will not attract flies.

There are several things to consider when choosing where to secure the horses.

Attention should be given to the weather and the prevailing winds. In dry, sultry weather the horse should face the direction of the prevailing wind. In stormy weather their tails should be turned to the gale. A site downwind of a group of trees should be avoided as the strong and gusty winds raise quantities of dead leaves which make some horses nervous. No horse likes dry leaves flying about and against him.

Should you be worried about bears, wolves, lions, etc, then picket the horses on the farther side of camp, so that should they break loose you will hear them passing.

Also, don't overlook the fact that your horses are working hard and are hungry at the end of the day. If your campsite can not provide them with an adequate meal, they may break away during the night and return to greener pastures. Once again, placing your tent in the direction from which you travelled will let you hear them as they go by.

Don't forget that horses can inflict harm to trees and the environment in the space of one night. This is why you must make an effort to protect the integrity of your surroundings.

In the past it was common practice for people to tie a horse to a tree. But bored horses tend to paw the tree's roots, which causes serious damage. They may also strip off the bark, which will kill the tree.

If you decide to place your horses on a picket line, choose a place with little or no vegetation, use a tree saver to protect the tree's surface, keep the horses at least six feet away from the trees, place the animals well apart from each other and at the first sign of any damage, move them to a new location. Be sure that your picket line is at least chest high, so as to discourage the horses from stepping over it.

Should you tether your horse, move him as soon as you can see the circle where he has been feeding, so as to reduce trampling and prevent over-grazing.

Never place your horses too near the tent, otherwise they run the risk of becoming entangled in the tent ropes during the night.

Watering

Riding is thirsty work. A man requires two to three pints of water daily to keep in good health. It is possible to train oneself to manage on less for limited periods but it is not advisable to do so. A horse on average, consumes ten gallons of water a day just to keep his various bodily functions operating properly.

Therefore one of the requirements of a good camp is a source of water for horse and rider. Safety, culture and custom will all influence this part of your camping experience.

Never take it for granted that just because the water is found in the wilderness it is pure.

The transparent water may look like innocence itself. Yet Long Rider history is filled with stories of travellers who became ill from dysentery, intestinal parasites and hepatitis or died from cholera, typhoid and typhus lurking in impure water.

One of the decisions about where to pitch your camp will be connected to the availability of water.

Remote pools often provide the worst water. Unless very inaccessible under boulders or in fissures of rock, they are nearly always foul with excrement of wild and domestic animals.

Henning Haslund made such an unsavoury discovery while riding across Mongolia in the 1920s.

"Late one evening we came to an almost dried up water hole in the sand. The water looked brown and slimy, and an offensive stench met us from afar off. In the middle of the little water hole we found a dead camel, but we boiled the water and put in an extra dose of tea and saccharine and at least it served to quench our thirst," Haslund wrote nonchalantly.

If chance forces you to camp near running water, camp above a village, not below it. But don't forget that there may be another village higher up river and out of sight.

Always scout the creek, stream or river not just for dead animals but for signs of industrial or agricultural pollution. Long Riders travelling alongside the Gila River in the United States, for example, were warned not to trust it because of the chemical pollutants which poured into the water from nearby ranches and farms.

Use a filter. Boil your water. Use sterilizing tablets. Treat it chemically with drops of iodine to purify it. No matter what method you choose, always use caution when drinking suspect water.

While most people remember to purify their drinking water, they overlook the importance of using clean water for cooking and washing. This often results in travellers becoming ill from the Giardia bacteria, which lurks in rivers, lakes and streams.

In addition to safety, there are also issues of courtesy and custom to consider when dealing with water sources.

Long Riders in desert countries learned that local tradition considered it very bad form to pitch their tent too close to a spring as it implied that others had to seek permission before obtaining a drink. Courtesy demanded that a tent always be pitched some little distance away from the spring, in order to demonstrate that the water was free for all to use.

Wells were another place where tradition dictated what happened. While no one would refuse a thirsty traveller a drink, he was expected to wait until the needs of local herds had been satisfied. If there was a public well, he was expected to quench his thirst there, rather than ask at a private dwelling.

But the days of public horse troughs and village wells are gone. This means that modern Long Riders have encountered a new challenge: where to find water for their horses.

Irish Long Rider Steve O'Connor was disappointed during his ride across Spain one hot summer, because he couldn't find water for his thirsty horse, Murphy.

"One of the surprising things I found was how difficult it was to get drinking water in rural areas at times. I discovered that many houses are empty during the day. Most gates had a sign saying, 'Beware of the dog.' In the past water was never an issue. But now local access to this precious commodity can no longer be taken for granted," Steve wrote.

If the chances come for you to camp alongside a river or stream, then you should look upon the water source as having different sections for various purposes. Your drinking and cooking water comes from upstream. The horses' watering place is next along. Still further downstream is where you wash dishes and bathe, being careful to keep any soap away from the animals.

Also, when a river is the source there are safety considerations to remember in terms of the horses. Make sure the river bank is in no danger of collapsing, that the horse won't become trapped in mud, that there is a wide approach and a safe exit from the water's edge.

In order to keep the water clean, and to protect the soil and plant life, always keep the horses at least 200 feet from the stream, river, lake or water source.

Sanitation

Fish and water plants are extremely sensitive even to biodegradable soap. To prevent contamination, do your washing in a basin at least 200 feet from the water source. Dump any waste water far from the water source.

Living outdoors means taking care of human waste and toilet paper. Set up your privy at least 100 feet away from camp. If you are going to be staying in camp for a rest, fastening a tarp to an adjacent tree can provide a degree of privacy.

Unscented, biodegradable white toilet paper is recommended. Bury it, and human waste, in a hole under about six inches of soil. Some Long Riders have carried small, folding military spades for this purpose. But more recently Long Riders have reported that a metal garden trowel equipped with a 4 inch wide blade works well.

The Chores

As you travel you will develop a routine that allows you to set up camp quickly and efficiently.

If you're riding solo, then all the work falls on your shoulders. But if there are two or more of you, then you will find that democracy is the only fair way to allocate the chores.

When Lady Florence Dixie ventured into the wilds of Patagonia, she travelled with her aristocratic husband, her equally noble born brother, and a number of local gauchos and guides. Though their table manners and bank accounts may have differed, they were all equals when it came time to work round the camp.

Lady Dixie wrote, "Roughing it may be all very well in theory but it is not so easy in practice. After a long tiring march, when you have been in the saddle twelve hours under a hot sun, it is by no means a light task, on the arrival at your journey's end, to have to unload your horses, pitch your tent, cook your dinner, clean your saddle and bridle, unpack your baggage, and place everything in order and neatness for tomorrow. It occupies a long and weary time. Before you can rest, everybody, no matter who it is, must take up his or her share of work. The thought of fatigue must be banished and everyone undertake to accomplish their tasks cheerfully and willingly. Only by doing so can things be kept going in the brisk orderly manner they should."

Certain things are consistent. Sharing the duties around camp is one of them.

When Clay Marshall and Hawk Hurst rode across the mountains of the western United States in 2013 they too learned the necessity of sharing the work load.

Clay recalled, "Once a rhythm is set, responsibilities are shared. Hawk and I would take turns starting the fire and collecting wood. Hawk would stay up late and stoke the fire; I would get up early and get it going again. We shared the labours of our cook pots and contributed for our subsistence with equal measure. The health of one affects the health of all. Learning to be at peace with the moment, we learned to give each other space. Every day is a new day, and new attitudes come with it. We had many accounts of apologies and forgiveness, and many accounts of being wrong, but we weren't afraid to admit it eventually."

Journeys are as different as the people who make them. But certain chores are consistent.

Nosebags require frequent cleaning; they should be removed as soon as the horse has done feeding and turned inside out to dry. Take turns appointing one person to watch the horses while they graze, are on the picket line, or are tethered.

Always take the time to protect your saddles, pads, panniers, bridles and other equipment. If you are in bear country, hoist your panniers and any food into trees well away from your camp. Porcupines and rats love to gnaw on leather which has been soaked with a horse's salty sweat. Cover your saddles and gear under a tarp against the dew or rain. Some Long Riders carry a small tent especially to protect their saddles and equipment.

Nightly Check

Just because you've halted for the day doesn't mean that you can stop making decisions. After dinner, decide if you are going to stay or move on tomorrow. If you're going to be riding, then discuss your next day's travel plans. Make sure everyone knows the route. Decide in advance if a midday halt is going to be made. To reduce the chances of a misunderstanding, use 24 hour military time to avoid mistakes between a.m. and p.m.

Don't turn in without looking at your supplies, checking the safety of your equipment and carefully inspecting the horses to make sure they are tethered or picketed securely.

This may sound as if you are on constant guard duty, being forced to rush here and there, and always busy. In fact, once you've laid out your camp and secured your horses, you will find that you will have time to relax and enjoy the scenery and serenity of being with your horses in the wilderness.

The simplicity and peace which arises at the end of such a day is ample reward for your hard work.

But a word of warning. Don't expect to sleep deeply. You may be dreaming away but your horse spends much of the night eating or moving about.

After one particularly restless night, Jeremy James recalled, "To sleep in the company of horses is no light matter. Horses are restless bedfellows. They chew. They sigh and yawn, and stretch and scratch and chew and chew. They lie down abruptly. They get up and sigh and blow through their noses and shake and scratch and chew and chew."

No matter if they are noisy bedfellows; you can rest knowing your horse is close by; unless, of course, you're worried about being attacked during the night.

Camping in Hostile Country

Look at any historical text, be it the Bible or Shakespeare, and you will find ample evidence of the evil which man has visited upon his brother throughout the history of our species.

Travelling with horses is subject to a great many hazards, which have been dealt with in previous chapters. But setting up a campsite places you and the horses in a vulnerable position; strategically, emotionally and legally.

First, let's consider the lesser of two evils; the hostility which a Long Rider may encounter from a suspicious or antagonistic government official. The uniforms worn by this type of threatening person vary. They may include city policemen, park rangers, Homeland Security or US border guards.

I mention the United States in specific in this example because of an email which arrived as I was writing this chapter. An American man in his mid-60s, who has been quietly travelling with his three mules for several years in the western portion of the United States, was stopped by the police in Gilbert, California.

The police were frustrated when they could not find any local ordinance which the equine traveller had violated.

"They couldn't charge him with anything else, so they put him in isolation in the mental hospital for evaluation to see if he was crazy," wrote the American Long Rider who reported the incident.

Other evidence of official hostility continues to grow within that country, with American Long Riders being prohibited from entering historic state or national parks, being issued with heavy fines if found sleeping along the road, etc. In terms of camping, if you are planning on travelling through American state or national parks, then be sure you know the grazing regulations in advance and abide by them. If permits are required, obtain them in advance.

It is almost a relief to return to the topic of traditional bandits who may merely want to rob you of your possessions, not strip you of your political liberties.

Circumstances vary too greatly from country to country to be able to issue a standard bit of advice. You must be ready to take different precautions depending upon the situation.

British Long Rider Christina Dodwell made many journeys across different parts of Africa, through the jungles of New Guinea, in the frozen taiga of Siberia, etc. No matter where she went, Christina relied upon her ability to establish a sense of common humanity and trust with the person in charge of the local town.

"In hostile territory, it is better to stay overnight in a village. The same people who would rob you in the bush are honour-bound to protect you and your possessions if you stay in their village. And there is a saying, 'It is safer inside the lion's jaws.' But don't unpack, as this creates an unfair temptation for people who have very little. If you leave your knife on a rock, it is really your fault if it disappears."

Long Riders in Mongolia have all reported how the nomads use powerful binoculars to constantly scan the steppe for signs of travellers. Thus, the landscape may look empty to you, but even though you have taken steps to camp out of sight or away from the road, your presence may have been detected without you even realizing it.

Like Christina in Africa, Tim Cope developed a practice of trying to pitch his tent close to a Mongolian nomad's ger/yurt before nightfall. He too felt that being open about his activities reduced the chances of his camp being attacked in the dark.

Bonnie Folkins has made repeated journeys in Mongolia. At first she too adhered to the idea of befriending the nomads and camping near their ger. However, several dangerous incidents taught her to readjust her thinking and camping practices.

"It is generally believed that if you see a ger and you are ready to set up camp, then you ride up and introduce yourself. The feeling is that everyone will be safer this way. This was my old way of thinking. Then while riding across the steppe with the Mongolian Long Rider Temuujin Zemuun, I was given a sharp reminder that the steppe wasn't as innocent of danger as it appeared, nor that the inhabitants should automatically be trusted."

Even though there appeared to be no one living in the vicinity for miles, when the time came to consider where to set up the tent, Bonnie mentioned to Temuujin the idea of finding a nomad family and camping nearby.

"Without hesitation he replied: 'No! Never! Not smart! People from ger get curious. Then want to visit, then want to see things, then want to drink vodka and make loud noise. Very dangerous!' So we chose a place on the brow of a hill, out of sight from the road and protected from the strong winds, yet with enough breeze to ward off mosquitoes. Then, to our great surprise, the bad weather shifted and faded in the distance. As we drove in the last tent peg, from out of nowhere, like Temuujin had warned, a nomad roared up on his motorcycle."

Curiosity and Common Courtesy

If someone visits your campsite on horseback, do not let them ride directly into the area reserved for your tent, campfire or living area. Suggest courteously that they secure their horse well away from your camp.

Standing Guard

Should you feel uneasy about your location, there are traditional safeguards which Long Riders have been practising for centuries which still hold true.

First, choose your campsite with care. In hostile country avoid camping on ground which can be overlooked or where one can be seen against the skyline.

If you don't want to be seen, avoid making a fire, remembering that a lighted match or the glow of a flashlight can be seen for a mile off.

Next, forsake the tent, as it betrays your exact location to marauders or enemies, whereas a Long Rider sleeping on the ground is difficult to locate.

Sleeping outside also heightens the chances of hearing any suspicious noises. If the camp is likely to be attacked, leave a small fire burning bright, but bed down at a safe distance away on defensible ground.

Double-check that your horses are tied safely. If they have bells, be sure they are worn on such a dangerous night.

Patrol the perimeter of the camp with a light, so that it is obvious you are aware and on guard. Make a strong mental note about the layout of the camp before you close your eyes. If you have a camp fire, have wood stacked up ready to keep it going during the length of the entire night.

Before retiring, point your saddle in the direction of where you will be travelling next morning.

Give a thought about where you lie down, as a startled man always jumps up in the direction his feet are pointing. Keep your torch/flashlight/headlamp and or your weapons close by your head. Do not take off your boots or zip up your sleeping bag.

If there is more than one of you travelling take turns standing guard, paying especial attention to the horses.

Avoiding Horse Thieves

As Bonnie and Temuujin learned, the Mongols use telescopes and binoculars to constantly scan the horizon, to study the landscape for signs of blowing dust that might denote the movement of cars, or to watch for signs of foreigners travelling with valuable horses.

Mongolia currently has a reputation where more Long Riders have their horses stolen than in any other country. Once your camp has been spotted, it is not unusual for a group of Mongols to ride to your camp, dismount and attempt to intimidate you. They usually ride away, after having carefully studied the layout of your camp and the location of your horses. Then they return after dark to steal your horses.

Mounted foreigners are often seen as rich and easy pickings. During a journey in Kazakhstan, Bonnie and two Kazakh Long Riders, Dalaikhan and Nurlan, received word that a group of ten mounted men planned to raid their camp that night.

They immediately took down the tent and by the time everything was packed up, the sun had set and night had fallen. Under cover of darkness, they rode away quietly, not stopping until they had put many miles between them and the raiders.

"After riding for at least seven miles, we put up one tent without a word or a light and all slept together – on alert all night," Bonnie recalled.

Under normal circumstances always bell your horses so you can monitor their movements by the pleasant jingling that occurs during the night.

If you suspect horse thieves may hit your camp, it is a safe precaution to keep the dominant leader of your horses saddled and picketed in camp. This will ensure that you are not left afoot. Plus, the other horses will be emotionally reluctant to leave their companion. And should you need to set off in search of your stolen horses, you can do so quickly.

One thing to keep in mind is the danger of a stampede. If horse thieves intentionally charge your horses through your camp you run the risk of being trampled to death.

The thought of having your horse stolen is a grim topic but it reinforces the idea of training your horse to respond to your private whistling or some small signal, because the horse that has learned at home that he will be rewarded with a treat when he responds to a friendly whistle is likely to come running after an emergency.

Breaking Camp

Dismantle your camp with care.

Have the horses been properly fed, watered, groomed and tacked up?

Have you remembered to cover your latrine? Have you cleaned up the area where the horses were picketed, kicking apart any piles of manure?

Did you pour water on your campfire to make sure it was out cold?

Have you packed away any trash, ready to carry it away and leave the campsite clean for the next traveller?

Did you remember to walk through the campsite one last time to make sure small articles may not have been mislaid or trampled into the dirt?

Summary

You may think that camping out with your horse is going to be a quiet affair. But it is full of surprises: the crackling of the fire, the sweet jingling of the horse's bells, the sounds of animals and birds going about their lives around you.

There is a thrill which comes from sleeping out in the open and under stars. You lie down remembering where you've come from, but knowing that like a bird on the wing tomorrow you will be gone again.

Sir Francis Younghusband was one of the most celebrated explorers of the late 19th century. As he grew older, his view of travel altered.

"When I started travelling, it was the outward aspect that interested me; now, it is the inner motive which draws me."

Camping under the stars, he wrote, "….releases us for a while from the prison of our little selves." He realized that as he stared up at the moon rise, he was seeing it with "the eyes of our forefathers" and that his restless heart had led him along "the same path which has compelled people from one century to another."

Camping, Younghusband wrote, liberates us.

"For a while we step out of the artificiality of urban existence and come a degree closer to the natural man, the state of being where wind and weather, heat and cold, hunger and thirst, earth and sky are closer to us. At the same time we are less distracted by irrelevancies. Let these thousand and one things be withdrawn and the inner world has a chance of coming into its own."

Many people are attracted to the romantic notion of travelling cross-country on horseback. Nothing illustrates the myth of this "pony picnic" idea like this drawing created in India during the days of the British Raj. Here several dashing Englishmen and an elegant memsahib can be seen enjoying life "under canvas up-country."

A startling example of the harsh reality of equestrian travel was captured on film in 1912, when Captain Johan Koch and his companion can be seen waiting for a meagre meal to cook during their gruelling equestrian journey across Greenland.

Hollywood is responsible for promoting plenty of equestrian fantasies. One of them can be seen in this 1930s film starring John Wayne. This particular fairytale involves the invisible pack horse. After chasing outlaws all day at the gallop, as if by magic Wayne and his friends are seen sitting down to a hearty meal, washed down by cups of steaming coffee. Note how Wayne's clothes, like his snow-white horse, are all spotlessly clean.

This is what real Long Riders look like. During their journey across the harsh deserts of Arizona and New Mexico, Walter Nelson (left) and Doug Preston became filthy. Doug's Levis are covered with dirt and soaked with horse sweat. There is a hole in his battered cowboy hat. Their camp is littered with all of the paraphernalia needed to survive in the harsh Despoblado Desert.

The tent provides protection from the elements, grants you independence, provides you with privacy from the prying eyes of strangers and offers a sense of safety in a world swirling with insecurity. Tim Mullan and Sam Southey found this design worked well when they rode across Mongolia, as it allowed them to stand and had plenty of room for their saddles.

Other Long Riders, like Günter Wamser (right), who rode from Patagonia to Alaska, prefer to use a tent which has separate rooms inside.

A good night's sleep will ensure that you feel emotionally rested in the morning. During her many long rides in Europe and Russia, Italian Long Rider Antonietta Spizzo has learned how important it is to have a warm, well-made sleeping bag.

Long Rider Sea G Rhydr found she preferred using a hammock during her "ocean to ocean" journey across the United States.

Most Long Riders carry a folding knife, which can be carried on their belt, and can be used for most chores. Because of the dangerous conditions which existed in Pakistan, I was licensed to carry this specially designed scimitar known as the "Asadullah Sword." A short matching dagger hung on a thong under my shirt, ready for instant use should I be attacked or kidnapped. The larger dagger I kept in my saddle bag.

One important item which is often overlooked is rope. In 1883 Swiss Long Rider Henri Moser made a remarkable ride across Russia, then on to Samarkand, Bukhara, Khiva and Tehran, before crossing the Caucasus Mountains and finally emerging at Istanbul. Then, as now, rope was a precious commodity, seldom seen, always useful and forever being stolen.

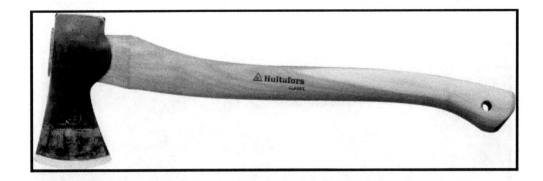

Most Long Riders do not encounter the type of problems, or timber, which require them to carry a heavy axe. The Hultafors Company makes a "classic hunting hatchet" which is light-weight, extremely tough and perfect for driving in tent pegs or picket pins.

Cooking over an open fire is increasingly restricted in some countries. American mountain man and Long Rider Hawk Hurst was lucky enough to enjoy this feast of roasted grouse and other delicacies during his ride from Mexico to Canada.

The Ortlieb Company makes a strong rectangular folding bucket which can serve many purposes, including giving a thirsty horse a drink. In addition, it can be used to wash and prepare food prior to a meal. Afterwards it serves as a sink to wash the dishes in. On rest days it can be turned into a tub to wash clothes in.

Never take it for granted that just because the water is found in the wilderness it is pure. Long Rider history is filled with stories of travellers who became ill from dysentery, intestinal parasites and hepatitis or died from cholera, typhoid and typhus lurking in impure water. Austrian Long Rider Horst Hausleitner can be seen purifying water he found in a remote water hole during his ride across Africa.

The first consideration for any campsite will be the horses. Several times Long Riders have found beautiful places to camp but rode on in favour of what would better suit the needs of their horse. Roland Berg and Sabine Matschkus found just such a place during their journey through Germany, Poland, Russia and Lithuania.

Avoiding horse thieves is a risk in some countries. While travelling alone in Pakistan from Peshawar to Chitral with my mare, Shavon, I always chose to sleep close beside her, so that I could hear her bell ringing during the night.

Chapter 73
Life on the Road

Tours or Travel

During the early 1970s a remarkable philosopher of travel named Ed Buryn wrote two books which told people how to successfully go "vagabonding." The first title was dedicated to travel in the United States. The sequel provided information about travelling in Europe and North Africa.

These were no mere "how to" guide books for hippies. They were the works of the greatest travel anarchist the late twentieth century produced. Buryn lit people's souls on fire. Decades later people are still sharing tales of how, after having read either of these two small books, they summoned up the courage to throw off the shackles of conventional life and set off in search of adventure.

Buryn didn't just liberate a generation and encourage it to travel. He was a ruthless writer who never shied away from telling his readers the harsh truth.

One of his thoughts exposes the chasm which exists between tourists and Long Riders.

"In fact people are bamboozled about travel. They love it but don't understand it. They do it but get nothing from it. The travel industry sells travel services not travel experiences. In fact the travel industry shields you from experiences because they reduce profits. Moving your body from place to place makes money but moving your heart or mind doesn't. The profits lie in conveyances that motate people, the lodgings that rotate them, and the restaurants that potate them. What happened is that an industry founded to provide travel conveniences and services has gradually convinced itself that conveniences and services are synonymous with travel. It's a lie."

Buryn left no doubt about the falsity of tourism.

"The primary damage is not on the wallet. The damage is heavy on the consciousness."

A prophet who practised what he preached, the far-roaming Buryn summed up his belief when he said, "Travel cheaply and live richly."

An Alluring Fantasy

Back in Ed Byryn's day life was still so innocent that young people routinely hitch-hiked across continents without a care about their personal safety. There was a war in Viet Nam but no never-ending "war on terror."

But times change and nostalgia shouldn't be allowed to exert an emotional influence on equestrian travel. If this book has taught you anything, it has proven that saying you're going to undertake an equestrian journey, and then successfully completing that trip, are two very different things.

To the outsider the Long Rider appears to be a romantic figure that suddenly appears as if from out of the past. This explains why strangers often express a longing to swing into the saddle and escape from the predictable drudgery of their lives.

During her ride to Scotland in 1939 Margaret Leigh was repeatedly told, "How much I envy you."

Human character doesn't change much. When Orion Kraus was riding through Central America 74 years later he heard the same deep longings, albeit in Spanish.

"When I introduced myself to people and told them about my ride, they would exclaim that they were jealous and say how it must be such a wonderful experience. I would smile and explain that it wasn't anything like the romantic image in their heads. But who was I kidding? I had started with the same idealistic vision," he wrote.

Reality versus Fantasy

Orion was right. We all painted idyllic pictures on a canvas of dreams.

But ask any seasoned equestrian traveller about what it's really like out there on the long grey road and you'll quickly get more than you bargained for.

That is because the Long Rider has learned that life changes when the horse's back becomes your only residence.

What sounded like an alluring dream has been revealed to be an ordeal.

After completing her journey across Great Britain, Vyv Wood Gee wrote, "Our idyllic vision of lazy picnic lunches dipping our feet in a stream while our ponies grazed lush grass alongside was rarely matched in reality. Slogging up and down steep mountains and struggling through deep peat bogs north of the border left little time to sit down and admire the view."

After the initial excitement has died down, you come face to face with the reality of making your slow plodding way across a vast landscape. When that moment arrives, what had sounded so thrilling in prospect in fact becomes immensely wearisome and monotonous.

This is just one of the reasons why few set off, and even fewer make it to their distant geographic goal, because there are unforeseen pitfalls waiting to demoralize an unwary Long Rider.

Knowing what lies ahead, being prepared in advance, heightens your chances of success.

What Does It Take

Prussian military strategist Field Marshal Count Helmuth von Moltke declared "no battle plan survives contact with the enemy."

No matter how hard you try to outwit life, once you swing into the saddle and set off, all of your carefully laid plans are going to be radically altered by unforeseen circumstances which are beyond your control. Equipment will break at the worst possible moment. Your beloved horses will be stolen. Trusted companions will desert. Bureaucrats will torment you with impossible demands. The list of possibilities is endless.

As the miles begin to fall behind you realize that you don't "conquer" the long grey road. It merely relents and allows you to pass, sometimes with relative ease, sometimes after demanding a terrible toll.

This is a hard task we are discussing, this equestrian travel, and it makes tremendous emotional and physical demands upon a person.

That is why even though throughout history there have been men and women who chafed under the restraints of society, who grew bored with the predictability of their existence and who longed to escape a humdrum life, more of them went to sea than ever became Long Riders.

So, you may be asking, what does it take to become a Long Rider?

Equestrian travel isn't like chemistry. There isn't an exact formula which states that so many grams of inspiration, plus a pinch of endurance, not forgetting a dash of courage will cook up a Long Rider.

But does history reveal clues? Have Historical Long Riders left behind hints? If we had to look for common qualities could we discover evidence? The answer is, yes.

If you are a person who loves comfort, conformity, routine and an active social life then you better find another way to travel, because the traditional pleasures of home must be dispensed with. Plain food becomes standard fare. There are periods of intense isolation. Exposure to hardship, suffering and various types of dangers become routine. The ability to adapt and endure is of paramount importance.

A person who undertakes an equestrian journey must be willing to forfeit the luxuries in exchange for personal liberty, outdoor excitement and the pleasure of roaming the world at will.

History demonstrates that the traveller's life is neither wildly exciting every day nor is it always monotonous, as something of interest happens every time the sun rises and sets. With experience comes the realisation that there is a balance between insecurity and tranquillity, that fear and spirituality are both found on the same journey, and that the long-term emotional compensations outweigh the immediate physical hardships.

Let us look at an equestrian journey from the perspective of its seldom-seen emotional interior, and see what Long Riders have discovered along the way.

The Benefits

Many books have been written telling readers how to tie various types of complicated knots onto the backs of hapless pack horses, or filling their heads with tales of how some dashing chap survived a series of astonishing adventures. None that I know of have thought to study the inner way of the Long Rider, to jot down the often-learned but seldom-spoken wisdom which a privileged few find and then hold close in the secret parts of their hearts.

There are in fact many incredible benefits which result from undertaking an equestrian journey. What is ironic is that though they are free to all, fewer and fewer humans partake of this privilege.

As I write this book at the dawning of the 21st century, the majority of people long to escape the mediocrity of their lives, just as their ancestors did. The planet is bursting with massive crowds of anonymous strangers, all living slightly different versions of the same dreary sameness. Monstrous cities become open air cages where citizens increasingly prefer to spend their time in the two-dimensional cyber world in an effort to escape the crushing tedium that symbolizes their predetermined lives.

Conventions must be followed. Bills must be paid. Routines must be respected. Expectations must be met. Drones must obey.

The great author Robert Louis Stevenson didn't see it that way. As far back as 1878 he told the world to get stuffed, bought a donkey named Modestine and then set off to explore France.

He wrote, "For my part, I travel not to go anywhere, but to go. I travel for travel's sake. The great affair is to move; to feel the needs and hitches of our life more nearly; to come down off this feather bed of civilization, and find the globe granite underfoot and strewn with cutting flints."

Cutting flints?

Oh, dear.

I wouldn't blame you if you were rethinking your idea about undertaking an equestrian journey. But don't be dismayed. Yes, there are challenges. But not as many, or as often, as you would expect.

Robin Hanbury-Tenison not only led twenty-four expeditions to every wild corner of the world, he is in addition one of the Founding Members of the Long Riders' Guild. What this seasoned explorer found was that the five equestrian journeys he made with his wife, Louella, differed from those expeditions which he had undertaken via other means.

During their ride along the length of the Great Wall in China, Robin made an extraordinary observation.

"I have always found on expeditions that for every one good moment there are nine bad ones when worry or discomfort predominates. The extraordinary thing about our long rides together had been that both Louella and I have found the proportions happily reversed so that nine tenths of our travel time has been supremely enjoyable. I do not believe anyone can honestly say the same for driving, walking, sailing, climbing, running, flying or any other means of travel."

The reasons for this contentment may surprise you.

Freed from Time

Thanks to advances in medical science, most humans now live far longer than their ancestors. Yet an extended life has not resulted in an increase of personal liberty. It has created a life style that is dominated by clocks and calendars. Instead of slowing down, modern humanity is increasingly in a hurry.

I'm not Einstein. Nor do I have any scientific pretensions. Yet equestrian travel history seems to demonstrate, for reasons I cannot intellectually explain, that time passes at a different pace during the course of a long horse trip.

First it seems to slow, as you find yourself sliding back into an ancient rhythm which, having been buried deep within your DNA, has been awakened from its slumber.

The pace of life on the horse proceeds so leisurely that the notion of time begins to become an abstraction. You are no longer chained to your watch. You're too busy observing the seasons. You are not anxiously awaiting the arrival of a text message. You've rediscovered the stars. You are not confined within four walls. You've become aware of the four directions.

The former demands of the world begin to melt away as you realize you are no longer a servant to words like boss, taxes and mortgages. A sense of exaltation begins to creep into your life. You realize that you are not travelling "back in time" in the nostalgic sense. You're riding in a world where sunrise and sunset matter.

The Welsh Long Rider Thurlow Craig wrote about how he made this accidental disconnection from time.

During one of his many journeys across the pampas in the 1920s, he observed, "The sun was shining brightly, it was a beautiful cool morning and there seemed to be quite a lot of scenery scattered around the landscape. I rode along playing a tune on the harmonica, thinking that there could be no better way of living than to travel, well mounted and equipped, in places I had never been before. There is something particularly exhilarating in the thought that you are going somewhere, but you don't know where, nor is there any hurry to get there. You are not working for anybody, not even yourself, and schedule is just a word in the dictionary and can stay there as far as you are concerned. You are not obliged to return over the same road, it is just a question of people and places passing before you. Hello. Good-bye. Gone. Maybe forever. But never mind, there is at present much more in front of you than you can yet have left behind. There will come a day when that is not so, and then you will live on memories. Now is the time to store up treasure, that then you will be able to mumble with toothless gums at your grandchildren, and inform them with a senile cackle that you have lived."

Personal Liberty

Your freedom extends beyond the release of any obligation to the clock.

Travelling on horseback grants you the liberty to explore the country as and where you wish. You are not restricted to the road. You are can detour and linger. You don't speed across the countryside encased in a metal cocoon. You are a moving part of a living landscape. You are not disconnected from humanity. Your need for grass, water and shelter brings you into constant contact with the lives of common people.

You are not an interloper. You are free.

Most people never experience this sense of breathtaking liberty. They never escape the world of man-made regulations.

Katie Russell did when she rode her mustang from Washington to Montana in the summer of 2011.

"We are halfway through the journey but the days are flying by. This feels like Life with a capital L. I keep singing, 'How you gonna keep her down on the farm, after she's been so free?'"

Half a world away, Tim Cope had found the same freedom out on the steppes of Kazakhstan.

"Some of the most impressionable times for me were when I was out alone with my three horses and dog, riding through a clear expanse of treeless plains, feeling as if I was etching out a path through the canvas of my own dream. To think that no one ahead knew I was coming, no one was expecting me, and in fact, no one but I knew we existed in that moment was a liberating experience, as if I had managed to break free of the parameters of our normal world that is so defined by time and place."

Reducing Your Needs

One of the earliest lessons any Long Rider learns is, "The more you know, the less you need."

This philosophy flies in the face of most modern lifestyles.

Anthropologists have recently completed a study which documented the number of possessions owned by average American families. Urged on by the demands of a commercial society, modern homes and lives are cluttered with mountains of items.

One of the authors of the study wrote, "The first household assemblage we analyzed resulted in a tally of 2,260 visible possessions in the first three rooms and that didn't include untold numbers of items tucked into dresser drawers, boxes and cabinets or items positioned behind other items."

During my own journeys in Pakistan and Afghanistan I observed people who, though they had remarkably few possessions, were undeniably happy. Not only did they demonstrate a sense of contentment with life which I had not observed in the United States, their sense of self-respect was not defined by the ownership of objects.

Long Riders learn to be content with very little. They have broken the chains which linked them to objects that previously dominated their existence. They have replaced consumerism with simplicity. They have realized the pointlessness of filling our outer existence with things, if our inner lives are empty.

Disconnecting from the World

Previous generations of Long Riders realized that the further they travelled, the stronger grew the feeling that they were becoming increasingly disentangled from the activities of the rest of the world.

For some, there was a gradual inkling that the journey had taken them to an unexpected emotional place in their lives.

Leonard Clark had been a hardened adventurer before the Second World War and the leader of a guerrilla underground during that conflict. Yet once the war was won, and he found himself lying on his back one night looking up at the stars blazing over Tibet, even Clark was moved by the realization of how far he had come from everything, and every place, he had previously known.

"The jangle of the bells on the necks of the quietly grazing horses spelled contentment for us on that glorious blue shining moon-illuminated night. All was quiet under the stars. There was a smell of night-moisture on the air. I felt myself being lulled into a peaceful state of mind. It is during moments such as this that the traveller receives wages for his work," Clark wrote.

The further one rides, the more often one finds that links to the outside world have been severed.

Charles Darwin recalled the deep impression a night he slept under the stars in Patagonia made upon him. He says the cold blue-looking sky, the stars, the silence, the horses feeding tied to their picket pins, and the sense of being cut off from all mankind, appealed to him more than the beauty of the tropics, the grandeur of the Andes or anything that he remembered on his travels.

Don Roberto Cunninghame Graham experienced this sense of disconnection while making his ride across the mountains of Morocco.

"By travelling a man, although his purse grows light, lays up treasures on which to live when he is old. What is a governor, compared to he who is Sultan of the world, when wherever night catches him, he rests and looks upon the stars? Stranger still how in a week or so the newspapers and books, the so-called intellectual conversation, news of the outside world, the theatres, churches, politics, and the things which by their aggregated littleness, taken together, seem important, fall out of one's life. The condition of one's horse, the weather, the storm, or coming revolution, all take their places and become as important as were the unimportant great events which a short time ago, served up distorted in an evening paper, wiled away our time."

Like Don Roberto, you may find that you've lost touch with the news and no longer care about the daily events that keep the world's curiosity entranced.

A startling example of this occurred on September 11, 2001, when two hijacked aircraft smashed into the World Trade Centre in New York and a third hit the Pentagon.

Edouard Chautard was making a ride deep through the back country of the island nation of New Caledonia, when he was made aware of events connected to the outside world.

"On September 11th, I was far away from everything. I was on the way to a small village to re-shoe one of my horses. Nothing in the world could bother me, I thought. But after arriving back in 'civilization,' I got caught again by the news of what had happened in New York," Edouard wrote.

Like other Long Riders before him, Edouard had reached a point where he had been preoccupied with following the journey of the sun, not the progress of the daily news.

Health Benefits

Others will not only envy your freedom but your health.

The Roman philosopher Seneca reportedly said, "Inaction weakens the body, exercise fortifies it."

Whether Seneca really said that or not, what is known is that by the late 19th century horseback riding was widely believed to improve one's health.

Captain John Codman was a celebrated author who, though in his 70s, was still making equestrian journeys across New England, sometimes during the height of winter. In his books, Codman praised the benefits of "equestrianopathy."

"I have been saying for years how amazing it is that horsemen invariably look much younger than they are," he wrote.

Nor was he the only advocate of healthy horse riding.

In France at the same time, Dr. Ghislani Durant published an important book entitled, *Horseback Riding from a Medical Point of View*.

"I concede that walking is an immeasurably fine invention," Durant wrote. "But saddle leather is preferable to shoe leather."

Durant then went on to list the various therapeutic effects derived from horseback riding.

"In the act of horseback riding, man follows the motions of the movable basis which supports him. Each time the animal which he sits upon alters its position the movements of impulse given to the body of the animal cause a displacement which is communicated to the rider. There is not perhaps a single muscle which does not come into play in horseback riding."

Durant also believed that "horseback riding restores and maintains harmony. The heart beats more quickly from the quickened motion of the blood." As a result, he said, riding "dispels ennui."

Codman and Durant both agreed that horseback riding stimulated the appetite.

But history is packed with stories of how strong and healthy Long Riders became during their journeys.

Gordon Naysmith was already a hardened tri-athlete prior to setting off to ride from South Africa to Germany. When he began the journey, Gordon weighed 85 kilos (187 pounds). By the end of the journey his weight had dropped to 56 kilos (123 pounds).

Many other Long Riders have also noted how much weight they lost during their journeys.

But Mefo Phillips put it best when she wrote, "We're as lean as lurchers, bursting with the good health that comes of being outside in the open for sixteen hours a day."

Not only will you become physically hardened; as your health improves your spirits will soar. One of the results of feeling stronger, inside and out, is an increased sense of self-respect.

A Heightened Sense of Intuition

One of the most well-known stories found in *Tschiffely's Ride* explains how the Swiss Long Rider realized that his horse, Gato, possessed the uncanny ability to detect and avoid quicksand. As the legendary ride progressed, over mountains, through deserts and across jungles, Tschiffely learned to rely not just on the horse's instincts but his own.

A sceptic might be tempted to dismiss Gato's abilities and actions as nothing more than luck. But other horses have demonstrated similar skills and other Long Riders have learned to trust them.

Evelyne Coquet made a series of equestrian journeys in the 1970s to various parts of the world. While riding through a bog-ridden part of Scotland, she nearly came to grief, until she learned to heed her horse.

"I feel that when a close relationship has built up between rider and horse, it is easy to tell the difference between a horse that is playing up and one who senses danger ahead. I have also noticed that many times, when deciding which route to take in the mountains, my mare always knows the best way to go and I should listen to her. If I make the decision myself, I have frequently found myself in a dead-end situation, whereas the route my mare wanted to take originally is always the right one!"

Other Long Riders also realized there was an inner voice at play whose existence they had either not suspected or had ignored. One such example happened in Canada. After having made several rides across that country, Long Rider Catherine Thompson realised the relationship with her horses had deepened because she had changed.

"My knowledge of how to deal with the horses was much stronger this year. Every day I learned to listen more deeply to my inner and outer instincts; learned to listen to my horses, where their ears pointed, the sudden tension that I would feel from Dakota below me and Coco behind," Catherine said.

What some have merely suspected, Jeremy James put into words and committed to paper.

In a special message composed while I was working on this book, Jeremy wrote to express his belief in how important intuition was to a Long Rider.

"I have had occasion over the past few days to be thinking about your *Encyclopaedia of Equestrian Exploration* and what a marvellous thing it is going to be.

While thinking about it, I began to ask myself questions about the whole business of horses and travel and thought that if I had to sum up what was the most centrally important aspect of the entire business, it would be, from my own experience anyway, to depend entirely and without reservation upon one's intuition.

I am quite sure you will have written about this and anybody of any sense would have found the same, but I strongly suspect there are many who set off without any real appreciation of how far intuition and intuition alone can take them. It not only gets you the right horse, but also sets your course.

Do you not recall riding through dense woodland or coming to places where you had a distinct feeling that to go down that particular way was dangerous? That there was something down there that was a threat and believing that, went the other way? I have; a lot. On the occasions I hadn't followed my intuition, I invariably became stuck.

It is as true on entering a village. Once you lay yourself open to the power of intuition, then any entrance to a village will let you grasp instantly what manner of people live in it and whether this is going to be a good place for you to stay or best to be on the other side.

I have realised that intuition can lead you to water, to feed and even to knowing when would be the optimum time to hit a frontier. I have had that experience too.

I remember waiting on the bridge at Ruse between Bulgaria and Romania, just standing at one end of it waiting because I sensed the guards on the far end were not going to let me pass. I stayed there for most of the night and then early in the morning, when I was certain the guards had changed, I took the bridge and I was right. There was a youngish guard on duty and when he saw me coming he got out of his hut and watched. When I handed him my passport and all of my horse's vet certificates he just waved me through and said something to the effect that I was lucky it was him, because the earlier guards might not have been as accommodating.

We slipped through like shadows and left no mark.

For my money, it's understanding the intuitive process that turns the whole exercise into something very fine, very gentle and lifts it from what might otherwise be a bothersome journey blighted by constant irritations and endless goings wrong, to one that becomes sublime and almost without effort.

The trick of course is to allow it to happen. Not to force it. So that in a short time, one becomes more and more keenly attuned to it and then it just becomes a matter of fact thing, you do it wholly automatically, and in no time you will be taking paths, tracks, diversions that no map, nor any guide could have put you as safely upon as your own innate instinct.

So there we go: above all things, intuition is the Long Rider's true astrolabe," Jeremy concluded.

In Touch with Nature

The Long Rider does not dominate his environment; he belongs to it. He greets Nature as a communion not a conqueror. He blends with the countryside. He feels his surroundings intensely.

Sadly, many millions of people will never experience the divine mystery which Nature inspires. Statistics reveal, for example, that fewer than half of British adults have ever started a campfire or ridden a horse. Robbed of their traditions, urbanized humans have lost touch with an essential part of our common heritage.

One of the benefits of being a Long Rider is the ability to re-establish relationships with earth, wind, fire and water.

German Long Rider Emil Trinkler discovered in the 1920s that it was the sights, sounds and smells of the remote mountains in Afghanistan that brought a sense of beauty and mystery into his life and travels.

"The afternoon sun was hot; we were surrounded by impenetrable mountains, but the higher we went the further we could see and the freer we felt. I have never felt as well as I felt there, where everything was unique, and where one could neither see nor hear anything human," he recalled.

Trinkler continued, "It is only when alone with Nature that man can understand it, whether it be in the high hills or in the deserts, by the sea or in the woods. It is only when we are free from everyday life and face to face with Nature that we appreciate the greatness of the universe. It is then that we realize what harm civilization has done for us and what a sad life, on the whole, we are compelled to lead, which makes us the more thankful when we are able to escape and become true men, finding inspiration once more in Nature."

Many a would-be Long Rider has wanted to set off so as to experience such daytime events; to discover the drops of morning dew glistening like pearls on a spider's web, to witness the dancing of the trees in an afternoon wind, to see the birds winging their way home through the declining sunshine.

But these are the blessings of the day.

There is another benefit of being a Long Rider; to be a part of the timeless night-time world as well.

Rediscovering the Night

It was an American naturalist named Henry Beston who wrote, "Nature is part of our humanity, and without some awareness of that divine mystery man ceases to be man."

Having been traumatized by his experiences during the First World War, Beston sought refuge in a small cabin situated on a remote beach along Cape Cod. With no neighbours for miles around, he sought spiritual retreat among the sounds of the waves and calls of the sea birds.

Beston made many observations which later went on to influence the birth of the environmental movement. He it was who warned that mechanized mankind had lost touch with the moon's sacred majesty and become afraid of the beauties of the night.

In his book, *The Outermost House*, Beston cautioned, "Our fantastic civilization has fallen out of touch with many aspects of nature, and with none more completely than with night. Primitive folk, gathered at a cave mouth round a fire, do not fear night; they fear, rather, the energies and creatures to whom night gives power; we of the age of the machines, having delivered ourselves of nocturnal enemies, now have a dislike of night itself. With lights and ever more lights, we drive the holiness and beauty of night back to the forests and the sea; the little villages, the crossroads even, will have none of it. Are modern folk, perhaps, afraid of night? Do they fear that vast serenity, the mystery of infinite space, the austerity of stars? Having made themselves at home in a civilization obsessed with power, which explains its whole world in terms of energy, do they fear at night for their dull acquiescence and the pattern of their beliefs? Be the answer what it will, to-day's civilization is full of people who have not the slightest notion of the character or the poetry of night, who have never even seen night. Yet to live thus, to know only artificial night, is as absurd and evil as to know only artificial day."

House dwellers view the night as a period of dark monotony. Long Riders who lie down upon mother earth look up and see a bright shining universe moving overhead. A special pleasure comes from realizing you are staring in wonder at the same bright points of light which amazed your predecessors.

That thought occurred to Gabriel Bonvalot, the French Long Rider who journeyed across Tibet in 1889. Lying down to rest on "the roof of the world," he wrote, "It is not long before we roll ourselves up in our rugs, and with the earth for a mattress, the sky for a ceiling, and the moon for a night-light, we ask for nothing better."

Twin Souls

There is one other remarkable benefit which I would be remiss not to mention: the astonishing emotional bond which springs up between horse and human.

To the uninitiated the horse is nothing more than an archaic form of transportation or a potential beast of burden. Such individuals have forgotten that many of the wise have recognized the close links between our species and our animal neighbours.

The Qu'ran, for example, reminds man that, "There is not an animal that lives on the earth, nor a being that flies on its wings, but they form communities like you."

As with numerous other injunctions prescribed in the Qu'ran, many Muslims fail to respect the rule which states that it is forbidden in Islam to treat an animal cruelly. Islam reminds man that animals are creatures with feelings. Their lives are to be considered worthwhile and to be cherished. They are to be treated with respect and kindness.

The fact that this wisdom is so often blatantly ignored says much about the arrogance of fools, confirms the cruelty of individual men, and verifies their lack of fear of any sort of Divine retribution.

There is no need to pretend that horses and humans are exactly alike. Horses live in a parallel universe to ours, where even though they are gifted like humans with sight, smell, hearing and touch, they comprehend the world differently, both as a species and as individuals.

It is the journey which draws the two species together. Unlike a brief sporting event, the trip requires horse and human to create a long-term inter-species relationship that allows them to survive as they search together for food, water and shelter. There is no other equestrian activity which requires the team to spend so much time engaged in an activity that is so geographically exotic, emotionally complex and stimulating to the senses.

The journey forces the horse and human to become immersed in the same world. They suffer the pangs of hunger together and then rejoice over a meal. They face the same perils with the same chances of escape or annihilation. They endure the same dreadful weather. They wander towards the same distant goal.

According to legend, Merlin transformed the boy King Arthur into different animals to enlarge his perception.

Journeys demonstrate that though man may not become horse, he has the capability to understand him. Though they do not speak in the same tongue, after having endured hunger, cold and danger, horses and humans achieve a state of mutual tranquillity that is deep and profound.

Many a Long Rider has returned from the journey humbled, after having realized that the equine slave he originally thought merely to ride ended up being the teacher who carried him step by step towards wisdom.

As Gato demonstrated to Aimé Tschiffely, horses often become our teachers in regards to the dangers of the physical world around us.

But there is another factor which results from being in his company. The horse is a sentient being. The further you travel with him, the stronger becomes his deep commitment and constant emotional support for you.

Once again, it was Aimé Tschiffely who recognized that even though a Long Rider may travel alone, he does not experience the desperate loneliness which many city dwellers often endure.

"I have been asked countless times if I did not find it boring and lonely to be on my own out in the wilds. I never felt the slightest dull when I was alone. I never wanted for better company than Mancha and Gato," he recalled.

Long Riders have also noted how their horses exhibited what is commonly believed to be another trait restricted to man: i.e. loyalty.

Baron Fukushima recorded the intense sense of allegiance his horses felt for each other. When one horse became sick and began to fall behind, the other horses stopped and refused to advance until their ill partner had caught up.

"I think the horses are like humans in that once you have similar goals, a bond is created and they worked together as brothers. The love shared between the horses is the same as that of a parent towards his children. The shared feelings between human and horse was the glue that held us together over the many difficult times and what made the journey a success," he wrote.

The wise Japanese Long Rider later explained that his amazing journey from Berlin to Tokyo could never have been accomplished by his desire alone, but only through the strong resolve of his horses.

This isn't to say that all horses are wise, loyal, kind, charitable, forgiving and just, no more than are all men. There are villains in both species.

But some horses have virtues which raise them above the common herd.

Though the Hindu Vedas, the Jewish Torah, the Christian Bible and the Muslim Qu'ran do not say so, by every law of logic and anatomy, if the soul exists, then the horse has as much a right to it as man.

Thus, as these various examples demonstrate, there are a number of benefits which may be gained from undertaking an equestrian journey.

Of course there are the practicalities of making the miles.

Emotional Readjustment

Departing on a long equestrian journey requires the traveller to learn new lessons and to readjust emotionally. The first such requirement is to move forward with eagerness, instead of looking back with homesickness.

In 1857 exploration author Francis Galton made this poignant observation, "Unless a traveller makes himself at home and comfortable in the bush, he will never be quite contented with his lot, but will fall into the bad habit of looking forwards to the end of his journey, and to his return to civilization, instead of complacently interesting himself in its continuance. This is a frame of mind in which few great journeys have been successfully accomplished; an explorer who cannot divest himself of it may suspect that he has mistaken his vocation."

Galton then warned would-be travellers.

"Make the bush your home. Interest yourself chiefly in the progress of your journey, and do not look forward to its end with eagerness. It is better to think of a return to civilization, not as an end to hardship and a haven from ill, but as a close to an adventurous and pleasant life."

No matter where you plan to ride, it is impossible to predict life. Because things never proceed exactly as predicted, a Long Rider must learn to keep worries in perspective.

"The most important thing my first long ride taught me was to stop worrying," remembered Bonnie Folkins after her return from Mongolia. "For the first 16 days, I did nothing but worry. The worry made me almost sick. I was anticipating things that never happened. I was not getting any sleep. I had to come to terms with the situation because the worry was affecting the quality of my life."

She advised, "Any time you see the quality of your life being affected or downgraded – halt – reassess – and tell yourself that whatever the thing is that is dragging you down has to be stopped."

Daily Schedule

Life on the road with horses requires one to adjust to a new set of circumstances and to learn to divide the day into four sections. Many have written about it but none summarized it as neatly as did Edwin Lord Weeks, who rode across Persia in 1892.

"The routine of daily life is a little trying at first, but easily learned; each twenty-four hours is divided into four parts, the period of hurry and activity in the early morning, a longer one of comparative tranquillity on the march, the brief hour of bustle on arriving at our destination, and then, nirvana, the dreaminess of sleep of the night."

Modern long rides may vary to some degree, but most of what Weeks wrote still applies today. To rise early is essential. As soon as the horses are watered and enjoying their morning feed, the traveller grabs a quick bite himself. If the tent has been used, then it must be packed away and the equipment prepared for departure. The horses are groomed, tacked up and standing ready. A last walk round the camp is made for lost or forgotten articles. Then it's time to mount and march.

Chances to graze during the day are never forsaken. A mid-day meal allows horses and humans both a chance to rest and refresh themselves. Then the trip continues until the early afternoon, at which time the necessity of choosing a camp site or finding shelter takes precedence.

It is a life that requires physical strength and emotional effort, so most Long Riders retire early and sleep deeply.

Rest Days

Travel is hard work, both physically and emotionally. That is why it is vitally important that every opportunity be taken to conserve the energy of the horses and riders.

Gabriel Bonvalot, whose legendary journey took him from Paris to Indochina, via Siberia and Tibet, understood the need to proceed with caution.

"Once the journey is commenced, no one is entitled to be intent upon anything but the discovery of the route; he has no right to tire his horse, to display his energy, to exhaust his strength, or to take a step which does not contribute toward the success of the enterprise. My companions have no difficulty in persuading themselves that the art of travelling may be defined, paradoxically, yet very accurately, as the art of resting," Bonvalot wrote.

Horses and humans must both rest.

Baron Fukushima wrote wisely, "The horses cannot speak. They can say nothing. But don't think they are unaware of the hardship they endure."

Travelling horses are unlike their soft cousins who reside in safe stables. After so many miles, so many mountain passes, so many deserts, so many hardships, so many miles, a road horse will learn to walk into a strange corral, eat his fill and then lie down and calmly go to sleep. Their overall condition depends on constant feeding, adequate stabling and enough rest to offset the hazards and hardships of the road.

While it's obvious that certain journeys will require horses to face physical hardships, such as crossing over high mountains, there is such a thing as emotional distress which also affects travelling horses.

Mary Bosanquet was the first to note and write about this back in 1939.

"One of the factors which make a long distance ride very hard on a horse is the fact that he has so little fun. A healthy horse, like a healthy human being, enjoys physical self-expression. He likes to go out prancing in the morning, play up a little, and show off to the other horses. But on a long distance trip he cannot do these things. He finds that it does not pay to waste his energy pawing in the valley. He must buckle down to the road and go steadily from the moment he starts out, if he does not want to be dead tired by the evening," Mary wrote.

As Mary accurately noted, road horses do not have a place where they can live safely and do as they like. Unless granted time to physically rest and emotionally recover, they will wear down and wear out.

Modern Long Riders should also pay special heed to the need to allow their horses to have quiet time – away from noisy humans.

As fewer and fewer equestrian travellers are seen on the road, it is not uncommon for large crowds to gather round them upon their arrival. What seems like a warm welcome to the Long Rider can become an emotional burden to a horse who is tired after a long day's travel.

Mary Pagnamenta wrote about the emotional toll it took on her horses after being patted and hugged by crowds of enthusiastic school children in New Zealand. Sea G Rhydr noticed that as the miles climbed on her journey across America, her pack horse grew so weary of being the centre of attention that she began laying her ears back in warning.

You must always give the horses an appropriate number of rest days so as to recuperate emotionally and physically.

Nor will you regret stopping yourself, as it won't take long before you become overworked by the demands of travel, the physical labour of horse care and the emotional stress which comes from dealing with a constant stream of strangers.

In 1857 English Long Rider Fanny Duberly rode across India, under horrific conditions, in the company of the British cavalry. She observed, "I do not know one of my acquaintances back home who can thoroughly appreciate a day of rest. When a halt day comes I cannot rest enough. Oh, the inappreciable luxury of a whole clear day, with no reveille to disturb me at two in the morning, no sleepy horses to rouse up and saddle, no tent to strike, no dusty march starting at dawn."

Fast forward to 2013 and another English Long Rider, Mefo Phillips, noted how little the requirements of equestrian travel had changed in all those long years.

"Oh what bliss, what decadence," Mefo wrote, "to lie in bed beyond 5:30 a.m."

Most Long Riders agree that one day off is not enough for either the horse or the rider. The horse does not have time for sufficient rest and feed, while the rider rushes about on his "day off", going shopping, doing laundry etc.

The first day the horse eats as much as he can, the second day he rests. The first day the Long Rider attends to overdue chores, the second day is when he too rests.

Chose your rest days carefully. Many Long Riders travel for five days and then stop during the weekend. This allows them to avoid the heavy weekend traffic.

But do not think that this is a rule carved in stone. Horses are not motorized transport. You have to keep a careful eye on them.

When he began his extensive ride from Mongolia to Hungary, Tim Cope used the five days, two days off rule, but learned that he had to adapt.

"In the initial stages of my journey, I was trying to travel too fast by horse by sticking to a five days on and two off schedule. But I learned that in the steppe, time is not measured by days, weeks or hours but the fall of the seasons and condition of the animals."

If you are travelling at high altitudes, in great heat or where the terrain is very challenging, then you may wish to consider riding for only four days, and then let your horses rest. The point is to be flexible, adapt to local conditions, but to always give your horses the chance to rest and relax as and when they need to.

Surprisingly, many Long Riders have written about how eager they become to return to the saddle and resume their journey. After spending time in agitated movement, attending to duties, collecting mail, and restocking supplies, often amidst large groups of people who make emotional demands, it is a pleasure to return to the calm of a life in the saddle.

Chores

I've spoken about chores before, but that was in the context of camping.

There is much more involved in horse travel than most people suspect. In fact you will find that the daily ritual of travel will include many things, but never boredom.

There is always something to be done, some task awaiting your attention or some concern nibbling at the back of your mind. It's not the easygoing pony picnic those at home think it is.

Cliff Kopas set off in June of 1933 with his bride, Ruth, to make a 1,500 mile honeymoon trip across the wilderness of western Canada. All they possessed were five horses and $2.65 in cash. But they had a dream and found it. Cliff wrote about how they spent a rainy rest day doing their "three R's," writing, resting and repairing.

Previous generations of equestrian travellers realized that the journey would require them to work hard.

German Long Rider Alfred Wegener was with the Danish expedition that crossed Greenland in 1912. He wrote, "For me, this expedition is surely very valuable. While before, I did have a certain type of energy, which here, for the purpose of comparison, I must call moral energy. Here, I am learning practical energy, the energy of activity. All these things that seem so unimportant, for example washing ourselves daily, overcoming an obstacle, irrelevant of what exactly it is, all these small things that make up daily life are things from which you can learn what practical energy is."

Horse travel demands daily labour on the part of the Long Rider. But as the Danish equestrian philosopher and author, Bjarke Rink, has noted in his book, *The Rise of the Centaurs*, "As city bred people develop urban culture, they automatically suffer a massive loss of ecological intelligence, which is ultimately the capacity to understand and survive in the natural environment."

In his study Rink explains that members of ancient mounted nomad cultures were "more interested in getting things done than in quarrelling over who did what."

These were tough travellers who lived a frugal life. To travel efficiently they learned to smooth out difficulties that occurred on the trail. This ancient principle still applies today. No one is exempt. Everyone pulls together.

Keeping the modern expedition moving smoothly will require you to manage your time efficiently. That is why the so-called "rest day" will usually find a Long Rider washing clothes that smell of horse sweat, shopping, making telephone calls, sending emails and updating a blog.

Use your rest days wisely, concentrating on accomplishing one set of tasks at each stop.

If you are travelling in a foreign country, then consider the extra time required to communicate in a different language and the patience needed to negotiate with an alien culture. Under such conditions, accomplishing one major task or objective a day is a reasonable expectation.

The romance rapidly fades when equipment breaks, your clothes tear, the tent needs patching and items need mending.

There is always a never-ending number of routine tasks which must be done on a regular basis. They include repacking or reducing the equipment, checking saddles for wear, saddle-soaping all the leather, cleaning the bit and exposing the saddle pads to the sun.

When the moment comes to stitch a broken girth or sew on a button, you don't want to waste time fumbling about.

That is why Robin Hanbury-Tenison wisely warned, "It was important that everyone knew exactly where everything was supposed to be. Nothing is more frustrating than looking for a vital spanner at a moment of crisis and finding it has made its way into the cooking box. This also meant we could unpack rapidly on arriving somewhere we were going to camp, and even more importantly, repack efficiently in the morning."

Dealing with the Mail

Previous generations of Long Riders were often out of touch for long periods of time. Not only were they isolated in remote geographic locations, when the rare chance came to visit a post office there was no guarantee that the traveller's letter would ever leave the building.

Before setting off to explore the Chaco jungle in 1900, British Long Rider George Ray attempted to post a letter home to England to inform his family of his safe arrival in South America. His experiences at the main post in Paraguay did not match the standards he had seen practised back in Great Britain.

"When I called at the post office of the capital I discovered another surprise. Upon asking for a stamp, the civil answer from the clerk was that he had none. On the lucky days they were available, the customer was also handed a brush and pot of paste and told to attach it himself. If you ask for a one cent stamp the clerk will cut a two cent stamp and give you a half," Ray recalled.

Today's world permits a stream of constant communications. People are no longer out of touch for months or years. Text messages, emails, mobile phone technology all allow a Long Rider to maintain contact with family and friends.

Yet occasions still arise when a visit to the post office in a foreign country is required, especially when physical documents, money orders, film, equipment etc., must be either sent or delivered.

Some countries maintain a reputation for widespread postal theft. This usually involves postal employees pilfering items from packages. In such nations, it is always safer to have documents and items transferred in a country by a professional delivery company such as UPS or DHL, as they track the progress of the package and ensure its safety en route.

Another common swindle is to steal the stamps off a traveller's envelope. In this case the clerk sells a traveller the stamps needed to send an envelope. Once the unsuspecting customer has left the counter, the clerk peels the stamps off, throws away the traveller's letter, and resells the same stamps to the next naïve foreign dupe.

Always make sure that you see the stamps firmly affixed to the envelope. Then demand that the postage be "franked," i.e. stamped with an official seal, in front of you. This guarantees that the stamps are no longer valid and will ensure that they stay on your envelope.

If postage theft and tales of widespread postal corruption are especially rampant, then contact the consul or embassy of your country and ask them to help send or receive your mail.

Another custom which has been practised by travellers for generations is to have letters sent on ahead to a distant post office. Such correspondence is known as "Poste Restante," a French term meaning "post remaining." The English describe this practice as "General Delivery." Regardless of the term used, it refers to the tradition of the post office holding a traveller's mail in safety until his arrival.

The amount of time post will be held differs according to the country. France will hold a letter for only 15 days. Australia extends the service for a month. Other countries hold letters for months on end.

To ensure that your letters arrive via poste restante, it is vitally important that they be properly addressed. Customs differ from one country to the next.

Some countries demand nothing more complex than:

Name of Recipient

Poste Restante

City, Country, Postal Code

Other countries, Australia for example, are more exact. To deliver a letter to, say, Adelaide, you would mark the envelope:

Name of Recipient

C/O Poste Restante

GPO Adelaide

SA 5000

Australia

No matter what country the letter is sent to, make sure the sender prints the words "Hold Until Arrival" along the bottom of the front and back of the envelope.

You can't just walk into any local post office and ask for your mail. It is important to determine in advance which post office in the city handles letters sent poste restante. Branch offices do not offer this service. It is handled by the GPO, meaning General Post Office, i.e. the main post office for that city.

You will be required to present proof of your identity, such as your passport, before your post is handed over.

Pocket Money

Long Riders often express surprise at how inexpensive this method of travel can be.

During his ride along the Oregon Trail back in 1949, John Beard noted, "We found that we did not need much money on the trail but that we did need thick skins and a keen sense of humour."

However every Long Rider has expenses.

Beginning in 1912 Long Riders hit on an ethical way in which to raise a little pocket money. Before setting off on their 33,000 kilometres (20,352 miles) journey to all 48 US state capitals, George Beck and his three fellow Overland Westerners, had a small postcard published. One side showed a map of their route. The obverse side showed Pinto, the Morab gelding who made the entire remarkable trip.

During the nearly three years that Beck and his friends were in the saddle, they would sell these postcards to curious strangers, hosts, supporters and friends they met along the way. The cost of a card depended upon the generosity of the buyer, but the amount normally varied between 5 cents and was hardly ever more than 25 cents. Nevertheless this small influx of loose change helped pay for grain and other small daily expenses.

When Messanie Wilkins set off to ride "ocean to ocean" in 1952, she departed with the lordly sum of $37, which she had made from selling homemade bottled pickles to her neighbours. She too hit on the idea of having a post card published. Like Beck, Messanie used the money to take care of her horse.

Publishing a post card is not an expensive proposition. They are small and weigh very little. Plus a supply of postcards can be sent on ahead and be awaiting your arrival at the Poste Restante in the next large town you visit.

If the card is adorned with a photo of you and your horse, as well as some explanatory information, it adds an air of authenticity to your tale when you meet strangers. Plus, the purchase of a post card will serve as a physical souvenir of your visit, especially if you sign, date, and inscribe a personal message to the person who has supported you via this small act of generosity or acted as a host for the night.

Your Diary

Few people set off on equestrian journeys. Even fewer ever write a book after they return. Keeping an accurate diary is critically important if you plan to express yourself by means of literature.

But your diary need not be seen as a potential form of profit. It is also a precious family document which will provide future generations with valuable information about your experiences and challenges. Not to mention the fact that glancing back at the travel-stained pages in the years to come will reward you with a flood of memories.

The rapid advancement of various types of new electronic communication devices has enabled people to jot down and instantly publish their random thoughts on every topic under the sun. But composing a text message which can only contain a maximum of 200 characters is not the same as having the discipline to write up a daily diary which contains vital details.

Riding all day is hard work. That is why making yourself sit down and update your diary requires discipline.

During his ride across India in 1947, Malcolm Darling explained what a tough task it was to set pen to paper after a long day in the saddle.

"A day's halt after much marching is an agreeable interlude, but there was plenty to do. I've never been so busy for so long. Every evening the day's doings have to be recorded in my diary and that is rarely finished before eleven. But the joy of the road never flags and each day brings fresh knowledge and a new experience."

Robin Hanbury-Tenison is the author of five equestrian travel books, not to mention many other books concerning exploration and conservation. During an interview about his long career as an explorer, Robin was asked, "What equipment do you always take on your journeys?"

Without hesitation, he replied, "The most important thing to take is a notebook, which should be written on each evening – at least two full pages describing what happened that day. If you don't do that you might as well not bother with the ride. Not only will you rapidly forget, but no one else will be able to share it."

Heed Robin's words well.

Don't rely on the treacherous notebook of your memory.

One Long Rider warned, "Never stir without paper and pen. Commit to paper whatever you see, hear or read that is remarkable, with your observations on observing it. Do this upon the spot, if possible, at the moment it first strikes, at all events do not delay it beyond the first convenient opportunity, for circumstances which often appear trifling to the traveller are very interesting to friends and readers. I have found since returning home that for want of a stricter attention to the above, that where I omitted to write down the details my memory almost entirely fails me and I have only a vague recollection of places I passed through."

Writing up your observations every evening is an important task. If you're maintaining a diary/journal then you should update it while the day's events are fresh in your mind. Avoid abbreviations. Write clearly, making sure to note the date and time of events. Record the name of the town, no matter how small or apparently insignificant. Ask for people's names and be sure to spell them correctly. Make notes about the availability of feed and water, for the possible use of other Long Riders.

A Stream of Surprises

To the motorist all towns along the road look alike. But horse travel is slow. It allows you to discover how different people are and how full of surprises life is. As at sea, the monotony of being in the saddle for months throws into extraordinary relief the slightest of happenings.

Journeys make a Long Rider learn to adapt. You have to think on your feet, control panic, evade danger, seize opportunity, rest when possible, flee when necessary, and realize that challenging days lay ahead.

Anticipating Delays

The length of the journey will influence how often you will be unexpectedly delayed. The reasons vary enormously. The point is that keeping to a strict schedule is neither realistic nor advisable. Flexibility in the face of adversity should be your rule.

Living an open-air life, you learn to readjust, to settle down to hard work, to expect discomforts, to focus on the future and not let the problems of today derail your dreams.

Time Bandits

But some problems can be foreseen. One such challenge will be the invasion of strangers into your personal space. An early lesson will be learning how to balance your need for solitude against the curiosity of others. Stories abound about Long Riders who become the unwilling focus of other people. The intensity of the exchange depends upon the country.

It is not uncommon for several strangers to ride up to a Long Rider's camp in Mongolia, dismount and proceed to interrogate the traveller for hours. Long Riders crossing the United States report increasing incidents where they are surrounded by sizeable and excited crowds. Because horses have all but disappeared in certain countries in the central portion of Africa, Long Riders have been followed by crowds which number from many hundreds up to an estimated thousand people, all of whom trailed along for miles anxious to stare and talk to the mounted strangers.

Thus, if your camp is not secret, it is but a troubled resting place and you become a public character open for inspection and discussion.

What must be remembered is that meeting a Long Rider is often a singular experience for most people. They are excited at seeing you, are curious about your journey and perhaps want to offer help or a night's accommodation. Many are also lonesome, and the idea of talking to a far-roaming Long Rider gives them a chance to express thoughts they are often reluctant to discuss with others.

DC Vision learned that being a Long Rider involves the art of being a good listener.

"Many people I met used two-way conversations as a means to a one-way monologue. I realized they were lonely. By visiting with me they had unexpectedly been shown a window onto the wider world. That's why I developed the ability to just listen, especially as they seemed grateful to talk."

There are two problems with spending time with strangers, either in the saddle or on the ground.

First, you're a traveller. If you spend your time stopped along the side of the road, gossiping with visitors, you're not going to cover that day's necessary mileage, find the campsite you need, care for your horse properly or have the time required to attend to daily tasks.

Next, even if you speak the local language, repeating your story, over and over and over again, becomes emotionally draining. This is why it saves time to have a small flyer or postcard, printed in the local language, ready to pass out to interested people. With a smile on your face, you can explain that all the information is provided on the flyer.

This brings up another aspect about stopping to talking to strangers. You need to courteously explain to curious pedestrians that taking care of your horse is your primary need.

Far be it from me to lecture, but if you stop to talk, you should dismount to save the horse's back. This is an ancient lesson long known to horsemen of old.

That is why Islam teaches, "Do not use the backs of your animals as chairs. Allah has made them subject to you, so that by them you can reach places that you would not otherwise be able to reach except with great fatigue."

If circumstances require you to stop and talk, then dismount out of courtesy to your mount.

If you feel inclined, you can invite the friendly stranger to meet you later that day at your next stop, where you can talk after you have off-saddled.

Keeping Hope Alive

This chapter is entitled *Life on the Road*. This is because what you imagined is not what you will find. The journey that once seemed like a dream is now a reality and finding the strength to see it through to its end becomes increasingly difficult as the miles and months grow.

Prior to his departure from Buenos Aires, the Argentine press had declared Aimé Tschiffely a "madman."

In an act of defiance, Aimé wrote, "Convinced that he who has not lived dangerously has never tasted the salt of life, one day I decided to take the plunge."

He climbed onto his Criollo and headed north towards New York.

But it's never how you think it will be. Weeks of great labour deaden your initial excitement. After a thousand miles you are beset with feelings of monotony. Tiredness turns into dismay. You have to learn how to distract yourself and keep your spirits up.

Robin and Louella Hanbury-Tenison have made five journeys. They are masters at keeping hope alive on a daily basis.

While riding through a particularly difficult part of the Albanian mountains, Robin recalled, "Louella and I are lucky. Fortunately we are never bored in each other's company and are both inexhaustible conversationalists, so that we tend to chatter inconsequentially as we ride along. We devised ways of distracting ourselves from the painful reality. One was to tell long stories of books or films only one had read or seen. This not only helps to pass the time, especially on long stretches of open country which, on a horse, cannot be avoided; it also helps us to get to know each other better and to air any idea which drifts into our minds."

The other thing to remember is that most fears don't materialize.

Jeremy James wrote, "I recall riding into Romania just after they shot Ceausescu in 1990. Communism had collapsed. I was told that law had disappeared, bandits were everywhere, bears stalked the forests and wolves howled in the mountains. Transylvania was a big and lonely place then. So what happens? You wind up staying with the bandits, take photographs of the bears, ride through the wolves and wonder what all the fuss had been about. It's the only real way to travel."

Finally, when troubles do arise, you learn to handle them.

Howard Saether sent an email to the Guild to report that he and Janja Kovačič had survived their foray across the infamous Chaco jungle of Paraguay.

"We made it through hell. It was tough," he said calmly.

Small Goals

There are a number of ways of maintaining your spirits during a long journey.

The first is to remember to relish the moment. You're not just rushing across the landscape, you're a part of the world, you're aware of the weather, and you come across secret places as if magically revealed. Take the time to recall how good it is to be on the journey.

One Long Rider recalled, "I spent the night here on the last full moon. It was the first time I slept outside without my tent in a long time because of mosquitoes. I remember looking up at the sky and the stars and hearing my horses eating, and having one of those feelings like 'Wow! I'm really doing it. I'm living my dream.' It was a good moment."

While it is important to always keep the final destination in view, the journey is made emotionally easier if you have short-term goals. By breaking the trip up into limited objectives, the completion of each smaller stage becomes a reward unto itself. Reaching these places which were once nothing more than exotic names on a map creates a sense of intense emotional importance to a Long Rider.

By the time his journey from Mexico to Panama was well under way, Orion Kraus had learned that valuable lesson. The passage from one province to another is an event of emotional significance, Orion discovered.

He wrote, "In a couple of days, I will hire a guide to take me over some mountain trails into Chiapas. I'm pretty excited as it is another marker on the way. I find that markers are good for me. They are little goals that I've set to show that I've accomplished something."

The reaching of such a goal is more than a means to interrupt the monotony of travel. It is a cause for celebration. Reward yourself. If you are in a city, then try to arrange for comfortable lodgings where you can bathe and sleep deeply. After having endured such grim fare on the road, enjoy a good feast. If the opportunity arises, observe local holidays and participate in festivities.

Don't forget to recompense the horses too.

Malcolm Darling understood that they too grow weary and are worthy of respect. At the halfway mark during his ride across India, a friend of Darling made sure to ensure that the hard-working horse was acknowledged and rewarded.

Darling wrote, "Paul knew that at a certain milestone my gelding, Corydon, and I would have reached the 2,000 kilometre mark in our journey. On coming to it we found three large carrots neatly set out on kitchen paper on the roadway in honour of the event."

But it's not enough to give your horse an extra carrot and a pat on the back.

Captain Otto Schwarz had more mileage than any other 20th century Long Rider under his saddle. He understood that travelling horses had special needs. They should not be rushed and they must be allowed time to rest.

"Especially on extremely long distance, it has been proven that it is not the length of the road but the tempo and speed that can hurt the horse," he wrote.

Otto also interrupted his journeys at certain points, usually after every 500 miles, so as to allow the horses the chance to spend between four and ten days to rest, depending on how difficult the previous stage of the journey had been.

These scheduled rest stops give you something to look forward to. But don't forget to be flexible. You're a Long Rider, not an endurance racer. If the weather looks bad, and you're in a safe, dry spot, sit out the bad weather, let your horse rest, and enjoy yourself for the day.

Handling a Crisis

In my book, *Khyber Knights*, I wrote, "I have always had an opposite taste, thinking the dreaminess of slow rivers and drowsy hamlets drains away our courage. I prefer the hard road that leads through deep valleys and finally up onto sunlit peaks, a road that can only be reached by high endeavour, a road that demands faith in one-self if one is to reach the mountain top and not stay drifting among the luxuries of the lower levels."

I wrote those words when I was younger and I was hungry to visit the lonely places in the world. What I was too naïve to realize is that life doesn't stop when you swing into the saddle. While you are staring in wonder at some incredible peak in a foreign land, those you love have been left behind to carry on with the routine duties of their daily lives.

Never forget those who loved you enough to let you go. They worry, while you wander. They are left hanging in an emotional limbo, while you ride along carefree.

If you have family or loved ones who care about you, then make an attempt to routinely reassure them of your safety.

You should also realize that an extraordinary number of emergencies may arise in your absence. Trouble doesn't stop back home just because you're off exploring the world on horseback.

Long Riders have faced everything from international dangers to personal dilemmas.

The Second World War was declared while Mary Bosanquet was riding across Canada. Because she was fluent in French and German, a rumour began to circulate that Mary was a Nazi spy. Gossip spread that Mary's horse trip was a carefully contrived trick which permitted her to roam and map the countryside at will, prior to a German invasion. The unfounded tale became so widespread that Mary was interviewed by the Canadian Mounted Police, who quickly established her innocence.

Other problems are of a more personal nature.

Gorm Skifter was half way through his ride from the Arctic Circle to Copenhagen, when, "he received an SOS on the wireless saying his father was in concussion after a riding accident." The Danish traveller was forced to rush home.

Likewise, DC Vision's 14,000 mile ride through the USA was interrupted because of a family medical emergency. DC returned home just in time to see his father before he died.

Other family matters also track down Long Riders.

One was served with divorce papers while in the midst of his journey. Another was hit with bankruptcy papers. Neither gave up.

American Long Rider Linda Losey had survived her own emotional crisis. That's why she took the time to send a sympathetic message to one of these travellers, for she too had undergone a deeply challenging time in her life. She wrote these encouraging words.

"We suffer, we push through, and one way or the other we get it finished. Except that it never finishes. The journey takes us to a better place."

Physical Fatigue

The journey may indeed take you to a better place – but not without a tremendous effort.

Perhaps if you are only travelling for a brief time, over easy ground, in good weather, then your journey may be relaxing; but the longer the distance the greater the amount of physical fatigue.

There are no exceptions to this rule. Even though he was hardened by years of travel and warfare, Leonard Clark remembered coming to the end of a long day's ride across Tibet, at which point he "groaned with gladness to slide from the saddle and stretch my legs."

Equestrian travel makes incredible demands on the rider's body. The sun pounds you till you slump in the saddle. Heat drains away your energy. Dust chokes your throat. Muscles which you never knew existed are on fire. Your joints throb with every swaying of the horse. Your bones ache and your legs grow stiff. Your fingers grip the reins till they cramp. Your eyes grow weary looking ahead for signs of relief.

Faint with fatigue, the moment arrives when what seemed like a dream journey has become an endless misfortune.

No one is immune to the physical payment demanded by the miles. The road teaches you the meaning of suffering.

Emotional Exhaustion

An equestrian journey is exciting to plan, and wonderful to recall years later, but it can be hell to endure it at the time.

Intense physical fatigue usually results in emotional exhaustion. Weariness overcomes not just your body but your heart. Some small stressful incident becomes the cause of your temper shattering. Disillusionment appears without warning. Curses rain down on yourself, your comrades, your horse, the whole bloody journey.

Tim Mullan and Sam Southey spent several years planning what they believed was going to be their dream ride across Mongolia. Soon after they arrived in Mongolia they were beset by unexpected problems. They had trouble with their visas, the government, the natives, the horses. After weeks of delay they finally set off, only to hit an emotional reef which threatened to wreck their dream.

In a brutally honest self-appraisal, Sam later wrote, "By the end of the first day I was left wishing I had never thought of this trip. Tim was apprehensive but asked me to work through my fear. 'After all' Tim had said 'we've waited seven years for this. We cannot give up now. We always knew it was going to be tough.' That was the problem though, I told people it would be tough but I never really knew what that would feel like emotionally until it started to actually happen. I wanted to be heroic about the trip but here I was crying in a toilet after my first hard day, wishing I was at home feeling content with life."

Dealing with emotional stress is part of a Long Rider's life. Unlike hikers and bicyclists who travel in a relatively carefree manner, equestrian travel involves a large daily dose of anxiety. Where will you find food and shelter for your horse? Will the next town be friendly? Can you cross that tricky border looming up ahead?

Worries vary from the minimum to the profound. One Long Rider recalled how 53 rolls of exposed film were ruined when his pack horse fell over while crossing a river.

"Such were the fortunes of travel," he wisely recalled.

Dealing with Disappointment

Just as you should reward yourself after you've reached a certain spot along your route so as to celebrate your physical progress, you should also protect yourself against the possible emotional disappointment which may arise when you finally arrive at a longed-for goal.

Distant names on a map present an alluring, albeit often deceitful promise.

Sometimes they meet our expectations.

"Before us now stretched Mongolia," the Danish Long Rider Henning Haslund wrote, "with deserts trembling in the mirages, with endless steppes covered with emerald-green grass and multitudes of wild flowers, with nameless snow peaks, limitless forests, thundering rivers and swift mountain streams. The way that we had travelled with such toil had disappeared behind us among gorges and ravines. We could not have dreamed of a more captivating entrance to a new country, and when the sun sank upon that day, we felt as though born into a new life- a life which had the strength of the hills, the depth of the heavens and the beauty of the sunrise."

Henning was lucky. Other Long Riders have discovered their emotional treasure was naught but a mirage.

After starving and struggling to ride over the Hindu Kush Mountains, Ernest Fox was alive with anticipation at reaching what had been described as a town full of food and comforts.

"They described it in glowing terms to us on the lonely march. Together, we deceived ourselves that we were riding to a rich metropolis, with a full bazaar and intriguing gardens. When we came over the last dreary rise we found a few humble huts nestled under some lean trees. It was very disheartening after our high expectancy."

It's when you're tired, body and soul, that your spirit begins to deceive you.

The Lure of Home

You would think that after so much effort, the idea of stopping the journey and returning home would be the last thing on your mind.

But the weather turns bad. A horse becomes ill. You lose the desire to explain yourself for the 100th time. Your money runs out. What had been an exciting adventure becomes dull and repetitive.

As the troubles increase, the rigours of travel may reach a point when they erode a Long Rider's original enthusiasm. The onset of physical and emotional exhaustion makes him long to return home, to see his loved ones, to enjoy a home-cooked meal, to sleep without worrying about tomorrow.

After riding for thousands of hard miles across Europe, English Long Rider Bill Holt hit that invisible spot where he didn't want to go on.

"Travelling slowly on horseback is different from travelling by car. I had seen every inch of ground in front of us all the way. It became monotonous, demoralising. I longed for the relief of something dramatic. And now all that mass of land was in my consciousness, weighing me down, and I was tired. I was suffering from continentitis," he explained.

Holt didn't give up. The reason for his success may be found in the unlikely country of Finland.

Sisu

Many Long Riders have contributed to the creation of this book. Some have shared a story. Others have passed along a warning about a particular danger. Many have added hard-won wisdom.

Only one has contributed a single word that means so much to so many.

During her "ocean to ocean" ride across the United States, Sea G Rhydr faced a host of problems including sick horses, hostile environments, a lack of money and a growing desire to stop and go home.

She didn't.

She persevered.

She reached the ocean, in more ways than one.

One reason that Sea made it through was thanks to a chance remark made by a stranger. A woman saw Sea riding along the road, stopped, got out of the car, walked back, and said that the tired Long Rider epitomized *Sisu*.

Sea had to ask what that meant.

Sisu is a Finnish term which means the ability to summon up strength of will, determination and perseverance in the face of adversity. *Sisu* is not the same thing as momentary courage. It denotes the decision to sustain an action against all the odds, regardless of the hardships, despite previous failures, in spite of how grim things may appear at the moment.

Travel, Travel, Travel

Most Long Riders reach a moment when their lives are reduced to one single, simple, stubborn purpose – to complete the journey. They may have never heard of the word *sisu* but they epitomise that philosophy.

Case in point is Scottish Long Rider Gordon Naysmith. During his historic ride across the African continent, Gordon suffered incredible hardships. He recalled that in Zambia conditions were so bad that he was lucky to make two miles an hour.

"It was the worst day of my life," he wrote in his diary.

He spoke too soon.

In Kenya he rode into the annex to hell.

"After three hours I had to stop because it is so bloody hot. Takes me twenty minutes to summon the energy to unstrap the water bottle. Absolutely no grazing here. No rain for over two years and even the scrub is dead. Terribly desolate place. Nothing but volcanic rock for miles. The occasional stunted thorn tree pushes its way to the sky. The sun beats down and nothing moves. By far the hottest day of the trip. I erect the tent as an awning and with the horse blankets down and me stripped to the buff I lie in a stupor for nearly three hours."

In his diary, Gordon pondered, "This is one of the few days when I was unable to think of one good reason why I should be torturing myself on this trip."

What Gordon knew deep down was that it wasn't merely physical strength that counted.

"The real test of our ability is not only to persevere but to cover distance under adverse conditions," he wrote.

To do that you must have a profound faith in the value of your journey. You must keep alive the fire that burns inside no matter how great the odds are against you.

"Travel, travel, travel. This alone matters. This alone will get you through. Nothing else prevails. This became our slogan when we grew tired, the way seemed hard, and the riding tough," wrote James Beard, when his journey along the Oregon Trail was in danger of failing.

"Don't you ever give up," wrote Frank Heath, during his 48-state ride across America. "If you do, that will be the regret of your life. You can make it somehow."

At one point Messanie Wilkins was down to 17 cents during her journey. She said, "You may be tired and hungry lots of times, but trust in God, keep going, and you'll get there," and she did.

Expect to become hard-bitten and scruffy. Expect to lose a lot of weight. Expect to go hungry and thirsty. Expect to lose sleep and border on exhaustion. Expect to smell like horse sweat, taste sand in your food, freeze at night and roast during the day. Expect the worst that the land can throw at you; then reach deep inside your soul, find some previously untapped strength, and ride on

The Ballereau Barrier

There is one exception to that rule. I call it *The Ballereau Barrier* in honour of one of the first Members who helped found the Long Riders' Guild.

Jean-François Ballereau has passed away. But he was one of the greatest French Long Riders of the late 20th century. He made a series of rides in Europe and North America. Then he determined to follow in Tschiffely's hoofprints from Argentina to New York.

Hard as nails, with thousands of miles under his saddle, Jean-François was no naïve novice. When he reached Columbia, he knew he couldn't hope to get his horses through the treacherous Darien Gap jungle which separates Panama from South America.

That is why Jean-François spent weeks carefully arranging to have his horses flown to Panama. According to the Panamanian consul and the Columbian authorities, the horses were healthy, their papers were in order, and there was no reason they couldn't fly to Panama and then proceed with the journey.

Jean-François hadn't foreseen the obstinate bureaucracy which awaited him. Upon landing at the Panama airport, a government official marched out and informed the startled French traveller that there had been a mistake. The veterinary documents were not in order. Under no circumstances would his horses be allowed into the country. In fact, if they so much as stepped onto the tarmac, they would be shot on the spot.

The Long Rider had only one choice. He flew the horses back to Columbia. Jean-François then spent fruitless months trying to contrive a way to continue all the while his finances dwindled. Finally, he realized he had been beaten, not by the terrain, or any of the other challenges he had long ago mastered. He had been conquered by an unforeseeable disaster.

Jean-François' journey provided a terrible lesson for all would-be Long Riders.

No matter how determined you are; no matter how skilled you are; regardless of how many hard-won miles are under your saddle; despite the validity of your cause; your journey may be destroyed by unexpected circumstances which are beyond your control.

One such example occurred as I was writing this chapter.

Brazilian Long Rider Filipe Leite had ridden from Canada to the border of Panama. Having been warned about that country's antagonism against Long Riders, Filipe spent months arranging to fly his horses to Peru. His plan was to then continue his journey across Peru, into Bolivia, and finally home to Brazil.

Then he hit the Ballereau Barrier.

"Oh Peru," Filipe wrote, "How many times did I daydream of riding my ponies through this majestic land? I would sit in my apartment in Toronto prior to this trip, imagining myself making my way up to Machu Picchu along the Inca Trail and riding on the shores of Lake Titicaca, the highest lake in the world. Unfortunately sometimes life gets in the way. As this Long Ride has shown me time and time again, life doesn't always go as planned. You can hope for the best but at the end of the day you must simply take what the universe hands you and make the best of it. Due to Peru's bureaucracy we were not allowed to ride everywhere I had planned."

Like a sailor encountering a tsunami at sea, one moment you're on course, the next you're struggling to stay alive. It happened to others. It stopped the best. It could strike you. Accept the possibility intellectually and prepare yourself emotionally.

Summary

A journey that fatigues you also teaches you many things. Water is sweeter than wine. Food, however meagre, tastes delicious. The coolness of a shadow is a blessing after the heat of the sun. The pleasures of a deep sleep are almost as satisfying as a sexual encounter.

Astride the horse, a new pattern emerges in your life. You have learned that happiness does not consist in having great possessions, but in sharing the world with a magical animal that is willing to accompany you on any journey you're brave enough to undertake.

When that moment comes, you realize you have passed an invisible line. You have crossed over. There is a rhythm of the road and you have found it. This is the moment when you realize that you could go on forever.

As American Long Rider Jeanette McGrath wisely said, "Remember it's about the journey, not the finish line."

To the outsider the Long Rider appears to be a romantic figure that suddenly appears as if from out of the past. This explains why strangers often express a longing to swing into the saddle and escape from the predictable drudgery of their lives.

The reality is far different. English Long Rider Steve McCutcheon looked clean and eager the day he left Delhi, India, on his journey to Peking. A year later, travel-stained and weary, he was photographed on Christmas Day, travelling alone along Pakistan's fierce Karakoram Highway.

Many Long Riders realize that the further they travel the stronger grows the feeling that they have lost touch with current events. This peaceful photo shows Edouard Chautard riding across New Caledonia on September 11, 2001, unaware of the terrible events which had happened in New York.

Jeremy James believes that a Long Rider's sense of intuition works as a type of astrolabe which helps travellers learn how to avoid trouble.

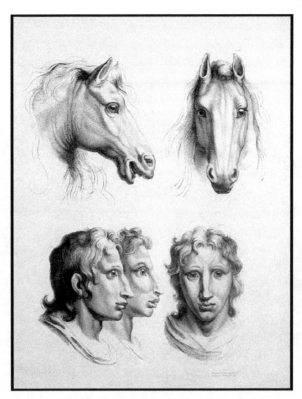

The journey draws the two species together, requiring horse and human to create a long-term inter-species relationship that allows them to survive as they search together for food, water and shelter. There is no other equestrian activity which requires the team to spend so much time engaged in an activity that is so geographically exotic, emotionally complex and stimulating to the senses.

As New Zealand Long Rider Pete Langford discovered, travel is hard work, both physically and emotionally. That is why it is vitally important that every opportunity be taken to conserve the energy of the horses and riders.

There is always a never-ending number of tasks which must be done on a horse trip, including cleaning and repairing equipment. The author is seen making an emergency repair to a set of saddlebags, on the road leading out of Gilgit, Pakistan.

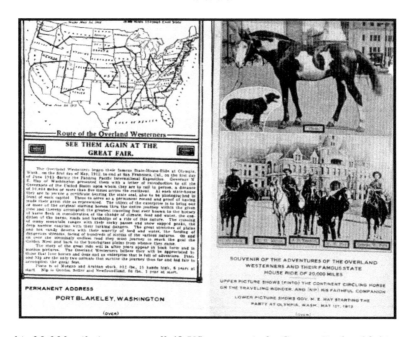

To raise money during his 20,000 mile journey to all 48 US state capitals, George Beck sold this small postcard. One side showed a map of their route. The obverse side showed Pinto, the Morab gelding who made the entire remarkable trip.

When Aimé Tschiffely set off to ride from Buenos Aires to New York he had no idea how difficult the trip was going to be. He epitomizes the Finnish term, Sisu, the ability to summon up strength of will and the determination to persevere in the face of adversity.

Jean-François Ballereau was the French Long Rider whose journey was stopped in Panama by unforeseen circumstances.

Chapter 74
Long Rider Ethics

Ancient Kings – Modern Lessons

You learn many unexpected lessons during an equestrian journey. I for one discovered the need to demonstrate kindness towards my horses thanks to a far-sighted and benevolent king who left his wisdom for me beside the road.

My long journey in northern Pakistan was nearing an end when chance forced me to spend the night in Mansehra, a small nondescript village a few days' ride from Peshawar. This was Pathan country, where a strict interpretation of Islam was the norm, so I wasn't expecting to have a surprise encounter with one of the world's most famous converts to Buddhism.

But soon after I set off that morning I unexpectedly came upon the Edicts of Ashoka.

Ashoka (304 -232 BCE) was an Indian emperor whose kingdom stretched from Persia in the West, through the Hindu Kush Mountains, to Assam in the East. The hill country I was riding through on my way down to the Kabul River had once been part of his vast kingdom.

Not content with ruling most of the Indian subcontinent, in 261 BCE Ashoka waged a brutal war of conquest against the people of Kalinga. It resulted in one of the bloodiest battles in history, with an estimated 250,000 killed on both sides in brutal hand-to-hand combat.

Sickened by the bloodshed, filled with remorse and ashamed of the part he had played in these events Ashoka embraced Buddhism and devoted the rest of his life to promoting the teaching of non- violence.

Born a king and raised as a warrior, he is not remembered for his military prowess, but as the author of *The Edicts of Ashoka*. These 33 inscriptions promoted the concepts of benevolence, generosity and purity among men. He also became the first ruler to advocate the protection of animals and to relinquish hunting.

Emissaries were sent as far away as Bactria, Greece and North Africa, proclaiming Ashoka's desire that mankind abandon war and embrace peace. Within his vast empire, Ashoka had the Edicts inscribed on boulders, cave walls, and on tall pillars. These inscriptions are dispersed throughout modern Nepal, Bangladesh, India and Pakistan.

More than twenty examples of the famous Edicts still exist in other nations, yet only one example can be found in Pakistan and it lay along my route. Soon after setting off from Mansehra in the morning, I was surprised to find a massive boulder resting serenely alongside the roadside. Carved deeply into its surface was the wisdom of the ancient king, Ashoka.

They had sat there for more than 2,000 years, enduring all weathers, so as to provide an important message from the past for travellers such as myself. Though I could not read the ancient script, I later learned one of the lessons Ashoka had left for me.

Man has a moral responsibility to treat animals with kindness, dignity and charity.

Nor was this the only time I encountered such an enlightened view.

During the time I lived and travelled in Afghanistan, Pakistan and India, I became aware of another ruler who became convinced that the finer elements of humanity might be found amongst all men.

Ironically, in a world full of instant news, one which rings out every few minutes with the words "ISIS", "Taliban" and "al-Qaeda," it would serve mankind well to remember that there is a vast portion of the Muslim world which has gone largely unnoticed. Unlike the chilling Puritanism of some movements, which helped inspire and finance the forces of political poison currently disguised as religion which are at work today, the Indo-Islamic civilization created the most tolerant and pluralistic example of Islam ever known.

The most important example of this alternative vision of the oft-misunderstood religion was the great Mughal Emperor Akbar (1542-1605). The hallmark of his reign was the emphasis he placed upon Hindu-Muslim unity and the concept of individual religious tolerance. Because he was convinced that spiritual truth was not the monopoly of any particular religion, Akbar organized the first global congress of faiths, fostered the spirit of enquiry and allowed every man and community to develop in its own spiritual manner.

Faith has no caste, nor national origin, taught this powerful ruler who placed the love of God above the rituals of religion. When a theocracy of Sunni extremists condemned Akbar's spirit of Sufi generosity, he transported the belligerent mullahs to Kandahar, and exchanged them for colts.

Like his enlightened predecessor, Ashoka, Jalaluddin Muhammad Akbar placed great stress on the purity of an individual's life. Though he too ruled an empire, he strove to replace anger with kindness and to promote tolerance among all men.

Akbar also prohibited the killing of horses, cattle and other domestic animals.

Companions of the Road

You might be wondering what two ancient kings of India have to do with modern equestrian travel?

Though they spoke in different languages and from long ago, each great emperor would have told you the same thing. There is a struggle in every soul between the forces of good and evil. It isn't confined to the battle-field, the world of commerce or the political arena. It has influenced events in equestrian travel as well.

While we can rejoice in the mounted Argonauts who bring glory to equestrian travel history, we cannot afford to ignore the wicked deeds done to horses by cruel humans who turned their journeys into excursions to Hell.

Some people have a lust for recognition. When such men and women take to the saddle, their craving for public attention makes them blind to the pain they are inflicting on their horses. As their addiction to adoration grows, they choose to ignore the extended agony of the animal and subject it instead to torment.

Having no hint of dishonour, these individuals reveal the egotistical monstrousness which lurks in mankind.

There is more to equestrian travel than tying knots and picketing horses. Discovering your ethical responsibilities is a vital part of reaching your ultimate emotional goal.

Mutual Love

Before venturing into the dark recesses of the Long Rider world, it would be encouraging to recall an example of the mystery which can link horse and human together in such a singular manner.

There are many examples of Long Riders who have taken the time to look into their horse's mind, to discover its little pleasures and to note its fears. These are the ones who win the horse's trust.

Professor Takeshi Shoji seemed an unlikely candidate to become such a Long Rider. After all, he was a psychologist practising in Tokyo who didn't learn to ride until he was 50. Yet despite his urban existence, the professor had been harbouring a dream for many decades. He wanted to make an equestrian journey across Japan.

The idea took root as the Second World War was concluding. As a young man Takeshi attended the Military Academy in Tokyo. Hundreds of horses were stabled there. When the war ended the academy was closed and the horses had to be re-homed without delay. Students were offered the opportunity to receive one of these horses for free, along with a single day's ration of food for the animal.

The young Takeshi was the first to volunteer. But because his home was far away, his request was denied as his superiors deemed it would be impossible for him make such a long trip on horseback under the extreme conditions created by the war.

For forty years the dream lay dormant. Then Professor Shoji learned how to ride and met Kage. This was an exceptionally strong Thoroughbred who had a reputation for biting people. Having been deemed unmanageable, Kage was given to the professor free of charge.

Some have attributed the change which came over Kage to Takeshi's knowledge of psychology. Whether it was science or intuition which helped Takeshi, who can say? But there came a moment when the horse bestowed his trust upon the human. A Japanese Centaur was created when these unlikely travellers set out in 1985 to ride 1,300 kilometres (800 miles) from Tokyo to Osaka.

Lacking practical experience, Takeshi took every precaution to protect Kage throughout the journey. He reduced his personal items to a bare minimum to decrease the weight Kage would have to carry. Knowing the horse would be forced to travel over hard roads, he had Kage shod with special plastic shoes to reduce the shock on the horse's legs. After the journey began, he faithfully stopped every hour so as to give Kage a ten-minute rest. Unless he felt the stable was safe, Takeshi slept next to Kage at night. After the first 100 miles had been completed, he asked a veterinarian to give Kage a complete check-up to confirm the journey was doing him no harm.

The doctor did not need to undertake a lot of complicated tests. He quickly announced that Kage was in perfect condition.

Some Long Riders have discussed the idea that as they journey together a strong feeling of emotional integration develops between horse and human. I have personally wondered if, as the miles progress and the day lengthens, road horse and Long Rider do not quietly fall into a silent rhythm wherein their breathing and heart beats become harmonious.

Kage's trust in Takeshi was tested when they reached the metropolis of Kyoto. In an effort to avoid the worst of the traffic, they had set off before dawn. But even at that early hour, the team found the roads were crowded with speeding cars and large threatening trucks. Their route through the city was complicated. The further they went, the more stressed Kage became.

It was at this moment that Takeshi realized he must not transmit any sense of fear or nervousness to Kage. The professor decided to place his trust in his horse. He loosened the reins, let his body relax in the saddle and said, "I'm here with you. I know you are afraid and so am I. We might die but we can die together."

They set off again, only this time Professor Shoji felt as if "we had become an animal with four eyes and ears whose blood vessels had been connected."

They completed the journey without incident.

Cruelty Unmasked

Not every corner of the equestrian world contains such quiet heroes. A different reality often lurks behind the mask of respectability. For example, one of the most repulsive equestrian travesties was cloaked behind the dashing finery of European cavalry uniforms.

This occurred in Europe in 1892 when 121 Austrian and 132 German cavalry officers challenged each other to a race. The German contestants were required to ride 580 kilometres (360 miles) from Berlin to Vienna, while their counterparts raced in the opposite direction.

A popular magazine of the time ran a cover illustration that depicts a misleading scene. In reality there was nothing debonair or gallant about the German and Austrian officers shown on the magazine cover, as these mounted criminals raced 46 horses to death in 71 hours.

Horrified reporters revealed details about the sufferings of the hundreds of other horses. "Some died on the road, while others, lame and almost ready to drop from exhaustion, were kept going by injections of morphia to deaden pain, and were sustained by doses of brandy, and all, with hardly an exception, were cruelly tried."

This act of national chauvinism resulted in editors around the world condemning the murderous event. As far away as Australia, one paper thundered, "We trust no magistrate in any English community would hesitate to convict a rider who attempted to accomplish such a feat for sport."

The public expressed outrage at this vain display of personal egotism and national pride. There was widespread demand for reform. Shortly thereafter rules were enacted to protect horses from being raced to death in endurance events.

Horse Killers

Sadly, as with any human effort, there are occasional outlaws who appear in the world of equestrian travel. When these villains appear, they abuse their horses, ride them too hard, do not feed them properly, and continue the journey even if the horse becomes wounded. Such actions are embodied in the Hungarian word *lóháldl,* which states that the horse is expendable.

Francois Xavier Aubry was the notorious French-Canadian whose legacy of equestrian infamy epitomized this concept in the 19th century. In 1849 he rode six horses to death and left half a dozen more permanently wounded on an eight-day journey from Santa Fe, New Mexico to Independence, Missouri.

But equestrian infamy is not a thing of the past.

In 1980 four Oxford undergraduates announced plans to ride a thousand miles across the desolate Andes Mountains of Peru.

Lacking any equestrian travel experience they spent three days learning how to load a pack mule from the Italian Army's Alpine troops. Another few days was spent with the British army, who taught them the rudiments of how to navigate with a compass. Armed with this tiny amount of knowledge the university students flew to Peru.

According to a report published in the London *Sunday Times*, it didn't take long for the expedition's horses to become exhausted, wounded and starving.

"The continuous rubbing of the saddles and packs was bruising the horses' backs. Attempts to prevent this by tightening the girths were frustrated by the animals' habit of deliberately blowing themselves out. The only remedy was a sharp punch in the ribs."

Nor was improper equipment the only problem, as the paper reported "The lack of fodder in the mountains exacerbated the horses' weakening condition."

Worse was to come. One packhorse fell off the trail and tumbled down the hillside. It survived but because it refused to move on, the English travellers traded it for a sheep for their dinner.

"By the time we spurred the horses into Huaraz, the remaining horses were in a wretched condition. The bruises on their backs had burst into purulent sores," one of the students told the English press.

Lacking enough horses to continue, the group's leader went to Lima and made an appeal for government support.

According to the British press, "Only the personal intervention of the Peruvian president, who gave them a permanent police bodyguard, enabled them to complete the 1,800 kilometre (1,100 miles) journey."

With the president on their side, it didn't take long before the Director of the Guardia police force issued an order for every local police station along their route to provide the gringos with horses. An armed police sergeant and corporal were commanded to accompany the tourists during the remainder of the journey. Thanks to the power of this draconian police order, and the presence of the two armed policemen, the Oxford students were able to hire or seize horses as they continued across Peru.

With an unlimited supply of horses now at their disposal, the students increased their rate of travel.

"In order to gain time we took to night riding, which increased our speed to 85 kilometres (52 miles) a day, riding 24 hours non-stop. By this stage the expedition had turned into an Odyssey. Two hours after sunset one day my horse, went into spasms for five minutes, then died of a heart attack. Less than five minutes later the sergeant's horse followed suit. An effort was made to revive this horse by blowing billows of cigarette smoke into its nostrils, but it was hopeless," the leader of the English students recalled.

The London newspaper stated, "The 49 day ride, which in the end depended on animals hijacked for them by local police, finished in Cuzco."

Though they claimed to be "valiant English Conquistadors," the four English Oxford University students hold the record for destroying more horses in a journey than anyone in history. During their brief ride across Peru, they killed, wounded or severely rode 81 horses and 19 mules.

Our sympathy goes out to the animals whose dignity has been outraged not by explorers but by exploiters.

No World Records

There have been occasions when a journey was reduced to a cruel spectacle in an ill-advised attempt to set a world record.

The most recent effort occurred in June of 2012 when an unemployed Texas air-conditioner repairman made a startling announcement. "I am planning to ride a horse around the world and intend to complete the trip in 1,000 days."

The man did not own a horse or saddle. He had no money and had not planned his route. He had no idea how he would travel overseas, even if he was lucky enough to reach his first goal of San Diego, California.

His motivation for making the trip was to gain entry into the *Guinness Book of World Records*.

In addition to knowing nothing about equestrian travel, the traveller was equally unaware that the Guinness website states, "We do not endorse speed records for travelling over large distances on horseback because of concerns over the welfare of the animals involved."

But a lack of information didn't keep the self-described "cowboy preacher" from proceeding with his plan.

Having had a saddle donated, the traveller adopted an unsuitable horse from the Humane Society of North Texas. The three-year-old stallion was underweight and barely broken to ride. The traveller set off in 100 degree July heat. Unable to carry the 200 pound rider, the small horse collapsed after only fifteen miles. "He lay down with me still in the saddle," the traveller told a reporter.

Determined to proceed, the traveller asked a local equine rescue organisation to supply him with a new mount. Having obtained a mare from the unsuspecting organisation, he proceeded to ride the animal so hard that on the second day she too collapsed.

The man's third horse lasted 300 miles, until it developed such severe saddle sores that the animal was too ill to continue.

Then it got worse.

Having obtained his fourth mount, the Texan had managed to reach the neighbouring state of New Mexico. While travelling through the desolate desert country near Alamogordo, he came upon a cattle guard. According to a spokesman from the White Sands Missile Range Fire Department, which had responded to a telephone call for help, the inept traveller had attempted to "walk or lead" the horse across the dangerous cattle guard. The horse broke its leg and had to be shot.

He had now lost four horses in two months.

Before he set off, the Texan had predicted, "The media attention to this ride will be enormous." He was right, but for reasons he could never have foreseen.

An international public outcry had begun when it was discovered that this man was destroying horses in his cross-country trip. Members of the Long Riders' Guild, animal welfare organizations, reporters in the United States and overseas, state police and equine welfare organisations all pooled their resources and tracked his movements.

Despite the string of injured or dead horses, he refused to accept any responsibility. Having been informed that there was no world record for equestrian travel, the Texan attempted to justify his actions by cloaking them under the disguise of religion.

"I'm doing the Lord's work out here," he told the press.

But with his every step now being monitored, and his supply of free horses having been removed, he returned to Texas in defeat.

Religious Deception

As I have previously stated in this book, a Long Rider soon realizes that "the horse is the key to the village." When you arrive on horseback, chances are the local inhabitants will extend courtesy and offer shelter out of love and concern for your horse.

Not all travellers are pure-hearted. Once a conman realizes the attraction of the horse, he can misuse the public's trust so as to obtain gifts and money in a fraudulent manner.

It is not uncommon for such individuals to invoke God as the justification for their journey, thereby tapping into the religious piety of those they meet.

The Texas "cowboy preacher" was one such example.

However that was a minor episode of this type of religious deceit. Others have also linked the concept of equestrian travel and spiritual devotion so as to mislead the public.

The most notorious case occurred in the United States in the summer of 2005 when a man who claimed he was going to ride from Mexicali, Mexico to Alberta, Canada, deliberately deceived the American public, repeatedly lied to members of the press, obtained money and equipment under false pretences, claimed to be raising funds for famous charities, misappropriated the reputation of cowboy organizations and fallaciously used the names of Christian groups without their knowledge or approval.

It was an unsigned email entitled "Fraud Cowboy" that tipped off the Guild. The message arrived at dawn on July 16th, 2005 and it didn't pull any punches. A reporter for National Public Radio in Las Vegas, Nevada had busted an equestrian traveller for fraud.

This discovery came about when a neighbour complained to National Public Radio that the so-called cowboy traveller who pretended to be sleeping under the stars was actually hiding in an air conditioned house on the north-west side of Las Vegas.

Thanks to the website the phoney traveller had created, it didn't take long for the radio reporter to discover that the false Long Rider claimed to have ridden from Mexico all the way to Montana. The reporter grabbed a video camera, drove across town, went inside the neighbour's house, aimed the camera out the window and telephoned the conman. The counterfeit traveller was standing in the front yard of his girlfriend's home in Las Vegas when he took the call.

When the reporter called the traveller on the cell phone number listed on his website, he asked "Where are you now?"

"Oh, sitting about 200 yards away from my camp here in Montana," the man replied.

"Can you describe what you see to me?"

"Oh, rolling hills, the Rockies and a lot of blue sky."

The conman was filmed talking into his cell phone in Las Vegas while telling the reporter this lie.

One of the reasons the man was able to carry out a deliberate campaign of treachery was because he cloaked his true intentions under the guise of Christianity.

Though he claimed to be a devout Christian cowboy, this architect of deceit systematically wounded and victimized a series of well-meaning people. One of the ways he did this was by his heavy handed misuse of the Christian community. Listed as one of the "Sponsors" of the Mexico to Canada ride was the "Cowboys for Christ" organization. Yet the founder of this Biblical organisation told the Long Riders' Guild that the counterfeit traveller was not connected to them, nor had they authorized him to list them as sponsors on his website.

Another well-known charity that felt the phoney traveller's sting was the "Happy Trails Children's Foundation," started by legendary western entertainer Roy Rogers. The conman had also falsely listed the Roy Rogers charity on his "Cowboys Helping Kids" website.

This case helped alert the public to this type of spiritual malfeasance.

Tradition Doesn't Excuse Cruelty

Another cause for concern occurs when a traditional equestrian culture or custom is used as a cover for cruelty.

Many Long Riders are motivated to undertake journeys because of heroes of the past. This inspiration takes various forms.

Vincent Gabriel Kirouac was 22 years old when he set out to ride from his home in Quebec, across Canada to British Columbia. Mounted on his horse, Coeur de Lion (Lion Heart), Vincent's mission was to promote the knightly virtues of chivalry, courage, compassion and loyalty. Instead of the clothes normally worn by a Long Rider, Vincent chose to wear a knight's helmet and tunic to highlight his mission.

As the journey progressed in the summer of 2012, Vincent was asked by a stranger to explain what chivalry meant. After pondering for a moment, Vincent replied, "I said it symbolized incorruptibility."

Despite the nobility of his mission, the young knight concluded his journey prematurely when he reached Saskatchewan. Coeur de Lion had developed a saddle sore. Instead of pressing on, Vincent put the welfare of his horse above his own ego. He publicly announced that he was finishing the ride so as to protect his mount. On his website he asked people to remember and pray for "All the horses that need comfort who have served man and may no longer feel useful."

Such gracious sentiments would have been of use across the Atlantic. Costumes cannot conceal cruelty, as was symbolized by another equestrian journey undertaken at the same time Vincent was in the saddle.

Two Hungarians, dressed as Hussars, announced they were going to ride to the Arctic Circle and back. They were stopped by police in Amal, Sweden and arrested on charges of animal cruelty. The men were released after spending two days in jail. But their four horses were impounded by Swedish authorities.

A veterinarian check ordered by the Swedish government revealed that the animals were exhausted, emaciated, poorly shod and had various injuries and saddle sores on their bodies. In addition to suffering injuries to his tendons, the pack horse had large open saddle sores on his back and sides. Another horse was lame.

Medical authorities estimated that the horses needed total rest for at least a month, and suggested they be put out to pasture for a longer period if possible. Soon after the Hungarians were arrested the Swedish government provided the Guild with the police report, medical documents and photographs of the horses' saddle sores.

After allowing the horses to rest and recover for more than a month, in mid July the Swedish Länsstyrelsen (government agricultural authorities) decided that the horses could be returned to the Hungarians, under certain strict conditions.

The horses were only released provided that the travellers promised to transport the animals back to Hungary via a trailer. The government authorities also stipulated that the horses were not to be ridden or used as pack animals for a minimum of eight weeks.

In order to regain custody of the horses the two men agreed to these terms. They trailered the horses across the border to Helsinki, Finland – then immediately broke their word to the Swedish government by saddling the horses and defiantly resuming the journey homeward.

In a statement to the public, one of the Hungarians wrote that he had regained control of the horses, "after 35 days of waiting for nothing." He soon bragged on his website that he and his companion were riding south towards Hungary on the injured horses "at an average of 50-70 kilometres a day."

After the travellers' return, the publisher of the Hungarian magazine Jövőnk revealed that the leader of the Arctic Circle journey had severely injured or killed horses during previous journeys in Turkey, Kazakhstan and Europe.

The journalist issued this stern condemnation of the disgraced rider.

"This man donned the clothes of a Hussar but never learned the most important historical lesson of Hungary's great horsemen: the horse was the Hussar's friend and not merely a means to try and become famous."

Other Outlaws

There have been other cases where equestrian travellers donned a national costume and abused their horses. In 2008 a Russian dressed as a Cossack nearly rode two horses to death in a mad attempt to reach the Eiffel Tower.

Another type of abuse involves appealing to the patriotism of the populace. After the tragedy of September 11, 2001, an American announced he was going to ride from Texas to New York so as to raise funds for the families of the firemen and policemen who had lost their lives in that tragedy. The ride was a ruse. The horse was trailered to the outskirts of a town. The man would ride in, collect donations and leave bills unpaid, all in the name of patriotism.

He was not a pilgrim. He was an entertainer. It was not a journey. It was a business.

Other renegades have ridden their horses even after they were covered with raw wounds. Some have starved their horses to the point of death.

These individuals are examples of a previously undetected part of the equestrian travel experience.

Equestrian Narcissistic Disorder

During my years researching equestrian travel I have collected evidence of what I term "Equestrian Narcissistic Disorder" (END).

Narcissism is associated with egoism, vanity, conceit, selfishness and an indifference to the plight of others. The "others" in this case refers to the horses which are exploited, abused, starved or killed by merciless travellers or mounted criminals.

There are many common traits found in the actions of individuals who exhibit the presence of Equestrian Narcissistic Disorder. These include an excessive need for admiration, a preference for showy clothes or historical costumes and a tendency to be an exhibitionist. They commonly overestimate their abilities, exaggerate their achievements, brag persistently and emphasise any trace of danger or hardship.

Because their personal goals take precedence over the horse's wellbeing, they proceed recklessly. If a horse is wounded, they are reluctant to halt the journey. They are often in a state of denial about the seriousness of setbacks, injuries or defeats. Even if the horse is killed or injured, they commonly refuse to express remorse or accept responsibility.

Having learned how to use the horse to secure the public's trust or to attract an audience, they use cunning to exploit others without regard for their feelings or interests. Their manipulative efforts thrive by continually enlisting the help of unsuspecting victims whom they meet as they ride across the country.

They tend to avoid Nature, targeting urban areas which in turn means they are inclined to follow main roads. Most prefer couch-camping in a host's house to sleeping in a tent.

Since they are searching for fans, not equals, they avoid contact with genuine Long Riders but take every opportunity to attract the attention of the press and social media. Their desire for attention becomes addictive. Desperate to be labelled the first, the fastest, bravest, sexiest, etc, they never volunteer information about other equestrian travellers to the media, as they are averse to being held in comparison.

Most are anxious to deny, ignore or belittle any spiritual aspects of the journey or cannot identify with such an experience. After the trip is completed, they are disinclined to share critical or even life-saving information with others, as this knowledge may benefit Long Riders whom they define as competition.

Having essentially ridden alone, they are unable to have friendship with their peers within the equestrian travel world. In his or her eyes, the completion of their journey reinforces a view of himself as being historically special.

Animal Ethics

The topic of unethical equestrian travellers has legal implications on an international level because it raises the sensitive topic of cross-species dignity.

During the time during which I have been writing this book, the media has routinely released stories which confirm the widespread abuse which is tolerated in a number of equestrian communities.

The leaders of the Tennessee Walking Horse community have been accused of condoning barbaric training practices. At the same time the horse racing industry has been revealed to put up with horrific abuse, including the extensive use of illegal drugs, which is often abetted and encouraged by financially corrupt vets. All the while the European dressage world continues to permit the pitiless practice known as *rollkur*.

The public has protested against these practices but an entrenched leadership, linked to lucrative financial incentives, follow the line of least resistance rather than implement any significant changes. As a result, the public sees, knows, and rages at this on-going equestrian abuse but their voices are either ignored or ridiculed.

Nor are Long Riders immune from this debate.

When the so-called Hungarian "Hussars" continued to ride their injured animals across Europe, the Guild contacted the Animal Welfare department of the European Union in Brussels. The EU provides the wolf with extensive protection but the lawmakers only provide protection to a horse if it is being used in an agricultural setting. Travelling horses, especially those who are on multi-national journeys, are afforded no protection from abuse.

In an email to the Guild, an EU official wrote, "the activities you describe are not covered by the current EU legislation and the general provisions of Directive 98/5 8/EC on the protection of animals bred or kept for farming purposes, are not applicable to horses kept for other activities such as leisure."

When the Guild accurately pointed out that the majority of Europe's horses were no longer involved in agriculture, that in fact they were primarily used for travel, leisure or sporting activities, Brussels agreed that an equine oversight existed. But no help was offered.

The scarcity of equine welfare codes has also been noted among Europe's professional mountaineering associations, which often use mules as pack animals. In a special report written for the University of Edinburgh, Glen Cousquer documented how "none of the existing codes of ethics for mountain guides, including the Mountain Code of the Union International des Associations d'Alpinisme or the Tyrol Declaration on Best Practice in Mountain Sports, consider man's responsibilities to pack animals."

Even the United Nations Code of Ethics for Tourism fails to mention the protection of animals.

From a purely practical point of view any traveller who fails to protect the welfare of his horses not only exploits the animals' health, but he also jeopardises the success of the journey.

Additionally, each Long Rider must also listen to his conscience and acknowledge his ethical responsibilities to the animals participating in the expedition. To treat these sentient beings as nothing more than a disposable source of raw power is to disregard the creatures' capacity for suffering. Thus every Long Rider has a moral duty to practise compassion with his equine travelling companions.

Protecting Horses and the Public

The Long Riders' Guild was formed to advance the ancient art of equestrian travel and to educate people on how to make a successful equestrian journey.

Another important part of our work is to alert the public to the need to exercise emotional and financial caution. The presence of a horse does not automatically denote a trustworthy rider.

The Guild is not an international police force. It is a brotherhood of equestrian explorers. Unlike the majority of the modern equestrian world, the Long Riders' Guild does not endorse competition, commercialism or nationalism. Being a Long Rider is not about how fast you can ride across a continent. It is about how the horse encourages personal and spiritual growth during a journey.

We collectively realize that accidents occur to horse and rider without premeditation or warning. In such a case the Guild requires that the journey be halted so as to allow the horse the time it needs to heal. There are many examples of ethical Long Riders who have stopped their journeys prematurely because they understood that the physical welfare of the horse takes precedence over their ego.

Times have changed. With the dawning of the twenty-first century, and with the availability of the Internet, those who misused their horses, deceived the public or lied about their exploits can hide no longer. Nor do their actions go undetected.

The Guild differs from the modern horse world in a critically important way. It enforces a strict ethical policy that never turns a blind eye to horse abuse. The Hall of Shame, published on the LRG website, is the only equestrian collection of its kind. The message it transmits is simple. If you abuse your horses while travelling, the Guild will take every reasonable action to stop your journey.

Validating Your Journey

There is another element to ethical equestrian travel. You may be called upon to provide proof that the journey was authentic and that your claim to have reached a distant goal can be confirmed by reliable evidence.

Being questioned by sceptics is nothing new to Long Riders or explorers. Two of the most renowned Polar explorers both survived gruelling and dangerous expeditions, only to have their integrity questioned after returning home.

After concluding the two-year long Discovery expedition to Antarctica in 1904, Captain Robert Scott was shocked upon his return to London. Despite having risked his life in the pursuit of obtaining valuable scientific research, the findings of Scott and his team were subjected to an extensive examination by several sceptical scientists. One critic went so far as to threaten Scott with a "scientific court martial."

Thanks to careful note-taking while in the field, Captain Scott's reports were found to be accurate and his critics were silenced.

Another Polar hero, Sir Ernest Shackleton, endured a more insidious type of attack. After a gruelling journey across Antarctica, Shackleton returned to England in 1909. He reported that along with two companions they had come within 112 miles (180 kilometres) of reaching the South Pole.

Shackleton was hailed as a popular hero by the press and knighted by King George VII. Unfortunately, there were those who envied his success. Motivated by spite, jealousy and prejudice, they began a quiet and insidious smear campaign which hinted that Shackleton had intentionally bungled his observations in order to claim that he had travelled "further south" than anyone else in history.

Shackleton was able to silence his critics and vindicate the accuracy of his claims thanks to the notes he and his team had carefully compiled during the journey.

The need for accurate observation was understood by Long Riders as well.

Many of the 19th century equestrian travellers had a military background. One such example was Major Clarence Dalrymple Bruce. He set off from Leh, Ladakh on August 29, 1905. He arrived in Peking, China on January 12, 1906.

The journey had required Bruce to ride over 18,000 foot high Himalayan passes and cross dangerous desert country. Despite the hardships Bruce never failed to make an accurate record of the day's event in a special document he created. It recorded the date, camp number, name of the place, the temperature at 6 a.m. and 7 p.m., observations on the wind and weather and notes on any geographical features of interest.

All of this scientific information was provided as a special Appendix in Bruce's account of his travels, entitled *In the Hoofprints of Marco Polo*.

One of the most extraordinary equestrian journeys of the 20th century was the inspiration for the creation of a remarkable set of documents and images which were intentionally created so as to provide absolute proof of the traveller's claim to have ridden 33,000 kilometres (20,352 miles) to all 48 American state capitals.

George Beck and his three companions realized in advance that no one had ever attempted such a journey before. That is why, even before their departure, they recognized the need to be able to confirm that they had ridden every mile, visited every state capital and met all 48 governors.

The Overland Westerners, as they called themselves, began their trip by meeting Governor Marion Hay at Olympia, Washington on May 1, 1912. They concluded the celebrated trip on May 24, 1915 when they met Governor Hiram Johnson at Sacramento, California.

Along the way Beck had carefully collected 48 "Certificate of Calls." These were official letters, issued by the governor's office, which verified the arrival of the Long Riders at that capital. Additionally, the mounted travellers also had a photo taken which showed them and their horses standing alongside each governor.

Friendship Book

Other Long Riders, both past and present, have recognized the need to document the accuracy of their journeys. These travellers did not keep military style records or collect letters from governors. They carried a special book which contained the names of the people they met, along with that person's signature, date and a personal comment.

An early example of this concept was the "signature book" kept by Frank Heath. He set off from Washington DC on March 31, 1925. He returned to the same city on November 4, 1927. During the course of his journey, Frank had filled seven signature books with names, dates and notes. The first and last signatures were from the same veterinarian who examined Frank's horse, Gypsy Queen, at the start and end of the journey. The mare was declared in excellent health.

The book also revealed that Frank had been on the road 948 days, riding an average of 11.98 miles per day. Gypsy Queen was under saddle an average of seven hours for each day on the road, making an average of 2.80 plus miles per hour.

The signature books also revealed that Frank had miscalculated how far he had ridden.

"These were worrisome days, while I was still trying to get my affairs straightened out after the conclusion of the trip. Originally I thought we had ridden 11,389 miles. That was the figure which I gave to reporters when I arrived at the Milestone marker in Washington DC where I began and ended my journey. But when I began reviewing my notebooks later, and discovered some errors, I had the seven notebooks reviewed by an expert mathematician. The distance was found to be 11,356 miles, a difference of 33 miles in 578 days under saddle. I am submitting this explanation to be frank. There is no intention of misrepresenting or exaggerating anything. In all subsequent articles or interviews I always gave the distance as 11,356 miles."

More recently Billy Brenchley and Christy Henchie kept a series of Friendship Books during their ride across the African continent. They made a point of obtaining the signatures of government officials in Tunisia, where they began their journey, and then seeking out signatures from other national officials as they rode through Libya, Egypt, Sudan, Uganda and Tanzania.

A Powerful Idea

Friendship Books not only provide vital evidence which proves the accuracy of your journey, they can also ease your way through local difficulties.

Though many Long Riders have collected autographs, it was Argentine Long Rider Benjamin Reynal who had the inspired idea of using a Friendship Book to enlist the aid of local police he encountered along the way.

He set off in 1998, determined to make an extensive exploration of his country. It took him nearly two years to ride 5,000 kilometres (3,100 miles) through 15 provinces.

At first Benjamin kept a Friendship Book so as to simply collect the names of his hosts and the places where he stayed. His first improvement upon the basic idea was to invite each person to add in a personal comment.

"One of the nicest things I have from my trip is a simple notebook that I call my 'Friendship Book,' because I can't find a better word to describe it. This was where I asked the people I met, those who helped me, or received me in their homes, to write whatever feeling, wishes, poems, etc they felt like. I did this just before leaving their house. The result was a beautiful compilation of notes, letters, poems and pictures of them," Benjamin explained.

Years after his journey was completed, he discovered that the "Friendship Book" was also "a perfect way of travelling back" to the trip.

However Benjamin accidentally discovered that the Friendship Book could become a strong strategic tool for a Long Rider.

"I have another hint about the Friendship Book that can be useful. As you know, in Argentina there is no long-term medical permit that is prepared for 'transporting' horses by riding them. In my country when you go to the veterinary office that issues permits for animal transportation, these documents are only valid for 48 hours. The document must also include all the information about the truck being used to haul the horses."

Knowing that he had so many provincial borders to cross with his two Criollos, Pampa and Federal, Benjamin realized that this bureaucratic system would create tremendous problems for him and that it was a waste of time trying to argue with local officials. That's when he hit upon the idea of seeking the aid of the chief veterinarian at the local Senasa (animal control) office. Benjamin explained his plans very carefully, the result being that the official issued him with a special permit that carefully stated: "travelling mounted, all the way around the country."

Benjamin knew this local letter was not applicable nationwide.

"Of course the veterinarian warned me that some officials might doubt the validity of the document. But something is better than nothing, I thought."

With this document in his pocket, and his Friendship Book in his saddlebag, Benjamin set off. That is when he quickly realized that the Friendship Book had a powerful but previously undetected purpose.

"With its growing collection of pictures, letters, stamps etc. it was a very fast, easy and truthful way of explaining your travels. I learned that after seeing the book 99% of the people wanted to help and become part of the trip."

Even more importantly, Benjamin made a point of collecting the signatures of all the policemen he met along the way.

"The reason for this is very important and I would recommend it to future travellers. If you get one policeman to sign your book and stamp it, as I did fifty times, then the next policeman you find will also want to sign, to be part of your trip, to have his picture taken with you."

Benjamin discovered the growing collection of police signatures unexpectedly created "a clear path" when trouble arose.

"One day I had to cross a very long bridge that went over a river. I could not go below it and the traffic was impossible over it. So I went to the small local police station and asked them for help. They got two cars; one was the only police car they had and the other was a private car. Then they stopped traffic and escorted me across the bridge. They were happy to do this, and I received such fast assistance after I showed them the Friendship Book."

In addition, Benjamin realized that as the collection of police signatures grew, chances diminished of anyone questioning the validity of the transport letter written by the government veterinarian at the beginning of the trip.

"No policeman or anybody else made any trouble after I showed them the Friendship Book. Their reasoning was: if he made it up to here, and he has some kind of written permit, and so many other policeman have signed his travel book, then all this must be valid and I am not going to be the one ruining this trip".

The Media

Long Riders have been attracting the attention of reporters for a long time.

After his arrival in Providence, Rhode Island, in 1925, Frank Heath gave what is believed to be the earliest radio interview done by an equestrian traveller.

Conducted before a live audience, a reporter for the Outlet Radio Broadcasting Station said, "I believe our audience would appreciate a few words from Mr. Frank Heath, the Horseback Traveller."

The Long Rider was allotted three minutes to explain his journey to all 48 states. When he was finished, Frank asked the announcer, "How was that for the first time?"

The live audience roared their approval.

During her ride across Canada in 1939, Mary Bosanquet was bewildered by the constant curiosity of the reporters who eagerly followed her progress across the country. She recalled her shock when upon arriving at a house in search of a place to rest for the night, hearing the radio announcer talking about a dark-haired English girl riding across Canada.

"My natural reaction to reporters is unfavourable," she recalled and she had an intense dislike for being "temporarily famous."

As technology advanced, it kept up with equestrian travel.

Messanie Wilkins was the first to attract the attention of reporters for the newly-invented television stations.

Initially it was the print media that took notice of the elderly lady riding alone from "ocean to ocean." Soon after she began her ride from Maine to California, newspaper reporters tracked her down. Messanie soon learned that giving interviews was a time-consuming business.

"The prospects of making that day's camp came to an abrupt halt when a car stopped. Out hopped two men and a woman. They were reporters from a paper in Portland, Maine. They asked all sorts of questions and I answered all of them which I thought weren't too personal. Finally I told them that the talking wasn't getting me any closer to California."

Messanie fumed, "I was a little fussed because we'd wasted almost an hour."

As her trip progressed, television caught up with a Long Rider for the first time.

"I was just about to saddle Tarzan," Messanie remembered, "when a big car drove into the yard. The three men in it said they had been looking for me all night. They were from a television network and had a movie camera with them. First one I'd ever seen. They set it up on an old fashioned tripod and then ran a line from it to the car battery. We kept running into them for the next couple of hours. They took pictures from both sides of the road, and once from the top of their car as they drove by."

After 17 months in the saddle, Messanie completed her 11,200 kilometres (7,000 miles) journey by arriving at the Pacific Ocean near Los Angeles in March, 1956. A few days later the lively spinster from the tiny village in distant Maine became the first Long Rider to appear live and be interviewed on a nationally syndicated television programme.

Messanie had one rule that she used to deal with the press, which any modern Long Rider would do well to remember

"I didn't want to be controversial," she recalled.

Benefits and Drawbacks

As Messanie learned, dealing with the media has benefits and disadvantages.

One of the major inconveniences is that granting an interview is time consuming. You can't afford to be disrespectful but you also can't sit up on your horse answering questions while valuable travel time slips by.

Plus, a Long Rider and her horses attract attention and can distract passing motorists. At least one major automobile accident occurred when an American Long Rider stopped alongside a busy road to answer questions, thereby diverting the attention of the nearby drivers, who crashed into each other.

It is always better for the horses and safer for you to arrange to meet the reporter at day's end, at some secure prearranged spot. Reporters recognize an interesting human interest story when they see a Long Rider. That is why they are usually willing to comply with this simple request.

Some reporters are more eager than others. During their ride from Kentucky to Oregon, French Long Riders Marc von Polier and Augustin Blanchard recalled, "We answered questions from a TV journalist while waiting in our underwear in a laundromat while our clothes dried."

Another consideration is that even though you are constantly on the move, the questions never change.

English Long Rider Richard Barnes heard and noted all the standard questions during his circular journey through Wales, England and Scotland in 1977.

"Where do you come from? What is the point of going by horse? What are you trying to prove? How many miles do you ride every day? How do you keep the horse shod? Where do you sleep at night? Don't you ever get lonely?"

Eventually you become tired of repeating the same answers over and over again.

During his 22,500 kilometre (14,000 miles) ride across the United States, DC Vision was interviewed by more than 600 newspaper reporters. In what has become the most popular "Story from the Road" ever published on the Long Riders' Guild website, entitled *A Journey to Simplify Life*, DC recalled how one interview stood out from all the rest.

"There was nothing extraordinary about the reporter's interview. It was essentially the same interview I had given over five hundred times, the same questions and the same rote answers. Looking back, I know I had crossed some imaginary line. I was no longer speaking to the newspaper's readers, but finally allowing myself to be honest. It may cost me the interview, I thought, but I was tired of portraying myself as what the external world expected of me. The question the young woman asked was, 'So why did you undertake such a long journey in the first place?' I looked at her and asked whether she wanted the rehearsed answer, or the truth."

What she heard stunned her.

"I took the trip because I wanted to prove to myself that I was still alive. My life no longer made any sense to me. I had everything that the television had told me for 25 years that I needed in order to be happy. But I felt like an M&M. I had this wonderful candy-coated shell, but there wasn't any chocolate inside of me. I didn't have any noticeable depth. I had become little more than a consumer and I couldn't face another 25 years living like that.

I was waking up every Monday morning wishing it were Friday, and soon realized that I was rushing away five out of every seven days. And I was a real stress junkie. I wasn't happy unless the pace at work was frantic. I was up to four and a half packs of cigarettes a day, 70 pounds overweight, and I didn't care if I was shortening my life. It's a slow form of suicide, and there are many of us out there who don't realize that."

A typical interview would last about 15 minutes. That interview at a county fairground in southern Idaho lasted six hours. The reporter even returned the next day to express her heartfelt thanks to DC for inspiring her to follow some of her unrealized dreams.

"From that day forward I have never told anyone what they wanted to hear, and have found it impossible to engage in small talk," he wrote.

One of the benefits of being interviewed is as news spreads about your journey, suspicions diminish and hospitality increases.

During his long journey through all of Argentina, Benjamin Reynal noted, "I did not expect medals or desire trophies. And the only reason I did some TV and newspaper articles during my ride was because it seemed fun. I was 24 at the time. But more importantly sometimes when I reached a house to ask for shelter, it helped me a lot if people already knew about my story thanks to the news. That lessened their fear and made them want to participate with the trip. So, at times it helped to be known. Other times I just wanted to disappear and be anonymous."

Times have certainly changed since Frank Heath spoke into a radio microphone 89 years ago. The concept of media has become a dominant factor in many people's everyday lives. It can also be an intrusive and emotionally distressing experience for a Long Rider.

Sea G Rhydr began her journey quietly in California. No one paid her much attention as she slowly made her way across the deserts of Arizona and New Mexico. By the time she reached Texas a few people had begun to follow the small blog she intermittently updated. Yet the closer she came to the Atlantic, the more intense grew the pressure from both the media and the public.

She recalled, "The publicity and the blog and all the rest of it are such a mixed bag. After I was interviewed on TV, people started stopping me and asking for my autograph. But the worse were the minivan Mamas. They'd pull off the road in front of me, blocking the way, yank their children out of the vehicle and line them up in front of the ponies. If they spoke to me at all it was 'You don't mind if we take a photo do you?' They'd take the photo; herd the kids back into the van and drive away. I can't imagine what that can possibly mean to them or the kids? Take a photo with the famous lady? Ugh!"

Like other Long Riders, Sea also learned that dealing with the press is "very time-consuming and annoying to the ponies."

"The day after the most recent TV experience it took me 10 hours to ride 12 miles, so I decided that I wasn't going to do that anymore."

Reporters and Vigilantes

As DC learned, most mainstream reporters are not interested in investing the time needed to conduct an interview with a deeper perspective. Deadlines have to be met. A quick story about the picturesque horse traveller is enough to satisfy the demands of an editor and the curiosity of the average readers. Such stories sell papers but don't make a long-term difference to the traveller.

In addition to the inconvenience, there is the problem of personal intrusion.

With the onset of the internet age, Long Riders need to be careful whom they speak to. There is a vast difference between a legitimate reporter and a nosy private citizen. Genuine journalists will be able to provide evidence of who they work for. A vindictive cyberstalker pretending to be a reporter will lack such credentials. If you feel any suspicion about the person's authenticity, don't hesitate to politely decline to engage in any type of conversation, telephone call or email exchange.

Even if the reporter is authentic, you are within your rights to decline an interview if it conflicts with your travel plans. You are under no obligation to answer questions about your private life. If you feel the interview is going badly, don't hesitate to conclude it politely.

Unless you deliberately sought out notoriety, you are not by definition a public figure simply because you chose to travel on horseback.

Summary

Some lessons from our collective past endure into the present. John Bunyan's book, *The Pilgrim's Progress*, is believed never to have been out of print since it first appeared in 1678. The book warns that one of the most insidious dangers that can befall a traveller is to lust for fame rather than to search for enlightenment.

One of The Guild's primary purposes is to ensure that the travelling horse is never deliberately abused.

Unfortunately there are individuals who would sacrifice the horse to satisfy their ego.

Thomas Lambie was a Christian minister and a Long Rider. He warned, "No one who mistreats a horse is fit to own one. The Lord's work shouldn't be a horse's burden."

Like his enlightened predecessor, Ashoka, Jalaluddin Muhammad Akbar believed man has a moral responsibility to treat animals with kindness, dignity and charity.

During his ride across Japan Professor Takeshi Shoji treated his horse, Kage, with great respect and kindness.

In 1892 Austrian and German cavalry officers raced each other 580 kilometres (360 miles) from Berlin to Vienna. As a result 46 horses were ridden to death in 71 hours.

Francois Xavier Aubry embodied the Hungarian word lóháldl, which states that the horse is expendable. In 1849 he rode six horses to death and left half a dozen more permanently wounded on an eight-day journey from Santa Fe, New Mexico to Independence, Missouri.

In contrast, Vincent Gabriel Kirouac made a journey across Canada to promote the knightly virtues of chivalry, courage, compassion and loyalty. When his horse, Coeur de Lion (Lion Heart), developed a saddle sore, the modern knight terminated his ride early.

A notorious example of placing ego before ethics occurred in the summer of 1990 when three Frenchmen made the ill-fated decision to take horses into Canada's barren Arctic Circle. They bought two horses under false premises. The untrained animals were over loaded, driven through the ice for 80 days and starved to the point of death.

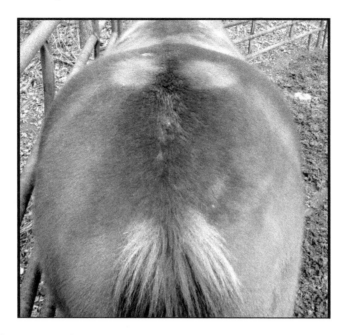

One of the characteristics of a person with "Equestrian Narcissistic Disorder" is that their personal goals take precedence over the horse's wellbeing. This horse was injured when the saddle was broken during a ride from Montana to Texas. Even though the Welsh traveller knew the saddle was inflicting pain and injury, he had grown so addicted to the public acclaim that he continued the ride to El Paso. There he enjoyed being hailed as a hero, before flying home and leaving the horse to an uncertain future.

Before setting off to ride to all 48 American state capitals, George Beck and his three companions recognized the need to be able to confirm that they had ridden every mile, visited every state capital and met all 48 governors.

Chronological List

	State	Capital		Date	Governor
1.	Washington	Olympia	1912	01 - May	Marion E. Hay
2.	Oregon	Salem	1912	11 - May	Oswald West
3.	Idaho	Boise	1912	18 - June	James H. Hawley
4.	Montana	Helena	1912	21 - July	Edwin L. Norris
5.	North Dakota	Bismarck	1912	12 - September	John Burke
6.	South Dakota	Pierre	1912	28 - September	Robert Scadden Vessey
7.	Minnesota	St. Paul	1912	27 - October	Adolph O. Eberhart
8.	Wisconsin	Madison	1912	25 - November	Francis E. McGovern
9.	Illinois	Springfield	1912	13 - December	Charles S. Deneen
10.	Tennessee	Nashville	1913	17 - January	Ben W. Hooper
11.	Alabama	Montgomery	1913	22 - April	Emmet O'Neal
12.	Florida	Tallahassee	1913	15 - May	Park Trammell
13.	Georgia	Atlanta	1913	05 - June	Joseph Mackey Brown
14.	South Carolina	Columbia	1913	24 - June	Coleman L. Blease
15.	North Carolina	Raleigh	1913	07 - July	Locke Craig
16.	Virginia	Richmond	1913	28 - July	William Hodges Mann
17.	Maryland	Annapolis	1913	18 - August	Phillips Lee Goldsborough
18.	Delaware	Dover	1913	August	Charles Miller
19.	New Jersey	Trenton	1913	28 - August	James F. Fielder
20.	Connecticut	Hartford	1913	10 - September	Simeon Eben Baldwin
21.	Rhode Island	Providence	1913	14 - September	Aram J. Pothier
22.	Massachusetts	Boston	1913	20 - September	Eugene Noble Foss
23.	New Hampshire	Concord	1913	26 - September	Samuel D. Felker
24.	Maine	Augusta	1913	04 - October	William Thomas Haines
25.	Vermont	Montpelier	1913	October	Allen Miller Fletcher
26.	New York	Albany	1913	12 - November	Martin H. Glynn
27.	Pennsylvania	Harrisburg	1913		John Kinley Tener
28.	West Virginia	Charleston	1913	29 - December	Henry D. Hatfield
29.	Ohio	Columbus	1914		James M. Cox
30.	Michigan	Lansing	1914	04 - February	Woodbridge N. Ferris
31.	Indiana	Indianapolis	1914	24 - February	Samuel Moffett Ralston
32.	Kentucky	Frankfort	1914	16 - March	James B. McCreary
33.	Mississippi	Jackson	1914	27 - April	Earl LeRoy Brewer
34.	Louisiana	Baton Rouge	1914	08 - May	Luther Egbert Hall
35.	Texas	Austin	1914	18 - June	Oscar Branch Colquitt
36.	Arkansas	Little Rock	1914		George Washington Hays
37.	Missouri	Jefferson City	1914		Elliot Woolfolk Major
38.	Iowa	Des Moines	1914	18 - September	George W. Clarke
39.	Nebraska	Lincoln	1914		John H. Morehead
40.	Kansas	Topeka	1914	15 - October	George H. Hodges
41.	Oklahoma	Oklahoma City	1914	13 - November	Lee Cruce
42.	Wyoming	Cheyenne	1914	23 - December	Joseph Maull Carey
43.	Colorado	Denver	1914	29 - December	Elias Milton Ammons
44.	New Mexico	Albuquerque	1915	25 - January	William C. McDonald
45.	Arizona	Phoenix	1915	03 - March	George Wylie Paul Hunt
46.	Utah	Salt Lake City	1915		William Spry
47.	Nevada	Carson City	1915		Emmet Derby Boyle
48.	California	Sacramento	1915	24 - May	Hiram W. Johnson

http://www.nationalcowboymuseum.org/research/exhibits/overland-westerners/default.aspx

Along the way Beck collected 48 "Certificate of Calls," official letters issued by each governor's office, which verified the arrival of the Long Riders at that capital. This list shows how they began their trip by meeting Governor Marion Hay at Olympia, Washington on May 1, 1912. They concluded the celebrated trip on May 24, 1915 when they met Governor Hiram Johnson at Sacramento, California.

Long Riders Billy Brenchley and Christie Henchie kept a series of Friendship Books during their epic ride across the African continent. They made a point of obtaining the signatures of government officials in Tunisia, where they began their journey.

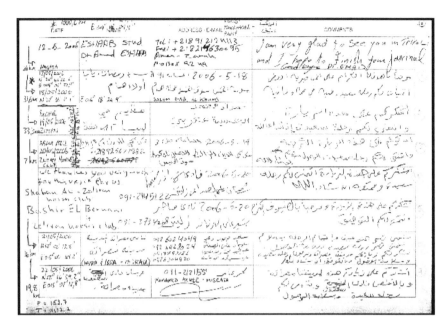

During the journey they obtained signatures from other national officials as they rode through Libya, Egypt, Sudan, Uganda and Tanzania.

Long Rider Benjamin Reynal rode 5,000 kilometres (3,100 miles) through 15 provinces of Argentina in 1998.

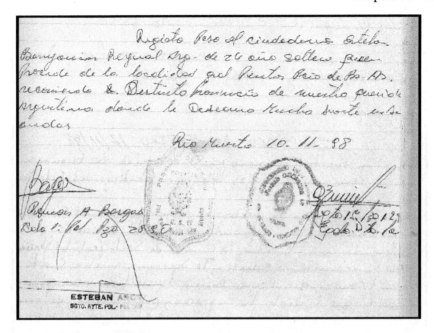

During his journey, Benjamin had the inspired idea of using a Friendship Book to obtain the signatures of all the local police he encountered along the way. This page shows a policeman's autograph, as well as the official stamp of that police station.

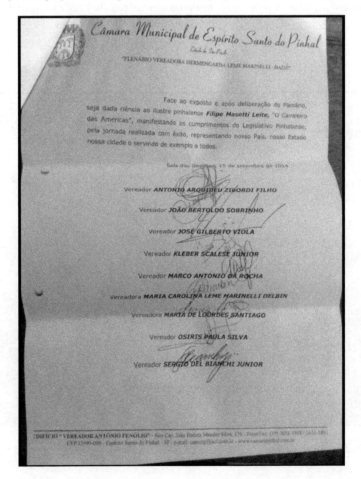

At the conclusion of a two-year journey from Canada to Brazil, Filipe Leite confirmed the validity of his ride by obtaining an official document signed by leading Brazilian authorities.

After riding from Maine to California, Messanie Wilkins became the first Long Rider to appear live and be interviewed on a nationally syndicated television programme. She was the guest of television celebrity, Art Linkletter.

It took more than a hundred years but in 2017 the legacy of the Overland Westerners was finally honoured. Meredith Cherry is the first woman to set out to ride the 48 state route created by George Beck in 1912. Starting in California, Meredith rode due north to Shelton, Washington. This small town marks the spot where the four forgotten travellers began their 20,352 mile mounted marathon. Meredith is seen holding the Long Riders' Guild flag in front of life-sized photos of Charles Beck and Jay Ransom (standing) and George Beck and Raymond Rayne (sitting). Rest in peace, Long Riders!

Chapter 75
The Long Quiet

Equestrian travel writers all too often focus on the external details. They tell you how to hobble your horse or which kind of saddle to use. While it is important to understand the mechanics of equestrian travel, these authors neglect to acknowledge the mystery which inspires so many people to undertake a Long Ride.

All brave souls who venture deep into the unknown sooner or later make this discovery: there are two worlds; the physical world which can be mapped and that other world which lies just beyond the edge of everyday events.

DC Vision, a Founding Member of the Long Riders Guild, made a 22,500 kilometre (14,000 mile) ride in the USA. This mounted philosopher knew there was more to a journey than mere mileage. He wisely said, "They either get it in ten miles or they never get it at all."

What he was referring to is known as the Long Quiet. What he did was explore the world within.

Different Minds

You probably take it for granted that the majority of humans are just like you; perhaps not.

In his book, *The Rise of the Centaurs*, the Danish equestrian historian, Bjarke Rink, delved deeply into the life style of the early mounted humans, who roamed at will across the vast grasslands which originally stretched like an Equestrian Equator from Mongolia to Hungary.

Unlike sedentary pedestrians, Bjarke conjectured that these horse-humans developed differently. Being constantly on horseback required them to be physically fit. Their sense of balance was enhanced. They had quicker reactions and their five senses were sharpened by a life lived out of doors.

In addition, Rink posed the possibility that long term equestrian travel could have an unforeseen mental impact as well.

"What happens to the infant's thought pattern when the family is eternally on the move? What happens to the human mind?" he wondered.

It may not be possible to dissect and diagnose the mind of an ancient Scythian nomad but many Long Riders have detected and noted an unexpected alteration in their mental outlook.

Tim Cope rode over the same ground where the original nomads once galloped. With several thousand miles already under his saddle, the further he ventured the more keenly aware he became of "an ongoing process" which was being created and influenced by "the moods of the natural ecology."

In words which could have been written by any horse-human, in any age, Tim spoke for so many when he said, "By moonlight, the silver glow, soft sound of horses breathing, the steppe again a moody dark sea, no words said, just this flowing floating, ever onwards stepping of the animals that was timeless and could have been anywhere on the vast Eurasian steppe. Distance and time for me becomes irrelevant in these conditions, a sense of soothing calmness and rhythm takes over."

On an obvious level riding amidst the glories of Nature keeps the rider's senses alive. You see, smell and hear more. Yet the "calmness and rhythm" which Tim felt sets the stage for the onset of inner reflection.

In 1997 a young American equestrian traveller named Bartle Bull set off to circumnavigate Lake Baikal. He had been expecting physical challenges. What surprised him was the interior inspection which he also underwent.

"Riding a horse through steppe and taiga can be monotonous, but there is no better way to see the country. The walker stares at the heels of the man in front. The motorist is stultified by the engine's throb and the speed of the scenery flashing past. The rider on horseback has both a need for vigilance and the opportunity for contemplation. This sensitivity to the details of the landscape gives meaning to the broader views and an intimacy with the character of the land. The rider sees over the country with eyes, half human and half animal. He thinks of footing, pasture, water, but his mind, sparked and resparked all day by the need to be alert, often reaches over the horizon," he wrote in his book, *Around the Sacred Sea*.

Making your way beneath a cathedral-like sky has other effects as well.

Changing Time

Unlike the Hollywood movies, Long Riders don't gallop across the countryside. They progress, day after day, country after country, at a steady, enduring pace.

As the sun rises, a peaceful progress begins which allows the Long Rider to hear the sounds of waking birds singing, insects chirping, animals calling. During the day clouds move silently overhead, all the while there is a constant peaceful rhythm of movement beneath the rider.

When he looks towards the horizon he is aware of the enormity of the landscape which surrounds him. On and on it seems to go, an endless Earth, all the while the horse moves along quietly at three miles an hour.

Hours pass and, not seeing another soul, the Long Rider speaks first to his horse, and then silently begins to commune with himself. The world is passing along so slowly that the traveller's senses begin to drift. Time slows down and a blissful blur descends upon the rider.

The journey has become a place of retreat. The Long Rider has ventured beyond an invisible curtain. Though there may be nothing to discover externally, the traveller has reached a point when the onset of silence and calm inspires contemplation.

As the sun sets, all the glories that feed the spirit have led to the discovery of hidden things residing within the rider's soul.

Learning to be Alone

Reading about Nature can be a pleasant experience. Actually surviving it can be quite frightening.

Louisa Jebb came face to face with this problem when she rode across the Ottoman Empire at the end of the 19th century.

"Cold and implacable the grim silent desert stretched away in front beyond the realms of space."

The landscape, she realized, was harsh and unforgiving.

"There is nothing human in nature. The earth, though loved so dearly, would let you perish on the ground and neither bring forth food nor water. Burning in the sky the great sun would merely burn on and make no motion to assist me."

It was while she was surrounded by this barren landscape that Louisa had an insight.

"If there is a link it is the response of its silence to the silence in you."

Louisa found that because of the intense solitude, "You were thrown back on yourself."

Human beings are social creatures and the majority of their lives are spent in close proximity to others of their kind. Consequently, many people are terrified of being alone. They avoid isolation. They fear solitude.

Equestrian travel often requires the traveller to spend long stretches of time on his own, frequently in absolute silence except for the steady sound of the horse's hooves. For many, this may the first time in their lives that they are totally alone. Some become frightened.

Others realize they possess the ability to cope with seclusion. Having learned the value of silence, they learn to draw strength from the solitude of the saddle. There is often a distinct feeling of distance emanating from such Long Riders. Their eyes are akin to quiet pools whose surfaces do not reveal what lies hidden deep within. They radiate strength and self-confidence.

Turning Away from the World

The value of halting the normal routines of life and learning to reflect inwardly may seem out of step with a world where everything seems gauged towards immediacy. Others have noted this difficulty.

After returning from his ride across a desolate part of Tibet, Leonard Clark wrote, "We moderns have lost the art of just living."

He issued that warning in 1950. Since then the world has grown more hectic, crowded, strident and intrusive.

Many Long Riders have encountered the wickedness of the world and all its cares, and grown bored to death with both of them.

Negley Farson, a war correspondent turned Long Rider, was an example of someone who was longing to remove himself from life's complications. With one companion, Farson set off to ride through the remote Caucasian Mountains. The area was sparsely inhabited but intensely beautiful.

"It is said that in the immense solitude of high mountains you come closer to knowing yourself than you will anywhere else on earth," Negley wrote. During that journey "clocks and hours stopped," and as they made their way through the mountains, "we lived in ourselves."

It isn't easy to reach such a spot in your life.

You have to realize that the horse isn't merely taking you towards a distant geographic goal. He is moving you at the same time away from the daily drama of world events. The journey allows you to leave behind the distracting chatter of others and turn off the noise of modern life.

The further the distance you ride the more intense becomes this experience. One Long Rider who learned this was Katie Cooper. She and her mule, Sir Walter, made a solo ride through the American Southwest which exposed them to harsh weather and long periods of silence.

"Walter and I travel through the world blissfully unconnected to technology, unaware of what passes for news or of any news we might be making. Local weather is the most important issue of the day. You know the feeling," she wrote. And other Long Riders concurred.

The Onset of Silence

Few equestrian travellers have realized that their journeys will expose them to such prolonged periods of silence and introspection. Prior to their departure, they are busy trying to learn the skills needed for their journey; how to overcome detractors, how to choose the right horse, how to use a pack saddle, how to summon up the courage to depart.

Once they are on the road things settle down into a peaceful pattern. That is when they notice that there are elements to the journey which they had not anticipated.

Margaret Leigh was one such example. She wrote, "We rode in silence, each alone with his thoughts. This tranquil movement through an empty world rocked me into a kind of trance, like that induced by sitting too long beside running water or moving tides. The slow unfolding of distant views is one of the greatest charms of travel on horseback. You proceed slowly, gathering impressions."

Day after day the gentle rhythmic motions of the horse induce a calming effect upon the traveller. The soothing progress brings on a peace of mind. Silent, alone in his own thoughts, the traveller learns to ride, react and receive. Without distractions, there is time to nurture ideas and to turn inwards with reverence.

The Inner Journey

Journeys rarely tell us what we expected to find.

Just as no two poems are alike, nor are any two journeys.

Many set off with no more purpose than to reach a distant geographic goal. These are the ones who carry their culture into the wilderness.

Horace, the Roman poet, had observed such travellers. He remarked more than 2,000 years ago, "They change their climate, not their soul, who rush across the sea."

Other travellers are deeply impacted when they leave behind the immense stimulation that is a part of everyday life.

Instead of street lights, they are bathed in starlight. Instead of inhabiting a world full of bright images flashing and crashing constantly across various-size screens, they are part of a planet where the sound of a crackling campfire, the taste of fresh water or the smell of the forest heal old wounds.

There is no time constraint, only time for transformation.

One of the Founders of the Long Riders' Guild understood this.

French Long Rider Gérard Barré wrote, "To travel merely for the sake of covering many miles does not allow for contemplation, except the possible contemplation of the map, the watch, or the GPS. What is important is not the amount of distance you ride. It is the immersion of your spirit into a state of mind which you cannot obtain except by forgetting normal society."

In Gérard's opinion the distance covered is therefore a secondary consequence of the search for a new truth.

"Looked at from this angle, I believe that the most important part of travelling on horseback is thus the conquest of self, of reaching one's 'interior Pole'," Gérard said.

A Prophecy

You wouldn't think that a fiery political rebel would be an articulate advocate of this state of peaceful equestrian reflection, but such was the case.

Count Vittorio Alfieri was an Italian aristocrat who had three passions in life – liberty, literature and horses.

"Without horses I am never half myself," wrote the man who defied Catherine the Great of Russia and Emperor Napoleon of France.

Having made several journeys in Russia and Europe, Alfieri set off in 1773 to ride from England home to Italy. He wrote in his autobiography, "I am under way again, and during this journey am opening myself up to poetic inspiration more than ever. My heart is filled with joy."

Considered one of Europe's most influential literary figures, Alfieri had realized that riding invites reflection. It was during this journey he recalled that "I learned the sublime art of silence."

The Count's journey became a mixture of travel and mysticism. Day after day, he was surrounded by views which inspired his poetic imagination. His mind, being at rest, became more receptive, his eye more observant. From the back of his horse he could speak with men, observe their ways, absorb their wisdom and perhaps read their hearts.

In a prophetic statement to future Long Riders, in 1799 Count Alfieri wrote, "Just because manners change, man, whether he lives in the year 1500, 1800 or 2000 will stay much the same."

As Alfieri predicted, modern Long Riders continue to travel in the same direction. Released from the press of the present, their journeys intensify their emotions and enhance their sense of clarity.

Thus these long periods of inner silence found on horseback bring many surprises, all of which are more profound than the passing attainment of reaching a distant ocean shore or riding into a foreign city. What is seldom understood is that during the course of an extensive equestrian journey many Long Riders experience epiphanies.

When asked her opinion, Bonnie Folkins said, "The Holy Grail is not an object. The Holy Grail is a state of mind. The Long Quiet arrives when the Long Rider least expects it. And the invisible bond that Long Riders share makes for a brotherhood of people who do not ever need to know or speak or write to one another to understand that they share a mystical link. The Long Quiet is why Long Riders never want to come home. To reach the Long Quiet is to touch on a metaphysical link to the wonders of the natural world – to the meaning of the natural universe."

Thus the secret of a successful equestrian journey is that you don't find what you thought you were looking for. It's what happens during the "getting there" that involves the ancient mystery of equestrian travel.

Finding the Long Quiet

Those who have discovered the Long Quiet have influenced events, literature and history.

Jonathan Swift is the famous author of *Gulliver's Travels*.

He wrote, "Vision is the art of seeing things invisible."

What no one remembers is the equestrian event which inspired this wisdom.

Swift was a Long Rider whose journey across Ireland inspired him to write about Gulliver's various journeys. Today a sanitised version of the original book is available as a sweet children's story. What is forgotten is that Swift's original story was a bitter political satire, published anonymously, which outraged the English establishment.

Most modern readers only remember the cute little people known as Lilliputians. What commercial publishers have long suppressed was the last of Gulliver's adventures wherein Swift recounts the tale of the talking horses. It turns man's definition of himself on its head.

To draw attention to the evils of materialism and elitism, Swift had Gulliver visit an unknown island inhabited by two kinds of creatures. The naked, selfish, savage and warlike humans were known as Yahoos. It was the horses known as the Houyhnhnms who enjoyed a peaceful society based upon reason.

Riding across Ireland on his beloved mare in 1725, travelling for long periods of time in peace and silence, inspired Swift to invent a land where talking horses were "the perfection of nature".

Had the author been walking or travelling in a coach, these profound ideas would probably never have come to him.

Nor was the impact of the Long Quiet restricted to literature; it is also linked to one of the greatest scientists of all time.

Charles Darwin led a life whose resonance is still being felt around the globe. It goes against common perception to think of this scientific titan galloping over the pampas of Argentina, exploring volcanic islands on horseback, and lying down to sleep on the bosom of the earth with his horse nearby.

Yet Darwin's diaries tell the story of not just a naturalist exploring the world searching for answers, they also reveal the inner man, the Long Rider who revelled in the freedom of riding on three continents, South America, Australia, and Africa.

Darwin wrote of "The pleasure of living in the open air with the sky for a roof and the ground for a table."

The young scientist discovered that long hours spent in the gentle rhythm of the saddle brought about unexpected ideas. Did his inner journey provide a sense of tranquillity that led to his reconsideration of science and evolution?

This introspection has practical applications, too.

More recently, the American Long Rider Len Brown also found inspiration in the Long Quiet.

While he was riding across the United States in 1982, Len wondered how he could make his horse more comfortable. He told the Guild that it was the hours spent in quiet contemplation that inspired him to invent the now-famous Orthoflex saddle.

Achieving that feeling described as the Long Quiet inspires creativity. It nurtures original ideas. It allows questions to arise unbidden. It encourages creative problem-solving. It enhances deeper understanding.

There are many more examples which prove the power of the Long Quiet.

You don't have to be a talented author, a scientific genius or an inspired inventor to connect with this elusive part of the equestrian travel experience. Like our ancient mounted ancestors, a special silent inter-species relationship between horse and human still enables us to venture beyond geography and to travel into an unknown country – ourselves.

Different Riders – Different Views

Long Riders young and old, past and present, have found a profound sense of peace during their time in the saddle.

Katie Russell was a young woman making her first equestrian trip in 2011 when she realized that the journey was affecting her in an unexpected manner.

"This thought came while riding yesterday. These days consist of a 4 to 6 hour meditation session: riding meditation where I am either here now, with my horse, or processing deep things inside, mostly forgiving myself for old wrongs. This meditation is bordered on each side of the day by plain old humbling labour: moving packs around, camp chores, horse chores. It is a strengthening routine on which I thrive. Add to that seeing beautiful new places and meeting beautiful new people, and I cannot think of a better way to spend my time."

Yet you don't automatically discover the Long Quiet just because you mount a horse.

Equestrian travel is the exact opposite of dressage, in that the former encourages free thinking, while the latter punishes you for the slightest deviation from a set of predetermined movements.

Free thinking, like free movement, isn't part of the plan, as organized equestrian events are populated by expert insiders schooled in confining disciplines. These are humans inhabiting a narrow world who are taught to cling to their beliefs, to worship the past and to only accept evidence which confirms what they already collectively believe.

In contrast history proves that Long Riders are the traditional human outsiders, the lone travellers who leave the predictability of the intellectual village, venture into unknown lands, both physical and personal, and during the course of their journeys shake off belief blindness.

But a new kind of threat is making it harder than ever for equestrian travellers to connect with this elusive and imperceptible personal space.

These days most of us are assaulted during our waking hours by an unprecedented flood of information. Television, radio, the Internet, mobile phones, SMS, Facebook, Twitter – they all conspire against tranquillity.

People addicted to social media, even if they ride a million miles, will never understand or attain the Long Quiet.

New Challenges

The stress created by the introduction of new technology is nothing new. Nor have Long Riders ever suppressed their suspicions of or sworn blind allegiance to the mechanical fad of the day.

English Long Rider Andrew Wilson expressed his concerns about mankind's increasing reliance upon machines while making his journey across the length of the Himalayan Mountains in 1873. A seasoned traveller, Wilson had seen much of the world. Living as he did at the onset of the Industrial Revolution, he realized that technology was not as benevolent as many automatically believed.

"A few individuals benefit by such discoveries as the use of steam have given to the people of this century. They may argue that this is a satisfactory and happy world. But unfortunately it is only a select few who can console themselves with that illusion. In every age and clime the voice of humanity has risen in wondering sorrow and questioning to the silent heaven," Wilson remarked.

Wilson's suspicions had been confirmed by the time Magdalene Weale set off to explore England on horseback in 1935. The once-radiant green countryside had been sliced into pieces by rampant railroads. Ancient forests had disappeared into the greedy maw of factory furnaces. Historic buildings had been destroyed so as to make way for the construction of shoddy commercial enterprises.

From atop a high hill in the county of Shropshire, Magdalene looked out across a countryside that had been blighted by the unrestricted growth of technological progress.

"The industrialism of the nineteenth century was a monstrous growth that consumed the green beauty of the countryside with its corroding breath," she wrote in anger. No building or any sense of cultural heritage was now safe, she believed, from the onset of "Industry which in its meanness knows neither reverence for the past nor pity for the great or beautiful."

James Wentworth Day was a renowned naturalist and author who made an extensive ride through Great Britain during the height of the Second World War. A man who loved Nature and the written word, he summed up the growing suspicion of machines when he succinctly stated, "the typewriter is the soulless emblem of this mechanical age."

Within the lifetime of these three Long Riders mankind had progressed from pen and ink, to the telegram, then the typewriter. Telephones and televisions soon followed. Today emails and text messages are the latest fad. But as history proves, the process of information exchange is on-going and today's miracle will be tomorrow's memory.

Yet it is the unexpected impact of recently-invented technology which presents a new type of threat to Long Riders: a diminishment or the disappearance of the Long Quiet.

Unintended Consequences

Once again mankind finds itself at a crossroads.

A new type of technical revolution is under way. Unlike our forefathers, who watched in amazement at the mighty power of the steam engine, our generation is witnessing the largest increase in expressive capability in the history of the human race. Thanks to the invention of the Internet, mobile telephone technology and social forums such as Facebook, more of humanity can communicate to other people than at any time in the history of our species.

As past lessons demonstrate, there have been unintended social consequences to the latest mechanical revolution.

Long Riders depart to learn more about themselves, their horses and Nature. Yet the intrusion of new communication technology acts like an invisible magnet which keeps the traveller hooked up to the sleepless hum of the internet and its various addictive offerings.

The wisest among the Long Riders had recognized and warned against such a development.

Richard Barnes explored England extensively. He had been inspired by the 17th century Japanese poet Matsuo Bashō, who in turn followed a tradition among the writers of Japan to go on the road on horse or on foot to contemplate and then convey the beauty of such things as a morning in the mountains.

Mounted on his trusty Cob, Remus, Richard slipped quietly though the country, unnoticed, unknown, looking for places where the modern world had not yet penetrated.

It was during his ride that Richard realized the journey had "Reminded me of some ancient thing within us."

"Travel is an art," he wrote, "which consists not only of fastening the buckles and keeping things together, but relating to what you see."

It was because he was riding alone, uninterrupted, that Richard had time to "free think", a term which he was the first to use.

The many books, poems and photographs he has published since then demonstrate the deep impact the ride with Remus had on Richard's life.

What Richard also discovered was that the discovery of inner harmony was contingent upon reflection and that the intrusion of modern events disrupted or reduced the chance of this from occurring.

"The popular attitude is that life has improved but time and time again you can see that something has been forfeited," he warned.

The Cost of Progress

For most of its history humanity relied upon the spoken word to communicate. After thousands of years of restricted communiqué, mankind learned to "draw sounds" when it began to put ideas, expressed as words, onto paper. Even after mankind had invented the concept of writing, it remained a rare skill practised by a handful of individuals.

During his ride across Central Asia in the 1870s, English Long Rider Frederick Burnaby observed the power of the written word when he watched a mullah prepare to write a letter in front of an awe-struck group of villagers.

"A dead silence reigned. Writing a letter was no everyday occurrence in that hamlet, and the man who was able to make a piece of paper speak was looked upon as a prodigy of learning."

In the blink of an eye humanity has gone from the point where communication was largely restricted to the rich and educated to a new stage in our collective development where billions of humans are compulsively interacting via technology which threatens to become all pervasive. From saying very little, modern society has become consumed with constant communication. Instead of riding in silence, travellers are now tempted to stay eternally connected.

This shift in priorities comes with a cost. Tranquillity is being forfeited.

Intrusive Technology

Like fire, communication technology is capable of changing itself from being a valuable servant into a deadly master.

What had originally been viewed as convenient and constant verbal communication has been transformed from a technical expedient into an emotional necessity.

The spread has been so rapid that there are now more mobile phones than people in Britain. The use of these machines has changed the way people act. What had started as a portable speaking device soon developed the ability to take photographs, send and share information instantly, constantly monitor world events and allow the owner to participate in international forums with millions of strangers.

As its abilities grew, so did the machine's disturbing power. What had once merely been a communications device encouraged the onset of obsessive behaviour.

A survey conducted by an American company, Lookout Mobile Security, confirmed that people were gripped by the incessant urge to interact with their technology. Owners routinely checked their phones for messages while driving, in restaurants, during church services, in the middle of the night, even in the bathroom. Other research found that mobile users can't leave their phone alone for six minutes and check it up to 150 times during a waking day of 16 hours.

Like heroin addicts and cigarette smokers, phone-users found comfort in repetitious rituals. No matter how relatively mundane the material being transmitted was, the act of scrolling, tapping and talking drew the user into a private space which excluded the rest of the world.

Robin Hanbury-Tenison was the first Long Rider to make note of the onset of this growing global problem. While riding across Albania in 2007 he met people who had an inability to stop using their mobile phone for more than a few minutes.

One of Robin's hosts, "suffers from what I had already noticed is a recent addiction of urban Albanians. My suggestion that he turned the thing off was greeted with incredulity. "

Robin concluded, "Mobiles are a drug in Albania."

There is a pleasure and pain principle at work.

Like lab rats who are rewarded when they press the right lever, humans who react to their machine receive emails, texts, news and images which act as a stimulant. Turning off the machine produces a sense of anxiety, leaving the human feeling out of touch or even socially isolated.

Internet Addiction

What had first seemed like a plot for a science fiction movie, i.e. the machines taking control of humans, has become an increasingly obvious reality. Doctors have realized that, like alcohol, the constant use of phones, laptops, tablets and computers are not only keeping people overly engaged, it is leading to a dramatic global increase in electronic addiction.

Scientists estimate that the number of people who are digitally dependent has risen at the rate of 30 per cent over the last three years. Internet addiction has become so widespread in Taiwan and Korea that both national governments consider it a national health crisis.

Especially frightening is the fact that technology encourages the young to sever their ties with the natural world. According to U.S. researchers, the average teenager spends more than 7.5 hours a day using a mobile phone, computer or watching television. Meanwhile, children in that country spend a daily average of 15 to 25 minutes a day in outdoor play or sport. The first technology addiction programme was recently begun in the United Kingdom, where the youngest known patient is four years old.

It is a frightening testament to the growing power of these machines that half of all the young people questioned for a recent study said they would surrender one of their human senses rather than give up their technology.

Disadvantages

Long Riders should be aware that communication technology creates personal and professional problems.

Whereas the journey should encourage the traveller to slow down, technology encourages the feeling that life is moving at an accelerating pace.

Despite the broad acceptance that quiet reduces stress, the small two-dimensional space of a mobile phone creates bright sounds and sights that saturate the brain, create stress and mute the dimensions of the real world around them.

Studies show that office workers often glance at their inbox 30 to 40 times an hour. Every time we shift our attention, the brain has to reorient itself. Contemplation is discouraged because of constant interruptions and continuous stimulation.

You can't look inwards for the Long Quiet if you're looking downwards at your mobile phone. With the onset of clamorous dissonance, the contemplative mind is overwhelmed and the inward eye is closed.

Taking your troubles with you

In the past explorers relished the idea of being able to escape from the tyranny of the mechanized world. They were beyond the reach of the post office. They remained in blissful ignorance of what was published in the newspapers. They were happy to find relief from the noise of every life.

That sense of contented calm is threatened or destroyed when the traveller is unable to disconnect themselves from the social networking scene. Electronic intrusion plays a sort of Russian roulette with the Long Rider's emotions, as the arrival of every email might bring disturbing news.

Instead of leaving their troubles behind, they lug them along and check them compulsively via Facebook, Twitter, etc.

Exploration Spam

It should be noted that the abusive stream of information flows in both directions.

When he set off in 1919 to make an extensive exploration of the Amazon basin, Alexander Hamilton Rice's expedition was equipped with the latest in communication devices, an Eddystone All World Receiver that derived its power from a pedal-driven generator.

Thanks to the radio, Hamilton Rice was the first explorer to send and receive messages from the field. What should have been a triumph for technology was viewed with scepticism by many.

"Whether it is an advantage by reporting daily is a matter on which opinions will differ. Technology now exists which permits a traveller to send daily updates of their difficulties, dangers and triumphs. This means that travellers are no longer in danger of being marooned. Yet the innovations which enable them to call for help in the case of an emergency are often abused on a daily basis," stated one group of explorers.

It didn't take long for more concerns to be voiced.

"The modern practice of frequent reports by wireless may be essential to finance an expedition, but has many disadvantages. Reports tend toward exaggeration in order to provide news; it causes worry at home if a regular report is not received; it makes great anxiety for the leader whether to report difficulties, perhaps only temporary, but which may provoke unnecessary organization of relief from home, or on the other hand to incur risk of blame by not reporting at once difficulties which develop into serious danger. Wireless calls for assistance have sometimes caused unnecessary excitement and anxiety, and induced rescue efforts involving further disaster."

Leaders of the exploration community concluded that the radio was a mixed blessing.

The development of new technology has provided an opportunity for the creation of spammer travellers. These are the vain and vacuous individuals who antagonize people by deluging them with dreary daily details about the trip, who kill any sense of suspense or mystery about their journey by blogging it to death, whose desperate need for approval results in turning the traveller into a crashing bore.

While he may be busy revealing the minutiae of his life, such a traveller is not really looking within himself. He is avoiding his soul and his horse.

Horses and Technology

Many Long Riders have acknowledged how the companionship with their horses was certainly one of the most satisfying emotional components of the trip.

Mary Bosanquet wrote, "I have experienced the sacramental experience of aloneness. I have been alone in happiness, alone in pain, alone in peace and in fear, alone in the mountains and on the burning prairies. My deepest gratitude is to the horses, for this journey is their gift to me. With them I have been alone but never forsaken, for companionship with animals is the most precious aloneness there is."

Farid ud-Din Attar, a Sufi mystic of the twelfth century, composed a famous poem which explained how a wise bird told a seeker, "I am a messenger of the world invisible. I know the way to the garden beyond the edge of time."

Many Long Riders have experienced a similar feeling of harmony with their horses. In the company of these natural companions, new scenes are ever opening to the traveller's view, his spirits become elated, and he is unconsciously taking in new energy and new life with every movement.

These feelings are more than psychological. The calming progression of the journey causes the heartbeats of horse and human to synchronise. A sense of calm ensues.

Technology introduces a note of disharmony which drives a wedge between you and the horse. He doesn't understand or need the stimulus provided by an electronic device. He represents wind, weather, starlight and freedom.

Long Riders have begun to write about how their horses recognize these interruptions.

Sea G Rhydr was the first to note this when she wrote how her horse, Jesse James, took offence when the mobile phone made a bid for the rider's attention.

"Jesse makes it very clear that he resents it mightily when I'm talking on the phone while riding him. He's quite right. He deserves my undivided attention while I'm in the saddle," Sea realized.

Over the course of countless generations humanity developed an intuitive ability that allows some of us to sense what our horse is feeling without the use of speech. This is a collective achievement of our species, one which developed after generations of first-hand experience. As machines progressively strengthen their grip on the human psyche, humanity's empathy with horses will wither like an unused limb.

There is one final consideration when considering the idea of chatting on your mobile phone or texting while you are in the saddle.

The horseman's grave is always open.

Mingling the cyber-world with the real one is life-threatening. Your attention should always be on the horse, the road, and the world around you.

Long Riders Voice Their Concerns

When Joseph Smeaton Chase set off at the dawning of the last century to ride from Mexico to Oregon, he had the time to ride and relax with his horse.

"All the morning we plodded quietly along, ruminating lazily to the pad, pad of the hoofs. After passing a minute hamlet, we rested for half an hour beside the road, under a sycamore in the fresh young leaves of which the horses discovered an interesting flavour. These roadside interludes are very pleasant. You tie your horse in the shade, take off the bridle, loosen the cinch, pull out your bread and cheese, and munch it to the rustle of leaves and the interrogative comments of hidden birds. The brook purls along, and your thoughts purl along with it. A draught of water and then the careful packing of the pipe-bowl and the first grateful puffs. You slip the bridle on, tighten up the girth, swing into the saddle, and ride on with one more little vignette added to the many such, of which one is turned up now and then by some chance occurrence, whereupon there comes back to you the whole scene, with your companion, if you had one, or your faithful horse, now perhaps obeying another hand, or none. What underlies this whole strand of thought is that silence enhances self-awareness and allows us to be in touch with our "inner" (and more real) life."

Those peaceful days are gone.

Equestrian travellers are increasingly expressing concerns about the effects of technology on their journeys.

One said, "The phone could so easily become a crutch. I felt it was a disadvantage when it allowed me to vent and share feelings in moments of challenge that I would have otherwise had to overcome alone."

Another regretted having exposed herself to the unrelenting curiosity of the public.

"I'm wishing I didn't have a blog or a following or any sort of publicity. Then I could have my bad days, mishaps and injuries in private like most people do. There are levels on which the blog and the Internet and the cell phone have made the journey much easier and other levels where they have added a crazy pressure and an awful vulnerable exposure to the whole experience."

The problem of how to deal with intrusive technology seems bound to become of increasing concern to future Long Riders. During her ride across the United States Sea G. Ryder gave a talk to a local school.

"One student asked how I manage to find time to do so many things in my life. My reply silenced the class: I told them I don't watch TV. I don't spend time surfing the internet. I don't text. I don't play video games. They looked at me in disbelief."

Sea continued: "For me, the computer is a highly addictive, mind and personality altering drug. When I'm spending a lot of time with my computer I'm less patient with people and my attention span is shorter in general".

Alienating Your Host

Katie Cooper also discovered how technology can exert a harmful influence on your journey. It can anger your host.

She wrote, "There is another way in which technology can be detrimental. Once in a while a host would offer the use of a computer during my stay. I'd usually accept, as it was the only way to post photos to my blog and I generally had a backlog to catch up on by the time I was offered access.

However, I noticed that the instant I logged on, the relationship with my host(s) suffered. It was as if an invisible wall sprang up between us. Just as Sea's horse Jesse James could feel Sea's attention captured by the phone and resented the abandonment, I could sense my host's initial mild surprise at my total shift in focus, turning to confusion, hurt or resentment as minutes became hours (it almost always took hours). I would be so engrossed that I'd shut out all distractions, including the presence of my host. It felt rude, even to me.

And no matter how delightful, entertaining, considerate and clearly grateful I tried to be after coming up for air, the relationship would be blighted. It never quite seemed to recover. They had watched me give a computer more undivided attention than I had given them."

As her journey across the United States progressed, Katie began to increasingly weigh the concepts of nature and technology against each other.

"I have a private journal entry from a stay in Louisiana at a place deep in a bayou swamp, the first I'd ever seen. It was evening. The moonlight was just beginning to cast shadows of the cypress trees on the black water. Frogs sang and unidentified insects whirred. I heard the plop of an alligator in the darkness. I sat on a porch and wrote in my notebook how my dislike of occasionally sitting at a computer at someone's house to catch up on the blog had turned to utter loathing. How it would instantly suck me in, capturing all my attention for those few hours as if the outside world did not exist. It left me feeling drained and depressed. I wrote, technology is doing this to all of us. And look here, at this place, this bayou; the pale light, the trees, the water, the scents, the sounds, the feel of grass between my toes. In a fit of conspiracy-theory pique, I wrote 'who would want to separate us from all this?' The longer I rode, the more I turned to the natural world."

Setting Limits

The Long Riders' Guild always supports the concept of incorporating new technology into equestrian travel. But we're not blind to its negative effects either.

Computerisation and the communication revolution were supposed to benefit us. Instead a new type of bondage has come upon us noiselessly. What was originally designed to assist us in communicating has become a time-sucking trap that has enslaved us to its beck and call.

The mobile phone in particular is a voracious predator. It devours your time, destroys your serenity and jealously diverts your need to be continually alert. It is not a single machine. It is a self-imposed leash you proudly wear and display. It connects you to the urban matrix you should be riding away from, not worshipping from afar.

The journey should allow you to draw a deep breath, to ponder ideas, to search internally, without being constantly distracted by external stimuli.

In order to do this, Long Riders should regulate technology rather than be consumed by it. Just as we are expected to be sensible about not overeating or drinking too much alcohol, we also need to learn to use technology judiciously.

Set limits. Evade the constant assault of information. Turn off the noise. Unplug the technology. Seek the Long Quiet.

Summary

My name is not Yoda. I don't pretend to be a Jedi master who can teach you how to wield a light sabre or use the power of the Force. Nor am I any type of New Age guru who claims to know how to lead you to inner contentment. I am a man interested only in the perfection of his skill, an equestrian travel historian who has taken the time to study the words of those who rode before me.

Long Rider history demonstrates that reaching the ultimate level of knowledge involves the inner self, not merely the application of practical skills.

Finding balance in the internet age will prove to be an unusual challenge for those who follow in our hoofprints. They will need to find peace within all the while they are distracted by the noise of an increasingly intrusive world.

Technology can serve us. Yet we should never forget the internal discoveries made by Swift and Darwin. It was in the realm beyond the limits of language that they touched the mystery of the Infinite.

Even today, modern Long Riders are uncovering secrets in their own lives which would be impossible to find elsewhere by undertaking explorations not only of distant lands but their own hearts.

To find the Long Quiet one must swing into the saddle, disconnect from distractions, venture into Nature and explore one's own soul.

In 1997 Bartle Bull rode around Lake Baikal. He had been expecting physical challenges. What surprised him was the interior inspection which he also underwent.

Katie Cooper learned that the further she rode the more "blissfully unconnected" she became from technology and the problems of the world.

Gérard Barré, a Founding Member of the Guild, wrote, "To travel merely for the sake of covering many miles does not allow for contemplation, except the possible contemplation of the map, the watch, of the GPS. What is important is not the amount of distance you ride. It is the immersion of your spirit into a state of mind which you cannot obtain except by forgetting normal society."

In a prophetic statement to future Long Riders, in 1799 Count Vittorio Alfieri wrote, "Just because manners change, man, whether he lives in the year 1500, 1800 or 2000 will stay much the same."

Riding across Ireland in 1725, travelling for long periods of time in peace and silence, inspired Jonathan Swift to write "Gulliver's Travels." One part of the book involved a land where talking horses were "the perfection of nature".

Richard Barnes wrote "Travel is an art which consists not only of fastening the buckles and keeping things together, but relating to what you see." He discovered that inner harmony was contingent upon reflection and that the intrusion of modern events disrupted or reduced the chance of this from occurring.

Internet addiction is on the rise. Robin Hanbury-Tenison first described seeing it in Albania in 2007. In 2013 Canadian Long Rider Bonnie Folkins photographed these Mongolian nomads fixated with their mobile phones as they made their way across the steppes.

In the film, "City Slickers," three businessmen embark on a cattle-drive vacation in the hope of resolving their personal problems. A wise cowboy cynically tells them, "You city folks spend fifty weeks a year getting knots in your rope. Then you think two weeks up here will untie them for you." Likewise, Long Riders need to learn to leave their troubles behind them by disconnecting the internet and social media.

Section Six – The Aftermath
Chapter 76
The End of the Journey

Down through the ages a tiny handful of humans in every era has made the fateful decision to swing onto the back of a horse and set off to explore the world.

Some ventured deep into dangerous jungles. Others rode to the top of massive mountains. Many crossed continents. They survived the summer heat of the Amazon and the frozen winter of Antarctica.

Their motivations were as diverse as themselves. Some were bold explorers. A few were spiritual pilgrims.

Despite their external differences, they shared one common trait.

The Welsh have a word for it.

Hiraeth.

Roughly translated, it means "a yearning for we know not what."

A Mounted Mystery

Not everyone finds what they expect.

Leonard Clark set off in 1949 to ride into eastern Tibet in search of a mysterious mountain which was believed to be higher than Mount Everest.

"The area concerned is so remote that it is not easy even to describe exactly where we are talking about," he wrote in his diary.

Known in the local dialect as Amne Machin, the region was populated by the fierce Ngoloks, a tribe of Tibetans who had a well-earned reputation as rapacious horse rustlers, expert caravan raiders and ruthless killers.

Clark was beset by trouble and uncertainty even before he left. Eventually he obtained the permission of the Chinese authorities to attempt what they thought was a mad scheme. Along with a group of well-armed companions Clark set off to find the mysterious mountain. He rode a Mongolian stallion known as the "Black Moon of Alashan."

The journey was more dangerous than had been anticipated but eventually Clark and his group reached the longed-for peak.

"It was called Tsebagase, which means 'Mountain God.' The half-dozen men in our party were top riders and our horses trained in mountain climbing. Still riding, we began climbing the stomach of the god, a slippery, rocky slope, and after many panting halts, during which we and our mounts breathed in jets of steam, finally reached the rocky pinnacle. Our altitude was now more than 15,200 feet."

Clark is the only Long Rider known to have reached this inaccessible spot.

"Tibet lay like a map unrolled at our feet. This sight alone was worth all the trials I had gone through since leaving home on the other side of the globe: a civil war, endless red tape and bickering with suspicious officials, finding a backer, disappointments, failures, sickness, trying to live out of a suitcase, intrigues, trying to live on what few dollars I had, bad food, delays of weeks, cold, and finally the long hours of, for the most part, dreary riding that had melted into endless days. But here it was at last."

Clark gazed down upon the junction of three Eurasian continental mountain systems, Kun Lun, Amne Machin and Bayan Kara. He rightly judged that, "this might be among the first mountaineering exploits accomplished in Tibet on horseback."

It was the only known equestrian expedition of its kind, before or since.

Even though Clark had travelled tens of thousands of miles to ride to the top of this legendary mountain he had not expected to find anything more than rocks, cold wind and a spectacular view awaiting him. He was in for a surprise that has never yet been explained.

"Dismounting we found a square-shaped temple measuring 12 feet by 12 feet. It was surmounted by a 30 foot tall tree trunk. Only Buddha knows how that pole ever got on a 15,000 foot mountain top in treeless Tibet. But there it was, held upright by ropes secured to the four corners of the Buddhist world symbolized by the shrine."

This sacred stone structure was eight feet high. The foundation of the temple was made of rough uncut stones, while the top half was made up of thousands of carefully arranged stacks of flat *Máni* stones. Each of these had been carefully decorated. Some had been chiselled with Tibetan Sanskrit religious edicts. Others were decorated with "painted pictures of Buddha, the Wheel of Life and various animals including elephants, tigers, yaks or demons from Hell."

Hanging from the ropes securing the tall tree trunk were hundreds of cotton flags with prayers painted on them.

The tree itself held the final surprise.

"Bound tightly round it with thick cords was a rusty gun, a sword, a turquoise studded saddle, and a whole horse's skin stuffed with wool with agates in its eyes."

Not only was the temple unexpected, Clark concluded, "It was the most elaborate we had encountered out of many hundreds seen so far."

Lessons of the Road

Many parts of an equestrian journey are predictable and some things you do expect.

Everyone will have to contend with the caprices of nature. Long Riders past and present have had to overcome a host of hardships.

Count Vittorio Alfieri was no exception. During his ride from England to Italy he was beset by problems.

"It is vastly easier to write about that trip than it was to make it. I encountered everyday perplexities and vexations which embittered the pleasure I should otherwise have had. One horse wouldn't eat. Another had gone lame. It was a continual sea of troubles and I had to bear it all."

Yet he eventually brought all of the horses safely home to his beloved Florence.

When trouble comes it seems as if the journey has become a relentless emotional and physical trial, specifically designed to break your spirit and destroy your dreams.

Then, after the immediate disaster or danger has been overcome, how easy it is to forgive and forget. The scorching sun and the torturing wind of the day are replaced by the comfort of a campfire and the shine of starlight.

Curiously enough, despite knowing that more hardships lie ahead, after a night's sleep a fever of restlessness takes hold of the Long Rider. He longs to resume the trek. He sighs with contentment when he is back in the saddle. He ignores the fact that privation may be awaiting him further down the road.

The elation of travel has awakened in his blood.

Life in the Saddle

Equestrian exploration is a very specific discipline.

In order to be successful certain skills must be mastered. Objects such as the saddle, the axe and the tent, which at first seemed exotic, become trusted tools that link the Long Rider in an unbroken line to the past.

Wisdom isn't marked on the map. Such understanding occurs incrementally. As fears fade, they are replaced by a desire to press on.

The longer the journey, the deeper the mark it leaves. Often a Long Rider passes some invisible point on the earth's surface. When this happens the saddle is transformed from being a symbol of an exotic escape into an altogether unexpected icon.

Frank Heath experienced this symbiosis during his 11,000 mile ride across the United States.

"Home?" he wrote in his diary. "I have no home except my saddle for a pillow and the blue sky for a roof. I feel free that way, as though I have more room in which to grow."

No one understood this more clearly than Mary Bosanquet.

Having set off from Vancouver in 1939, she had ridden solo across Canada. As she neared her final destination of New York City, she lamented the conclusion of a journey that had become a quest that transformed her.

"In ordinary life the houses in which we live are our geographical centres. We go out of them, but only to return. We are like ships at anchor, riding to the length of the anchor chain, but not leaving the harbour. And so we come to belong to the places in which we live. No matter how much we travel from place to place, we are still only scudding from harbour to harbour, only changing our position from one stationary point to another. But in these months with the horses, only the journey has been constant. For I no longer travel to arrive. I no longer belong to lights and fires, to pleasant meal times, to books and pictures and windows curtained at night, but to roads and rivers, to fields and forests, to weather and sky," she wrote.

Mary had, she realized, become comfortable with swinging onto her horse and riding, "Out of the unknown, into the unknown again."

Proceeding Slowly

Mary Bosanquet and Frank Heath had both learned to make the road their home. They never rushed forward thoughtlessly. They never put their horses at risk. They became acclimatised and rode with thoughtful dignity.

They did not dwell on the hardships. They took an interest in their progress and enjoyed every moment of the journey.

They did not look forward to the end with eagerness. Nor did they think of a return to civilisation as an end to hardship but as the closure of an adventurous and pleasant life.

By travelling in this manner, unrushed, at the speed of the horse, they still managed to cross the North American continent with what later seemed to be surprising speed.

Filipe Leite put these principles into practice when he set off in 2012 to ride 16,000 kilometres (10,000 miles) from Calgary, Canada to his family home in Santo do Pinhal, Brazil. After two years in the saddle he found himself on the border of Bolivia and his native country of Brazil.

As he neared the end of his journey, Filipe wrote, "As I look at the map, it is hard to understand just how I got here on horseback. It seems impossible! But when you focus on one day at a time and when you put all of your energy in the moment, it is amazing how far you can get."

Filipe's efforts were rewarded by a tremendous outpouring of public support from the people and government of Brazil. He was invited to be the guest of honour at the nation's largest rodeo. When he rode into the arena, 60,000 people gave him a standing ovation. The country's leading sculptor created life-sized statues of Filipe and his three horses. And 500 horsemen rode out to meet Filipe and act as his escort as the Long Rider approached his home town on the last day of the journey.

Soon afterwards Filipe wrote, "For the past 803 days I have lived as a vagabond, a saddle tramp. Riding from ranch to ranch. Pitching my tent on top of mountains and in national parks. Carrying everything I own in my packsaddle. Bathing in cold rivers. Sharing meals with those who have nothing and those who have it all. I have felt the gut-wrenching fear of facing off against grizzly bears and drug cartels. I have slept on top of my saddle blankets hundreds of times. Many nights I went to bed thirsty and hungry. I have woken up drenched from heavy rains, ridden through snow, sandstorms, and earthquakes. These past 803 days have been lived intensely. The boy who left Calgary 16,000 kilometres ago is not the Long Rider arriving in Espírito Santo do Pinhal today. After crossing ten countries with the help of my horses, I have finally come home, to my birthplace, a much stronger person."

Never Ending

Mary, Frank and Filipe all reached a point in their travels where the rhythm of the journey had become so strong that they didn't want it to end. They had learned the value of simplicity, had experienced the wealth of human kindness, had learned to sleep in a different place every night, had learned that the perfect journey is never finished, that there is always one more track to explore, one more mirage to follow.

Magdalene Weale summarized that feeling when she wrote, "I experienced one of those rare moments of exhilaration which life occasionally offers. I galloped across the top of the world, the air like wine, the hills flashing by as we sped along. I felt as if I could go on like this for ever."

The trip, which had at first represented such an incredible challenge, had become part of Magdalene's life. Instead of hardship she had discovered solitude and peace.

All these Long Riders and many more had reached a point in their journey where only an ocean could have stopped them. They longed to ride on forever.

Then sorrow caught up with them.

The Realisation

Suddenly it is over.

You spend your last day in the saddle looking at the faithful horse that has carried you so far. You hold the reins in your fingers and marvel at the simple beauty of these strings of freedom. Everything looks fresh, alive, and you know you're going to miss it – for the rest of your life.

Long Riders often experience a sense of shock at the end of their ride.

At the conclusion of Bernice Ende's second journey she had spent 16 months riding through 14 western states in America.

"Did we really just travel 5,000 miles, me, my horse and dog?" she asked herself incredibly.

Other Long Riders have also been taken by surprise.

"I could not believe that this was the last day of my journey," Margaret Leigh wrote, "because by this time it seemed the normal condition of life."

Looking back on the journey, the days seem to have gone by so fast. The distant goal has been reached. But instead of a sense of triumph, there is often a feeling of regret.

You realize that there will never be another day like this. Tonight you will not fall asleep under a wild moon. Tomorrow you will not sit astride your proud steed.

The victory is bittersweet.

After riding 6,000 miles from Mongolia to Hungary, Australian Long Rider Tim Cope endured such a moment.

"I felt sad and panicked that the journey was coming to an end. What would I feel and how would I live without my horses that had become such a big part of my life? Without them I feared I would feel empty and incomplete, a pedestrian in an alien world. In the evenings I spent as much time as possible with them, taking in their characters, and even appreciating their own individual smells."

Preparing to Return

The beginning and the conclusion of a journey are both important events. However they arouse different emotions.

Whereas you set off with a tinge of excitement, it is often common to feel a bit of fear when you receive your marching orders out of paradise. People feel uncertain, apprehensive, unresolved, bewildered, sad and exhausted when their journey ends.

They are going to be required to go from a life of freedom back into the cramped and conventional world. Instead of looking for grazing, they will be looking for a job. Instead of worrying about the weather, they will be concerned about money.

During his ride through the Atlas Mountains of Morocco, Don Roberto Cunninghame Graham had gone hungry, been kidnapped and held prisoner in an isolated fortress. Despite these hardships, he detested the idea of going back to London.

"To return again to all the cares of life called civilised, with all its listlessness, its newspapers all full of nothing, its sordid aims disguised under high-sounding nicknames, its hideous riches and its sordid poverty, its want of human sympathy, and, above all, its barbarous war brought on it by the folly of its rulers, was not an alluring thought," he wrote.

Before the final day arrives, you should give serious thought to how you want your journey to end, because many years later your memories of that special day will be as vivid as if they were yesterday.

The Quiet Arrival

Most people never depart on a life-changing journey, preferring to stay huddled at home. For those who do set out, the arrival at a distant destination may represent a variety of internal meanings including personal redemption, the renewal of hope or the solution to a spiritual dilemma.

For some it may be an intensely private moment whose origins stretch back many years.

There are no odometers on a saddle. There is no magic mark in the dust. Often there may be no obvious landmark to mark the conclusion of the trip.

Colonel Frederick Burnaby was one of the most celebrated Long Riders of the late 19th century. After a perilous ride across Central Asia, he eventually reached his childhood dream, the Oxus River which Alexander the Great had crossed.

"Finally, after riding along a narrow path we arrived upon the banks of the Oxus, and I gazed on the world-renowned stream which in my boyish days it had been my dream to visit. The mighty river – the Oxus of Alexander – lay at my feet, its banks bound together by a bridge of transparent ice, which separated the subjects of the Khan of Khiva from those who pay tribute to the Czar."

There was no great or obvious landmark to crown Burnaby's journey, just a few high reeds growing on the riverbank.

Likewise when Malcolm Darling rode across India in 1947, his journey also ended at a river. Cliffs of white marble a hundred feet high rose like icebergs on either side of the Nerbudda River. The trail led down past these "gates of heaven." Upon reaching the gleaming river Darling reflected in silence.

"The dream was fulfilled. Unmoved, the horses drank deep."

More recently New Zealand Long Rider Ian Robinson made solo journeys across Mongolia, Tibet and Afghanistan. Each of the trips had a demure finish.

"I often felt on my rides that no one knew where I was and no one really understood what I was doing," Ian explained. "My arrivals were very quiet, just making it to a point in the middle of nowhere to be met by no one I had ever seen before."

The Big Finish

For others the conclusion has been a moment of public celebration.

After riding across Siberia, Kate Marsden returned to London, where she was introduced to Queen Victoria.

When Aimé Tschiffely completed his legendary ride from Argentina to the United States in 1927, he was greeted as a hero by the American President and received a ticker-tape parade as he rode through New York City.

A few years later, when Mary Bosanquet arrived in New York in 1940, she was met by an escort of mounted police, who led her through Harlem, the Bronx, down the length of Central Park, and onto the mounted police barracks on Forty-Eighth Street.

"What was my amazement upon arrival to find myself met by the town band and escorted in glory to the town hall, where a large crowd was awaiting me. The Boy Scouts kept them back with ropes and a policeman directed them. Never in my life have I experienced such importance."

After riding the length of the Oregon Trail in 1948, John and Lulu Beard rode into Independence, Missouri, where the historic path had originally begun. Awaiting them was "A large mounted group of men and women, all in Western dress, who escorted us into the heart of the city. There we were greeted by the mayor and presented with a signed photograph sent by President Truman."

The End of the Rainbow

Sometimes everything falls into place perfectly.

In 1994 German Long Rider Günter Wamser decided to undertake the ambitious plan to ride from Patagonia to Alaska. A seasoned traveller, Günter originally thought the journey would take a few years. Instead it became an Odyssey of endurance which lasted twenty years and covered more than 25,000 kilometres (15,535 miles).

Using two sturdy Criollo geldings, it took him five years to travel across Argentina, Chile, Bolivia, Peru and Ecuador. He resumed his journey in 2001, spending four years crossing Panama, Costa Rica, Nicaragua, Honduras, El Salvador, Guatemala and Mexico.

Disaster struck at the American border when his faithful Criollos were refused entry into the United States. After finding them homes in Mexico, Günter adopted four formerly wild mustangs and headed north again.

In 2007, he and his travelling friend, Austrian-born Sonja Endlweber, began riding the mustangs north along the Continental Divide Trail, heading through New Mexico, Colorado, Wyoming, and Montana. They crossed Canada and in the summer of 2013 Günter reached his goal at last: Alaska!

Two other Long Riders had ridden all the way to the top of Alaska, only to discover that Prudhoe Bay is the site of a gigantic oil field and an extensive refinery. The area is bleak, off limits and definitely not horse friendly.

But after twenty years in the saddle, Günter was determined to conclude his journey at a point where his horses would be safe and his soul would be at peace. Luck was with him.

"Wind accompanied us on our last climb. On the top of the ridge we should be able to see the small village of Healy, our final destination. Gentle rain had joined the wind. Braving the elements we finally crossed the ridge and were taken aback. There was Healy, framed by a perfect, colourful rainbow. Welcome, I whispered. We couldn't have wished for a more beautiful finish line."

After arriving at the small village Günter reported, "We found exactly what we were hoping for: no welcoming committee, no party, no music, just a lush green pasture. We took the halters off one last time and the horses rolled with pleasure before they joyfully galloped across the huge pasture. Their intuition had told them that the nomadic way of life had come to an end."

Disappointment

Long Rider dreams don't always come true because things don't always turn out the way you expect.

You underestimate the budget. Borders refuse to open. Horses become ill, are stolen or die. A companion deserts. Illness knocks you flat.

At some point you realize you're not having fun anymore. You're riding out of duty. That's when you know it's time to stop. The line of travel you had drawn with such confidence on the map back at home will never be completed.

Or if it does you may not be happy with what you find when the journey ends.

At the tender age of 17 Tom Cashner nurtured a dream of becoming a cowboy. When he read a newspaper account about a man in Texas who owned a large cattle ranch, Tom bought a horse and set off from his home in Canton, Ohio. He was headed towards Texas to find work as a cowboy.

Along the way his beloved horse, Streak, was killed by a truck and Tom changed his name to "Tex" in honour of his pilgrimage. After having ridden 2,750 kilometres (1,700 miles) the road-weary youth arrived at Ardmore, Texas in June, 1951. He immediately began a search for the ranch owner, who someone had told Tex would employ him as a cowboy.

"I went to the newspaper. They got hold of Charles Goddard by phone and he came to meet me at the newspaper office. He was not what I had expected. Instead of a tall, row-boned, tanned rancher, I was introduced to a 70-year-old business man in a suit and a tie. It was a big let-down for me. Goddard told me that there was no facility at the ranch for a single man. All his hands were married men and lived near the ranch. So much for the western movies with the ranch hands, trail rides, etc. I never even got to see his ranch, though he did take me to lunch. 1,700 miles was a long way to go for lunch. Many thoughts raced through my head – Streak's death, the rain, the sun, the sweat, the cold, my dreams gone. My only consolation was that I had set a goal and made it, at any cost," Tex recalled philosophically many years later.

There is another element which comes into play at the conclusion of an equestrian journey; fate.

No one knows more about that than the English Long Riders Robin and Louella Hanbury-Tenison.

After riding across both islands of New Zealand, their planned conclusion was destroyed when Cyclone Bola ravaged the island nation. A metre (3 feet) of rain fell in two days causing one of the worst disasters in the country's history.

"The landscape had changed beyond recognition. Houses stood isolated in a sea of mud. Countless thousands of animals lay drowned and bloated or stood shivering on patches of higher ground. It was not until the next day that we were able to see the full extent of the damage. There was now no question of our riding any further. Apart from the immorality of adding to the problems faced by the rescue services if we ran into trouble, the whole landscape was now so waterlogged that progress would be impossible."

After riding across Spain along the ancient pilgrim trail to the cathedral of Santiago de Compostela, Robin and Louella's moment of triumph was again denied them.

"It should have felt different, knowing and welcoming in a special way. We expected the people living there to indicate somehow that they knew how excited we were, not by lining the streets and cheering but perhaps by giving us a special smile or wave. Such, however, is not the Galician way and there was nothing save the now rapidly-reducing milestones to show how near we were to the end."

As they rode their horses towards the famous church, what had been a chilly reception turned into official hostility.

"In the last square, the Plaza de Cervantes, we stopped to water the horses and rest them for a moment. The sun was just catching the spires of the Cathedral ahead of us, church bells were ringing all over town and the moment seemed just right as we mounted and rode the last few hundred meters. At that moment a whistle was blown loudly and one of the municipal guards in a peaked cap began to run towards us. You and your horses are not allowed here, the guard shouted furiously."

After being allowed to take a hurried snapshot in front of the cathedral, the Long Riders were ushered off the church property.

But it was China which dealt the Hanbury-Tenisons their largest surprise. Weeks of hard travel along the legendary Great Wall was supposed to have been concluded with the Long Riders receiving a warm welcome from high-ranking government officials. But a wrong turn led to disappointment.

"Instead of arriving to a delegation of Chinese officials, we found ourselves inside a giant steel mill industrial complex. After total solitude we were plunged into a bizarre world, a man made desert of slag and rubbish. It was hardly the ending we had expected for our romantic ride along the Great Wall. Some of the chimneys were pouring out black smoke which smelt deadly. A dreadful sense of anticlimax began to overcome us. Then we looked at each other and laughed. After riding 2,000 miles along the Great Wall, instead of receiving the plaudits of the local population and the world press, we found themselves under arrest by a factory guard. Finally freed, and at our last camp, we fed and watered the horses and then quietly congratulated each other on having made it."

Broken Dreams

Not everyone returns to happiness. Sometimes you become vulnerable to bitter disappointment.

While the annals of The Long Riders' Guild are full of daring tales written by intrepid men and women, few equestrian explorers can match the James Bond-like escapades of the Scottish Long Rider, Parker Gillmore.

Gillmore was already a seasoned world traveller, big game hunter and prolific author whose journeys had taken him to dangerous parts of North America and Africa, when the British government offered to send him on a secret mission for Her Majesty, Queen Victoria.

The date was April, 1879 and the job was simple.

Gillmore was to mount up at Cape Town, South Africa, ride more than a thousand miles alone into the heart of the African continent, whereupon he was to negotiate with local native rulers, urging them to allow their warriors to become part of the English army. When that bit of mounted diplomacy was accomplished, the amateur ambassador was to ride back and report on his success.

Mind you, there was one bit of bother.

Forty thousand warriors in the deadly Zulu army, under the command of their wily leader, King Cethshwayo, had gone on the warpath against the English redcoats. As if that weren't bad enough, the overly-optimistic British force which initially took the field suffered a deadly defeat while camped at Isandlwana, where nearly every soldier was killed. Thus Africa was ablaze in what amounted to a genocidal gang war when Parker Gillmore was asked to ride into this blazing cauldron of danger and deceit.

In the company of his faithful horses, Bobby and Tommy, Gillmore made a ride across Africa that defies belief. He was stalked by lions and narrowly escaped war-like natives. Raging rivers blocked their path and Gillmore was tormented by an "African fever" so severe that at one point he passed out under a tree for nearly twenty-four hours.

At last, after a ride that should have made him a hero, the near-dead Gillmore rode back into civilization, where he was promptly informed that the Zulu war was over, hence his services were no longer required, and that during his absence his beloved wife of twenty-five years had died and been buried.

Yet the most notoriously ill-fated conclusion of any journey happened in San Francisco. In the spring of 1912 George Beck, his brother Charlie, their brother-in-law Jay Ransom, and a family friend, Raymond Rayne, set off to ride to all 48 American state capitals.

Calling themselves the "Overland Westerners," they reached Sacramento, their 48th and last state capital on May 24, 1915. They had been in the saddle for three years and one month, a record 1,127 days of that time spent riding. They had gone through 17 horses on the 33,000 kilometre (20,352 miles) trip. During this time they had spent just $9,000 between them. After their photograph was taken with the governor of California, they set out for the last stop, the Panama Pacific International Exposition in San Francisco.

Arriving there on June 1, 1915, they expected the boisterous crowds gathered to celebrate the opening of the Panama Canal to great them as homecoming legends.

Instead an Irish cop yelled at them to "Get them hay-burners off the street."

Little Sheba the belly-dancer was big news. Four saddle-sore heroes were not. They came expecting glory. They found only disenchantment.

Judging the Rewards of Failure

The topic of "failure" is of vital importance to those of us who participate and study the ancient art of equestrian exploration. And whereas the public is always eager to hear a tale about a bold victory, those of us who have journeyed know that success often hangs by a slender thread.

One of the most unique explorers to express his thoughts on the topic of failure was Long Rider Sir Ahmed Mohammed Hassanein FRGS.

At the dawning of the 20th century the vast desert of Libya remained one of the last unexplored places on Earth. Because travel was restricted by the distance camels could trek between wells, vast portions of the Libyan interior were still blank spots on the map. One of the most elusive places yet to be seen by an outsider was Kufara, an oasis located deep within the Libyan Desert.

A German explorer, Gerhard Rohlfs, was the first to penetrate the desert and reach the remote town. But the oasis was far more than a mere source of water. It was also the capital of the Senussi Islamic sect. Rohlfs, who barely escaped with his life, had all his scientific observations and equipment destroyed by the deeply suspicious tribesmen who inhabited Kufara.

Enter Ahmed Hassanein, the dashing Egyptian diplomat turned explorer.

Educated at Oxford where he won fame as a fencer, the Egyptian of Bedouin descent returned home and initially served as a diplomat for King Faud. But Hassanein's love of adventure came to the fore in 1920 when he accompanied the lovely English travel writer, Rosita Forbes, to the Kufara oasis in Libya.

Failure certainly played a major role in that journey, as their caravan missed a vital oasis and nearly died of thirst in the desert.

Yet failure on the way did not prohibit Hassanein from befriending the Muslim leaders of the elusive Senussi Brotherhood once he reached Kufara. It was during his first trip to the legendary desert town that he became aware of rumours of a "lost oasis" which lay even deeper in the desert.

Despite his earlier problems, in 1923 Hassanein mounted his horse and led a small camel caravan on a remarkable seven month journey across the centre of Libya. More than two thousand gruelling miles later he emerged with marvellous tales of having not only located the "lost" oasis of Uweinat, but having also discovered a cave which contained ten-thousand-year-old drawings. Attributed to djinns, these Palaeolithic images depicted a flourishing, but now extinct, pastoral world inhabited by giraffes, ostriches, gazelles, even cows, but no camels. Yet the most startling image depicted human beings swimming in what had become a forbidding desert.

Hassanein correctly realized that the rock drawings indicated the existence of a sophisticated pastoral culture which had gone extinct before the camel had been introduced.

The Egyptian explorer was hailed as a success after his expedition returned. National Geographic magazine published his story. He was awarded the Founder's Medal of the Royal Geographical Society. And cunning businessmen offered to pay him substantial fees if he would lecture to the public, dressed in traditional Bedouin clothing. He declined to prostitute his beliefs in the name of profit.

This was largely because Hassanein had been deeply touched by the desert.

After riding his horse, or walking, for thousands of miles across an often empty landscape, he had realized that there was little to discover externally, but a great deal to discover in himself. Such revelations came about thanks in no small degree to the intense silence and calm which surrounded him, as he made his slow way across a desert that remained untouched by the invasion of the noise and tumult of the modern world.

Knowing that his predecessor, Gerhard Rohlfs, had "failed" in the public's eye, Hassanein gave careful thought to how explorers should define success or failure.

In his classic book, *The Lost Oases*, Hassanein wrote, "To the outside world the work of an explorer is either failure or success with a distinct line between them. To the explorer himself that line is very hazy. He may have won his way through, amassed all the information that he sought, be within a score of miles of his journey's end; then suddenly, his camels give out. He must abandon the best part of his luggage. Water and food take precedence; the boxes containing his scientific instruments, his records, have to be left behind. Maybe his plight is still worse, and he must sacrifice everything, even his own life. To the outside world he would be a failure; generous critics might even call him a glorious failure, but in any case he has failed. Yet how much is that failure akin to success!

Sometimes on those long treks the man who fails has done more, has endured more hardships, than the man who succeeds. An explorer's sympathy is rather with the man who has struggled and failed than with the man who succeeds, for only the explorer knows how the man who failed fought to preserve the fruits of his work."

Defining Success

In this day when it is all too often argued that there are no "white spots" left on the map, critics falsely claim there is no longer any purpose to explore. Why go there, they say, when you can gaze at a faraway spot thanks to Google?

The lure of exploration cannot be explained to those whose souls have never heard the elusive song which lured Hassanein into risking his life – twice – in the Libyan Desert.

For those of us who have responded, and gone, we know that the mere act of setting off is in itself a victory.

As for "failure," that is a term all too often misunderstood, and frequently used, by those who stayed behind in the comfort and safety of their homes.

Many Long Riders have felt the past calling to the present. They have longed to venture into unknown lands and satisfy their desire to see things first hand. Not all their dreams and journeys were realized.

Louis Meunier had read about the German Long Rider Emil Trinkler, who had ridden across the centre of Afghanistan in the early 1920s. Inspired by the previous journey, in 2005 Louis set off with an Afghan companion, Hadji Shamsuddin, to make a perilous journey across that war-torn nation. The landscape was harsh and the danger of being killed or kidnapped by hostile tribesmen was ever present.

Finally, after having completed the majority of the ride, Louis rode into Herat, Afghanistan – on the verge of death. Doctors discovered an infection in his liver which required him to return to France immediately via an emergency medical rescue flight.

Once his life had been saved, and he was lying in a Paris hospital with time to think, Louis wrote to the Guild to say, "I felt great frustration that we had not been able to complete our journey. However, then I remembered that I had enjoyed a great experience. I knew my life had changed since I set off for this unforgettable journey across Central Afghanistan. Not only did I experience what had long been a dream of mine, I discovered more of my beloved Afghanistan on the back of a great stallion, all the while travelling in the way of the ancient Turkoman horsemen."

What had seemed like a failed journey was in fact only the beginning.

"This journey has been like an awakening which has left a deep impact on my soul and will surely influence my life in the future. As I sit here in the bed resting, I can look at my maps, notes and pictures and imagine myself back on the saddle. But I don't want to live in the past. I have to make new projects. I wish to go back to Afghanistan again," Louis wrote.

He did return to Afghanistan, where he rode his mighty stallion, Tauruq, in buz khazi games, explored the Wakhan Corridor and organized the first climbing of the tallest peak in the country.

What should have been a bitter disappointment became the inspiration for other adventures. Louis may not have found fame or a pot of gold. But he did discover personal contentment and happiness.

A Safe Conclusion

As this chapter demonstrates, there is a need to consider how you conclude your journey.

Will your ride end alone in a quiet place? This is often what happens when people ride "ocean to ocean" across the United States.

Do your plans require you to finish your ride at a symbolic spot, a historical monument or a public building? If so then you should have allowed plenty of time to arrange for the conclusion of your ride to be planned well in advance. Government representatives are always busy, so if you wish to invite them to attend in an official capacity then you should have given them plenty of advance notice. One traveller who made a dramatic journey across the United States failed to understand this. Consequently when he arrived at the state capital, there was no one there to meet him.

Don't forget the press. On the last day of an extensive journey Long Riders experience a range of emotions including euphoria and exhaustion. Care should be used if you are interviewed by the media.

Finally, there is always the practical side of things. With cameras rolling, photos being taken and newspaper reporters asking questions, your attention will undoubtedly be diverted. This is an excellent opportunity for thieves to loot your gear while you are distracted.

Summary

Mary Bosanquet spoke for us all when she wrote, "Last things, last things. How they hurt."

No matter what year it states on the calendar when you chance upon this page, one thing will have remained the same. Long Riders, past and present, will look back upon their journey as being a magic moment in their lives.

Captain James John Best realized this at the conclusion of his ride across Albania in 1838.

In words which still ring true today, he wrote, "This ended the equestrian journey, which was the most exciting and enjoyable excursion I had ever made in my life."

When you step down from the saddle on that last day, remember this Navajo prayer.

"May it be beautiful before me. May it be beautiful behind me. May it be beautiful above me. May it be beautiful all around me. In beauty it is finished."

Leaving New York State in 1875, Willard Glazier was the first known Long Rider who intentionally rode "ocean to ocean." Despite being kidnapped and nearly murdered by Arapahoe Indians, crossing the Rocky Mountains and surviving numerous hardships, he finally reached the Pacific Ocean near San Francisco, California the following year.

Many Long Riders make journeys of an intensely private nature and shun the spotlight. After completing a gruelling solo ride from Canada to Mexico, Allen Russell enjoyed a moment of quiet triumph at the Mexican border in 1975.

Other journeys conclude with celebrations. William Reddaway made a unique journey to the four corners of England, during which time he visited 30 historic cathedrals and abbeys. Because he raised funds for a children's riding programme, well-wishers were on hand to welcome William and his horse, Strider, home.

When Tim Cope completed his historic 9,500 kilometre (6,000 mile) ride across the steppes, government officials from Australia, Hungary, Mongolia and Kazakhstan met him at Opusztaszer, a national heritage park on the edge of the Eurasian steppe near the Danube River.

Ed Lines, Phil Sutton, and Nick Warner celebrate after completing their 3,200 kilometre (2,000 mile) long ride through the Andes Mountains.

After riding 16,000 kilometres (10,000 miles) from Canada to Brazil, a statue was erected in honour of Filipe Leite and his three horses.

The Overland Westerners rode more than 20,000 miles, only to find that the media ignored them. Within a few years their epic ride had been forgotten. George Beck, (bottom left) the group's leader, succumbed to a tragic death and Pinto, the horse who had made the entire journey, also came to grief.

Though he nearly died during his ride across Afghanistan, Louis Meunier turned disappointment into triumph. He returned to the country and made an award-winning film about the Kyrgyz nomads, who live in yurts at an altitude of 4,500 metres in the remote Wakhan Corridor, a thin strip of land hidden in the mountains between Pakistan and Tajikistan.

At the end of the road you experience euphoria and exhaustion. You also realize that the journey which pushed you to the limits of your endurance will haunt you for the rest of your life.

Chapter 77
Saying Goodbye to your Horse

No animal has affected mankind on so deep an emotional level as the horse. Since the days of our prehistoric past, the horse has galloped through our collective consciousness. Considered the most noble of all animals, the horse is often credited with representing the traits which frail humans aspire to, including courage, loyalty, dedication and unconditional love.

Authors have at times attempted to preserve the names of great horses for the sake of posterity. One such scribe was Bernal Díaz del Castillo, a soldier who accompanied Hernán Cortés in the conquest of Mexico against the Aztec Empire. At the age of 84 Castillo recorded his adventures in a narrative entitled, *The True History of the Conquest of New Spain.*

Considered a masterpiece by scholars, the aged warrior recounted many of the 119 battles in which he fought, concluding with the defeat of the Aztecs in 1521. Unlike other authors of his era, whose bias prohibited them from writing about the lives of the diverse native peoples residing in the area now known as Mexico, Castillo observed and noted important ethnic details. Having come from humble origins, he was also quick to praise the bravery and sacrifices of his fellow common soldiers.

But we must be thankful for more than that, for Castillo was no mere pedestrian with a quill pen and a long memory. He was a lover of horses and found within his book is a priceless equine roll call.

Like many of the Spanish, Castillo believed that next to God, the Conquistadors owed their salvation to their horses. That is why, though decades had passed, when the time came to recall the events in Mexico, Castillo took great pains to write about the horses with such exactitude.

He refers to them by name, such as Cortés's horse El Morzillo, whom the natives worshipped as a god. He recalled their colours, such as, "Cristobel de Oli, an admirable dark bay." He remembered their qualities, such as "Motilla, the best and fastest." He wrote of them as friends and comrades whom he had ridden, fed and led to water.

Humanity has at times preserved the names of other famous war horses such as Bucephalus and Marengo. Other scribes have recalled the deeds of renowned equine athletes such as Man of War and Seabiscuit.

But dull human eyes have never thought to gather the names of the indomitable Road Horses that made history. Their gallant deeds and incredible journeys have been overlooked.

Long Rider Horses

Seriy and Shavon, Pinto and Pompeii, Mancha and Gato are just some of the horses who demonstrated amazing endurance, astonishing courage, incredible stamina and undying loyalty during the course of extraordinary journeys.

What sets them apart straight away from the flashy race horse or the fire-breathing charger is their ordinary exterior. Mancha, who made the famous journey from Buenos Aires to New York, had a Roman nose and a bad temper. Shavon had been employed pulling a vegetable cart through Peshawar, before I set off with her to explore Kafiristan. Seriy was the most unlikely of all equine heroes. He was barely 14 hands high but that didn't stop him from carrying his rider at a brisk trot 9,500 kilometres (6,000 miles) across Siberia, in the dead of winter, to a meeting with the Czar in St. Petersburg.

To look at these horses, many would have said they weren't fit to ride and certainly not worthy of respect.

For example the arrogant hidalgos of Argentina mocked Tschiffely's Criollo geldings, calling them old and ugly. Later, after the unlikely trio had reached New York, the same haughty aristocrats changed their tune and began loudly describing Mancha and Gato as equine immortals. They may have been ugly according to the standards of the show ring but that didn't stop the Argentine Congress from passing a law in 1999 celebrating

September 20th of each year as "Día Nacional del Caballo" (National Day of the Horse) – because that is the day Aimé arrived in New York in 1928.

Yet Long Riders don't need national holidays to comprehend these things. They have learned that road horses have qualities which only the wise can detect.

Lawrence Burpee was one such example. When he sat down to write his book, *Among the Canadian Alps*, in 1914 the young naturalist praised the sturdy horses which had made his journey a success.

"A good Canadian mountain pony will follow unerringly a trail that is indistinguishable to even an experienced guide; he will carry an able-bodied man, or a much heavier pack, all day over a trail that would kill an eastern horse; he will pick his way through a tangle of fallen timber with an instinct that is almost uncanny and he will do all this on the uncertain feed of mountain camps. He is a true philosopher, a creature of shrewd common sense, pluck, endurance, and rare humour, a good fellow, and a rare friend."

Bill Holt understood this about his beloved horse. Trigger had been employed pulling a tinker's junk cart along the lanes of Yorkshire when Holt saw him. Something about the white horse struck Holt so strongly that he ran after the tinker and bought Trigger on the spot.

Holt had not planned on making an equestrian journey. He certainly didn't comprehend that his snap decision would bring a faithful mount into his life that would carry him for thousands of miles across Europe in the 1960s.

"I did not realize at the time that it was he who had adopted me. He had come to bear me away. His was a love of freedom. He had brought to me the means of a release from the bondage of a humdrum life. It was he who had rescued me. It was he, not I, who led the way and showed me a world I had never seen before," Holt wrote in his classic book, *Ride a White Horse*."

The Bond

And so it goes. Many historians have remarked upon the various useful services horses previously provided for mankind. In bygone days they dragged the plough, pulled the tram, hauled goods, went to war and carried the mail. It was a time when the majority of humans were physically and emotionally closer to horses.

A different attitude now prevails.

As the motor age progresses fewer humans interact with horses at any level. Recreational riders usually have little real companionship with the high-priced, well-groomed and stabled animal that others often feed and care for. When a person rides at most three or four hours a day, the horse thinks one thing, the man who saddles him another.

Yet one thing remains consistent.

Time after time, in journey after journey, hardship, fatigue, and hunger have brought horse and human closer and closer together.

The two travellers may be from different species but they shiver together in wind and rain. They jointly endure bitter cold and blazing heat. Together they starve and then rejoice over a meal. They face the same perils with the same chances of escape or annihilation.

Theirs is a community centred upon cooperation, sharing, sacrifice and support for one another.

Bill Holt expressed the thoughts of so many Long Riders when he wrote, "When a man has lived with a horse, eaten with a horse, swum with a horse, slept with a horse, travelled alone with a horse for months on end, the world seems empty without him."

An intimate companionship grows between man and mount that is well nigh impossible for motorized people to understand, but Long Riders continue to experience it.

In 1998 Benjamin Reynal made a 5,000 kilometre (3,100 miles) journey through 15 provinces of Argentina. Accompanying the 24-year-old Long Rider were his two faithful Criollo horses, Pampa and Federal.

"The relationship with my horses was simply phenomenal," he recalled. "They followed me everywhere, even sleeping by my side, one metre away, while having kilometres of open land to go to."

But there is more to this relationship than just loyalty.

The Guide

A mounted brute calculates the animal's value in terms of its efficiency. For him the horse is merely there to provide the physical means of locomotion.

To the uninitiated the horse is also a source of friendship and camaraderie.

A few Long Riders learn that the horse sometimes serves as a vista into another world. Though speechless, he becomes the spiritual kernel of the journey.

Mary Bosanquet recognized there was more to her horse, Jonty, than what strangers observed on a superficial level. She struggled to express a vague feeling that her horse had become a catalyst, a mysterious agent of change.

"He is freedom and fearlessness. He is the secret of the wilderness and all that is lost to cities," she wrote.

Jeremy James had no hesitation in stating his belief that in certain cases the horse is the teacher who leads the rider towards an elusive goal that has no connection to external geography. For Jeremy the horse has the power to evoke a sense of involvement on a loftier plane shorn of the impediments of daily humanity, where any sense of self-adulation is exposed as meaningless and paltry.

After a life spent with road horses, he believes it is a privilege to participate alongside them in the harmony of the natural world.

"Four legs take us further, beyond our sight," Jeremy explained. "Our fellow voyager becomes more than our friend, more than our transport; more, much more. He becomes not only our physical ally but our spiritual mentor, our touchstone with the elusive agents of nature. Unfettered by stable, by frontier or by fence, he is doing what lies in the depths of his heart – to go beyond the horizon as his ancestors have always done, and to be there by dusk. He reveals a world so different, so changed from our own; it's as if you have penetrated another dimension, seen through his eyes, heard with his ears, felt with his senses. Between you and him, a communion develops: a psychic dependency. He and you become one, alone with the earth and the stars: your aims are simple. Today you will skirt the horizon. And tomorrow. And the next day. And when you wake at sunrise, he's on his feet long before you and will have comprehended that which you have planned, he has already got it. To my mind the whole purpose of travelling by horse is this other-worldly dimension it affords you."

As Jeremy predicted, the horse has often changed the fundamental identity of the Long Rider. In such cases there is a mixing of horse and human; a merger of instinct and reason. The two halves induce a third, a rare and perfect whole.

But what of the horse?

How they view the journey

Long Riders are a diverse lot.

Don Roberto Cunninghame Graham, a highly cultured and tremendously erudite man, did not believe the horse understood the emotional significance which the rider experienced.

"They have carried me on journeys that to them could have no meaning and that to me have been the best remembered time of my life," he wrote.

Frank Heath on the other hand was a former cavalry soldier who had little formal education but possessed a deep insight into horses.

He wrote, "I am glad that I am not so stuffed full of dogmas of so-called unquestionable facts that I cannot believe my own eyes. I am glad that because I walk on two legs, can read, write and reason, that I can understand and appreciate the fact that horses have deep instincts that guide them correctly."

According to the laws of Nature the horse relies on senses which humans have either lost or never attained. On the surface he appears to be emotionally self-contained, inhabiting a world which lacks deception. Thus we can only guess what he feels in his heart.

But you don't need much imagination to realize that horses love to travel. In return for some hay, a measure of grain, a drink of pure water and a kind word, they exhibit a source of perennial optimism. They exalt in their freedom, as is evidenced when other horses, trapped like convicts behind fences, run up and stare enviously at the road horse that is passing by on an adventure.

The Nomadic Horse

Nature didn't design large horses to spend their lives cooped up in cramped stables like rats in a lab cage. They were bred to live beneath the sky and run in the sunlight.

A road horse is a return to that earlier time.

Circumstances may cause the road horse to endure driving rain, biting flies and small meals. But in return he has been blessed with a dazzling dose of freedom.

The constant walking makes him incredibly fit. The animal has a robust appetite, develops the ability to sleep anywhere, becomes hard, lean, resilient and resourceful.

In addition, the constant motion awakens the wanderlust in horses. Like their riders, they acquire a love of travel and are always anxious to start a new day full of adventures.

But with the journey concluded, a question arises. What will these unique, brave and curious horses do next? Like their human companions, the answer depends upon the individual.

Some settle down contentedly.

Magdalene Weale noted that her borrowed mare wasn't at all unhappy about returning home.

"Sandy quickened her pace, sensing instinctively that this time she really had come to the end of her wanderings. Unlike her rider, she had no regrets."

After travelling for thousands of miles under the wandering moon, other road horses have a problem adapting to life in a stable.

Basha O'Reilly's horse was one such example.

"My Cossack stallion, Count Pompeii, who carried me from Russia to England, took a while to understand that the journey was over. Every time I took him out for a hack and went home again, I could feel him thinking, 'But we were here last night! Have you lost your compass?' He is used to it now, but still hankers for travel, I can tell," Basha said.

Likewise, after Vyv Wood Gee and her daughter, Elsa, concluded their journey across England and Scotland, Vyv recalled how their horses reacted in a similar fashion.

"Lancer, Rowan and Mikado seemed to enjoy our trip as much as we did. Within hours, literally, of returning home, rather than revelling in the lush grass, they were looking over the gate apparently wondering why we hadn't set off and asking where next."

In cases such as these the horse has reached the point where it believes that tomorrow will be just like today. It thinks it will spend tonight in a different field and then move on with the sun. It never suspects that the journey has an ending.

When told, if the horse could speak, it would undoubtedly say, "I've served you well and loyally. And I am eager to continue. My only regret is that I am no longer needed and we cannot travel on together."

Now comes the moment in the journey when the future of the horse must be decided with dignity and justice.

Three Emotions

No matter what century or country, all Long Riders share certain things in common. Through everything the horse has provided unchanging companionship and unbroken trust. He has been tireless and kind. He has suffered and helped you. As a result the two of you are bound by feelings of friendship and the memory of dangers shared.

Yet all the while you've been riding, anguish has been stalking silently behind you. Like two sides of a river, you have never met. Now, after having survived it all, Fate saves her harshest trick until last. Destiny has pronounced a decision from which there is no appeal.

The time has come for the Long Rider to learn that the journey is a trip through three emotions; Hope, Trust and Remorse.

There is sorrow in the final discovery that, for many Long Riders, this incredible companionship must now end.

A Long Rider's Obligation

A moral fault line runs through our journey; sentiment versus necessity.

How do we balance our personal needs against theirs? Are horses partners or victims? Powerful or powerless?

Though religion and science can conflict, both offer similar evidence about the necessity of providing justice for your horse.

The Sufis speak of *zikr*, a spiritual state of mind and heart wherein devotees seek to realize the presence of God. Such striving of one's self in God's way, via an ordinary daily activity, can be seen in the Long Riders love and devotion to his horse. Goodness, kindness, generosity, courage and devotion to duty, as opposed to vanity, cruelty and unworthy motives.

Even if he is not religious, a Long Rider shows that though the horse may be devoid of civil rights, he is nevertheless a divine gift and deserving of our sympathy and practical service. The Qu'ran cautions mankind to remember that every species that lives on Earth forms communities like humans do.

Brigid Brophy on the other hand was no mystic. She was an outspoken British novelist, critic, feminist, pacifist and campaigner for social reforms. An article she wrote for the Sunday Times in 1965 is credited with having inspired the formation of the animal rights movement in Great Britain. She took a decidedly different route from that of the Sufis but ended up arriving at a similar conclusion.

"I don't hold animals superior or even equal to humans. The whole case for behaving decently to animals rests on the fact that we are the superior species. We are the species uniquely capable of imagination, rationality, and moral choice and that is precisely why we are under an obligation to recognize and respect the rights of animals," Brophy wrote.

Disregard religion and ignore science; you'll still realize that adventure and adversity equals duty.

After such shared suffering, there can be no victorious end if you treat your horse with shame.

Every Long Rider must discharge this ethical obligation conscientiously.

By ensuring the horse's welfare you guarantee that the journey concludes with integrity.

"For any member of the Long Rider's Guild, this is the sacrosanct principle. It underpins any expedition on horseback. In all that is written in the hundreds of books that the Guild publishes and the thousands of pages which its web site provides, this conviction remains unassailable. The well-being of the horse is paramount," concluded Jeremy James.

Weighing Your Options

Many famous tales have been told about friends who depart together on a journey. Over the months they survive many challenges and forge an unforgettable relationship. But there is a difference among travellers.

When Jason returned with the Golden Fleece, he said goodbye to his fellow Argonauts. He didn't sell them.

At the conclusion of her journey from Vancouver to New York, Mary Bosanquet wrote, "To part with a horse who will not miss one is bad, but to part with a horse who will miss one is as bad as anything I know."

The question then becomes, what do you do with the horses?

According to Mongol custom, a horse that had survived combat was retired to a life at grass. You may not have that option. Depending upon what country you are in, the choices confronting you can range from acceptable to horrific.

Separating the Horses

The first challenge depends upon how many horses you have. Do you keep them together or separate the group?

René Descartes was a 17th century French mathematician and philosopher who knew a lot about numbers but was an ass when it came to horses. He argued, "The reason animals do not speak as we do is not that they lack the organs but that they have no thoughts."

This type of species chauvinism contended that because animals could not articulate words, then they did not suffer emotional distress when separated as humans do. They were mute beasts, nothing more.

Luckily science has since demonstrated that animals use tools, experience empathy, exhibit compassion and feel grief. Because of these new findings the European Union animal welfare policy begins with the premise that animals are sentient beings and must be treated with an attitude of morality.

But any Long Rider could have set Descartes straight a long time ago.

Horses may not have the capability of expressing speech but science has proved that they have excellent memories which enable them to learn and memorize human words. They are also skilled communicators among their own kind. They whinny if one of their fellows wanders too far away by accident. They form tremendous bonds of loyalty to one another during the course of an extended journey.

Most importantly, they display signs of extreme emotional distress if separated from their travelling companions.

Many Long Riders have witnessed their horses suffering intense separation anxiety. For example, in 1889 American Long Rider Thomas Stevens confronted the problem during his ride across Russia. When his companion went home, the other man's horse was sold. This forced Stevens to travel on alone. That decision devastated Stevens' road horse, Texas.

The horse was so inconsolable at the loss of his equine companion that the American could not ride him. He had to lead Texas by hand for two days, so as to keep the distraught horse from returning to search for his missing companion.

Friends for Life

Various Long Riders have confirmed that the bond which is formed among their horses is so powerful that when the journey is over, road horses often tend not to mingle with non-travelling horses.

Years after her journey, Basha O'Reilly's stallion, Count Pompeii, still routinely ignored other horses. After riding her gelding, Igor, 13,000 kilometres (8,000 miles) across the United States, Lucy Leaf's gelding, Igor, also preferred to live alone.

Jeremy James had two geldings, Gonzo and Sir Karo. Though bonded to each other, they too ignored other equines.

"I know mine never made friends of any other horses even though opportunities for shared grazing and so on were put before them; no, they stuck together, as though they shared something the others did not, which, of course, was true."

The most dramatic example of this equine exclusion was connected to Aimé Tschiffely's Criollos, Mancha and Gato. At the conclusion of their famous journey, the horses were given an honourable retirement at a large estancia in Argentina. They were inseparable until Gato died at the age of 32 in 1944.

Dr. Emilio Solanet, Tschiffely's friend and the protector of the horses, wrote to the Long Rider to explain how Mancha coped with the loss of his friend, Gato.

"I feel sorry for Mancha, who will have nothing to do with any other horses. I am sure that horses sense what it means when a companion dies. They know that he can't be found anywhere. Mancha never calls Gato. He is not restive, and does not fuss as formerly he did when temporarily separated from his friend. Now intelligent Mancha is sad and lonely. He keeps on his own although I have put twenty other horses into his favourite field. It is useless; already a week has passed since Gato died, but he takes no notice of any of them, and roams about alone, far away from the others," Dr. Solanet explained in his letter to Tschiffely.

The Long Rider does not need scientific evidence to realize that a travelling horse experiences stress, apprehension and fear when separated from his trusted friends.

Despite what Descartes believed, an intense emotional bond is created among travelling horses and separating them presents a serious problem.

Keeping them together depends upon the options available in the country where the journey is concluded.

Running Free

Straight away, you can forget the Hollywood mythology of just setting the horse free in a sea of green grass where it will run and play among other horses. That might work as a fairy tale ending to a fictional movie like *Hidalgo* but not in the harsh reality of the modern horse world.

After riding her beloved mare across the United States for 16,000 kilometres (10,000 miles), Tracy Paine considered that option.

"I think Dawn loved and trusted me," Tracy wrote. "But she had retained the instinct to be with her own kind. That is why I thought about setting her free among the wild Mustangs out west when our journey was over."

Then Tracy recalled that wild horses are rounded up every year by government authorities. Cruel methods are often used. The captured horses are held in pens for years and are then auctioned off to an uncertain future, which might include being shipped to a meat factory. Because of this Tracy realized, "Dawn's fate would have been uncertain."

She opted to keep Dawn rather than grant a freedom that might have cost the horse its life.

A Home for Life

Some Long Riders are blessed with the option of providing a permanent home for their horses.

After riding his mare, Gypsy Queen, 18,000 kilometres (11,000 miles) to all 48 American states, Frank Heath told the press, "People have tried to buy her but she is not for sale at any price. I've promised her a life of ease after she finishes the trip."

And he made sure she got it. Frank protected and provided for his horse for the next eleven years. When she became critically ill, he asked a veterinarian to euthanize her. He then donated her skeleton to the veterinary medicine department of the University of Maryland and gave all his notebooks and papers connected to the trip to the university library.

Bringing Them Home

One thing to keep in mind is that it has never been easy to bring horses home.

Long Rider Arthur Young made a series of journeys in England, Ireland and France in the late 18th century. During his initial journey across England in 1776, he was the first to note how local farmers had discovered the benefits of feeding carrots to horses. Young next made an extensive journey across revolutionary France. There he witnessed the immense poverty of the majority of the population, and contrasted that against the wealth of the aristocrats. Young recorded how one nobleman's stable was "580 feet long, 40 feet broad and was filled with 240 English horses."

Despite his reservations about the unstable political situation in France, he returned there again at a critical juncture in the country's history. Once again mounted on his faithful mare, Young set off to explore the kingdom on horseback. This time the journey quickly fell to pieces. Only a hundred miles into the long trip, the mare became unexpectedly blind. Despite the difficulties, the loyal Long Rider refused to abandon the animal.

"After riding her three thousand seven hundred miles humanity did not allow me to sell her."

In October of 1788 the loyal traveller managed to bring the horse back to the safety of England.

Clarence Dalrymple Bruce also managed to save his horse against tremendous odds. He set out in 1905 to ride his small Kashmiri hill pony from Ladakh, India to Peking, China.

"I was loath to part with the little fellow so brought him back to England, where he now spends his days running in a field at home, wondering no doubt, where all the grass he sees comes from."

The cost of shipping horses overseas has always been expensive and remains so today.

After buying horses in Australia, Edouard Chautard and Carine Thomas rode 5,000 kilometres (3,000 miles) along the Bicentennial National Trail. They then decided to ship their three horses home to New Caledonia.

"The price was $5,000 per horse. We had to go to the bank to ask for the money. We now have to pay every month for three years for that loan," Edouard informed the Guild.

Returning by Relay

Bringing the horses home via motorized transport also involves a great deal of expense.

After completing their "ocean to ocean" ride from California to Virginia, Jeannette and Richard McGrath were faced with the necessity of raising enough money to pay to transport the horses home to Wyoming, a distance of several thousand miles. They came up with a novel solution.

Jeanette wrote, "We called horse transports, previous hosts, horse organizations, rodeo grounds, vets, horse traders, personal friends, trailer companies, and contacts of contacts of contacts. Ideas were plentiful, but our challenge continued to be cost. Anyone who transports horses understandably wants to be paid for their time and gas at a profit. We only had enough money left for gas. This began to confirm the gut feeling I had had for months that we would indeed be going home via a relay. So we started to focus our efforts on calling our old friends. We got out the atlas and plotted our course home. We continued to call previous hosts all across the country until we had plenty who were willing to drive and had access to a large enough trailer. Then we got down to the details; where we were meeting, how many miles each person was asked to drive, how long it would take, where we would meet the next driver and at what time, how far we would go each day, where we would stay for the night, etc."

Though it was a logistical challenge, the McGraths brought all their animals home safely.

Gifting the Horse

When Clarence Dalrymple Bruce completed his historic ride from India to China, he had enough money and political influence to ship his Kashmiri hill pony home to England. Many Long Riders were not that lucky.

At the end of a long and dangerous ride, they find themselves in a strange country. They are physically and emotionally exhausted. They are almost always financially impoverished. In such cases some decide to give their horses to friends.

One such traveller was W.C. Rose, who made an astonishing ride from Mexico to Argentina in the late 19th century.

"And now," Rose wrote, "I crave to be permitted a few lines in just praise of my noble mare, Pepita, which carried me faithfully and well during my long, long ride. She was a bronco, stood about fourteen and a half hands, was as swift as an arrow, surefooted as a goat, and almost indefatigable. She was a beauty, endowed with great intelligence, and of a very amiable and docile character. She twice saved my life, and, as I have said, carried me all the way from Mexico to the Argentine. When, after the termination of our journey, I made a present of Pepita to my friend Pedro, he said it was the greatest token of friendship I could have given him. He was right; parting from Pepita made me weep like a woman for the first time in my life."

Some Long Riders presented their horses to a person who was full of respect for the journey that had been done.

After Baron Fukushima completed his journey from Berlin to Tokyo, the Emperor of Japan expressed admiration for the Long Rider's hardy native horses and then guaranteed their safety for life.

Other Long Riders have discovered places which could provide safe havens for their horses.

When his journey from Mongolia to Hungary was concluded, Tim Cope wrote, "I knew that I wanted all three horses to be together, and selling them was not an option for me. These were the heroes of the journey, the brave, strong and uncomplaining equines who had felt the brunt of our experience from start to finish and they were my companions, my friends."

Even though people had offered to buy or keep the horses, Tim opted for another solution.

"Out of the blue it was suggested that I could give them away to the children's home at the village of Tiszadob where I had stayed previously. The feature of this place was a 19th century castle with expansive lush pasture all around the grounds. A backwater of the Tisza River was just a few hundred metres away, and due to the moist air, rich soil, and leafy forests nearby, the grass was particularly good."

Tim learned that the director of the orphanage believed that interaction with horses would help the children who had lacked vital physical contact with their family during their formative years. A lack of funds had kept the orphanage director from purchasing horses for such a therapeutic programme.

"Despite the fact that the children's home was not the open steppe that I had always imagined for them, it eventually felt like the right decision. At Tiszadob they would be spoilt, and because there were no other competing horses they would always have attention, and ample pasture, hay and grain," Tim concluded.

Other Long Riders have given their horses to someone who can use them for work in exchange for feeding them.

The journey made by Marie-Emmanuelle Tugler and Marc Witz led them from the luxuriant sub-tropical forests of Southern Brazil to the mythical Incan ruins of Machu Picchu in faraway Peru. Knowing they could not take their horses and mule back to France, they found suitable homes for them.

"The horses, Tipi and Coco, went to a large ecological farm, where they will take tourists for weekend rides. As for Brioza, she is joining a large herd of mules, and twice a month she will carry goods to the nearest village. Sad but reassured, we left our travelling companions with whom we have been so happy, so serene, so confiding for six months and 3,200 kilometres (1,900 miles)," Marie-Emmanuelle explained.

The conclusion of a journey places a Long Rider at a tactical disadvantage if he is overseas. Time and money may be short. The desire to return home may be pressing. In such circumstances it is easy for a smart stranger to take emotional advantage of a tired traveller.

Do not be deceived by appearances. Question the possible new owner thoroughly. Inspect the property carefully.

If possible, ask for a written agreement which states that the horses are being donated provided certain conditions are met. This might include not separating or selling the animals without first notifying the Long Rider. Updates on how the horses are doing may also be a term of the agreement.

Harsh Realities

Finding a kind-hearted person who is willing to give horses a home for life is rare.

All too often the traveller cannot foresee the unpleasant circumstances which await him.

Sometimes the animal doesn't work out and the journey never begins

Katie Cooper's first attempt was ruined when the mule she had chosen was found to be unsuitable.

"I struggled for months and months against what I knew deep down had to be done."

Despite her deep devotion to the mule, Katie realized, "Butch needed another kind of life, one more suited to who he is."

But that didn't prevent her from being "ripped by grief and loss as the trailer disappeared down the dusty road, carrying Butch to his new home."

Many times injuries occur during the course of the journey which prohibits the horse from continuing.

Tim Cope's original pack horse was such an example.

"Kok my sturdy pack horse had stepped on a five-inch rusty nail that had lodged deep in his hoof. I treated him for two weeks to no avail before deciding to leave him behind."

Immense distance often plays a role in the horse's future.

After Parker Gillmore survived his incredible ride across South Africa, he knew he could not take his beloved horses back to Scotland. He was forced to sell, "my faithful horses, to whose endurance I give full credit for accomplishing my most arduous and trying journey."

Government restrictions hamper many dreams of taking the horses home.

After Donald Brown completed his ride from the Arctic Circle to Copenhagen, he encountered such bureaucratic obstructions. He was particularly distressed at the loss of his remarkable mare, Pilkis.

"Pilkis seemed to sense the finality of this farewell and went slowly with drooping head, wondering perhaps at the selfishness of men that they separate good friends at their convenience. But due to the stringency of veterinary regulations for import I could not take her to England as I had hoped."

A lack of money has forced many a Long Rider to realize he cannot afford to keep his horse.

After completing a gruelling ride across the deserts and mountains of the American West, Clay Marshall realized he could not keep his horses.

"Sadly my life in the civilized world couldn't support the needs of an equine family. My wife and I lived in the city. We didn't own a barn, pasture, or even land and we didn't have the time and money to give the horses the attention they need. Even if I could have afforded it, I wouldn't pay for one of my horses to waste away in a stall the remainder of their days."

The goal is to end the journey with an upright heart and a happy horse. In each of these cases, the Long Rider found a suitable home for the animals. Because they were forced to sell their horses, the decision left scars on the travellers' souls.

Other individuals have had no qualms in sending their horses off to a cruel future.

Easy Come, Easy Go

There are all types of sins. The Bible warns against seven notorious examples; anger, greed, laziness, pride, lust, envy and gluttony. It forgot to include the misdeed of deliberately delivering your horse to a pitiless fate or an unkind master.

Sometimes fate forces a Long Rider to sell a horse. It can't be helped.

But that doesn't excuse those individuals who purloined their honour by selling their horses without a thought to their future welfare.

A case in point was the Welshman who travelled with two horses from Canada to Texas in 2008. These beautiful Quarter Horses had been located thanks to the help of American Long Rider Allen Russell, who spent weeks searching the countryside until he located two splendid animals. The horses left Allen's Montana ranch in wonderful condition.

The Welshman rode them hard. Failing to heed Allen's advice, he tied the pack horse to the horn of his saddle. When it pulled back, the strain was so great that it broke the tree of the riding saddle. The traveller ignored an emergency message sent by Allen and the Guild warning him not to proceed without changing saddles. The Welshman didn't care and he refused to slow down.

The reason behind his behaviour was based on the fact that he loved being in the media. He had become so addicted to the publicity he was receiving in the American press that his only goal was to reach the big party planned for him in El Paso.

The horses arrived covered in saddle sores and bearing raw marks where the hair had been rubbed off their bodies. The traveller put them in a stable and effectively walked away from them. He started attending various celebrations thrown in his honour. After nearly two weeks of enjoying his status as a star, living as a guest in a posh hotel, and attending parties, the Welshman announced he was flying home. His only effort to provide for the horses included a half-hearted attempt to sell the injured horses to a car salesman. When that failed, he bought his ticket and prepared to board the plane. The horses were to be left in the stable, their future entirely unknown.

Allen Russell had been following the course of these events. He had repeatedly tried to speak to the traveller at his El Paso hotel but his telephone calls were never answered. Finally, Allen got through.

"He said he had to leave the next day and that he had done all he could to find the horses a home. I spent considerable time stressing to him that he owed the horses more than this and asking how he possibly thought he would be able to find them a home when he was gone if he hadn't been able to do it when he was there." Allen later wrote.

Allen continued, "If you look at his blog, it is full of stories about his basking in glory, his plush hotel room, his rush to be off to the restaurant and bar with his admirers. There is next to nothing about caring for the horses. He doesn't mention them again or of any effort to secure their futures while in El Paso. He has no idea of the confusion the horses felt as they waited in unfamiliar surroundings for the man they had given their trust and accepted as their leader to guide them. Day after day they had given their all to him and in trade only asked to be treated decently."

Thanks to an emergency effort made by Allen and the Long Riders' Guild, a suitable home was found for the horses at the last minute. But by then the Welshman had flown back to Great Britain.

"If I had not done what I did he would have left the next day with no future secured or even prospects for a home for the horses," Allen recalled. "If that is not abandonment then I don't know what is."

Allen summed up the situation when he wrote, "My opinion is anyone who forms such a relationship with two fine horses like these and after they carry his sorry ass to success pays their debt by deserting them is no good in my book. It proves there are more horse's asses than horses."

Unfortunately this is not the only such episode.

For example, there was the American who rode his horses 20,000 miles to all 48 American state capitals. At the onset of the journey in 2002 the Guild suggested that the horses be named George Beck and Frank Heath, in honour of the Historical Long Riders who had previously made that journey.

At the conclusion of the trip the traveller stunned the Long Rider community by listing the horses for sale on Ebay. He was prepared to separate them and sell them for a fast buck to the first buyer, no questions asked. Once again the Guild interceded and helped ensure the horses were kept together and went to a safe home.

But things didn't work out that well in Mongolia.

In 2010 an Australian set out to ride across Mongolia from east to west in no more than 90 days. The result was a catastrophic journey.

Because he hoped to travel 2,500 kilometres (1,550 miles) in record time, the 176 pound rider rode the small Mongolian horses extremely hard. Upon arriving outside the capital of Ulan Bator, an eyewitness stated that the two horses were so thirsty they could not eat. Upon observing the condition of the dehydrated horses, this Mongolian immediately drove twenty-five kilometres to get water from a well and bring it back to the distressed animals.

In addition to being parched, both horses were extremely thin and one of them was suffering from saddle sores which have been described as unbelievable. A witness described the traveller's saddle blanket as "a putrid piece of carpet." Another eyewitness said the horse's injuries were, "the size of dinner plates and going to the bone." In addition to these open wounds, the injured horse was also being eaten alive by insects. According to an official statement, "I could see the bones and there were hundreds of worms (insects)."

Despite their injuries, local Mongolian horsemen were prepared to purchase the horses and nurse them back to health. Fearing that he would lose money, the Australian decided instead to sell the wounded horses to a local salami factory.

Some things are so fundamental that they should be obvious. Yet none of these men understood that the need to protect the integrity of the horse doesn't stop when you step down from the saddle. In each of these cases the traveller turned the journey into a publicized stunt wherein ego and public acclaim become more important than the horse-human relationship.

One cannot reduce equestrian travel to that of a product. It is never a jar of jam or a dossier of dust-covered facts ready to be presented for scientific inspection. At the heart of the matter is the mutual journey carried out by two sympathetic beings, a Long Rider and a Road Horse.

I speak with great conviction because I have been forced to part from a horse I loved. I learned from painful experience that it is never the mileage that matters. The miles never blind us to the heartache of leaving an equine friend.

Adieu to Shavon

No life is free of criticism. Older siblings mock us. Teachers browbeat us. Bullies torment us. Friends ridicule us. Some of the criticism, though painful, has a grain of truth lodged within, and therein helps to improve our lives. But many things are said for reasons which aren't exactly noble. I've come in for my share of criticism too. And while I've lived long enough to accept and learn from most of it, one unfounded barb left a wound that never healed.

A smug American woman once falsely denounced me for deserting my horse.

In my book, *Khyber Knights*, I explain how I made a very dangerous solo journey on my beloved palomino mare, Shavon. Having left Peshawar, I had ridden her to the remote mountain kingdom of Kafiristan, in the far north-west of Pakistan. There I was stricken by hepatitis so severe that I was on the edge of death.

The nearest medical assistance was a long day's ride away in the distant town of Chitral. I was too weak to mount without assistance. The journey was made through desolate mountains, under a blazing sun. After fading in and out of consciousness, at one point I passed out and slipped from the saddle.

When I regained consciousness, I was lying face down in the dust. Shavon was standing over me, shielding me from the sun. If she had wandered off, I would have died on that desolate road. With a terrible effort, I got back into the saddle and urged Shavon to walk on. It was the horse who brought me to Chitral and saved my life.

The only local doctor didn't waste anytime telling me that the hepatitis was so severe that I was close to death. He predicted that if I didn't fly back to Peshawar, via the irregular plane that arrived in Chitral on occasion, I would be dead within two weeks.

I was young and unwilling to listen to reason. Perhaps, I mistakenly thought, I could ride on in a few days' time.

I was so weak I could barely walk but I made it back to the hotel, where Shavon was picketed outside. A nearby corn field had been harvested but the still-tender corn stalks were standing. Being too weak to stand, I lay on my stomach, and with a small pocket knife I laboriously crawled along the row of corn stalks, slowly cutting one corn stalk at a time. When I had a large pile, I dragged them with the greatest effort over to my hungry horse.

It was the water that defeated me.

I found a bucket and, having filled it with water, attempted to lift it and take it to the thirsty horse. When the disease first hit me, I had been too weak to even summon the strength to close the fingers on my hand. Two days later I was little better. I didn't have the strength to lift the water.

That was the moment I sank down on the ground, leaned back against the wall of the hotel and tasted the bitter bile of defeat.

Of course Shavon didn't understand any of this. There had been no valley of hunger, no desert of thirst she would not cross for me. She had carried me through all weathers, never slipped, never faltered, never complained, and when the moment came, rescued me from a lonely death.

I owed her my life.

And now I knew I had to leave her.

Because of her unusual colour and great beauty, a wealthy rug merchant was anxious to purchase her. When I walked away from her, Shavon cried out, calling to me, urging me to come back, pleading with me not to leave her.

Later, when I was tortured and imprisoned in Pakistan, I never cried. But I wept for Shavon. It wasn't just the hepatitis that nearly killed me. It was the grief of leaving her in that mountain fastness which unmanned me.

I had not ridden an equine slave. I had been privileged to travel with a golden-haired triumph. And circumstances beyond my control had forced me to leave her.

After my book was released an American woman, living in comfort and surrounded by her ingrained cultural perceptions, accused me of emotional indifference. Having ignored the fact that I was at death's door, she said I should have put Shavon in a trailer and brought the mare back to Peshawar. What the fool failed to realize was that the concept of a horse trailer did not exist in that country and that the long and hazardous road I had just travelled led over one of the country's most infamous mountain passes.

This woman never understood the practicalities or the emotions involved in my situation.

There was no way to take Shavon back to Peshawar, short of riding her and I couldn't do that. So I found her the best home I could.

My life has progressed since then. I lost my parents. I was disappointed in love. The hurt fades.

Shavon's memory is with me always.

Her name invokes a wound that never healed.

No outsider can fathom what happened between us. Her image still dwells within my eyes and abides in my heart. And if, like me, you set out on the long grey road then you too may be forced to leave behind your treasured horse.

The Emotional Cost

I am not the only one.

No Long Rider can come to this tragic parting without learning the meaning of real sorrow.

Other Long Riders have written about the depth of their emotional attachment to their horses.

Canadian Long Rider Bonnie Folkins said that parting with the horse which carried her across Mongolia to be akin to "a good-bye that we suffer like a death."

The toughest equestrian explorers, who have ignored hardship and sneered at danger during their journeys, have experienced incredible remorse when they are forced by necessity to leave their gallant horse behind.

George Younghusband rode his faithful pony, Joe, through the jungles of Burma. After arriving at the river which held the ship prepared to take him back to civilisation, the Long Rider boarded. Seeing his friend sailing away, Younghusband wrote that little Joe galloped up and down the beach, calling out to his departing friend until he was out of sight.

Selling

There is an old Long Rider saying, "Horses are our life. They are not our livelihood."

This concept is based upon the fact that your horse has carried you further than you thought possible. He has been your trusted ally in unknown territory. You have built a life together. You have felt his soft breath across your face.

How can you leave such an animal?

But harsh reality sometimes forces us to do so.

Italian Long Rider Count Alfieri once said, "Without horses I am never half myself." This explains why he wrote, "I abhor trafficking in horses."

Jeremy James also expressed his emotional distress when forced into this situation during his ride across Eastern Europe.

"If there's one thing in the world I really hate it's selling horses; I can't stand it. If I had my way I'd keep every horse I ever saw and have a great big place full of them, but I suppose that's a bit of a dream. Besides, I haven't got the money."

The Practicalities

Like all aspects of equestrian travel, if circumstances dictate that a horse must be sold then there are realities which cannot be ignored.

Normally, a horse owner living in his own country has the luxury of making sure the animal looks its best. The horse is advertised in such a way as to highlight its beauty, training and performance. Time is often on the side of such a seller.

Those are not the type of circumstances which Long Riders normally encounter.

If you are in a foreign land the potential buyers know you are cornered and under pressure. That is why you can count on them to exploit you financially and emotionally.

First, do not think that your horses will be accorded any degree of fame because they have just completed a remarkable journey. Quite the contrary, crafty buyers routinely ignore the animal's obvious robust health. They tell the Long Rider that the journey has rendered the horse "weak."

Next, never expect to sell the horse for the same price that you originally paid. Throughout history equestrian explorers have learned that profiteering is a highly developed skill among horse dealers.

Fynes Moryson was the 16th century Long Rider who spent ten years riding through Germany, Bohemia, Switzerland, Netherlands, Denmark, Poland, Italy, Turkey, France, England, Scotland and Ireland. In 1592, having ridden from Vienna, Austria to Padua, Italy he discovered that the locals refused to give him a fair price for his fine horse.

"When I came to Padua the horse dealers, finding I must sell my horse, agreed among themselves most craftily. Every day they sent a man who would offer less than had been offered the day before. After fourteen days I was about to accept the price being offered, when by chance I found an Englishman who was returning to Germany and gave me a fair price for my horse."

Fynes got lucky. The majority of Long Riders have been forced to accept a financial loss rather than run the risk of keeping the horse in the hope of a better price at a later date. The expense and uncertainty of this practice are too great.

It doesn't help your chances if there is a glut of horses already on the market.

After completing a gruelling ride across the deserts of the American Southwest in 1926, Clyde Kluckhohn was told that "people would not take a horse as a gift that year." He was lucky to find a ranger who offered him fifty dollars for all his horses, his saddle and equipment.

Another problem Long Riders encounter in foreign countries is that potential buyers have no actual currency.

The first part of Tim Cope's journey took him across Mongolia. But he was not permitted to take his horses out of the country. To Tim's surprise, his idea of selling the horses to local nomadic herders was complicated for an unexpected reason.

"The problem with selling is that you usually need to sell quickly. But nomads make such decisions very carefully and very few of them need any more horses. Worst of all I found it very hard to find any herders who had any cash. Most were willing to swap in exchange for another horse, a sheep, a yak or maybe a saddle with stirrups."

As a result, Tim lost "at least 50 per cent of the value" of his horses when he finally sold them.

When the time comes, always write up a dated "Bill of Sale" for each horse being sold. Include the physical details of the horse, including age, sex, colour, markings and the condition of its health. This is to protect you against a case of "buyer's remorse," if the horse is returned and the money demanded back. Note the price being paid and state if the purchase price is being done by cash, cheque or in trade. Be sure the buyer, seller and a witness all sign this dated document

The "Long Rider International Equine Bill of Sale" provided in Chapter 17 of this encyclopaedia will serve this purpose.

Deadly Deception

The ancient Latin phrase "Caveat Emptor" translates as "Let the buyer beware." It is usually used to emphasise the point that the buyer is often not in full possession of all the facts.

Long Riders should instead memorize the phrase "Caveat Auctor," which means let the seller be on his guard.

Should circumstances force you to sell your horse, your legal rights and the horse's life may both be forfeit.

This was the tragic circumstance which DC Vision, one of the Founders of the Guild, encountered at the conclusion of his four-year journey through the United States.

After having ridden his Shire mare, Louise, 23,000 kilometres (14,000 miles), news of a family medical emergency reached the young Long Rider in the small town of Birch Tree, Missouri. The distraught traveller had already arranged for a local horseshoer to re-shoe Louise, so DC was deep in thought when the blacksmith asked if he might be of any assistance.

"I responded impulsively that I needed to sell my horse. Louise and I had been inseparable for four years. She was the closest sentient being I had ever known, so the announcement of needing to sell her was heartbreaking. But I knew I had no choice," DC later recalled.

The horseshoer instantly agreed to purchase the beautiful mare and promised to provide her with a good home.

"The farrier led the way in his pickup truck to his house, where he paid me $500 for my beautiful mare. She was worth thousands of dollars on the market, let alone my emotional attachment to her, but I knew this was to be our fate that June day."

While DC unloaded his saddle and gear off Louise, the farrier spoke privately to his wife at the door of their home. He then returned with a cheque, handed it to the unsuspecting Long Rider and announced that he was going to transport Louise to a nearby pasture.

"When I turned to put the check in my bags, he loaded my horse into the trailer. 'Wait, I have to say good-bye to her!' As I walked the hundred feet to the trailer, he drove away."

Confused, and not knowing what was happening, DC could feel the atmosphere had changed. Sensing something was wrong Louise began to whinny in a nearly human scream, turning to face DC, kicking at the trailer.

"Being so helpless, I began to cry. But I was immediately brought back to the situation at hand when the wife screamed at me 'Get your fucking gear out of my yard or I will call the police!' I began walking imploringly towards the woman so as to beg her to tell me what was happening. She slammed and locked the door."

A few minutes later the sheriff arrived. DC explained the situation to the law officer, who told him since he had taken the money for Louise they were in their legal rights to demand the traveller leave the property.

The distraught Long Rider asked if the sheriff could tell him where the pasture was so that he could walk there and say goodbye to his horse.

"Son, he doesn't own a pasture. Look, I know you are upset, but you might as well know the truth. You've been lied to. He's taking her to the auction to sell for meat for dog food."

There are miracles, albeit little ones, even in the Long Rider world.

DC reached his home in time to see his father before he passed away.

Just as importantly, DC later learned that an elderly farmer attended the auction where the nefarious horse-shoer had taken Louise.

"The farmer loved draft horses. When he spotted a magnificent Shire draft mare enter the auction ring that day he bought her on impulse, took her home and let her loose in his pasture. He just wanted to wake up each day and see a big draft horse out there while he drank his coffee," DC later recalled.

That lucky draft horse was Louise, who lived eight more years in the farmer's field.

Slaughter

Before making an equestrian journey, it pays to learn if the inhabitants of that country eat horses or export them to other nations to be used as meat. These practices make selling horses a dangerous proposition if you are trying to ensure their long-term safety.

As Keith Clark made his way across Chile he saw beautiful horses on their way to destruction.

He wrote, "It was heartbreaking to see a lorry carrying half a dozen really good horses going north to be slaughtered. There are plenty of horses around the town of Cochrane. So if a rancher needs money he sells a horse for slaughter. And it's usually the big, strong horses in good condition that fetch the most money."

Mongolia and Kazakhstan both have a strong reputation for consuming horse meat. Whereas the Mongols normally eat horses in winter, the Kazakhs consume them all year round.

Tim Cope was terribly aware of these cultural and dietary practices. Whereas in the past nomads valued a horse for its abilities, Tim learned that times had changed. Instead of caring how strong or beautiful the horse was, modern Kazakhs were interested in how much fat and meat was on the animal.

That is why, after buying his horses in Kazakhstan, he had no illusion about what fate awaited the animals if they were left behind.

"I have dreamed of getting these horses out of the country because the destiny for EVERY horse in Kazakhstan is horse meat sausage. While I understand this culture very well, I am still infuriated when onlookers view my horses purely from a meat point of view."

He advised other Long Riders riding in Kazakhstan to try to avoid selling a horse in a town or city because "the horses will most likely end up as meat." He also warned that the province of Bayan Olgiy has a strong reputation for horse meat consumption. His advice is to try and find a nomadic herder to sell the horses to.

Bonnie Folkins, who has also ridden in Kazakhstan, offered another valuable insight. Although the idea of donating the horses might appear to be noble, she strongly advises against trying to give the horses away as gifts.

"The mentality is completely different there," she warned. "People in Kazakhstan will not understand that sort of philanthropy. They will think you are foolish for giving away expensive horses and in turn will not treat you with respect. In fact, they may even be somewhat suspect if you do this. If they are given away as gifts, whoever ends up with the horses will simply try to sell them for profit and may not treat them well."

Bonnie advised, "If you have good horses, they will command a reasonable fee. If they are purchased by respectable dealers, farmers or trades people, they will be treated kindly and such people will take the animal's best interests to heart. Anyone making such an investment will be prepared to make a sacrifice and be committed to keeping the horses in good health and sound condition."

Honouring the Horse

According to ancient legend, the Native Americans in Patagonia believed that a mythical land called Trapalanda lay hidden behind the Andes. This was an equine version of Shangri La, where a vast plain of tall, lush green grass awaited the spirit of departed horses. In that land they ran free and were never tired.

Many modern cultures continue to honour the horse.

The Yakut people who reside in Siberia do not attempt to dominate the horse. They treat the animal as their brother, believing that they have ancestors in common. This respect and reverence is so deeply ingrained that Yakuts frown on speaking roughly to a horse and striking the animal is a cultural taboo.

A Life of Cruelty

Yet there is no point in pretending that other countries share these values. Many Long Riders have noted the cruelty inflicted upon horses by people with varying views on animal kindness.

G.W. Ray was one of the first equestrian travellers to note the lack of sentimentality. After arriving in Buenos Aires in 1889, he was horrified at the wide-spread horse abuse which he witnessed.

"Surely no suffering creatures under the sun cry out louder for mercy than the horses in Argentina? Some of the streets are very bad and filled with deep ruts into which the horses often fall. There the driver will sometimes cruelly leave them, when, after his arm aches in using the whip, he finds the animal cannot rise. The horse is left to die in the public streets. Looking on such sights seeing every street urchin with coarse laugh and brutal jest jump on such an animal's quivering body, stuff its parched mouth with mud, or poke sticks into its staring eyes, I have cried aloud at the injustice. I have been very near the police station more than once when my righteous blood compelled me to interfere. The policemen and the passers-by only laughed at me for my pains. It has been my painful duty to pass moaning creatures lying helplessly in the road, with broken limbs, under a burning sun, suffering hunger and thirst, for three consecutive days, before kind death, the sufferer's friend, released them," Ray wrote.

There were other things which Ray witnessed which were so horrific that he added, "I had better leave knowledge of those events in the inkpot."

The Indian subcontinent is also notorious for horse abuse.

Before he became famous for writing books like *1984* and *Animal Farm*, English author George Orwell worked and travelled in India and Burma. There he witnessed how the horses employed to pull passenger carts, known as a *tonga* or a *gharry*, were subjected to unspeakable abuse.

"Their master looks on the whip as a substitute for food. Their work expresses itself in a sort of equation – whip plus food equals energy. Generally it is about sixty per cent whip and forty per cent food. Sometimes their necks are encircled by one vast sore, so that they drag all day on raw flesh. It is still possible to make them work, however, it is just a question of thrashing them so hard that the pain behind outweighs the pain in front. After a few years even the whip loses its virtue, and the pony goes to the knacker."

Nor has such cruelty been eradicated in India.

Horses are still employed to pull carriages in Bombay. According to one recent news report many of these horses are routinely abused.

"Most live a life too gruesome to describe. To make them turn left and right, spiked bits are clamped in their mouth; so their mouths bleed all the time. You think they are chewing food. They are actually swallowing their own blood. Most are cold shoed, which means rather than finding a shoe that fits the horse's foot, owners get the hooves brutally hacked to fit into smaller shoes. This makes the horses unstable on their legs, their hooves begin to rot. The iron shoes slip on wet streets. When they fall or flail, they are flogged to shock them into quickly standing up. This makes them slip again. Their legs are swollen and stiff. Even their off hours are agonising, standing in filth, unfed, and in seasons like this, knee deep in rain water for hours. Where the horses are in enclosed areas, as in the Ambedkar Nagar slums, 4 to 6 horses are squeezed together in rooms 10 feet by 8. They can barely breathe. They stand there for hours, defecate, trying to beat off swarms of flies without any space to move."

The reporter concluded, "The horse has not changed. He is still loyal, loving, devoted to his master, a friend to whoever shows the slightest affection. But you and I have changed. We see the horse today as just another creature to exploit, make quick money off."

Such cruelty is not restricted to a single continent or practised by only one nation.

In 2008 reporters documented how the once thriving Romanian horse population was being savagely eradicated.

"Ribs showing clearly through their tattered flanks, the starving horses corralled on the edge of the eastern Romanian city of Galati are just a few days away from death. Once, they would have pulled wooden carts along the city's streets or worked in the fields, as horses have done in Romania for centuries. But now they have been abandoned by their owners, victims of a disastrous attempt to bring the country into line with European Union law by banning horse-drawn carts from main roads. Over the past month, hundreds of stray horses have been found roaming the streets and parks of Romania's major cities. Many are half-starved and barely able to walk; some have died where they were discovered, unable to get back to their feet. But there is little demand for an ailing animal in a country where an estimated one million working horses have been officially labelled an anachronism."

Cases such as these drive home the truth of what Brigid Brophy once said.

"Whenever people say, 'We mustn't be sentimental,' you can take it they are about to do something cruel. And if they add 'We must be realistic,' they mean they are going to make money out of it."

Long Riders must recognize the fact that there are savage countries which tolerate brutal customs.

I myself journeyed through equestrian exploration hell in Pakistan.

On my last journey in Pakistan my pack horse fell ill in a part of Pakistan inhabited by a tribe of pagans. While I sat beside my sick comrade, he died suddenly at midnight, so the next morning I paid hundreds of rupees to have him properly buried. In my naïveté I believed the task had been done as promised. So I was puzzled when later that night I heard the sound of drumming, singing and merriment off in the distance.

It wasn't until I was riding out of that country that I was informed that all the drumming I had heard during the night was the sound of the pagans celebrating my loss. The curs had taken my money, chopped up my horse, gathered together in a secret place, and while singing and dancing, fed the whole village on my grief.

The Last Resort

As all these examples demonstrate, NEVER let your horse fall into unholy hands.

That was a lesson which the nation of Great Britain learned in 1930.

At the onset of the First World War the British army only had 25,000 horses ready for combat. This caused the War Office to begin an urgent search for at least 500,000 additional horses and mules. To fulfil the need the countryside was emptied of equines. Knowing their animals were going to be taken off to war, many farmers preferred to shoot their horses rather than let the army have them.

That option would later come back to haunt the British.

At the conclusion of the First World War the British high command left an estimated 20,000 horses behind in Egypt. Instead of being shipped back to England, Australia or New Zealand, from whence they came, these equine warriors were sold for a pittance to Egyptian horse dealers.

After that the Allied war horses began a life of unspeakable degradation, starvation and cruelty. For the next twelve years they endured a living hell and were abused beyond words.

The horses were forgotten until 1930, when Dorothy Brooke, the wife of a British cavalry general recognized that the starved horses pulling carriages through the streets of Cairo bore the brands of the English army.

"These once proud animals were hungry and weak, lame, ill-shod, blind and suffering effects from the extreme climate. The majority of them drag out wretched days of toil in the ownership of masters too poor to feed them."

Brooke alerted the British press, who in turn informed the horrified people of Great Britain. Funds were raised and many of the surviving horses were rescued.

Previous generations of Long Riders were perfectly aware that many countries treated horses with unspeakable cruelty. That is why before he set off to ride from Kashmir to Peking in 1905, Clarence Dalrymple Bruce and his companion made a solemn pact.

"Before commencing the journey we had decided to leave no animal to die behind by inches. The friendly bullet was invariably to be their destiny."

Dalrymple Bruce made his decision perfectly clear to the natives he had hired to accompany him to China. Under no conditions whatever would any horse be left behind or remain alive unless the Englishmen were confident that it would be placed in the care of an individual who could be trusted.

The idea of putting your horse down may seem shocking and abhorrent to modern readers.

If Fanny Duberly were alive she would express another point of view because during her journeys in Russia and India she observed "horses that were left to linger until nature puts an end to their pain, instead of being mercifully and instantaneously destroyed."

That is why she advised, "The principle is good, which teaches men to refrain from taking God's great gift of life, but I saw enough of animal suffering to teach me that death is often the greater blessing."

The ultimate outcome of your horse's future depends upon actions.

Don't believe honeyed words and false promises. If in your soul you have doubts about the other person's sincerity, listen to your instincts.

Never let your horses fall into cruel hands.

If you cannot, absolutely cannot assure yourself that you can find safe, decent homes for your horses then put them down rather than permit them to be abused.

Allow your horse to retain its dignity.

A bullet is kinder than years of starvation and torture. A lethal injection is preferable to a delayed life of misery. Euthanasia is better than a cooking pot.

When the time comes to say goodbye to your horse remember this old English prayer.

The Horse's Prayer to its Owner and Driver

Farewell.
I've served you long and true, through the many miles my back has carried you as you rode on safety's wing.
Ah, the memory of our journey, now for ever flown, as aged together we have grown.
But why thine eyes in tears?
I do not wish your tender heart to move.
Nay, do not look so sad, nor stroke my head;
We now must part, must bid a long adieu.
Take pity now when you decree my fate.
Timely save me, if you can, ere the last hour of my allotted life.
Do not yield me up to others who will tie me close or abuse me.
Sell me not to a barbarous creature who will gore my side with the spur or waste my noble strength on some
*   empty immorality or vile exercise.*
Find for me, if you can, one who knows the blessings of honesty and humanity.
And ere you go, hear my last request.
Do you teach others, like yourself, to know our value and to use us fair.
For ever have you proved the horse's friend.
Finally, when my strength is gone, instead of turning me over to a human brute to be tortured and starved,
Take my life in the easiest and quickest way, and your God will reward you in this life and in Heaven.
You will not consider me irreverent if I ask this in the name of Him who was born in a stable.
Amen.

Saying Goodbye

How the world gives and takes away.

You remember what you have both gone through.

But the last day has dawned. The friend who has changed your life is leaving.

You can't believe this moment has arrived.

Life won't be the same

Many a brave Long Rider has struggled to sum up what won't go into words.

Sven Hedin, who had a reputation for absolute fearlessness, wrote, "I was particularly sorry. But now the moment of parting had come. I hated the merchant who came to fetch my horse; and there were tears in my eyes."

Despite having made five equestrian journeys in various parts of the world, Robin and Louella Hanbury-Tenison were still emotionally distraught when the horses they rode through Albania were taken away.

"You never get used to saying goodbye. Once the lorry arrived, things happened in a too-quick blur. One moment we were kissing our horses goodbye – then they were loaded and gone. Louella and I, tears streaming down our faces, watched the lorry until it was out of sight."

Many a Long Rider has found him- or herself standing there, alone in the road, feeling forlorn, lonely and unsure of what to do next.

Grief

The Ancients believed that horses were capable of experiencing grief over the loss of their human companion.

Homer wrote that when Achilles' charioteer was killed in battle, "Hot tears flowed from the horses' eyes to the ground as they mourned for their charioteer."

Another legend states that Julius Caesar's horse "shed tears for three days before the hero's death."

In the Middle Ages one book attested that "when their master is dead or dying, horses shed tears, for they say that only the horse can weep for man and feel the emotion of sorrow."

I cannot confirm or deny such stories. However I can write with conviction regarding the many travellers who have been haunted by the decision to leave a horse behind.

After riding across Spain in 1852, George Cayley had to sell his beloved stallion. That decision, he wrote, "pinches my heart and leaves a wound that would rip me apart were I armour-plated oak."

Jeremy James learned about bereavement, his heart sat like a stone in his chest when circumstances forced him to leave behind pieces of his spirit.

"I felt caught in a whorl of anguish and grief. Our time was up, something said. In my heart I knew it, dare not say. Ten days later I sold the horses. The last time I saw Ahmed Pasa he was walking off behind a wall. He never knew what was happening. I know he didn't, thought we'd be back for him, later. Simsek knew. I saw it in his eyes and he broke me, like a reed. That night I wept into my pillow…..feelings of loss and recrimination. What had I done?"

It's hard to comprehend the dimensions of the heartache a Long Rider often experiences. But let me try to touch this pain with my limited number of words, so as to explain what it is that aches so deeply all these years later.

There were two horses in my life, Shavon and Pasha. I did not truly comprehend their value until they had left my life. They are gone now and something special that was once part of me is also departed.

As Jeremy and I both learned, nothing in truth can replace a Long Rider's equine companions. You are bound forever to your horses by a treasure of common memories. Theirs was a friendship which neither time nor distance can mar.

The feeling of brotherhood lasts longer than the journey which produced it. This is something which no Long Rider can explain but every Long Rider has felt.

Afterwards

This is a unique type of pain that resonates across the ages of your life. You wonder how the horses' lives were resolved. You worry that you could have done more, could have protected them from pain, could have ensured their safety. You spend the rest of your life judging your actions, trying to heal the psychological aftershock of a shattering and irreparable blow.

What happens afterwards? Most never learn. Sometimes it's better not to know.

One Long Rider learned her horse had been killed by wolves in Mongolia. Another found out his horse had been shot after it bit a man.

In 2008 Finnish Long Rider Tony Ilmoni rode 7,000 kilometres (4,300 miles) from Kyrgyzstan to Peking, China. When the journey was concluded Tony tried unsuccessfully to export his horse back to his home. Because of bureaucratic problems he failed.

"Corruption was the main reason why my horse never left China. And my bad conscience did not leave me either. So in September, 2011 I decided to go and look for my horse Gustav. Fast forward: I did find him after a lot of hassle. He was in a small village close to the Kazak border. He was not in good shape," Tony informed the Guild.

Once again he attempted to bring the horse to Europe, but there was never any news that this effort succeeded.

Summary

Equestrian travel has never been about riding in circles, winning blue ribbons, garnering the acclaim of the mob.

A journey marks the soul's solitary progress across the physical plain of our temporary existence.

This passage on horseback becomes a metaphor for life.

Early on, our desire is threatened when people try to talk us into not setting off.

Being consumed with fear themselves, they envy our determination to undertake what they know they lack the courage to try. So they fill our ears with tales of certain death, appeal to our sense of responsibility, attempt to burden us with guilt.

Not knowing if we will live, die or succeed, we suppress our concerns and set off into the unknown anyway.

Along the way we encounter unexpected dangers, endure hardships, suffer loss, overcome superstitions, conquer dragons, face our fears, find ourselves – or not.

All too often we are betrayed, disappointed and deceived along the way by those we trusted, loved and respected.

Sometimes we fail.

Occasionally we die.

But the journey, like life, has unexpected turns.

If we succeed, we are blessed, enlightened, changed from what we were into someone we only suspected dwelt within.

During the ride the horse has been an inspired leader, strong servant, trusted guide, brave companion, fleet messenger and faithful friend.

He has done more than merely carry us.

He has enchanted our heart.

But hidden behind the veil of nature is a touch of sorrow.

We have kept him from harm's eye.

Now, with our journey ended, our greatest desire is to provide him with the two things he most rightly deserves, protection and freedom.

Instead we watch as he is led away by a stranger into the unknown.

After he is gone we are like a tree with only one branch

We are left with an affliction of love.

Events link the two of you like the shores of an immense sea.

Though you may never meet again; all roads lead back to his memory.

Perhaps he will talk to you in your dreams.
Good Saint Hippolytus, the patron saint of horses, protect him.

Humanity has preserved the names of famous war horses and recalled the deeds of renowned equine athletes. But the contributions of road horses, such as Gato and Mancha, have been largely overlooked by historians. During the Second World War Tschiffely revisited Argentina, where he saw his faithful Criollos for the last time.

An intimate companionship grows between the Long Rider and the horse. Mary Bosanquet wrote, "On a journey like this a traveller does not possess his horses; they possess him, body and soul."

After having lived together through so many adventures, horses display signs of extreme emotional distress if separated from their travelling companions. Road Willow and Road Snow, who accompanied Kohei Yamakawa across the length of Japan in 2014, are examples of such intense equine bonding.

Travel awakens the wanderlust in horses. Within hours of completing her journey across England and Scotland, Elsa Wood-Gee's horse, Mikado, was anxious to resume travelling.

Road horses often develop tremendous emotional bonds for their equine companions that last for life. The most dramatic example was Mancha and Gato. They were inseparable until Gato died at the age of 32 in 1944. Afterwards Mancha ignored other horses. This picture shows Mancha at Gato's grave. Mancha was 37 when he died in 1947.

Ideally a Long Rider wants to provide a home for life for his faithful horses after the trip is concluded. That was what Marc Kempf did after he spent nearly five years travelling 23,500 kilometres (14,500 miles) though Canada and the United States with Speedy and Chris.

Bringing a horse home from a distant country is fraught with difficulties. Luckily Clarence Dalrymple Bruce had the money and political connections needed to ship the small pony he had ridden from Kashmir to Peking back to his home in England. There it was looked after by the Long Rider's daughter, Daisy.

Arthur Young was not as fortunate. While riding through France in 1788 his mare went blind. "After riding her three thousand seven hundred miles humanity did not allow me to sell her." He managed to bring her back to England.

After completing their "ocean to ocean" ride from California to Virginia, Jeannette and Richard McGrath were faced with the necessity of raising enough money to pay to transport the horse's home to Wyoming, a distance of several thousand miles. They came up with the novel solution of enlisting friends to drive them and their animals home via a system of relays.

Some Long Riders give their horses away as gifts. After completing his ride from Berlin to Tokyo, Baron Fukushima presented his horses, Ussri, Altai and Hsing An to the Emperor of Japan.

Logistics often prevent a Long Rider from keeping the horse. After riding the length of China's Great Wall, Louella and Robin Hanbury-Tenison had no option but to sell their horses, Tang and Ming.

Injuries sometimes interfere with plans to keep the horse. Jo Kimmins bought her horse Malachy in Spain and travelled across the country with him. But at the conclusion of the journey the horse became ill, which forced Jo to find him a home in Spain.

Throughout history Long Riders have been exploited by crafty horse dealers. Fynes Moryson spent ten years riding through Europe in the 16th century. He recounted how he was nearly cheated when it came time to sell his horse in Italy.

It doesn't help your chances if there is a glut of horses already on the market. After completing a gruelling ride across the deserts of the American Southwest in 1926, Clyde Kluckhohn was told that "people would not take a horse as a gift that year." He was lucky to find a ranger who offered him fifty dollars for his horse, saddle and equipment.

Long Riders should memorize the phrase "Caveat Auctor," which means let the seller be on his guard. After riding his Shire mare, Louise, for 22,500 kilometres (14,000 miles) DC Vision was deceived. Instead of providing the horse with a safe home, the unscrupulous buyer immediately attempted to sell the horse for dog food.

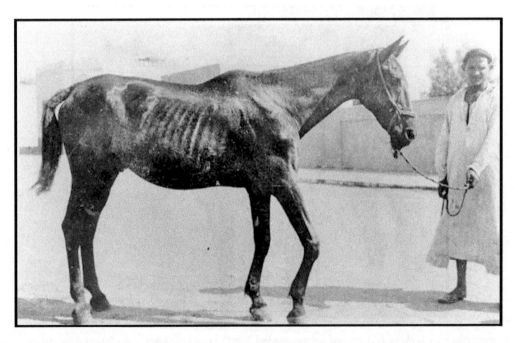

Never let your horse fall into unholy hands. This is one of the 20,000 army horses left in Egypt by the English army. When discovered in 1930, the horses had spent years suffering unspeakable degradation, starvation and cruelty.

After riding his stallion, Ahmed Pasa, across Turkey, Jeremy James wondered, "How do you say farewell to the companion of your finest days?" He concluded, "Here is a conflict between the heart and head that scars your soul."

No Long Rider can come to this tragic parting without learning the meaning of real sorrow. I experienced incredible remorse when I was forced by necessity to sell my gelding, Pasha, at the conclusion of my last trip in Pakistan.

What happens afterwards? Most never learn. Sometimes it's better not to know. After riding his horse, Gustav, from Kyrgyzstan to China, Tony Ilmoni later discovered that the horse was not being looked after properly by its new owners.

Chapter 78
Who You Have Become

When the trip is over, the land remains the same. Not so the Long Rider.

You set off like a shy child. But now the seasons of the journey have altered you in an invisible manner.

You sit at the table amongst those who knew you prior to your departure. Though you returned physically, you are no longer one of them. There is a distance in your eyes.

You hear them speaking to you, using the same name as when you left. But they no longer know you.

The journey challenged you, broke you, rewarded you, liberated you, renewed you and erased you.

Later, when you look in the mirror, thoughts come unbidden.

What marks a man, you ask yourself? What scores his soul, you wonder?

I am not me any more, you conclude. I am not who I was. A stranger has returned bearing my name.

As Sea G Rhydr said at the conclusion of her journey, "I'm simply not the same person who rode out of California in the pouring rain in October, 2011 and rode into Maine in November, 2013. There is no way to do something this crazy and soul-bending and not be changed deeply."

The Journey

Even though Long Riders travel in a straight line towards a distant goal, the journey marks a turning point in their lives, the sharpest turn many of them will ever encounter.

The journey has two levels, the outer and the inner. The former is a transitory geographic goal. The latter is a link to the eternal.

That is why English Long Rider Richard Barnes wrote, "Travel is an art, not only of fastening the buckles and keeping things together, but relating to what you see."

Richard understood that the journey can be experienced by the senses but never fully explained by words. It becomes a symbol of the unity of worlds visible and invisible.

Long periods of time spent in the saddle envelop the traveller in silence, listening, remembering and, hopefully, understanding. Though the traveller rides alone, he realizes that he is linked with those who rode in previous centuries.

"Exploration is no longer about planting flags and staking claims: it's a right and a duty for every generation to satisfy its longing for meaning and purpose," said Duncan J.D. Smith, a noted travel writer and a friend of the author.

Yes, a potential flame can burn in every heart but it cannot shine amidst confusion. The joy of riding in freedom has different effects. Self realisation comes to some.

Choices

Few Long Riders realize there may be emotional implications associated with their return.

Prior to their departure they were too busy protecting their dreams from the critics who stay behind to give any thought to a distant homecoming.

It is never easy to ride away from the mentality of the herd.

The poet e e cummings warned, "To be nobody but yourself in a world which is doing its best, night and day, to make you everybody else means to fight the hardest battles which any human being can fight, and never stop fighting."

But the act of departure signals more than the start of a long march towards a distant geographic goal. It is a declaration that the Long Rider is responding to a desire to live in a way different than that which was dictated to him at birth, by parents, culture, religion, sex, politics and economics.

Even before he swings into the saddle the Long Rider's eyes have been opened. He realizes he faces a choice between collaboration and resistance. Should he listen to those who urge him to seek safety within an urban existence? Does he follow the herd and direct all his energies toward obtaining the comforts of life?

Not being satisfied with what appears to be his predetermined destiny, every Long Rider has to resolve to change it.

Messanie Wilkins was a simple soul who felt that her heart was caged. Somewhere inside her was a song which others could not hear. She was the daughter of a poor farmer, not a poet. That is why she did not attempt to describe her "ocean to ocean" ride in fancy terms.

It was certainly a quest for personal freedom, but in her plain-spoken way Messanie simply said," I knew that I had been born restless."

Like other Long Riders, Messanie was responding to an ancient message implanted deep within her DNA that urged her to undertake a migration away from predictability. She instinctively knew that even on a planet where every place had supposedly already been explored, the last great unresolved mystery was to be found hidden within her own soul.

Such freedom is worth a little hardship.

When Thomas Stevens was making his ride across Russia in 1898, he made a point of riding to the estate of the famous author, Count Leo Tolstoy. That wise man told the Long Rider, "All travellers are pilgrims; and while the person who travels for pleasure or on business is not to be compared for righteousness to the pilgrim, yet all travellers are worthier than stay at home people. Their virtues consist in their contempt for a life of ease."

Long Riders are the modern mounted pilgrims of the sunrise. They have set themselves a goal which seems far beyond their reach. They are often scared before setting off because they are literally riding into unknown country on many levels. But they have determined to pay the price to find their soul's desire.

If one author summed up their common courage, it was Long Rider Sir Richard Burton, who wrote, "Do what thy manhood bids thee do, from none but self expect applause; He noblest lives and noblest dies who makes and keeps his self-made laws."

Challenges

Many dream of making an equestrian journey. Few ever summon the courage to set off on the difficult path towards self-reliance. When they do, it doesn't take long for the romance to be stripped away remorselessly.

Awaiting those who depart is the bare and barren truth. A host of physical and emotional challenges will force them to confront the limits of their strength. They learn to endure hardships and heartaches. Adversity teaches them perseverance. Overcoming illness bestows confidence. Ignoring hunger develops an iron resolution. Facing the unknown gives them courage.

Ian Robinson rode alone across Mongolia and Afghanistan's Wakhan Corridor. But it was his solo journey in Tibet that taught him the meaning of fortitude.

"No journey, no place has ever challenged me as Tibet did. My 3,500 kilometre (2,100 mile) solo horse trek across this unforgiving land in 2002 and 2004 brought me to my knees physically, emotionally and spiritually. Suffering extremes of altitude, cold, isolation and in constant conflict with the Chinese authorities made my pledge to deliver the ashes of a Tibetan Lama, Khensur Thabkey Rinpoche, to the holy Mount Kailas in Tibet's far west a test of endurance, both of body and mind," he recalled in his book, *You Must Die Once*.

Long Riders like Ian aren't imbued with magical powers. They aren't born with special talents that qualify them to undertake such difficult trips. When confronted with ordeals they have to resist and find a way forward. They must overcome uncertainty and summon the will to continue.

As the miles fall behind them, a mixture of courage and curiosity grows stronger as the outline of who they once were grows dimmer. The deeper they dig within themselves, the stronger becomes the desire to complete the journey no matter what. A growing sense of individual identity fuels their desire to accomplish something special in their lives.

Italian Long Rider and poet Vittorio Alfieri summarized this sense of bravery when he wrote, "Often times the test of courage is not to die but to live."

Changes

Lao Tzu, the Chinese philosopher credited with founding the concept of Taoism, warned, "The farther one travels the less one knows."

Wisdom is not automatically gained by self-sacrifice. Discomfort is no guarantee of knowledge. Many a fool has ridden 10,000 hard miles and returned home just as ignorant as the day he left.

Thus, a journey may be arduous but not be counted a success on another level. What is surprising is that no matter where their diverse journeys have taken them, Long Riders who return often have a surprising number of discoveries in common.

Roger Pocock spoke for many when he said that an equestrian journey gave him an increased sense of energy, strength, well-being and alertness.

"If there is any healthier or pleasanter way of life than this, I can only say, I have never enjoyed it," he wrote after completing his solo ride along the Outlaw Trail from Canada to Mexico.

Many have reported learning how few material possessions one needs to be happy. The stark reality of life in the saddle has demonstrated the value of simplicity. While food, shelter and friends remain high priorities, "things" have greatly diminished in importance. The more you know, the less you need.

After having won through so many hardships, travellers have learned to be grateful for yesterday, to live for today and remain hopeful for tomorrow. They accept good fortune, or bad, with equal equanimity.

One part of their apprenticeship has been the need to survive in all weathers. Constant exposure to the elements has taught them to respect and reconnect with the natural cycles of the seasons.

And then there is the horse.

"What strange mystery is there," pondered Jeremy James, "that lies between the horse and us, that long silent way that has so fundamentally altered us?"

Looking back upon his journeys Jeremy recalled the horses that had enriched the lives of so many Long Riders. He also remembered the physical trials lived through with those equine friends.

"How many thousands of streams did we ford? How many steep banks did we slither down? How many quagmires? How many insecure bridges spanning streams have we gingerly crossed? How many days of being soaked in the saddle, how many miles burned in the sun or dried by the wind? How often did we hear the music their hooves made upon the road?"

Unlike a competitive event, the horse had not separated the traveller from those he met. It revealed to the Long Rider the essential unity of mankind, as the horse's soothing presence enriched countless lives along the way.

Lessons

I have spent time with many of the greatest Long Riders. As a rule, I met them alone at our first encounter. That is because they radiate intensity. They have the dignified bearing of those who stand apart. There is always a distance in their eyes. When they speak, you hush and listen. They were sleepless souls awaiting another dawn departure. And every meeting still echoes in my memory.

The path they chose to follow was complex and often hidden. They had elected to push beyond the boundaries of their previously-known lives. The further they rode the more narrow notions they left behind.

Competitive riders are about control, the search for robotic equine perfection, the glorification of ego, the worship of money. The vast majority of so-called "explorers" are publicity-hungry adventurers seeking thrills and recognition.

Long Riders belong in neither of those camps.

They crossed rivers and rode over mountains to find personal secrets. Some shared their discoveries.

George Cayley recalled, "The exquisite delight it gave me to realise romance was not confined to the men and times of long ago but still surrounded us in our daily lives if only we had the facility to see them." He penned those words in 1853.

At the end of his ride across the middle of America in 1976, Robert Schweiger stated simply, "I had accomplished what I had set out to do. I had ridden every step of the way. No sham or shame, no flamboyance; just one hoof beat after another, every step of the way. Financially, the trip netted nothing. Measured in dollars and cents it could be termed a failure, but a dreamer doesn't sum up success by the coins in his purse."

Andi Mills also made momentous personal discoveries riding across that country in 2007.

She wrote, "The first one thousand miles drove home the realization that the destination is not nearly as important as the journey to reach it. I learned the cavernous difference between 'needs' and 'wants.' I learned not only to endure and overcome difficulties, but to truly embrace them for the valuable lessons they teach me. I learned to be content in my circumstances, no matter what they might be at the moment and most importantly, I learned that true contentment is a choice. By the time my journey came to an end, I no longer held any illusions about myself. I knew exactly who I was and exactly who I was not. How many people live and die, not knowing that simple truth?"

Starting in 2009 Bonnie Folkins made several challenging journeys in Mongolia and Kazakhstan. Having studied extensively prior to leaving, it wasn't the hardships of equestrian travel that shocked her.

"I wanted to see what my limits were and I found I didn't have any," she wrote.

What surprised her was the deep emotional impact the journeys had on her.

"They offered me a second life."

She continued, "In the beginning, it never occurred to me that by doing an equestrian journey and becoming a Long Rider I would become part of an international family of people of all ages – passionate about horses to the point that we abandon all and take off for the unknown. And once horse travel is in your blood it is like an addiction – something that you cannot imagine ever giving up. All Long Riders know that – like an unspoken mantra. We share concerns and take great interest in one another and, down to the finest detail; we do our best to help one another. We become brothers and sisters even though we know we will probably never meet. Most importantly, we know in our hearts that we have the same heart-felt bonds with our horses because of the sacrifices they have made for us over so many miles and through all weather. I am not a religious person but I can say I am spiritual. Spiritual means different things to different people. Long Riding has increased my spirituality and has therefore made my interior life extremely meaningful."

Diverse people, in different ages, riding on various continents, yet each had passed a stern personal examination. Each represents a link between the present and the past.

Perspective

In the beginning of most journeys, the overwhelming emotion is apprehension.

Friar Giovanni Carpini rode from Frankfurt, Germany to Karakorum, Mongolia and back in the late 1200s. Prior to his departure, the elderly man had absolutely no hesitation in expressing his chances of success and survival.

"We left with many tears not knowing whether we travelled towards death or life."

The journey was so dangerous and gruelling that upon his return to Europe several years later, Carpini was welcomed as one raised from the dead.

Anyone who rides a great distance and survives an assortment of perils will certainly return with many a tale to tell, as travel has represented a period of discontinuity from previous activities and beliefs.

What is unique is when the traveller recognizes that he has undergone an internal alteration as well, that there has been a realignment of his emotional compass.

"It is a rare fish that knows it swims in water," an ancient proverb states.

Nevertheless many Long Riders have recognized the power of this period and understood that it has influenced their reflective consciousness. They realised they had returned enriched with more principles and were more receptive. They understood that they had not escaped from their previous problems. Only now they were more able to put them into perspective.

Hetty Dutra made such a discovery after making her way along the length of the Nez Perce Trail into Canada.

"Did it change my life? What changed was my happiness with myself. I learned to like myself and trust myself and my instincts."

Bit by bit the effect of the journey sinks into the deep parts of your soul and leaves an impression ever afterwards which renders everything else feeling tame by comparison. It has taught you things about yourself that you could not have learned in any other way. One vital lesson learned by many is the need to balance the reality of daily action against inner tranquillity.

DC Vision underwent a remarkable transformation during his four-year journey across the United States. Initially he saw the horse trip as a way of escaping from life's ambitious addictions.

"You have to bear in mind that the journey wasn't about high adventure. I took the trip because I wanted to prove to myself that I was still alive."

As the years and miles both grew, so did DC's belief that he was journeying in more ways than one. Alone one night in a desolate portion of the far west, he penned what he called *An Ode to the Long Rider.*

"I threw another unnecessary calendar onto the night's campfire then took out the journal from the pack to write down a line or two. From the saddle you will always get the entire sensual impact that fossil fuel explorers in their boxes simply have never found. There is an ancient natural heartbeat matched at this pace, where rider, mount, and environment find their communion. Only when you leave routine existence will you find this grace, and the completion of the journey will reveal this union. The men, women, children, and horses of The Long Riders' Guild have explored millions of miles across all types of terrains. Our intention will never be to settle down into society's constraints, for we have found the untravelled places within ourselves where expansion cannot build," he wrote.

Millions of tourists set off on holidays every year. Few come back wiser from the experience. Their goal is to get a tan, not to take their destiny into their own hands. They travel in such a way that every facility has been extended. They do not return with a new vision of their lives and the world won through hardship.

One man did. He had an awakening after making a ride of discovery that was timeless and true.

Tschiffely

A journey may be counted a true success only if wisdom is discovered along the way.

I have written on many occasions in this book about the historic trip Aimé Tschiffely made from Buenos Aires to New York. The majority of those previous references were related to the technical expertise he learned about equestrian travel and later shared in his famous book, *Tschiffely's Ride.*

What I have neglected to explain was the immense emotional after-effect which the ride had on Aimé.

I have recounted how Aimé Tschiffely had been laughed at by fools who derived pleasure from denouncing his planned journey, even if they themselves were incapable or too cowardly to attempt to undertake it.

Luckily for the rest of us, Aimé ignored the critics. But that was to be expected from this quiet and serious man. Even before he left Argentina, he had travelled extensively, lived rough, seen the best and worst of humanity and developed a passion for personal freedom. He wasn't out to impress anyone. He owed fealty only to himself.

As we all know, Aimé encountered many challenges, endured unimaginable hardships, almost died from tropical diseases and was nearly murdered several times during the trip.

Yet the dangers and distractions of the physical world did not blind him to the beauties and mysteries of life.

At one point he and his faithful horses, Mancha and Gato, found themselves 11,500 feet above sea level atop a mountain in Central America. It was in this nameless spot on the map that Aimé had an epiphany.

"During the night the moon was so bright that I though it was early morning, and as I could not sleep, I went to keep the horses company. They seemed glad to see me and followed me when I went where the grass was better and where they had feared to go alone, their instinct for danger having kept them near me while I slept. Here I was, as it were, between two continents and two mighty oceans, with my faithful friends of thousands of miles both making the best of a bad meal beside me, but I knew they were satisfied, for experience had taught the three of us to be contented, even with the worst," he later wrote.

The journey changes many of us. The older we get, the stronger and more obvious become the marks as they draw nearer to the surface.

I can name you names, but I won't, of Long Riders who became increasingly silent.

This explains so much about Aimé's later life, how he detested and shunned the traditional horse world, relished anonymity and sought solace within books. It is true that he made a short equestrian journey across England in the early 1930s. But the majority of his life was spent researching and writing. Those who knew him said that his principal quality was an overriding humility. He seemed to possess a huge inner strength that did not need to throw its weight around. Instead of seeking to be defined as a thrill-seeker or hero he was renowned for his intense modesty.

Though he had no children, Aimé wrote several books aimed at a younger audience. One of his lesser-known works was a thinly disguised autobiography. Entitled *Ming and Ping*, it recounts the story of a young man who ventures into the jungles of South America in search, not of riches, but of wisdom.

The book was written many years after the famous horse trip was completed. During that time Aimé had resided in London, where he witnessed, "the strife for wealth and fame, the hurry and worry of mankind, some rising, some falling, foolish pleasures, the struggle of humanity."

The explorer in *Ming and Ping* was clearly Aimé, speaking via another character.

One night in the jungle the explorer wrote, "When he remembered the futility of existence in cities, the hurry and scurry to get nowhere, the fight and scramble for power, money and worldly possessions, and all the vain-glories and inconveniences of social life, he envied his Indian hosts."

He continued, "I have never said that I despise civilization, but since you have mentioned the word, let me tell you that, in my opinion, whatever it may be worth, civilization should be man's highest aim. But if by civilization you mean machinery, unnecessary luxuries, modern weapons of death and destruction, scientifically trained armies, and so on, I much prefer to remain what you call a savage. However, if by civilization you mean improvement of the mind, and betterment of living conditions for all human beings, without regimentation or interference with any nation's or individual's liberty, I am all for it."

Aimé's last journey took him to Spain in 1952. He went to every part of the country, living simply as he had always done, eating and drinking with the locals, immersing himself in the culture, speaking the language like a native and still looking for answers. He was nearly sixty years old, far from home, once again the wandering stranger, when he held his life up for inspection.

In his book, *Round and About Spain*, he asked, "For the thousandth time in my life I came to the conclusion that I must be a failure. After all, what do I possess? Health? Yes. Common sense? Perhaps. Ambition and vigour? I thought again. Vigour when it comes to doing certain things. Ambition, for what? To be what? To end as what? Ambition to LIVE, to learn and to see as much of the world and its people. Amass wealth at the expense of sacrificing LIFE, and perhaps honour, self-respect and even friends? No!"

The Brevity of Life

As I sat here writing this chapter of this book, the bell in the nearby church tower rang nine times. It marked the beginning of yet another morning here in the tiny French village which I call home.

Every peal of the bell reminded me of the brevity of my life.

Aimé died in hospital the year I was born: 1954. He hadn't been unwell. He went into hospital for minor surgery – and passed away without warning a few days later. He left behind no great fortune, only the legend of a horse trip. His widow, Violet, was left to struggle alone for many years.

My own life was but a few weeks old at the time he departed. Though I have been connected with Aimé for many years no one has ever asked me how much money he made. They have all spoken instead of how his heart of fire lit a spark in their lives, how he inspired them to undertake great journeys, how he showed them the way, how he held aloft a light to drive out the shadows of cowardice,.

We are here but a moment. Where we came from, and where we ultimately return to, remains a mystery which defies the attempts of priests and atheists to solve. All we know is that for a twinkling of the universe's eye, we are here, cognizant, awake, alive – and capable of doing great things with our lives.

Most are content with being defined as someone's offspring, sibling, spouse, aunt or uncle, friend. People rush to be associated with a sports team because it identifies them as members of a local or national herd. They seek friends on Facebook because it provides them with a collective identity. They use others to define themselves because they lack the courage to stand alone.

The mystery of their existence is as visible to them as it is to anyone else, but they prefer to delay contemplation of the inevitable. It is always summer. Time is everlasting. They live their lives as if they are exceptions to the doom that awaits us all.

As the bell chimed nine this morning, I was struck by what it meant. Nine less breaths in my body. Nine less seconds of consciousness. Nine fewer moments of realization. Nine seconds closer to oblivion. Nine less chances to take the most precious gifts I have, time and health, and do something meaningful with my life.

When you put your life into perspective, and factor in horses, you should ask yourself if what you do reflects who you are and what you symbolize. Does winning a blue ribbon, because your horse could make a certain movement or jump over painted sticks, constitute your legacy?

Journeys have always symbolized more than mere geography. They are the migration of our soul searching for answers. From Ulysses to Tschiffely, a brave few have set off in search of more than a mere destination. What they have been seeking is a meaning to mysteries.

Nor should we ever confuse the courage it takes to travel alone with the collective adrenalin which results when one takes part in a military campaign.

War is a bed of lies whose aim is state-sanctioned murder. Throughout history leaders have manipulated their people's fears, appealed to their greed, inflamed their patriotism, all the while they urged the populace to turn fire and sword against their neighbours. History is replete with empires whose leaders told their citizens that theirs was a righteous campaign, that God justified their actions, that indescribable riches awaited them in the nearby capital of their enemies, that unless they opposed another philosophy their nation, values, personal safety and families were doomed.

Afghanistan, where I began my career as an equestrian explorer, is a perfect example of this cocktail of pride and folly.

Alexander's Greeks, Genghis' Mongols, Victoria's English, Gorbachev's Russians and Obama's Americans are all different variations on the same tune. In every case, mankind rushed to war, believing they did so for a valid reason, and after having lost a vast number of lives, they all went home again.

That is war. That is a collective delusion.

That is not a journey.

The Earth abides. We do not.

As the bell rang nine times this morning, I was reminded of how many people have lived in this ancient village. Joan of Arc rode by the door of my ancient house in 1429. How many countless thousands have been born, walked these narrow cobble-stoned streets, and died in this little hamlet since her departure? Who remembers them? What did they accomplish?

What we do reflects who we are.

Undertaking the journey is about far more than reaching the shore of a physical ocean.

The water may have halted your physical progress, but in an indefinable way, you can never be stopped again – because you are no longer the person you once were.

Peace

In a purely physical sense many Long Riders conclude the journey after having defied perils, ridden through black nights and felt the blood running hot through their veins. The journey proves they were not among the complacent.

Having faced challenges and overcome them, the Long Rider realises he doesn't have to prove anything to anyone. He has stood up to the test. As a result the traveller has returned not only safe but strengthened with a formidable power of the spirit.

He has ridden the miles, yes. But in addition his soul has been replenished, a longing fulfilled, a thirst satisfied. Having ridden through the Terra Incognita of his own life, the traveller has found solace, quiet, freedom and clarity.

Like Tschiffely, many a Long Rider set off as an underdog. Along the way the traveller found self-esteem, courage, patience and resilience. He has learned not to care what may befall him tomorrow because of what he survived yesterday.

After riding across India in 1947 Malcolm Darling realized, "I know who I am. Until a man knows who he is, he cannot know what he can be."

For many a sense of restlessness has been driven out, replaced by a feeling of serenity.

Long Rider Samuel Butler explored New Zealand in 1862. He articulated this sense of serenity accurately in his book, *Erewhon*, when he wrote, "There came upon me a delicious sense of peace, a fullness of contentment which I do not believe can be felt by any but those who have spent days consecutively on horseback."

Others realised how a long-held desire for something missing had been replaced by a sense of arrival.

Ella Maillart, recalling how she rode from Peking to Srinagar with Peter Fleming in 1935 said, "It was a journey where nothing happened, but this nothing will satisfy me for the rest of my life."

Some achieve a serenity of the spirit when they comprehend that an essential inner need has been found; they have found themselves and become their own friend.

Bonnie Folkins realized that the journeys had affected her in an unexpected manner.

"Zen asks us to stop trying to intellectualize and define, and to concentrate on the pure living experience of the moment. When I read that I realized that I had found nirvana – something that takes experienced lamas 30 years to achieve, if ever. There is no question. That is what the ride did for me. It gave me a sense of peace and fulfilment that no other experience has offered me in my lifetime."

In all these cases, and many more, an illumination has transformed the traveller. A simple journey has brought them into contact with higher truths. Along the way they have met a mysterious creature; themselves.

Summary

Equestrian travel is, on the one hand, simply a manner of transportation. Yet as history has repeatedly demonstrated, Long Riders are far more complex than that.

They consistently refuse to join the mainstream. Instead they set their own standards and maintain their own individual ideals. Over and over they demonstrate that it's not about settling for who you are. It's about believing in who you can become.

What the Long Riders in this book represent is hope; hope that all of us can do something special with our lives, hope that we can make a difference, hope that we too can find excitement in an all too predictable world.

Eventually the waves of time will wash away all these lives and the memory of many of these journeys. But for the Long Riders who made these trips that will not matter because they will have sanctified their existence by their mighty efforts.

Mary Bosanquet understood that. She spoke for all the Long Riders when she wrote, "Whatever comes, I shall have done one thing for which I thank God. An urgent, vital day. A day that says, live while you can, and die when you must; take all that comes and give everything you've got, only don't fear, don't waste; be alive while you can."

Prior to departure Long Riders learn to protect their dreams from critics. One friend told Erich von Salzmann that if he attempted his journey he would end up, "chained to a pole by an iron-neck chain, and, worst of all, not a whisky & soda in sight." Salzmann set off anyway in 1903 and rode 6,000 kilometres (3,700 miles) across China, the Gobi desert and Turkestan.

A host of physical and emotional challenges force Long Riders to confront the limits of their strength. Ian Robinson's 3,500 kilometre (2,100 miles) solo horse trek across Tibet "brought me to my knees physically, emotionally and spiritually."

Many Long Riders are surprised at the deep emotional impact the journey has on them. After riding across Mexico and Central America, Orion Kraus realized, "I didn't really want this trip to be for anyone else. It was personal. The goal of reaching Panama was not as important as the path that got me there".

Long Riders like Mefo Phillips realize their lives have been enriched by the horse. "I understand: I'm no one's sister, no one's mother, no one's wife, no one's child, no one's employee, no one-time cancer patient, and no responsibilities at all. I'm caught in a rhythm, a cadence of travelling; a conscious thought there's nowhere else I'd rather be than here with my amenable horse, Leo, swinging along with his ground-eating stride."

After he completed his ride, Robert Schweiger realized, "I had accomplished what I had set out to do. I had ridden every step of the way. No sham or shame, no flamboyance; just one hoof beat after another, every step of the way. Financially, the trip netted nothing. Measured in dollars and cents it could be termed a failure, but a dreamer doesn't sum up success by the coins in his purse."

Hetty Dutra realized that her ride along the Nez Perce Trail had given her a new perspective. "Did it change my life? What changed was my happiness with myself. I learned to like myself and trust myself and my instincts."

Countess Linde von Rosen learned how to balance the reality of daily action against inner tranquillity. "I am thankful for every step I have ridden on the path of life. Through a network of roads and destinies we all wander towards the same goal."

During his journey across South America André Fischer realized, "I changed not only outwardly (10 kilos less, brown burned, long hair and occasionally times with wild beard), but still more in my inside."

Despite being the most famous Long Rider, Aimé Tschiffely detested and shunned the traditional horse world, relished anonymity and sought solace within books. Instead of seeking to be defined as a thrill-seeker or hero he was renowned for his intense modesty. He decried, "The futility of existence in cities, the hurry and scurry to get nowhere, the fight and scramble for power, money and worldly possessions, and all the vainglories and inconveniences of social life."

Journeys have always symbolized more than mere geography. They are the migration of our soul searching for answers. From Ulysses to Tschiffely, a brave few have set off in search of more than a mere destination. What they have been seeking is a meaning to mysteries. The author is seen on one of his early journeys, riding in Hunza, which served as the inspiration for the mythical Shangri La.

Chapter 79
Between Two Worlds

Not many of us live long enough, or experience enough, to be able to look back and see the arc in our lives.

The Arcadian moment in my life occurred when I crested the Shandur Pass.

Beginning in 1936 an annual polo competition is held on "The Roof of the World," the wide plateau that sits atop the 3,700 metre (12,200 feet) high Shandur Pass located in the northwest corner of Pakistan. Rival teams come from the distant towns of Chitral and Gilgit, which lie on either side of the remote mountain pass.

The Shandur plateau is covered in snow for most of the year. But in early July thousands of people make a pilgrimage to witness what is considered to be the most dangerous polo game in the world. There are no rules, so injuries are common. Because of the rarefied air players have been known to have heart attacks and die in the saddle.

When I made my last journey in Pakistan, a single-lane dirt road made its way through the Karakoram Mountains from faraway Gilgit. Another earthen path, wide enough for a single vehicle, likewise twisted along from the rival town of Chitral. Via these two tracks a host of local tribesmen had made a pilgrimage to the world's highest polo ground.

Prior to the match the polo horses had been carefully brought to the top of the Shandur via Bedford trucks. My companion and I were the only ones amongst that migration who had ridden there, having come all the way from distant Peshawar.

The journey across Pakistan had already forced us to climb other mountains. But nothing in my previous experience had prepared me for that day's ride.

We had started at sunrise, setting off from the village of Sor Laspur with light hearts. One minute we were talking and cantering across flat ground, the next we were climbing as the mountain slammed us into a new reality. Compared to that ascent the Malakand Pass had been a joke and the Lowari Pass fit for children. We did not scale the Shandur Pass like arrogant caballeros; we crawled up her flanks like lowly insects, one slow painful step at a time.

From the moment we put hoof and foot on that road our legs and lungs complained. The little village of Sor Laspur lay 1800 metres (6,000 feet) above sea level. Horses and men took one burning step for each of the 6,500 more feet that lay between us and the crest of the cruel pass that loomed over the hamlet.

Two hours into the attempt we stopped to rest. Sor Laspur looked like a toy town lain out below us. Mounted again, we rode but said little. As the day grew longer, the air grew thinner. One thousand feet to the hour is reasonable progress for laden horses. Yet we were soon stopping every ten minutes, letting the horses suck in great draughts of increasingly cold air. We rode, then walked, rode, then walked, all of us panting like dogs as we crawled towards the top.

The only noise on that great long road was the jeeps. Because the Shandur is barren of so much as a single tree, everything needed by the spectators, participants and horses was being hauled in by jeep. Food, firewood, hay, cooking oil, tents, blankets, you name it, were being brought up that mountain for the greatest sporting event of the far north.

As the hours passed we made our way like ants across one giant turn on the road, then up another. By late afternoon the cold had become so severe we halted the horses. It was impossible to believe I had ever been too hot in Pakistan. That was a dream somewhere long ago. We dug into our saddlebags for our jackets.

The horses laboured as they carried us up, up, up, with every breath an effort and every step a victory. At last the sky was so close there seemed to be nothing between us and Allah. I could have touched Him, if I had possessed the courage to look up and reach out.

We crested the Shandur Pass at dusk. It was the quintessential equestrian moment in my life.

There before us was a vast alpine valley, a giant green bowl of wind-blown grass. In the middle rested a dark blue lake never sullied by boat or man. On all sides, save for the notch where we stood, were lofty, jagged peaks edged with snow and forming a protective ring around this sacred, secret place.

Neither of us needed to be told to rein in. What we saw would have halted a world-weary king. The last rays of the sun were colouring the sky like a rainbow. Great clouds overhead were the colour of orange sherbet. The mountain tops surrounding us were a delicate shade of blue. The sky itself had turned rose. Yet breathtaking as that was, it was the vast grassy arena that riveted our eyes. The giant camp laid spread out before us like a carpet of fire. Lantern and cooking fires beckoned and winked, urging us to join the great multitude below.

I drank in that vision and then shut my eyes tightly, storing the image of that valley behind them forever.

The former life I had led in civilized parts seemed to be part of a distant dream. I remembered the futility of existence in cities, the scramble for money and worldly possessions, the hurry to go nowhere, the vainglories of social life. I didn't care what governments did or what news was preoccupying the distant world. For a moment I was at the edge of Eden, at peace, with only the tinkling sound of the bells on my horse being gently blown in the cold alpine wind.

A sense of tranquillity came over my soul and a magical fire was lit from which years later the embers still glow.

Life isn't like the movies.

No one rides happily into the sunset.

After witnessing the polo game, I rode down the far side of the mountains and reached the distant town of Gilgit. Then I headed south alongside the wild Indus river. Eventually I completed my journey and returned to my adopted home of Peshawar. The moment I stepped down from the saddle for the last time my life became a long torment. I stood there, that most helpless and most ungainly of creatures, a dismounted Long Rider.

The Dream

To understand what has been lost, one must appreciate what was discovered.

The Long Rider has been floating along in a world that has little to do with the constraints of time. In such a world there are no nasty intrusions as can be seen in any daily newspaper. Harping critics fade away. The path of the sun takes on a new importance.

The demands that obsess the majority of people, such as jobs and bills, no longer control the destiny of the Long Rider. Instead of being encased inside a motorized steel cocoon, forced to commute to a forgettable job, the Long Rider finds himself drifting through a serene and natural world wherein the primary purpose is to find those ancient needs of our mounted ancestors: grass, water, food, fire, shelter.

Imagination and curiosity are awakened. From the back of a horse one can speak with people, observe their ways, hear their opinions and perhaps even read their hearts.

The saddle is no longer an inanimate object. It has become the key to an undiscovered mystery which unfolds day after day. As the journey progresses the feeling of freedom becomes overpowering. You long to prolong the sense of personal liberty.

As her journey across the western United States was drawing to a close, Katie Russell worried, "How can I return home, back to my old life now that I have tasted this freedom, this gypsy life? The faithful horse tied outside my tent, the rhythm of the days: routine and yet new each day – a stimulating combination of organization, spontaneity, and practice that makes the days fly by in a precious blur."

Trouble occurs when dreams crash into necessity.

Few Long Riders realize that returning from their journey will subject them to a painful emotional challenge, that the longer one has spent time in the saddle the harder it will be to adjust to the demands of domestic routine, that the transition process is often extremely difficult.

The Mirage called "Home"

There comes a time, especially amongst first-time travellers, when an invisible influence eventually exerts a silent message. Though they were initially anxious to depart, a longing to return home begins to seep into the Long Rider's psyche.

Equestrian travel is filled with physical hardships and emotional challenges. Sitting alone by the fire, many a Long Rider has had time to wonder what fun his friends were having back home or if his family was worried about his welfare. At first it's easy to refuse to listen to these whisperings. But as the miles grow, and the troubles continue, a longing often develops to be re-united with loved ones, to revisit favourite haunts with pals, to enjoy a delicious meal, to sleep in comfort, to give up wandering.

If allowed to grow, these thoughts eventually tip the scales. The Long Rider is overcome with loneliness and longs to return home.

After having overcome a tremendous number of troubles during his second ride across Europe, Jeremy James found himself at such an invisible emotional crossroad.

"Each time I stopped," he wrote, "I found it harder to get going again. Although so much of it was glorious, the riding kind, the people friendly, I longed to be able to stop, to finish, to put my hand on a door handle, turn it, walk in and call that home my own. I wanted to reach into a barn for a bale of hay for Gonzo, not have to look for it all the time."

In his book, *Vagabond*, Jeremy writes about wanting to reach "the end of the rainbow," all the while realizing that he was "half caught in the past, half in the present, as in the eye of a storm with all things now and then whirling round."

These inner storms aren't apparent to outsiders. To them the Long Rider appears to be a carefree wanderer.

That explains why one stranger told Richard Barnes, "I would give you a thousand pounds to swap lives for a day."

Yet as Richard's long circular journey around Great Britain began to draw to a close, he began to have second thoughts about what awaited him at home.

"I had to ask myself what price I could put on this journey. When I set off I was hungry for wilderness and solitude, travelled in search of experiences which would not come my way at home."

Now, after having spent so much time in the saddle, Richard realized that he had grown apart, that his solitary experiences were going to be hard to relate and harder still for others to understand.

"Getting closer to home was different to everything that had gone before. It was good to see my friends, but I felt quite remote. Maybe homecoming was not to be so simple and to try and fit inside four walls after being outside for months would be a problem," he wrote in *Eye on the Hill*.

Richard had no way of knowing how correct he was.

The Painful Passage

When the five original Long Riders from three countries met at the first international meeting of the Guild, we made a number of surprising discoveries. Like returning soldiers, it was the first time we could converse with someone who understood what we had experienced physically and emotionally. As a result, we talked non-stop for three days.

What we learned was that despite the immense geographic and cultural differences which lay between our journeys, we had all undergone a shocking number of similar events before, during and after the journey.

While we were in the saddle, never had our lives burned so brilliantly. When we reached our distant destinations, we felt victorious. And then the darkness fell upon each of us individually.

How little did we realize what was in store for us? No one had warned us of the unexpected effects which our journeys would have upon our unprotected souls. None of us had been told that everything changes the moment you step down from the saddle the last time and re-enter the pedestrian world.

At that meeting, for the first time in our collective lives we revealed how we had each suffered when the journey ended. The rhythm of our lives had been shattered. Our horses were gone, leaving a huge hole in our hearts. We were lost, lonely, emotionally confused and diminished. Some of us had struggled financially. Some had been homeless. Some felt the future was empty. All had been wounded.

Even if you have a secure home to return to, few Long Riders realize the emotional difficulty of moving their wild souls back inside four walls.

The 3 Ds

The journeyer passes through three stages; discouragement, danger and, finally, disorientation.

The first section of the Encyclopaedia explains how nearly every would-be Long Rider has to overcome the resistance of those who oppose their plan to set off on an equestrian journey. This opposition has been documented through the ages. Pedestrians always have a long list of reasons why it is inadvisable for a seeker to depart from the safety of the village. Marco Polo was undoubtedly told he would never live to see distant Cathay. Finding the courage to ignore this discouragement is the first big D.

The extensive fourth section of the Encyclopaedia is devoted to a study of all the various types of dangers Long Riders may face; i.e. bandits, bears, bugs, bureaucrats, deserts, mountains, rivers, swamps, etc. The list is the most comprehensive ever compiled. What it does is to provide an in-depth look at what may await the traveller. Overcoming all these various types of dangers is the second big D.

If you travel far enough you eventually find yourself standing at a lonely spot.

The last big D is the one you confront when you return home.

It is this sense of disorientation which is the final act of a true journey.

The Shock

Gone are the long quiet days of just you, the horses and the desire to reach a distant geographic goal. You have ceased your long effort to ride into the unknown.

The conclusion of the journey forces the Long Rider to re-enter a world full of mundane bills, trivial problems and boring people. This emotional transfer often inflicts a tremendous sense of disenchantment on the Long Rider.

The great Long Rider Sir Richard Burton didn't hide his contempt for domestic life.

Prior to setting off in 1856 on his dangerous journey to Mecca, he joyfully wrote, "One of the gladdest moments in human life, methinks, is the departure upon a distant journey to unknown lands. Shaking off with one mighty effort the fetters of habit, the leaden weight of routine, the cloak of many cares and the slavery of home, man feels once more happy. The blood flows with the fast circulation of childhood; afresh dawns the morn of life."

In stark contrast to Burton's love of departure was his loathing of "the hell of returning."

Many Long Riders have written about the intensity of their homecoming. Until recently they were overdue on the other side of the world. They smelled wood smoke, heard the tinkling of the horse bells and saw the stars blazing overhead. Now they have re-entered a sterile environment divorced from Nature. Instead of moving forward, they are going nowhere.

Upon returning from her ride across Mongolia, Canadian Long Rider Bonnie Folkins captured the feelings of many a Long Rider.

"So, there you are, in the middle of nowhere, almost in a trance, something like what a Buddhist monk might be trying to achieve by meditation, and then it comes to an abrupt end. The shock is devastating. It is like being awoken from a dream by a bucket of cold water; the cold water being the reality of society."

After spending two years riding thousands of miles across Europe, Bill Holt returned to England feeling like an outsider.

"My finger nails were torn, my fingers calloused with holding the reins, my jacket roughly mended, and my boots were badly worn. It felt odd to use a chair and table."

Christina Dodwell experienced similar feelings when her dangerous ride across Africa was concluded.

"Everything was so strange, yet so natural; it was like recovering from amnesia, seeing and hearing familiar things, having to learn again everything that had been forgotten or lost somewhere in the recesses of my mind," she wrote.

The Initial Excitement

At first you are too preoccupied becoming reacquainted with the luxuries of modern life to take any notice of forthcoming problems. After spending months or years in the saddle, riding from dawn to dusk, experiencing various degrees of discomfort, you can truly appreciate the comforts of life.

One Long Rider recalled, "Ah, that first night back. Real food, cheery faces, the joy brought on by not worrying over the welfare of the horses."

For others, it is the joy of knowing that hunger was a thing of the past.

In 1906 Aubrey Herbert, and his Albanian comrade, Riza Bey, rode from Baghdad, across the Syrian Desert, to Damascus, where the two famished men cantered up to the best hotel in the city.

"For three weeks we had been tanned by the sun and stung by the wind, sand and rain. Our clothes were fastened with string. With his gun slung over his shoulder Riza marched before me into the ordered quietness of the dining room. I followed, as well armed as he. There I sat down, penniless and unknown, and ordered a royal luncheon. Silence fell upon the room. Luckily for me our English Consul was there. He backed my name upon a piece of paper for all the money I wanted and for three days I revelled in luxury and baths," the travel-stained Herbert recalled.

It was thirst that afflicted others. After riding through the steaming Burmese jungles in 1887, George Younghusband wrote, "I shall never forget that most delicious bottle of beer after drinking nothing but the water of affliction for months."

But it's not all champagne bubbles and laughter. At first you can't believe the hot bath, the delicious meal and the soft bed. Then the disillusionment begins to creep in.

After riding from Peking to Srinagar, Swiss Long Rider Ella Maillart said she felt as if she had returned to "a life to which I feel myself a stranger."

In the company of her friend, Peter Fleming, the two weary travellers discovered that their longed-for drink wasn't as delicious as they had anticipated.

"In the dining room at the hotel we amused ourselves like true savages, while prim couples manifested open disapproval of our shabby clothes, untidy hair and buccaneer-black faces which no hat had ever shaded. But our amusement soon wore thin. It was too depressing to be so near that world, all dressed up as though it was going to act in a comedy. After months and months of anticipation it was almost without pleasure that we clinked our champagne glasses."

It isn't just the displeasure of society giving you the cold shoulder that Long Riders find distressing. Many have grown so accustomed to a hard life, and to sleeping on the ground, that beds feel uncomfortably alien.

"I went to sleep early," Louisa Jebb wrote, after completing her rigorous ride across the Ottoman Empire, "but the comfort I expected from lying in a bed was by no means confirmed, for the soft mattress and cool sheets frightened away slumber. I felt inclined to sleep on the floor."

Horses

What you notice immediately is what's obviously missing; your horses.

Modern life is composed of fragile relationships involving family, love, marriage, work and social friendships. Yet any of these alliances can disintegrate with little warning.

The horse is the heart of the journey. His emotional continuity makes him a compelling and reliable friend. No matter how wrong things may have gone, he has always been there for you.

It is extremely difficult to cope with the loss of your constant companion. You and the horses have formed a relationship that has been torn apart.

This helps explain why many Long Riders report dreaming about their horses, thinking they can hear them grazing nearby. Others have said how much they miss waking up to the sounds of the horses snuffling at dawn.

From a life full of equine sounds and smells, the returning traveller finds himself surrounded by an uncomfortable silence.

One Long Rider reported that it took her two months to readjust, during which time she was prone to burst into tears and cry uncontrollably at the thought of the horse she had adored and been forced to leave behind in a far-away country.

After completing his journey across the American Southwest, Clay Marshall also had trouble adjusting to the absence of his horses.

"Driving a modern vehicle without the reins and significantly greater horsepower took some getting used to upon my return, along with the other comforts and luxuries of civilized life. A clean-shaven face and clean, modern clothes were especially strange for me those first few days; surreal even. One of the hardest parts of my transition, however, was not having the horses around."

Even if you bring the horses home, they too have trouble adjusting to a sedentary life.

Robin and Louella Hanbury-Tenison rode two Camargue geldings from the Mediterranean to their farm in Cornwall, England.

"When, after a week's complete rest, we paid them our daily visit we thought they seemed restless. Thibert looked worried and Tiki appeared to be trying to tell us something. We realised that they felt it was high time we were all moving on. They were quite rested now and ready to carry on the journey which had become second nature."

Other Long Riders have reported the emotional difficulties which horses and humans encounter after returning.

Sea G Rhydr spent two years riding "ocean to ocean" with her horses, Jesse James and Luna. At the conclusion of the journey she placed them in a large pasture close to the house she had moved into. As Sea learned, being nearby isn't the same as being in the saddle.

"The hardest thing, and the thing I didn't expect, is the feeling of estrangement from the herd. The ponies live outside and I live inside and we're not doing anything together any more. I go out to feed and water them and they're polite but that's about as far as it goes. We're losing our common tongue. The mission is over and they're not really interested in just hanging out once in awhile. They don't want to be patted or scratched. They're bored and we're not going anywhere. After all this time of living, sleeping, travelling, grazing and communicating as a herd on the move we've stopped. Our security and companionship is no longer with one another and that's hard. Harder on me than it is on them, I think."

Living with Less

One of the first things you notice when you unpack your few possessions and put away the saddlebags is how many objects surround you. Having lived on so little for so long, the re-entry into a world of obscene excess has a shocking effect.

The majority of modern humans lead lives which involve an increasing amount of consumption and materialism. Thanks to discount stores and 24-hour online shopping, never in human history have so many people owned so many products.

This increase in personal possessions has produced unforeseen consequences. For example, the size of American houses has dramatically increased. Whereas in 1950 the typical home was 983 square feet, today's new home averages 2,480 square feet, and it's still not big enough to accommodate the family possessions. A study made by the University of California found that seventy-five percent of the families interviewed could not park their cars in the garage because it was filled with an overflow of superfluous things. This in turn led to the development of the nation's lucrative $22 billion personal storage industry.

Sadly, a great deal of what Americans purchase never finds its way into a home or a storage unit. Instead it goes into the garbage. According to a study by the Natural Resources Defense Council, Americans throw 40 percent of the food they buy into the trash.

Though they are surrounded by an avalanche of belongings, there is strong evidence indicating that increased consumer activity hasn't made Americans happier. On the contrary, even though purchasing has dramatically increased since the 1950s, people in that country report a decrease in happiness. Dwarfed and dehumanised by his possessions, the man who has it all realizes he has nothing.

When asked what they missed most, many Long Riders report that they had been happy with what little they had.

One Long Rider wrote, "Last night we were dirty, isolated and free; tonight we are clean, sociable and trammelled. Four walls imprison us. Everything seems unreal, unnecessary or dressed up. Have the non-essentials of existence become the realities? And as it had been difficult while we were still in it to get disentangled from it, so now we were experiencing a difficulty in entering it again – a difficulty in once more taking up and using the things we had discarded for a time. It was if we had never used them, so strange did they seem, and so little did we understand their meaning."

Thus after the first flush of enjoyment has passed, you find yourself back in the land of work and worry. That's when you begin to remember why you left. A sense of estrangement arises when you view the artefacts of your previous existence. Did you really need all those clothes? How had you managed to live a fuller, richer life without all these things?

You begin to ask yourself what is really essential in life. How much of so-called civilisation is something sordid hiding under a high-sounding nickname? In a world where a handful of people are hideously rich, while billions starve, it begins to dawn on you how little it took to make you happy.

Katie Cooper wrote, "I didn't even unpack, or take anything but a mattress out of storage for the first three weeks. I simply laid the sleeping bag down on the mattress and continued living out of my bags. One set of clothes, a hand-towel and a metal cup. It just didn't seem like any more was necessary."

Reverse Culture Shock

After having survived what one Long Rider called "the turbulence of re-entry," many travellers undergo what is known as reverse culture shock.

Long Rider Jonathan Swift was the author of *Gulliver's Travels*. When that fictional character returned from living among the talking horses known as the Houyhnhnms, Gulliver experienced severe problems re-adapting to life back home in 18th century England.

The distraught traveller felt a strong sense of alienation, which in turn sparked an intense sadness and feelings of bereavement. It wasn't long before Gulliver's feeling of deep loss grew into frustration, anxiety and finally anger.

Modern Long Riders don't have to contend with talking horses, but like Gulliver, they report feeling various negative emotions when they return.

After living outside, houses feel too hot, dry, stuffy and oppressive. After enjoying long periods of silence, they are surrounded by noise. After being grateful for a simple meal, they are confronted with mountains of food that does not live up to their expectations.

Massive emotional readjustment is often required because the onset of reverse culture shock may manifest itself in feelings of personal guilt, deep disappointment or resentment at the privileges and excesses which are a part of the modern consumer-oriented society.

One Long Rider reported, "To be separated from my horse, to sleep within four walls, to eat my meals within a restaurant, was intolerable. I could not understand how the people in the city lived the unnatural life they led. There was nothing I could do about the empty feeling inside me, a tight, stretched feeling of the whole body, with a painful void where the heart and stomach should be. I miss going somewhere."

Many travellers eventually question the validity of their former lifestyle, values and beliefs.

A Lack of Understanding

It is not unusual for returning Long Riders to feel they have achieved something significant. Without being boastful, they are entitled to a sense of pride. Many express the belief that they have discovered their true identity.

While this may be cause for personal celebration, it often invokes an odd sense of isolation. Though they bear the same external name, after having survived so many challenges Long Riders often come home so emotionally altered that their family and friends hardly recognize them.

Before long the traveller realizes that he is no longer a part of his previous world. He has turned his life upside down by riding thousands of miles but life back home has been proceeding as if the journey had never occurred.

Upon your return it is not unusual to discover that your friends have never moved, either emotionally or physically, from the day you left. You'll discover the same people; sitting on the same bar stools, talking about the same old things, following the same predictable routines.

Keith Clark noted this effect when he completed his difficult ride in the Andes Mountains, then returned to his local pub in Yorkshire to catch up with old friends.

"It's as if I left in mid conversation and then came back and just picked up where it was left off. Absolutely nothing has changed," the stunned traveller recalled.

One of the tough emotional lessons returning Long Riders learn is not to expect to find either sympathy or understanding back home.

Though strangers often expressed an embarrassing amount of interest in your journey as you rode through their country, people at home display a shocking lack of curiosity about your adventures.

A lot of people will pay polite attention to your tale, for about a minute, and then you had better be prepared for a long list of standard reactions to your trip.

First they generally ask if you had a nice horse holiday. Then they will enquire if you are going to get a job and/or grow up. It doesn't take long for a Long Rider to learn that conversation with old friends is invariably disappointing and boring.

Jeanette and Richard McGrath spent two years making an "ocean to ocean" ride across the United States. The trip forced them to overcome tremendous tactical, emotional and financial difficulties. But despite all the hardships and delays, the young newly-weds realized their dreams when they rode their horses up to the edge of the Atlantic Ocean in 2011.

While the McGraths had foreseen the difficulties involved in making their trip, what they hadn't counted on was the tremendous stress they would encounter when they returned home.

"It was extremely difficult readjusting to 'normal' life," Jeanette explained in a message to the Guild. "Our stomachs and minds were churning with excitement, concerns, and emotions."

In addition to locating a home and finding jobs, they also had to become accustomed to being apart.

"That was really hard since we'd spent 24/7 for 2 years together."

Plus, the Long Riders discovered that their friends had moved on emotionally and were not really interested in hearing about their exciting equestrian journey.

"It seemed like hardly anyone cared that we were back. No one related. They would just look at you, nod and smile, and say, 'Oh that sounds like fun.' That is not exactly the descriptive word I would choose. They just don't get it."

Months after their return, Jeanette made this important observation about what a Long Rider should expect when the journey is over.

"Most people don't understand why we sacrificed so much, and they never will unless they accomplish such a huge dream. We had learned to live with zero privacy, a measure of fame, completely the centre of attention, and an object of entertainment wherever we went. It was the complete opposite when we got home. We were completely alone and no one was asking us multiple times a day to tell our stories. It was very lonely and deflating. Not that we sought out the attention or fame. In fact it got quite old. But you learn to adapt and live with it. It was just as hard to learn to live without it again."

Sceptics

When people have created a strong preconception of something, they will have nothing else. That is why it's been said that people will believe anything about an equestrian journey, except the truth.

They don't want to hear how boring it often was. They are anxious to spice up their lives by hearing how you escaped being eaten by wolves, outwitted bandits and rode through earthquakes.

When disappointed, some people take the truth as a personal affront, and refuse to believe the messenger. They want fables, not harsh reality.

On the other hand some Long Riders have been viciously condemned when they shared their stories, as the truth they brought home cast doubt on previously treasured collective convictions.

A famous example was the contempt heaped upon Marco Polo when he returned home to Venice. Instead of believing his stories about faraway Cathay, he was roundly denounced as "Marco of the Million Lies."

Another Long Rider, James Bruce of Scotland, was likewise viciously savaged.

Bruce was a wealthy Scottish aristocrat with a passion for exploration. He spent more than a dozen years in North Africa and Abyssinia, during which time he resolved to discover the origins of the Blue Nile. On November 14, 1770 Bruce reached the spring from which the fabled river originated. Using a half coconut shell as a cup, he drank from the source.

Upon his return to London Bruce was expecting to be hailed as a hero. Instead his stories were greeted with incredulity. Critics claimed he had never even been to Abyssinia. He spent several years creating a five-volume series entitled *Travels to Discover the Source of the Nile*. But despite this evidence, his critics once again ridiculed his honour and reputation.

Instead of responding to the cruelty and injustice, the emotionally-wounded Long Rider retired from public life. He treated his detractors with silent contempt, disdaining to make any reply to publications impeaching his veracity. When his friends urged him to defend himself in the press, he firmly replied, "What I have written I have written!"

Later travellers proved the substantial accuracy of Bruce's account of what is today Ethiopia and his books are considered to be of great historical importance.

The Biology of Belief

One reason Bruce was denounced was because public opinion was shaped by those who dogmatically dictated "what idle theory was to be believed, and what solid information was to be rejected."

As one friend wrote, "These brazen images Bruce refused to worship. In their presence he maintained his statements, and they frowned upon him with pompous incredulity. With just indignation, he sneered at their impertinence and folly; but they knew their power, and they deliberately banded together to run him down."

Though none of his critics had ever been to Abyssinia, they felt justified in destroying the traveller's reputation.

Why?

The collective attack upon Bruce contains an important lesson for returning Long Riders.

We commonly accept the fact that various types of animal life congregate in large groups; herds of zebras, schools of fish, flocks of birds, packs of wolves, etc.

It is also known that some animal life exhibits swarm behaviour, by flying in formation, running en mass, etc. Animals enact swarm behaviour for various reasons, including migration and to escape predators.

Humans are also capable of unconscious swarm behaviour.

Staying with the ethnic herd provides a reassuring sense of identity, working within a corporation ensures a feeling of economic comfort, trusting the leader of the political pack frees one from having to make difficult personal decisions, moving in the same mental direction as your fellow countrymen acts as a political panacea in scary times.

There are an estimated 316 million Americans. Most of them automatically brand themselves identically by what they own, wear, eat or drive. Would the unconscious force of 200 million of them exert an undetected influence? Could such collective power demonstrate the power of what I term "the Biology of Belief"?

Unlike other mammals, human beings are prone to vanity. While believing in their special individuality, the vast majority of them spend their lives akin to mayflies. In a blaze of short-term existence, they are born, grow, mate, decay and die. Be it 24 hours or 80 years, their lives are less than a blink of the eternal eye. How many of them do one true thing, stand alone, take a great risk, defy a tyrant, brave the dark, set off on a journey into the unknown?

The vast majority of them live and die without having had the courage to act alone.

Through a series of accidents I have become the witness and chronicler of this tribe of wild rovers known as Long Riders. There is loneliness and a sense of isolation in most of them. They are outsiders looking in at settled society.

Upon reflection, I believe one reason there are so few Long Riders is because only a minority of humans are capable of breaking free from this herd mentality and venturing off on their own, be it in a geographic, spiritual or political manner.

There is, I suspect, some sort of "switch" buried deep within their DNA which prompts the Long Riders to wander, on many levels, away from the security and comfort to which their fellows are addicted.

This might explain why there are an extraordinary number of rebels, mavericks and outcasts, as well as poets, authors, scientists and reformers, amongst the ranks of the Historical Long Riders; i.e. Oscar Wilde, Charles Darwin, Jonathan Swift, Father Eusebio Kino, to name just a few of the very famous ones.

These individuals raise interesting questions about our definitions of belonging.

And they help explain why, as Lord Byron's poetic hero, Childe Harold, states, "Our destiny calls and we must go."

Long Riders have been described as introspective, moody, rebellious, adventurous and romantic loners.

But setting off on that road often leads to unforeseen complications with the ones we love upon our return.

Resentment

As Bruce discovered, those who step across the invisible line and break the taboos of society are punished in a variety of ways.

The Long Rider has expanded more than just his sense of geographic knowledge. For him time has run rapidly, in contrast to those left behind for whom time stands still. The journey has awakened all of the Long Rider's senses, as opposed to those who make their way through life in a waking sleep, whose senses are benumbed because of a lack of anything to call them into use.

Upon his return home, the traveller often involuntarily invokes a strong sense of unease and discomfort.

The majority of people are afraid to fly from the nest. Theirs is a life half lived, enclosed within walls, divorced from Nature, terrified of hazards; their allegiance is given to maintaining the settled order of things. They often display deep suspicion of a returning traveller and subject him to social stigma. One such example was the man who accompanied one of the equestrian expeditions which tried to reach the South Pole.

At the age of 24, Apsley Cherry-Garrard was the youngest member of Captain Robert Scott's expedition to Antarctica in 1910.

During the austral winter he and two companions made a dangerous trek in order to secure unhatched Emperor penguin eggs, believing them to be of great scientific importance. In total darkness, and in temperatures ranging as low as minus 60 degrees Centigrade (minus 77 Fahrenheit), they travelled nearly a hundred miles to reach the penguin colony.

The exhausted explorers managed to obtain three eggs. The return journey was so severe that most of Cherry-Garrard's teeth shattered from chattering in the frigid temperatures. Dr. Edward Wilson and Lieutenant Henry Bowers, Cherry-Garrard's companions on that trip, later died in Antarctica.

Upon his return to England, the sole survivor dutifully took the precious penguin eggs to the Natural History Museum in London. Cherry-Garrard had risked his life to obtain those eggs. The museum's employees made him wait in the hall; then dismissed him. It was just another Tuesday morning to the men at work. Cherry-Garrard was an oddity who had upset the office routine of drones that worshipped the clock and ignored the compass.

After completing incredible journeys and overcoming a host of dangers, Long Riders return shining with life. They don't realize they have become out of tune with their former friends.

Everyone makes choices. The friends who remained at home could see freedom, could smell it and knew it existed, but chose to hide in their homes while the Long Rider followed a desire to pursue the stars. The friends became captives of their possessions and remained loyal to collective illusions. Their horizons were reduced by inertia and the love of comfort. Diverted from exploring the path of life, they became relentlessly ordinary.

Upon his return, many a Long Rider has discovered an emotional gulf exists between him and his friends. On occasion the traveller is surprised to find himself the butt of jokes, ridicule, contempt, envy, anger and misunderstanding.

Count Vittorio Alfieri learned that bitter lesson after he rode home to Italy.

"I returned to a cold and bitter reception from those I thought were my friends. I learned that returning from exile was no guarantee of a warm welcome from those who lacked the courage to stray far from the hearth, that any effort, even if unintentional, to excel them becomes a cause of mortal offence," the Italian poet wrote.

Nor should you underestimate the emotional toll which may come into play with your immediate family.

Many people sacrifice their dreams in exchange for financial security. Some betray their hopes because they are crippled with fear. Others become compromised and trapped by accident. Regardless of what hindered their escape, they harbour a sense of heartache and pain when they look back upon what their life might have been.

When they hear the stories of a returning Long Rider, they know their dreams have fallen apart and that they have lived a life-lie. Remorse overcomes them when they realize they have wasted their chance. What was it they wanted to buy that was worth all their dreams?

In such circumstances, anger often arises among the family. Many will not even acknowledge what the Long Rider did or grant it any significance. The traveller is often accused of shirking his duty and of not living up to expectations. Awkward conversations ensue. Family gatherings become painful.

One such instance involved the Long Rider Arthur Elliott.

He had been wounded while fighting for England during the First World War. Afterwards he never married, preferring to work with horses. In 1952 he set off to ride from Land's End, England to John O'Groats, Scotland against the strong opposition of his siblings and extended family.

During the subsequent ride, Arthur was severely injured, but rode on regardless. He ultimately reached his distant destination. Upon his return, Arthur's younger brother, who was the father of six children, was resentful and jealous.

These unexpected displays of negative feelings fade with time but leave a shadow on your soul.

When his journey from Mongolia to Hungary was over, Australian Long Rider Tim Cope suffered an emotional shock at how he was treated.

"They were coarse and unhelpful and I realized that whilst they marvelled at my adventure they did not identify with it. I had become a novelty. It was already fading to something as intangible and ungraspable as the embryo of the idea in the first place. I knew a part of me was dying," Tim recalled.

The majority of people will never understand and sometimes not even respect you for what you have done. But some will.

In response to seeing a Member of the Guild riding by, one citizen shared this poignant remark.

"After an adulthood of doing the 9 to 5, taking on a career that pays and does not interest me and giving up on so many of my dreams, I am so happy that someone out there hasn't."

Inarticulate

You paid more than money for what you learned during the journey.

You sacrificed comfort. You endured isolation. You had to fight to reach your goal.

Upon your return you feel free; but at what cost?

Many Long Riders report that after an initial dose of enthusiasm, they grow increasingly silent.

One returning Long Rider wrote, "I don't know what to say. Words fail me. Things have changed on the inside, but I can't describe how."

Another reported, "People are generally not interested in hearing about your experiences. They cannot relate. And most are too busy to ask questions because it doesn't have anything to do with them. And you really do not want to go there because you know they will not understand anyway. The only people who understand are people who have done long rides or people who genuinely want to do a long ride."

Money

Alexander Selkirk was the Scottish sailor who was marooned on a remote island in 1704. After spending four years in isolation, he was eventually rescued and returned to England. His adventures served as the inspiration for Daniel Defoe's fictional hero, Robinson Crusoe.

Even though he had lived a primitive life on the island, once back in London Selkirk made a startling remark.

"I am now worth 800 Pounds, but shall never be so happy, as when I was not worth a Farthing[1]."

How could a man who had been deprived of everything civilisation deemed essential equate that experience with happiness?

Modern society is aimed at convincing people to search for employment. While food and shelter are primary necessities, many humans spend their life force seeking to obtain trifles or to be entertained. Repetitive and uninteresting jobs are offset by hours spent in escaping reality via television and the internet. People who are content with planned and predictable lives don't see the necessity to break away from what is a banal existence. They prefer comfort to challenges. Aspirations wither and adventure goes unheeded.

Compared to the majority of lavish modern lifestyles, the Long Rider is a financial primitive because his needs are modest. But what lies at the heart of the matter is the attitude which many equestrian travellers take towards the decision to make a living or to live a fulfilling life. Like Selkirk stranded on his remote island, Long Riders learn to be satisfied with what they truly need instead of what a materialistic society says they require.

---

[1] Editor's note: A quarter of a penny.

After completing his journey to all 48 states, Frank Heath made an important insight. He contrasted the world's obsession with obtaining wealth against the traveller's discovery of inner treasures.

"Whenever I meet people I have to answer many questions or be thought snobbish. The question that upsets me above all others is, 'What did you get out of making the journey?' What is the use of trying to answer a person who counts life in dollars and cents?" Heath wrote.

Setting off on an extended equestrian journey is expensive on many levels. Most travellers work relentlessly in advance so as to save the necessary funds. Homes are mortgaged. Sacrifices are made. Luxuries are dispensed with. Many a Long Rider, me included, has sold precious personal possessions to finance an equestrian expedition.

It is not unusual for a returning Long Rider to be emotionally exhausted. Yet just when time is needed to recover, necessity forces the traveller to undertake an urgent search for money and employment.

A few are lucky enough to resume jobs left temporarily vacant. Others return penniless. There may be concerns for feeding the family and providing for their welfare.

One Long Rider recalled the monetary hardship she and her husband faced when their journey ended.

"It was very financially stressful. We saved for years to go on the ride, spent two years without an income, and came back with zero money to our names. It was tough starting all over again but it was a choice we made. We most certainly don't regret it; quite the contrary. But it didn't make it any easier getting back on our feet."

During this difficult time of transition, it is reassuring to remember that true happiness has little to do with income or the obtaining of possessions. Studies have shown that the more materialistic people become the greater their sense of wellbeing diminishes.

It is important to remember in the immediate aftermath of returning that what is essential to the human spirit is not the size of a person's bank account but the discovery of their true self-worth. Financial hardships will be overcome. Meanwhile, the long-term gratification derived from completing the journey becomes increasingly valuable as time goes by.

Long Riders have reached for something more important than monetary wealth. They have pushed beyond the bounds that life tried to impose upon them. They may not return financially enriched but they can take great comfort in the value of their experiences.

The Emotional Let Down

It is fine to advocate optimism but that doesn't mean that we can afford to be blind to the negative feelings which many Long Riders endure when the trip is done.

After participating in what feels like a journey out of time, most Long Riders are more content to be on the road than in a room.

Abbé Évariste Huc endured tremendous hardships during his ride across China, Tartary and Tibet in 1844. But he had no hesitation in expressing his regret upon returning to settled society.

"During the time we had been in the desert our tastes had been insensibly modified, and our temperament accommodated by its silence and solitude, and, on re-entering cultivated lands, the agitation, perplexity, and turmoil of civilization oppressed and suffocated us; the air seemed to fail us, and we felt every moment as about to die of asphyxia," Huc explained.

From being constantly on the move, there is a sudden lack of physical progress. The feeling of inactivity is bewildering. Life feels arrested.

After completing his rigorous ride through the Caucasian Mountains in 1929, Negley Farson wrote, "I have seldom felt lower in my life."

Other Long Riders report confusion about goals and experience feelings of perplexity about their future.

When Gordon Naysmith completed his epic 20,000 kilometre (12,000 mile) ride from South Africa to Austria, he was physically, mentally and emotionally exhausted.

"I went into town to visit a couple of pubs I used to frequent but the atmosphere was not the same. I found I was missing the drive of the trip a lot. It seemed there was nothing to look forward to except to go back to work and write more computer code."

Some become dejected.

Ella Maillart experienced intense emotional hardship when her ride from China to India came to an end.

"I felt lost, only half alive," she wrote in her diary. After being plunged back into contemporary life, she wondered, "You ask yourself unceasingly, who am I?" In despair she said, "I long to take a standing leap beyond the bitter days that go by the name of return."

After he completed his ride across Spain, it was the literary Long Rider Somerset Maugham who articulated the feelings of depression which often accompany a traveller's homecoming.

"You have returned. The previously impossible has become matter of fact. After living life so intensely, you find yourself listless, surrounded by ennui. Having survived brutal realism, you find yourself enveloped by fantasy. Having your senses so deeply enriched, you find yourself in a spiritual desert. After the silence of the saddle, you return to an ant nest of noise and distractions. After your commune with nature, you find a host of mechanical distractions. After such excitement, you return to a limpid life. All the streets look exactly alike and all lead nowhere. You become resigned to what you have lost; all the simple pleasures which you discovered in the saddle. The journey is over but still it inhabits your dreams. An odour caught by chance brings back a flood of memories. You remember the starry darkness. The sound of the horse bells chiming softly in your dreams and you wonder which part of your life is real. Your initial feeling of homecoming turns to ashes. There is longing and regret."

The Body's Reaction

One reason Long Riders experience emotional trauma is because their bodies are undergoing a chemical change.

Travelling across the countryside on horseback invokes a sense of spaciousness. Living in the open air is energy-enhancing. Being physically involved with horses is invigorating. Witnessing the passage of the seasons stimulates the emotions.

American specialists who x-rayed the brains of travellers found that this combination of heightened stimulus contributed to a sense of wellbeing. There is also evidence to suggest that the human body receives a chemical rush from travelling, as the journey into the unknown constantly produces adrenalin.

Richard Halliburton, one of the most famous travel writers of the 1920s, wasn't aware of the chemical complexities his body was experiencing when he returned home from his many dangerous adventures, one of which was the first airplane flight over Mount Everest.

But Halliburton was enough of a writer to realize that his body was undergoing serious biological changes. He wrote, "One is loath to return again to the world with its complexities and its unhappiness." He complained about being "beset by the depression that always follows intoxication." Everyday life, he complained, was "drab and insipid." He longed to return to being a "Horizon Chaser."

Like Halliburton, Long Riders often experience an emotional slump after having spent long periods of time in the saddle. When the daily dose of constant vibrancy is withdrawn, their energy levels drop. Instead of elated feelings of happiness, they report a lack of motivation.

Stress

Even though Long Riders experience a tremendous emotional high when they conclude their journey, the physical and emotional changes which they then undergo often produce increasing levels of stress, anxiety and depression.

Having survived the dangers of the journey, they must now overcome the challenges of the homecoming. Like soldiers returning from a war zone, Long Riders and various types of explorers report experiencing depression, anxiety and nightmares. Several astronauts, for example, have suffered mental anguish after completing their missions and then turned to alcohol to relieve their depression.

Equestrian explorers aren't immune from such invisible interior wounds.

During his historic ride from Mongolia to Hungary, Tim Cope revelled in the fact that every day he was being "challenged to learn." He was constantly, "feeling the air, in touch with the way the world works and aware of everything around me."

His senses had become so heightened that he noted, "In the winter time you even realise when the days shorten by one or two minutes."

Then, after his return to Australia, the young Long Rider found himself feeling like an exile at home.

"If I'm in an apartment for a week I totally lose touch with what the moon's doing, where the stars are, what the weather's doing, and I start to lose my strength. To live in the city, in a world of abundance and disconnection where everything is controlled at the touch of a button; for me that feels like death," Tim wrote.

Grief

Few Long Riders realize that they are likely to undergo a grieving process when the journey is concluding.

They have been deeply involved in an immersive experience which required them to be concerned with deeper and subtler things. Suddenly they return to a world full of striving and scheming and sorrow. They may find themselves surrounded by love but not by comprehension. The painful process of reintegration requires them to resume their well-ordered place in life. Feeling orphaned and lost, many experience a vast and secret misery.

Francis McCullagh was a young man who rode with the Cossacks in 1905. Upon finding himself on a spotlessly clean ship heading back to "civilisation," he wrote this lament.

"I hated these snug berths with their immaculate linen. I pined for the sleep in the open air with the solemn moon overhead, the free wind of heaven blowing on my face, the large vague sounds of the night coming wafted gently like fairies' whispers o'er the dim swaying harvest fields, the tethered horses nosing around in the vicinity, sometimes tumbling awkwardly to the ground asleep, sometimes kicking and whinnying. It may seem a humiliating and unmanly confession to make, but I must confess that my anguish was such that, instead of going to bed like the good bourgeois I now was, I sat for half the night on that cold deserted deck, weeping in secret, like a child."

Time moves on and names change; but Long Riders still suffer.

As I was writing this chapter another young Long Rider also had to deal with what is sometimes termed "the pilgrim's death," the moment when the journey ends and the traveller realizes with a sense of shock how much he will miss the experience.

After having been inspired by Aimé Tschiffely, in July 2012 Filipe Leite started a 10,000 mile journey from Canada to Brazil. The ride took him through ten countries and lasted two years. After enduring tremendous hardships, Filipe's historic journey was concluded when the Brazilian Long Rider reached his hometown of Santo do Pinhal in August, 2014. In his moment of triumph Filipe admitted, "I cried for three days as the trip slowly came to an end."

On the Outside

Have you ever asked yourself, "What happens to heroes?"

In Tolkien's classic tale, *The Lord of the Rings*, Bilbo and Frodo Baggins depart on one final adventure, sailing away with their friend Gandalf the wizard and Galadriel the Elven queen for the mythical land of Tol Eressëa.

Yet what happened to the other heroic Hobbits; Samwise Gamgee, Meriadoc Brandybuck and Peregrin Took who were left behind?

They woke up one morning to find themselves back in the domesticated, predictable, boring Shire, with no more adventures waiting to be undertaken, no more dynamic friends to chat to, no more great mission waiting to be done. Eventually the night arrives when the three former travellers find themselves sitting alone at a table in the local inn, talking quietly to themselves about adventures and topics which the other Hobbits could not comprehend, may not believe and had no interest in discussing.

Like those three Hobbit travellers, Long Riders need to understand that there are rhythms to a man's life. During the journey the solitary rider has been an island on the move, carried along by forces over which he had limited or no control. There have been times when his self-destruction seemed assured. Yet, like Sam, Merry and Pippin, by a miracle he has survived.

Then the day dawns when the Long Rider wakes up in his version of the Shire. That's when the question arises, "What do you do if you survive, after you win, when you're still living?"

Tragedy often stalks those who cannot relinquish the wild side of life and whose very being has been fundamentally altered.

The Lure of the Road

The journey required the Long Rider to be reckless of safety, to leave behind possessions and to dispense with comfort. Having returned home, the traveller finds himself standing at an invisible crossroads. According to "society," the time has come to settle down.

The problem for some is that the journey was the highlight of their life and anything else proves to be anticlimactic. Some Long Riders attempt to readjust to the trivialities of an everyday existence. For a while they are content to cherish their memories. But as the bonds of conventional life begin to restrict them, the desire to return to the intoxicating life of the road attracts them like a magnet.

The Scottish Long Rider Mungo Park had nearly died during his first equestrian expedition into Africa. That didn't keep him from being drawn back to the unexplored Niger River. Homesick for the unknown, an inexplicable desire to ride into the jungle again resulted in his death in 1805.

Like Park, a handful of Long Riders abandon all pretence at routine and home life, preferring to remain in the natural world instead of being hampered by society's conventions. One such modern example is American Long Rider Bernice Ende.

As I write this chapter, Bernice is out on the road – again. She has spent the last ten years in the saddle and has ridden 22,000 miles to date.

Even though an equestrian journey is fraught with loneliness and replete with peril, Bernice is compensated by a feeling of freedom and stirring excitement. This helps explain why Bernice said she no longer desires the comforts of a conventional home, preferring to sleep in a tent alongside her horses.

"I don't want to be in a house anymore. I want to see the stars and the moon and what the wind does to the leaves and grass. I want to feel the heat and the cold on me. I want to feel alive," the sixty-year-old former ballet teacher explained.

As Bernice demonstrates, there's a difference between living and existing. According to her, it's not about things; it's about life.

Long Rider Realignment

Prior to writing this chapter I entered into a special correspondence regarding this topic with Long Rider author and philosopher Jeremy James. He shared these special observations with me.

"I think the rides re-set our gyroscope."

One reason this occurs, Jeremy believes, is because the Long Rider becomes attuned to the magnificence of the world and is no longer deceived by the notion of distance.

"Yet distance is what we know best about, footfall by footfall. A kind of equanimity takes over, all tied up with the breath of a horse and the long distance, the Long Quiet as you term it; where nothing can touch it or us."

Eventually the journey "gets deep into the psyche, into the bone as it were," of the traveller.

The troubles encountered by some returning Long Riders result, Jeremy believes, not necessarily because of a sense of disorientation. "I suggest perhaps it is a re-orientation."

"The rides do not disturb so much as set us free," Jeremy explained.

He continued, "It is a curious matter, this re-engaging business. Truth is I suspect that we never really recover from our long rides. We are corrected by our rides. They align us with a different perspective."

"There's something about the harsh purity of the journey that takes one out of the mainstream," he wrote. "When I think of the Long Riders I know, they're all a bit like it. It's as though we caught a glimpse of something and knew it to be true and fine. It's a peculiar loyalty to something high, something profound which cannot be answered in the common run."

Jeremy acknowledged that the strain of trying to readjust to our previous position in society may come at a cost because, "We never really fit in anymore. Not for want of trying. Something far more intrinsic and deep has happened and will not let us go.

And although we might say we no longer seem to be able to comply with the norm, it does not mean we become useless. Rather, we become our own masters, and in our own way, which, as it happens, does not usually follow with what might have been before."

Certainly it can be disorienting in that we lose certain pre-conceived, run-of-the-mill concepts. But that is enrichment, he contends, not a fault.

"Like you, I have not, nor ever will regret the journey. It was the finest thing I know I have ever done. And if it's brought me hardship later, it's because I didn't understand that to begin with. I wish I had known this, then. It would have helped me to understand myself and more, to appreciate what the horses had delivered at full velocity. Without their dimension, their constant company, their depth of field, I know for certain, my world would have been a more curtailed, a narrower place."

He concluded by urging Long Riders to realize that the journey has two stages; the awakening and the realignment.

"What I might say is that if we, as the oldies as it were, can say to aspirants that the same will happen to them, then instead of being thrown by it, as we have been, to grasp it for its grace."

Restoration

As Jeremy and I both learned to our dismay, a Long Rider needs to give thought to his return.

You need to allow time to readjust to what feels like an artificial world. Most Long Riders say that the first two months are the hardest.

It helps if you have a quiet place where you can retreat, re-think and restore your sense of emotional balance.

Reward yourself by enjoying all of the luxuries you missed. Take pleasure soaking in a hot bath. Eat everything you ever day-dreamed about while you were starving in the saddle. Read a good book. Sleep late for two or three days running. See a movie. Visit old friends. Place all these well-earned moments deep within your memory banks.

Don't become isolated. Be willing to discuss your journey but do so carefully.

Because the journey just ended, it seems impossible that the details will ever fade from your memory. But every traveller forgets events, names, places, dates and details. As soon as you conclude your journey summon up the discipline to organize your journal, arrange your photographs, edit your film, work on your book and thank all the people who assisted you.

In this way the aftermath of your journey helps keep you emotionally preoccupied, and extends your trip in a new manner, all the while you have time to readjust to your new circumstances and surroundings.

Benefits and Discoveries

Returning is not all bad.

Many Long Riders come back with a sense of gratitude for what they have learned and experienced during the journey.

On an obvious level the completion of a difficult and dangerous equestrian trip permits the traveller to put aside all questions of physical courage.

But other discoveries are more subtle.

Though they may not undertake another journey, many Long Riders have become aware that in addition to having made history in their own life, they glimpsed the eternal along the way.

Andi Mills experienced such an epiphany after completing her ride across America.

"Of course, I came home in a flurry with a million things to do right away. Today is the first time I have taken a deep breath and stepped off the carousel long enough to look around. You were right, CuChullaine. I am not the same, I will never be the same and it is a good thing. I feel different. Deeper and richer and I feel as though I have more dimensions if you can understand that. Instead of being smooth, I have a different texture. Instead of feeling like a small part of a small world, I feel like a big part of a big world. Instead of watching life go by, I got to touch it and smell it, and be part of it in a very intimate way. Instead of seeing sand, I saw grains of sand. Instead of seeing a mountain, I saw the rocks that made up the mountain. What a special gift that is."

Choices and Changes

Long Rider Oscar Wilde warned, "To live is the rarest thing in the world. Most people exist, that is all."

Recent studies in England bear this out. Uncompromising in conformity, unquestioning of authority, cramped at every turn within the tame limits of the commonplace, 63% of people surveyed say they have not achieved their childhood dreams and live a life that is curiously aimless.

DC Vision's journey caused him to deeply question the values and customs he had been taught.

"By the time survivors of life reach their middle ages they have been beaten to passivity by bills, bullshit and bodies melting into gravity. The script most people carry at this point in life is little more than a laundry list of schedules, routines, escapism via the internet and favourite television shows. Addictions are hardened to the point of shiny diamonds, and change is not a welcomed visitor. This is the script of billions of your neighbours," he wrote.

His trip on horseback was, he believed, "the greatest gift I ever gave myself. Out of the journey rises a phoenix, a dreamer taking their first yawn in the early dawn, not quite awake, but not deep asleep either. This is the time that you first become aware of the script, that historical self that you are being called to evolve from."

Once your eyes are open, you can never close them again.

It also helps explain why many Long Riders undergo various types of major life transformations shortly after returning, including a change in job, career, marital status and housing. They are looking for new answers to life's complexities.

The Courage to Continue

The journey has caused you no longer to take life for granted. The homecoming requires you to remain loyal to what you have learned and who you have become.

How do we stay aware? How do we keep our integrity intact? How do we continue to follow our heart if we are not in the saddle? How do we use the emotional resilience and courage from the journey to move ahead in our life?

In 1942 the poet T.S. Eliot wrote in England, "We shall not cease from exploration and the end of all our exploring will be to arrive where we started and know it for the first time."

Nearly seventy years later, Colleen Hamer discovered the truth of that statement when her ride in faraway Nebraska was concluded.

"Coming home was very hard at first. It seemed like every dysfunction in my life and relationships were magnified 100 times. I think I felt lonely for the person I had been on the road. Then I came to realize that the road didn't change who I was. It just allowed me to be the person that I truly liked and respected. There is a new strength that comes from me now," she wrote upon the completion of her journey.

Time

Some Long Riders, like Alexander William Kinglake, are blessed with immediate insights when they complete their rides.

Kinglake rode through Syria, Lebanon, Palestine and Egypt in 1835. His emotional experiences were so powerful that upon his return to London he was seized with a blazing urgent desire to write. His book, *Eothen*, described why he left.

"There comes to him a time for loathing the wearisome ways of society; a time for not liking tamed people; a time for not dancing quadrilles, not sitting in pews."

What he found instead was, "Day after day, week after week, and month after month, your foot is in the stirrup. To taste the cold breath of the earliest morn, and to lead or follow your bright cavalcade till sunset through forests and mountain passes, through valleys and desolate plains – all this becomes your mode of life. If you are wise, you do not look upon the long period of time thus occupied by your journey as the mere gulfs which divide you from place to place to which you are going; but rather, as most rare and beautiful portions of life, from which may come thought, temper, and strength. Once you feel this, you will grow happy and contented in your saddle-home."

Kinglake was lucky.

Most Long Riders need time to put their journeys into perspective.

It takes time to delve into the deep dark corner of the saddlebag of your memories.

Something has to evolve within you before you finally realize what the journey means.

It is when you see the journey from a distance, after the dust has settled on the saddle, that you begin to discern the magnitude of how it changed you, instilled courage, taught you to endure, to believe, to strive, to ride towards what seemed like an impossible goal – and to reach it.

Sea G Rhydr realized this when she wrote, "In many ways I feel that I shall be unfolding the answers to these questions for the rest of my life."

Summary

The Long Rider sets off on a voluntary migration. There will have been many times when the rigours of the road will have caused him to regret departing on such an agonizing journey.

And his return may subject him to a profound emotional ordeal.

Yet he has learned the importance of independence and the need to live fully.

Most people merely accept their lot in life. The Long Rider has set an example. He has refused to settle into a life of servitude. He has done what others could only talk about but feared to do. He is an inspiration.

He proves that people have a choice in life; to reside in the safety of the beehive or to soar alone like an eagle.

The Arcadian moment in my life occurred when I crested the Shandur Pass and saw all the lantern and cooking fires beckoning in the valley below. What I didn't know was that a long emotional torment would begin when my journey was over and I became that most helpless and most ungainly of creatures, a dismounted Long Rider.

After having ridden from Peking, when Ella Maillart and Peter Fleming (left) arrived in Gilgit they were excited to become reacquainted with the luxuries of modern life. But it didn't take long for Ella to realize she had returned "to a life to which I feel myself a stranger."

After returning some Long Riders have been viciously condemned when they shared their stories. Even though James Bruce discovered the source of the Blue Nile, his critics unjustly ridiculed his honour and reputation.

Not every Long Rider receives a heroic welcome. This photo shows Arthur Elliott coming home to an empty flat above a lonely petrol station on a cold, rainy autumn day. No fanfare. No dinner. Instead he endured resentment from jealous family members who disapproved of his journey.

Many Long Riders undergo physical and emotional shocks when they return. After riding across China, Tartary and Tibet, Abbé Évariste Huc found the turmoil of civilisation was oppressive.

After spending two years riding from Canada to Brazil, Filipe Leite was given a hero's welcome. Larger than life statues were created in Sao Paolo to commemorate the journey and 500 horsemen rode alongside Filipe when he arrived at his hometown. Yet despite being a moment of victory, Filipe admitted that he wept when he realized the journey was coming to an end.

Some Long Riders, like Bernice Ende, find they cannot resist returning to the saddle. She has made eight trips and ridden more than 20,000 miles.

Alexander William Kinglake was one of the lucky ones. He had immediate insights when he completed his ride. But in most case it takes time for the traveller to fully understand the implications of the journey on many levels.

Sceptics may condemn the Long Rider's desire to explore the world. In response, Don Roberto Cunninghame Graham wrote, "How many men of cultivation and education have seen the pampas, prairie, desert or steppes, and throwing off the shackles of their upbringing stayed there for life and became Indians, Arabs, Cossacks or Gauchos. But who ever saw an Indian, Arab or wild man of any race come of his own accord and put his neck into the noose of a sedentary life and end his days a clerk?"

Chapter 80
Honour

What does "honour" mean to a modern Long Rider? And why is it important?
To find the answer, we must look East, to the "Land of the Rising Sun."

The Baron

Bushido is a Japanese concept corresponding to the notion of chivalry. It is a code of ideals which demonstrates the struggle between the two sides of human nature. The samurai who practised *bushido* are often mistakenly believed to have been exclusively warriors.

There were exceptions.

Baron Yasumasa Fukushima was a special human being. A highly literate scholar and a skilled linguist, Fukushima was sent to Germany to act as military attaché. When his tour of duty was over, instead of taking the ship home to Tokyo he decided to travel overland – on horseback.

On February 11th, 1892, the Baron departed from the Japanese Embassy in Berlin on one of the longest equestrian journeys of the late 19th century.

Some scholars have said they believe the Baron's ride was actually a military reconnaissance mission that allowed him to observe the development of Russia's Trans-Siberian railroad.

What has been overlooked is that the code of *bushido* encouraged samurais to undertake long pilgrimages, known as *shugyo*, to distant places. Spiritual enlightenment, they believed, could be achieved through endeavour and personal discomfort.

Fukushima's 14,000 kilometre (8,700 mile) journey became a legend and proved the validity of that concept.

The Long Rider travelled for 488 days – across two continents, through Germany, Poland, Russia, Siberia, Mongolia and Manchuria – before finally returning home to Japan.

It is indeed ironic then that this modest man received a hero's welcome when he reached Japan. Upon entering Tokyo on June 29, 1893 he discovered the city had arranged a gigantic welcoming party complete with a huge triumphant arch. The weary traveller's personal possessions were held in such reverence they were placed within a Japanese museum.

Even more surprising than these outpourings of public support was the intense personal interest which the Emperor of Japan showed in Fukushima. Among other notable attributes, the sovereign was a keen horseman. He invited Fukushima to several private meetings at the imperial palace, at which time the ruler questioned the Long Rider about his journey and horses.

It was during one of these meetings that the Baron told the Emperor, "14,000 kilometres means that each hair on the horses has the value of 1,000 gold pieces."

Several days later the Imperial Minister visited Fukushima to explain that the Emperor had offered to provide a permanent safe home for the Long Rider's horses.

Despite these unprecedented honours the Baron neither demanded nor expected any reward. The journey had required him to be supremely practical; but in addition he had become deeply spiritual. According to the concept of *yugen*, a samurai can achieve self-realisation by the simple perfection of an everyday task.

The journey had forced the Baron to transcend fear. He had achieved a quietness and tranquillity which led to the composure of his mind. Having come in contact with the centre of his soul, he had no need for the acclaim of a crowd to justify the meaning of his life.

In fact, he had reached a point where his own identity had faded into the background.

An important clue about the Baron was discovered on the back of a photograph which was taken of him in Russia. Fukushima sent this photograph to his wife prior to his departure into the wilds of Siberia. It reveals a vital clue about the nobility of his spirit.

On the back of the photo he wrote, "When foreign people look at you, they shall see the Japanese spirit in a brave warrior."

This sentence is deceptive. It is the Baron reminding himself to remain humble. He did so by remaining too shy and modest to use the word "me" when he described himself.

His poetry, his sensitive insights, his ability to place immediate situations into a deeper historical context, mark him as one of the most amazing Long Riders in human history.

Very few Long Riders have ever attained this higher philosophical plane

When I, a foreigner, try to define what it was that created a true samurai, I believe there must be much more than simply an excess of courage. To reach true harmony, there must be a soothing poetry of the soul to balance the hard bravery of the heart. Perhaps this is why the mighty Emperor spoke to the Baron so honestly? And the humble people reacted to the exhausted traveller so warmly? Because they could both detect the humility which radiated from this good man?

A Mounted Brotherhood

It would be a mistake to think that the Baron simply hatched the idea to ride home to Japan without any type of outside inspiration, and after having arrived at such an unlikely plan would have been able to achieve his goal without the assistance of others.

In fact one of the remarkable points about the Baron's ride is how it demonstrates the strength of the equestrian brotherhood symbolized today by the Long Riders' Guild.

Three of the most extraordinary Long Riders of the 19th century were part of a chain of events that resulted in the Baron reaching Tokyo.

The American Long Rider Januarius MacGahan rode from Fort Perovsky, Russia, across the Kyzil-Kum Desert to Adam-Kurulgan ("Fatal to Men"), Kyrgyzstan in 1873.

Two years later MacGahan advised British Long Rider Frederick Burnaby on how to reach Khiva.

It was Burnaby's famous book, *A Ride to Khiva* that inspired Fukushima seventeen years later.

Prior to his departure, Fukushima met Sven Hedin in Berlin. Sweden's greatest explorer and Long Rider gave the novice traveller valuable advice concerning his upcoming trip.

Three heroes from three countries helped their Japanese comrade.

Fly to your Brother's Aid

The concept of receiving wisdom from a wise elder reaches back to the days of the Trojan War. Prior to leaving his home, Odysseus entrusted the welfare and education of his son to his friend, Mentor. It is his name which has come down through the ages to represent a trusted teacher and guide.

Though the idea may be old, the practice remains alive today.

What began with five Long Riders from three countries has now spread to more than 40 nations. In every case, one equestrian traveller inspires, encourages, warns or educates another. One helps you. After your ride, you in turn share your hard-won wisdom with those who follow in your hoofprints. The Guild has always been about aiding our fellows, not winning at their expense.

Several notable modern examples of this philosophy have occurred while I was working on this book.

As I write this chapter a young man named Kohei Yamakawa is attempting to complete the first modern equestrian journey across his native Japan.

But like the Baron, Kohei did not set off without the assistance of other Long Riders.

Hideyo Tsutsumi, the first Japanese Member of the Long Riders' Guild, is acting as Kohei's mentor.

While Kohei didn't lack enthusiasm, he was in an absolute vacuum when it came to equestrian travel. In the intervening years since the Baron made his ride all knowledge of the topic had been wiped out in Japan. Nor was there any suitable equestrian travelling equipment such as saddlebags or a pack saddle.

Due to the special historical importance of this journey, the Guild organized an international effort to assist Kohei. Kelly de Strake, the owner of the Custom Pack Rigging Company, donated an adjustable pack saddle and other valuable equipment to the Guild, so as to equip Kohei with the best equipment available.

Senior Long Riders from various continents then donated the funds needed to pay for the cost of shipping the equipment to Japan.

Nor are other examples lacking.

Prior to her departure across Africa, Esther Stein travelled to London to meet renowned Scottish Long Rider Gordon Naysmith. Having ridden 20,000 kilometres (12,000 miles) from South Africa to Austria, the knowledgeable Long Rider presented the younger traveller with a treasure-trove of otherwise unobtainable information.

And in an unprecedented show of international equestrian brotherhood, Long Riders from five countries helped Filipe Leite prepare for his 10,000 mile journey from Canada to Brazil.

This outpouring of generosity and support prompted Filipe to explain his feelings about being a Long Rider.

"There is no competition. The horse unites us," he wrote.

Inspiration

As these examples demonstrate, Sir Isaac Newton was correct when he wrote, "If I have seen further than others, it is by standing upon the shoulders of giants."

Luckily Long Rider history is filled with examples of travellers who drew inspiration from or were helped by their peers.

In 1938 James Wentworth Day became inspired to make his journey across England after having read the equestrian travel books of Long Riders William Cobbett, Arthur Young and George Borrow. When he wrote his own book, he acknowledged that he "had ridden in their hoofprints."

In 1907 newlyweds Quincy and Nell Scott rode 3,800 kilometres (2300 miles) from St. Paul Minnesota to Seattle on their honeymoon. When John and Lulu Beard planned to ride in the opposite direction in 1947, the Scotts offered them emotional support and this valuable advice.

"There are none who really know, as Nell and I do, how deep is the satisfaction of a journey like yours, as also how tough are some of the experiences that go with it. Rain, snow, hail, lightning, mosquitoes, rope burns, rattle-snakes, quicksand, dry camps and strayed mounts; we know the whole picture and are living it over with you."

One of the most remarkable examples of friendship occurred in 1964 when English Long Rider Bill Holt rode up to the door of the world-famous author Somerset Maugham. Having made his own equestrian exploration of Spain in the 1890s, Maugham had always loved horses. Now retired, the great writer was living in Cap Ferrat, France.

Holt later wrote that even though Maugham wasn't expecting him, the elderly Long Rider received him and his horse warmly.

"I arrived on his 91st birthday. When he saw Trigger Maugham smiled, came over to us, shook hands with me and asked about my horse," Holt wrote. "I am very fond of animals, he said. Always be good and kind to him. He gently caressed Trigger's nose. 'If I had known that a horse was coming to visit me this morning I would have dressed ready to mount. Do you mind if I give Trigger some sugar?' and then fed him."

The Last Enemy - Yourself

These are inspiring stories. But life isn't always filled with noble deeds or honourable people.

When he wrote his great classic on exploration in 1852, Francis Galton cautioned travellers to remember failure in travel could happen for a number of reasons. "An exploring expedition is daily exposed to a succession of accidents, any one of which might be fatal to its further progress."

While Galton was primarily concerned with avoiding prowling lions, he did not consider the ethical accidents that might befall the unwary traveller.

Few realize there is an invisible crevasse that lies across everyone's path

After having survived every sort of physical disaster, they are tempted to violate their conscience

Some compromise their honour day to day. Some fall prey to self-deceit. Some sell their souls.

The Final Trap

Every returning Long Rider can justly take pride in his accomplishments. But there is a thorn hidden under the rose.

Long ago a Sufi mystic wrote, "If you wish to find the hidden treasure destroy the castle of egotism."

That wise man understood that the lure of egotism attracts man like honey draws a bear. Self-centeredness is the weak point of man. It diverts a person away from that which is spiritual and leads him toward darkness and arrogance.

In an age when people use Twitter and Facebook to reveal their every secret, in an age when people will go on television and do anything to gain fame, Baron Fukushima serves as a beacon of modesty, strength, resolve, iron will, courage and dignity.

This marks the sign of one who is in touch with the centre of his soul and does not need the acclaim of the crowd to justify the meaning of his life.

This special ability is very important today, as we are sadly seeing a glorification of macho egotism.

Fame

Dr Johnson defined honour as "nobility of soul."

That nobility is endangered when a passion for fame becomes the primary motivation.

After completing his historic ride from Peking to India, Peter Fleming described how he and his companion Ella Maillart detested the media's attempts to exaggerate their equestrian accomplishments.

"We were united by an abhorrence of the false values placed – whether by its exponents or the age at large – on what can most conveniently be referred to by its trade name of Adventure. From an aesthetic rather than an ethical point of view, we were repelled by the modern tendency to exaggerate, romanticise, and at last cheapen out of recognition the ends of the earth and the deeds done in their vicinity."

Fleming understood that there is no subject on which people are more apt to deceive themselves than the lust for fame. He knew that the media can't be trusted to decide what is right or wrong; only his own conscience could make that decision.

Increasingly people are tempted to define their self-worth solely by their public visibility. Yearning to be noticed and admired, they lose touch with their morality by becoming uncontrollable narcissists.

Wisdom for Long Riders can be found in peculiar places, even the theatre.

Jeremy Irons is one of the few actors who won the Triple Crown of Acting, winning an Academy Award for film, an Emmy Award for television and a Tony Award for theatre. In a recent interview he expressed sadness by what he sees as young actors' ever-increasing drive to chase fame instead of good roles.

"I think that there is this idea that what you should go after is fame. That is a hugely mistaken idea because fame means absolutely nothing. This whole culture of wanting to become famous is a sign of a society that's lost its way and will only judge people as being valid if they're famous, which of course is all bullshit."

The first man to walk on the moon proved that if honour is to be effective it cannot be imposed from the outside. This incredible man knew that reputation may be an external judgement; but honour has to be an internal one.

A Cautionary Tale of Two Armstrongs

Is the journey about serving self or helping others?

The very notion of a hero has been distorted in today's modern world. But two men bearing the same last name help put things into perspective.

Each rose to the pinnacle of greatness within his respective field. Each handled fame and celebrity in exactly opposite ways. Neil Armstrong shunned it like poison. Lance Armstrong desired it so greatly that he cheated to get it.

Neil Armstrong made history on July 21, 1969 when he stepped onto the moon and said, "That's one small step for [a] man, one giant leap for mankind."

I joined an estimated 600 million people who witnessed that moment on television.

At the time no one gave much thought to why Armstrong had been chosen by NASA to become the first human to walk on the moon. Most simply assumed it was because he was an excellent pilot. What was not commonly known was that Armstrong was an intensely modest man. An intelligent, brave, humble, self-effacing and articulate man, he shunned publicity, seldom granted an interview, would not pose for photographs and refused to sell himself out to the media circus.

In the years after his famous flight, he handled fame with extraordinary good sense and dignity.

He died at the age of 82 while I was writing this book. I never dreamed of being an astronaut. In fact I've always been happy being no higher than the back of a horse. But Armstrong made the impossible seem attainable. If a regular fellow from Ohio could do that, then what might I achieve?

We need to understand that there is a difference between explorers and exploiters.

Neil Armstrong had nothing to prove to anyone.

Move forward into this new century and we can see ample evidence of a society that is addicted to the attainment of celebrity at any cost. Because of this the very notion of a hero has been distorted.

In stark contrast to the Astronaut Armstrong, Lance Armstrong is an example of a win-at-all-costs competitor who eagerly embraced the bogus cult of celebrity. Addicted to adulation, Armstrong was a fame-hungry "hero" who bullied and deceived his way to the top. Lance Armstrong desired it so greatly that he cheated to get it.

Though he won the Tour de France bicycle race a record seven consecutive times, he was later disqualified from all those races and banned from competitive cycling for life because of doping offences. When caught he issued a litany of disingenuous indignation.

Do we follow the example of the soft-spoken Armstrong who insisted he was only doing his job when he went to the Moon?

Or do we succumb to the siren's song of celebrity which led another Armstrong into the ethical wilderness?

Before he died during his last expedition to Antarctica, Sir Ernest Shackleton warned, "I think nothing of the world and the public. They cheer you one minute and howl you down the next. It is what in oneself and what one makes of one's life that matters."

Tim Cope understood the wisdom of Shackleton's words, when he wrote, "Although times change, we are faced with the same challenges and traps as travellers that existed in the past."

Both realized that after they were gone people would measure their lives and conclude that it wasn't about where they travelled as much as what they stood for.

Addicted to Adoration

In an earlier chapter I discussed the ethics of equestrian travel. That study focused mainly on the human's obligation to protect his horses. I have also written about how a traveller should not deceive the press or cheat the public.

But sadly there have been occasions when equestrian travellers have become so enamoured with fame that they have ignored, erased or censored information about other Long Riders. These acts of deception were made in an effort to make the traveller appear bigger, bolder and braver to the press and public.

Instead of using the ride as a portal to inner discovery it became a search for celebrity. Making a name took precedence over principle.

They had not heeded the advice of the noted explorer, Colonel John Blashford-Snell who stated, "He who believes his own publicity is heading for a fall."

Betraying Beck

Long Rider Lewis Freeman was the author of more than twenty travel books. He warned, "It is a callous traveller who, in strange lands and seas, does not render hearty homage to the better men that have gone before him."

As Freeman realized we have a responsibility to others. But not all honour it. Some practise self-delusion and deceit.

Fame can be a blessing and a curse. Once some people get a taste of it, they become addicted. Because fame fills some starving corner of their psyche, they are unwilling to share a crumb of recognition with another Long Rider.

One extraordinary example of this behaviour occurred in 2002 when an American man contacted me. Where, he asked, could he make an equestrian journey that would be of special historical significance?

I explained how George Beck and his three companions, the Overland Westerners, had completed an extraordinary equestrian journey to all 48 state capitals between the years 1912 to 1915. While the trip was astonishing, it was the devastating emotional result which gave it a special poignancy. Having arrived in San Francisco at the end of their fabulous ride, Beck and his friends mistakenly believed they would be greeted as heroes.

Instead they were ignored by the press. They were so broke they had to sell their horses and ride the train home to Shelton, Washington as hoboes. Beck later tried to write a book about the journey but failed. Despondent, the man who had ridden 33,000 kilometres (20,352 miles) fell down in the dark while walking home. He drowned in six inches of water.

Shortly after his death, Pinto, the extraordinary horse Beck had ridden during the entire course of the journey, was taken away to the Olympic Forest. He was put to work as a lowly pack horse, and like his master, passed away without receiving the honour or recognition that was due him.

When the American man spoke to me in 2002, I explained all this and suggested that if he wanted to undertake an epic ride, then visiting all 48 state capitals, and honouring George Beck would be a noteworthy achievement. He agreed to undertake the challenge. Thereafter the Guild located a suitable horse, which was named George Beck in honour of the dead hero. The Guild also created a special website for this trip and donated our services as webmasters. I personally contacted many state governors, urging them to meet the traveller when he arrived at their capital.

It all seemed to be going well, until as the miles had mounted, and the media increasingly smothered the traveller in attention, the American began to grow emotionally distant.

After having circled around a great portion of the nation, the traveller reached Olympia, the state capital of Washington. This was the first state building and governor which Beck and Pinto had visited during their great journey. Just as importantly, Shelton, the tiny village where Beck and the Overland Westerners had begun their magnificent journey was only 30 miles away from the capital.

During the course of the journey, I had been in constant contact with the city officials at Shelton, who were in turn anxious to honour "their" tragic Long Riders when the modern traveller rode in.

He never did.

Even though he had already ridden 10,000 miles during the journey, and only 30 miles separated him from visiting Beck's home, the traveller broke his word and rode away in the opposite direction from the very Long Riders who had put him in the saddle.

Thus Beck and Pinto were brutally dismissed by the traveller who had become addicted to public adulation.

Brotherhood or Commerce

Acknowledging the contribution of others is one of the keys to being a successful Long Rider.

Yet the concept of comradeship is the last thing on some people's minds.

An extraordinary example of this type of personal behaviour occurred on a deserted road in Syria.

The Swiss Long Riders Hans Jürgen and Claudia Gottet had set off in 1987 to make a 13,000 kilometre (8,000 mile) ride from Arabia to the Alps. The journey north had been hot, gruelling and lonely.

Imagine the Gottets surprise when they saw another equestrian traveller approaching them, riding south from the direction of nearby Turkey.

It was an extraordinary moment in modern equestrian travel history when these the two parties met on the deserted road. The Irishman was a well-known author who was riding from Paris to Jerusalem. In his subsequent book he erased the Gottets from his tale.

Like others, he was anxious to impress the public and the press with the false impression that he was first, the fastest, the bravest, etc.

Stunters

Sir Richard Burton wrote, "Man should seek honour, not honours."

That philosophy was enacted by a Long Rider whose journey should have made his name a household word, but who chose anonymity instead of celebrity.

Diamond Dick Tanner was the first man to ever attempt to ride around the world. After he crossed the United States in the 1880s, he stopped his journey in New York City, stepped down from the saddle and returned to his small Nebraska hometown, where he spent his life working as the local doctor. Diamond Dick was a hero of the Old West. He found the Long Quiet and then walked away; became a quiet country doctor and never discussed his past.

Unfortunately travel and exploration have long been populated by people whom the legendary English mountain climber, Wilfred Noyce, described as "stunters." In his book, *The Springs of Adventure*, he explained that the reason he risked his life he attempted to scale Mount Everest and other dangerous peaks was because, "What do I conquer? I conquer myself!"

What Noyce objected to were those individuals whose goal was merely to become famous. He provided one such example in his book.

"Those who go out in order to cull a reputation can be called stunters. In those happy days it was not so difficult to find something novel and exciting. In the 1890s it was sufficient to ride a bicycle around the world. John Foster Fraser and three companions did and wrote a book. 'We took this trip round the world on bicycles because we were more or less conceited, liked to be talked about and see our names in the newspapers'."

Aimé Tschiffely warned against what he called "headline grabbers." He cautioned the public to be wary of "vain men who have written so-called confessions to be sold to gullible readers".

Much of equestrian travel involves ritualistic behaviour. Some acts, like feeding and brushing, reach back to the dawn of man's relation to the horse. That is why, even though every modern Long Rider journeys in the present, he is always aware of the past.

And you would not think that anyone would pretend to the press and the public that "no one else would dare do this."

But you would be wrong.

Case in point is the Australian man who recently rode across the United States. The moment you visit his website, it opens by him singing to the sound of a twanging guitar.

"There's 330 million people in the USA and only one horseman dares to do what this man does. In the middle of nowhere, when there shouldn't be a soul in sight, the lone rider sits with a rifle by his side," he falsely claims.

Oh dear! We wouldn't want to disturb his fantasy by reminding him of petite Catherine Thompson who was riding through the wilderness of Canada at the same time. And let's not forget that Bernice Ende was close by, making her seventh consecutive ride in the United States and having ridden more than 20,000 miles without so much as a murmur.

Ah, but that type of information doesn't help a hustler. Hugging the road so he can be seen by the media and hogging the limelight is what the stunters are in search of.

It was Sir Richard Burton, again, who wisely wrote, "He knew it all by heart, but his heart knew none of it."

Ethical Exploration

There are other types of individuals who occasionally infest the equestrian travel world in an effort to aggrandize their ego or enlarge their bank account. The first clue is that their stories are chiefly concerned with the incredible dangers they supposedly survived.

One fellow claimed he was trailed by a mountain lion for four days. Another supposedly got lost in the Mojave Desert, and when he finally spotted a lone pool of water, he could tell it was poison by looking at it. Another wouldn't discuss his journey until he had seen the resumés of the North American Long Riders who offered to help him.

Nor is it only men who perpetrate these offences.

When Long Rider Ana Beker was making her ride from Argentina to Canada in 1952, she was shadowed in El Salvador by an impostor named Barbarita Ricci. The interference became so annoying that the Argentine ambassador issued a statement in the national press which explained the fraud. "The said Senora Ricci is neither an Argentine citizen nor did she leave the Argentine Republic to undertake the ride in question."

More recently a South African woman boasted that she was going to re-ride Tschiffely's journey from Argentina to New York. Armed with a photocopy of his book as a guide, she set off on a journey filled with dubious actions. Instead of following Tschiffely's route north, she turned east into Brazil. There she put her horse on a boat and floated him across the country, claiming that there were no roads in Brazil. She attempted to enter Mexico illegally. When border guards detected her, she fled back into Guatemala. There she left her horse, flew over Mexico, landed in the United States, obtained another horse and proceeded north. Two horses had died prior to her arrival in New York City; nevertheless she was quick to enlist the press to trumpet her accomplishment.

For some, the desire to undertake an equestrian journey is a false display of ruggedness. Those are the ones who stress the hardships.

They prove that the accumulation of miles is no guarantee of success. The horse can never deliver them for the true goal of the journey will forever elude them. They will never arrive. Their journey is endless because, being blind, they never truly set out.

A real Long Rider comes back not with tales of suffering but with an address book filled with the names of new friends.

In his book *As a Man Thinketh*, James Allen wrote, "Circumstance does not make the man; it reveals him to himself."

Filipe Leite understood the true value of the journey he had made. After he stepped down from the saddle, he wrote, "To be a Long Rider is to not be afraid to ride into the unknown; to face your greatest fears and to live out your dreams. In a world where people follow the herd more and more, the Long Ride shows that there is another path to be followed. It is not the path that has been beaten down by the stampede of all those who crossed it before. It is a path full of problems, emotions, but also happiness. It is a path that leads to a life worth living. You don't take that path for a piece of paper but for yourself, for your soul, for the lessons that will be learned. My Long Ride has given me moments and memories I will carry with me forever."

The Value of Virtue

The heritage of generations speaks to us in a half-lost language.

Socrates chastised the Athenians for loving riches more than honour.

Long Rider Messanie Wilkins was the daughter of a simple Maine farmer who lacked much education. But she was wise enough to say, "Being greedy had always been against the grain with me. I didn't intend to change my character for profit."

The ancient Greek philosopher and the farmer's daughter both had a moral compass that allowed them to understand that the only way to make your ride unique is to see it as an inner journey, where the actual benefit is to you as a person.

Chivalry in a New Age

The concept of a mounted brotherhood is nothing new

Genghis Khan didn't inherit a kingdom. He founded his equestrian empire by obtaining the loyalty of nineteen men from nine different tribes, including Christians, Muslims, Buddhists and Shamans. Yet their mutual commitment and loyalty transcended kinship, ethnicity and religion.

Thus throughout history, mounted men have attempted to recognize the finer qualities in their lives.

In Europe chivalry, whose root word is "cheval" (horse), was seen as the guardianship of the concepts of wisdom, sincerity, benevolence, courage and generosity.

In Islam the Sufis developed a similar spiritual path known as *futuwwah*, which was an attempt to foster true fraternity among mounted men.

Likewise in Japan the samurai adhered to the corresponding concept known as *bushido*.

But has honour waned since the era of horses passed? Is nobility a birthright or is it defined by one's actions?

Events throw light on the character of Long Riders, past and present, which demonstrate that they are striving for perfection, not pretence.

New Zealand Long Rider Ian Robinson has made challenging solo rides in Mongolia, Tibet and Afghanistan.

He wrote, "Although it is fine at times to be praised by others and congratulated on an achievement, if this is our main concern then we lessen what we have done. One wonders how many great adventurers there are and have been but their exploits are unknown to all but a few, and just because no one knows doesn't reduce the accomplishment and the pride. Modesty is still a valued quality."

After his life-threatening ride across the Libyan Desert in 1923, Sir Ahmed Mohammed Hassanein wrote, "I crave no statue in a public street or a page of history to enshrine my name."

He realized "how few will understand" but looking back on his dangerous journey Hassanein remarked that he had not gone in search of gold or fame but to find a place where "there were no footsteps but my own and my thoughts were my treasures."

Summary

Clay Marshall didn't ride as far as many have done, but he learned more than most.

"I want people to learn from my mistakes. I have learned more about horses in the last three months than the rest of my life combined. I know now just how naïve I truly was prior to this trip. I want to share my experiences, mistakes, and lessons learned with anyone who might listen."

Along the way he learned that Long Riders are Comrades not Competitors and that at the end of the day what matters is personal validation.

It's not enough to strive for mere miles. Mastery of technique is an empty vessel.

We don't want to beat the Baron and Aimé. The true goal is to strive to be like them.

During his long and illustrious military career, Baron Fukushima was awarded many medals for bravery including the Order of the Sacred Treasure by the Emperor of Japan, the Order of the Red Eagle by the Kaiser of Germany, the French Legion of Honour, the Grand Star of Austria and was made a Knight Commander by the Queen of England. Yet despite these acclaims he remained a paragon of modesty and virtue.

The practice of aiding other Long Riders remains alive today. Hideyo Tsutsumi, (seen holding the Guild flag) is the first Japanese Member of the Long Riders' Guild. He is acting as the mentor of Kohei Yamakawa, who is attempting the first modern equestrian journey across Japan.

Diamond Dick Tanner was the first man to ever attempt to ride around the world. After he concluded that journey in the 1880s, he stepped down from the saddle, returned to his small Nebraska hometown, where he spent his life working as the local doctor.

Long Rider history is filled with examples of travellers who drew inspiration from or were helped by their peers. Don Roberto Cunninghame Graham (left) was instrumental in helping Aimé Tschiffely get his equestrian travel book published.

In 1907 newlyweds Nell and Quincy Scott rode 3,800 kilometres (2300 miles) from St. Paul Minnesota to Seattle on their honeymoon. When John and Lulu Beard planned to ride in the opposite direction in 1947, the Scotts offered them emotional support and valuable advice.

During his epic journey from the tip of Patagonia to the top of Alaska, Russian Long Rider Vladimir Fissenko (right) met renowned explorer Thor Heyerdahl in Peru. The world-famous author spent the day riding with Vladimir and urged him to press on with the difficult journey.

One of the Founding Members of the Long Riders' Guild was Marshal Ralph Hooker (right). He had made several important rides in the 1950s and at 95 years old was the world's oldest equestrian traveller when CuChullaine O'Reilly organized the first international meeting of equestrian explorers.

Captain Otto Schwarz (left) rode 48,000 kilometres (30,000 miles) on horseback across five continents, making him the most well-travelled Long Rider of the 20th century. Yet he was always eager to assist other Long Riders. He is seen showing fellow Swiss Long Rider Basha O'Reilly various maps of his journeys.

The concept of comradeship was demonstrated by English Long Rider Alistair Boyd. He had ridden across Spain in the early 1960s, only to become so enchanted with the country that he has spent the rest of his life riding and writing in Don Quixote country. When American Long Rider Katherine Boone came across Spain in 2001 Boyd hosted her.

When Edouard Chautard and Carine Thomas(right) set off to ride Australia's Bicentennial National Trail, they received valuable assistance and advice from Australian Long Riders Sharon and Ken Roberts (left), the first people to ever ride the length of the BNT.

In the early 1970s British Long Rider Gary Davies (right) was taught about equestrian travel by legendary Welsh Long Rider Thurlow Craig. At the conclusion of his 9,500 kilometre (6,000 mile) ride from Mongolia to Hungary, Australian Long Rider Tim Cope came to London in 2007. There he was congratulated by Gary and other Long Riders.

After surviving a perilous ride through Central Afghanistan in 2005, French Long Rider Louis Meunier (right) acted as mentor when New Zealand Long Rider Ian Robinson rode into the remote Wakhan Corridor in 2008.

Beginning in 2005, British Long Rider Jakki Cunningham (left) has led three equestrian expeditions from the south of France to England. In each journey young adults, such as Luke Tucker are taught how to become Long Riders.

Robin and Louella Hanbury-Tenison (right) are Founding Members of the Guild who epitomize the concept that Long Riders are Comrades not Competitors. They hosted British Long Rider William Reddaway when he made a unique journey to the four corners of England, during which he visited 30 historic cathedrals and abbeys.

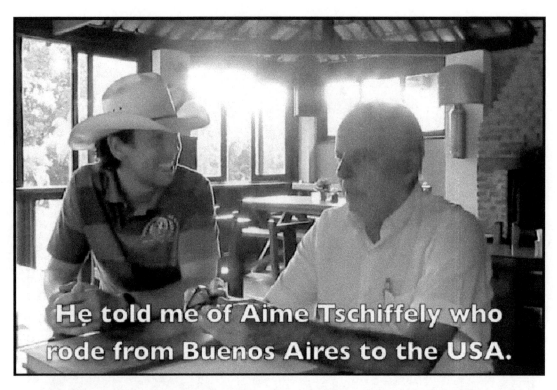

Brazilian Long Rider Pedro Luis de Aguiar (right) was inspired by Aimé Tschiffely and later made a record ride in South America. When Filipe Leite set out in 2012 to ride from Canada to Brazil, Pedro was one of the many Long Riders from around the world who mentored the young traveller.

Epilogue
The Future of Equestrian Travel

For 6,000 years the relationship between horses and humans has been one of the key factors in mankind's progress. It is an extraordinary success story of inter-species integration.

While it is true that the distant echoes of the past permeate this book, equestrian travel is not a stagnant relic but a vibrant work-in-progress. It is a topic which is not solely dedicated to the narrow study of where we came from but the exciting idea of where posterity will ride to.

Like our Long Rider ancestors, we still have to face paradoxes in life. But because circumstances vary through the ages we must ask new questions. To comprehend what may come we must acknowledge how recent events have shaped our immediate environment and what problems may be lurking round the corner.

I am not comfortable portraying myself as an equestrian Nostradamus. Nor do I wish to aspire to the role of futurist as exemplified by H.G. Wells. However during the course of normal equestrian research I began to detect a pattern among apparently disconnected events. This pattern, if carried to its logical conclusion and then ignored, might result in widespread equestrian suffering and dampen the cause of equestrian travel. Hence my decision to publish this brief review of recent historical facts and events, in the hope that my conclusions, though yet to be fully confirmed, might serve as a warning to Long Riders in the future.

The Dawning of a new Age

No one realized at the time that the inaugural parades of two American presidents would have such a symbolic resonance.

William Taft was elected president in 1908 and rode to his inauguration in a horse-drawn carriage. Four years later, his successor Woodrow Wilson chose to travel the same route in an automobile.

These two journeys represented the oncoming shift of the 20th century American horse world, though few at the time realized what they were witnessing.

In 1890 millions of horses, ponies and mules were employed in America. They worked on farms aiding agriculture. They toiled in cities delivering goods and people. They strained to maintain contact with the remote parts of the country. There were an estimated 30,000 horse-drawn fire wagons alone, each of which employed at least three horses.

The United States horse population reached its peak of 21,550,000 animals in 1918.

Consequently, by the time President Wilson stepped into his automobile, equine-related occupations or services influenced the majority of American's lives. By 1930 less than one-third of the nation's equines remained alive.

The advent of inexpensive automobiles and tractors at the dawning of the 20th century had combined to create an unprecedented equinocide.

Hollywood to the Rescue

The cycle of events shapes each generation.

With the loss of horses as agricultural implements, allies in the theatre of war and as companions in exploration, men began a fifty-year migration away from the saddle, preferring instead to seek personal adventure and outdoor activity elsewhere. Yet a resurgent interest in horses was about to be ignited by an unlikely ally.

In a deliberate attempt to capitalize on a growing sense of national nostalgia, the emergent television industry created an unprecedented cinematic wave of black-and-white western programs. This calculated marketing ploy resulted in a record 39 different cowboy shows flooding into American homes during 1959. With names like

Maverick, Rawhide, Cheyenne, Gunsmoke and Lawman, an impressionable audience of first-generation children television viewers were subjected to fantasy equine tales starring Trigger, Silver and Champion.

Sensing the potential profit, Hollywood followed suit during the subsequent decades by generating movies, such as National Velvet, My Friend Flicka and the Black Stallion, wherein horses were depicted as personal rescuers, best friends and emotional surrogates, not as domestic drudges or disposable military commodities.

As the values expressed in this high-calorie diet of Hollywood hot-house cinematic equine fantasy took hold, this generation of American children unknowingly become part of the emergence of 20th century post-domestic horse ownership, one wherein horses were increasingly viewed for their emotional rather than practical value.

Decades of Fertility

The once-young television viewers of the 1950s became collectively known as the Baby Boomer generation. When they reached maturity, they gained the financial independence and disposable income necessary for them to devote their excess cash-flow into turning children's equine fantasies into personal horse ownership.

This rise in private pleasure horse riders resulted in Americans bestowing a new definition to its equine population. Whereas many 19th century Americans had viewed the horse as a working animal, modern Americans begin viewing their horses instead as a representation of personal prestige, social distinction and historical affiliation.

Few of these animals served any practical or traditional purpose, i.e. travelling, ploughing, logging, wagon pulling or war. They were instead employed by Baby Boomer owners, who having grown up on cinematic tales of Roy Rogers and the Lone Ranger, had bought horses because they were increasingly viewed as status symbols, emotional allies, companion animals, sporting competitors or endangered links to a mythological Western past.

Ironically by the mid-20th century equestrian travel was on the verge of extinction, with fewer than a dozen journeys being made during the 1950s around the world.

All the while as horses began to be viewed as personal adornments, a corresponding massive increase in amateur back-yard breeders resulted in a significant spike in the American equine population, thereby reversing the decline in equine population brought about by the advent of the automotive age. By 2006 there were an estimated 9,924,000 horses in the United States.

Thus in the last decades of the 20th century the American horse population enjoyed years of unfettered fecunddity as the Baby Boomer generation graduated from being individual owners of single horses into enthusiastic amateur breeders of large privately-owned horse herds.

There were 78 million American Baby Boomers born between 1946 and 1964. The success of their ranchette lifestyle was reliant upon several financial, climatic and social factors, none of which appeared to be in any danger of declining. Yet much like the unforeseen demise of the era of cheap gasoline, Baby Boom Breeders did not predict that changes in the climatic, social and political arenas might eventually bring about personal financial hardship based upon their previous equestrian decisions.

Changing Social Needs

Regardless of any one horse breed's popularity, with the dawning of the new 21st century a shift in equine desire began to be noted among the aging Baby Boomer population, now known as the Grey Wave. The year 2008 was a banner retirement year, as the oldest Boomers reached 62 and began collecting Social Security benefits.

As their physical abilities and youthful equestrian fantasies were replaced by diminished physical capabilities and ageing bodies, a dramatic decline was noted in terms of the popularity of show events. One contributing factor may be attributed to aging female Baby Boomers, many of whom were now grandmothers, and who felt a decreased desire to compete in the fashion- and body-conscious ring against a younger generation.

Meanwhile, subsequent generations of younger American females, did not share their predecessors' limited social options or view horses as being a statement of social privilege. This further decreased the general need for all horses.

Shifting Demographics

Humans have spent more than 99% of their time on earth in non-industrial societies. In 1900, less than a sixth of the world's 1.5 billion people dwelt in cities; yet by 2050 70% of humanity will be urban.

As humans become increasingly sedentary, the importance of horses has been further reduced by the overall decline in the number of people who have any desire to be involved with horses on a regular basis.

New Zealand is one example. By the 1880s New Zealanders had six times as many horses per capita as Britons; one for every three people in New Zealand compared to one for every 18 in Britain. But membership in the New Zealand Pony Club has steadily declined with membership today being about half of what it was 15 years ago.

This growth of urbanization did not go unnoticed by the Long Riders' Guild.

In 2005 my wife Basha and I were invited to a confidential meeting with the Director of the British Horse Society. He had asked us to come and discuss how the Guild saw the future of the English horse world.

Our journey to his office took us through the ancient city of Coventry. Because we took a wrong turning, we ended up in an economically-depressed area. It was largely inhabited by Indians and Pakistanis, the vast majority of whom were dressed in traditional South Asian clothes such as turbans and burkas.

When we met the Director, and he asked us about Britain's equestrian future, I described the urban scene we had just stumbled across. How, I asked him, was he going to make horses appeal to those people?

He had no answers. Instead of discussing the possibility that a massive social change was well under way in England, the group's leaders decided to focus instead on continuing to broadcast the message which had been originally formulated by the traditional, tweed-coated, fox-hunting, land-owning, Tory conservatives which had formed the organization.

As a result their influence is restricted to an increasingly marginalized portion of the overall British population.

A Lost Generation

It wasn't only Coventry which had lost interest in horses. As the new century began to advance experts in various fields expressed collective alarm at the manner in which children's lives had been radically altered in so short a time.

Even before computers became common household objects, George Orwell had warned, "The trend of the age was away from creative communal amusements and toward solitary mechanical ones."

That sad prophecy has been fulfilled in homes and play grounds around the world.

In 1970 40 percent of all American children walked to school; now fewer than 12 percent do. In Great Britain the area in which children may roam without supervision has decreased by almost 90% since the 1970s. Numerous countries report the rapid decline in outdoor hobbies. And a study released in 2014 by Britain's National Trust revealed that fewer than one in ten children regularly play in wild places compared to almost half a generation ago, a third have never climbed a tree and one in ten can not ride a bicycle.

Instead of playing and pretending outside, children have been engulfed by new technologies and immersed in a relentless barrage of electronic imagery which is impossible for them to ignore. The result is that the majority of children prefer to stay indoors. In Great Britain, for example, eleven- to fifteen-year-olds now spend, on average, half their waking time in front of some sort of screen. Other countries report that their children devote an average of 42 days a year online.

The result is young people are increasingly disengaged with the natural world and a generation of "manchines" are largely ignorant of the joy of unbridled exploration.

We do not need to criticize the benefits of electric marvels; but we need to realize that children need to be encouraged to actively participate in the outdoor world as well.

This disconnection from nature is not only linked to the advance of the Internet age. There has been an increase in the social philosophy of "risk aversion," wherein well-meaning adults in authority discourage children from playing and exploring in the natural world. Whereas previous generations were free to frolic outside for hours, or ride their pony in search of adventure, nowadays the activity of children is increasingly structured by fearful parents and restrictive teachers.

Riding horses builds self-confidence and courage. It teaches children to accept responsibility. It also encourages love, not only for the horse, but for nature itself. Sadly this new culture of timidity has adapted a safety-first attitude for children that has drained the world of any hint of risk, leaving a flat sameness.

Luckily France has recognized the importance of introducing horses and nature into the lives of children. The nation has launched an operation entitled "Pony School" whose goal is to welcome 250,000 children to discover ponies and equitation.

While that is an encouraging sign, other factors have also undermined the strength of the global equestrian world.

The End of Easy Money

While things were changing at the playground, other painful adjustments were also occurring at the work place.

The rise of late 20th century equine sporting events was linked to the public availability of the personal horse trailer, the affordable pickup truck and the presence of cheap gas.

In 1970 a gallon of gasoline sold for .40 cents in the United States. By 2008 the cost had increased until the average price per U.S. gallon reached a high of $4.11. A new 1971 Chevrolet pickup truck cost $2,229. In 2015 the Chevrolet pickup truck costs $26,105.

While costs increased, the crash of the financial sector and an extended recession brought increased unemployment. Falling real-estate and stock markets eroded personal savings, all of which further undermined individual efforts to maintain the expensive privilege of owning horses.

Climatic Challenges

While these financial ordeals were taking place, another unexpected threat emerged to threaten the American equestrian status quo: Mother Nature.

The world was stunned when an area of the Arctic sea ice twice the size of Great Britain melted and then disappeared over a couple of weeks in 2007. The following year the same thing happened again.

Further south, increasingly hotter summers and long periods of drought affected the physical environment of the equestrian world.

Due to global warming and a drought brought on by climatic changes, America's once bountiful and cheap hay suffered an unexpected reverse. As supplies declined severely, hay prices reached the record price of ten dollars a bale in parts of America.

As long-term drought dried up grazing land and drove up hay prices, ranchers sold off huge portions of their herds because they couldn't afford to buy food for the animals. In Wellington, Colorado, one rancher reported that $5,000 worth of hay was stolen from his field during the Labour Day weekend.

The decrease in America's once inexpensive and plentiful basic equine food left many of the nation's horses starving or living on reduced rations.

In the early summer of 2012 I sent emails to Long Riders, either on journeys or residing in various parts of the United States. Could they, I asked, observe and confirm my suspicions that the weather had become unseasonably hot. And had this, I wondered, impacted equestrian travel conditions? The reports they sent back left no doubt. The country was being baked alive. As a result the price of hay was sky high and it became harder for Long Riders to find grass and water while travelling.

A Changing Horse-World

The decline and eventual climax of 20th century benefits which had governed the modern equestrian world for decades resulted in a devastating and radical alteration of practices. The implications were soon clear and appeared in the most basic parts of the horse's life.

In Great Britain, for example, a continued poor economic climate has meant that horses, which can cost up to £100 per week to look after, are suffering as people cut back on veterinary costs, routine care, shelter and feed. Organisations have reported a rise in hoof and worm problems, as horse owners cut costs by reducing veterinary checks.

Continued higher prices on hay have reduced the numbers of new people who might be tempted to get involved with such an expensive animal.

When people have to decide between feeding their kids and feeding their horses, the horse will always lose. In 2010 I predicted a dramatic increase in the number of abandonment cases. Sadly, I've been proved all too accurate.

Abandoned Horses

As expendable income plummeted so did the demand for horses.

In the United States the Equine Welfare Alliance released a comprehensive analysis of the various economic forces that had caused major shrinkage of the horse industry in recent years. The study analyzed the cost of alfalfa, grass hay, corn and gasoline as well as the impact of the extended recession. The study concluded that these factors had resulted in a 50% reduction in foal registrations in all breed registries.

Nor did nostalgia still exert its traditional strong appeal.

The American government has an estimated 47,000 wild horses living on federal land. But only 5,400 had been adopted by 2005

As prices plummeted, websites and newspapers began to run a new type of advertisement. Page after page of horses were being offered for free to a good home by people desperate to find an emotional solution to a new type of equine crisis.

Among the hundreds of examples listed was a Thoroughbred gelding named Wall Street. His owner listed him as a "recession casualty."

"One owner! Hand raised from birth. Hunter jumper trained. Sweet and loving gelding. Lost my job and my husband's job too. Wall Street loves attention. He retired in 2008 from showing but loves to trail ride and has been turned out since then. I want him to have a good and loving home. He is very close to my heart but I can't pay my bills."

On both sides of the Atlantic equine rescue operations began documenting yearly increases in equine abandonment. In 2009 the Washington, D.C. based Unwanted Horse Coalition estimated 170,000 to 180,000 horses had been abandoned in that country.

Conditions continued to deteriorate. In 2014 the Irish media reported horses could not be sold for £5. That same year the town of Bridgend, Wales was overrun by a pack of 250 horses which had been abandoned by gypsies who could not afford to feed the animals and let them loose in the countryside.

With more equines than were actually needed, a combination of global economic meltdown, irresponsible breeding, spiralling bills, and rock-bottom sale prices resulted in untold thousands of horses and ponies being abandoned or suffering from neglect.

Thus, the mythology of the last fifty years has brought the modern equine population to a level of unpredicted growth and unprecedented danger, one wherein hundreds of thousands of horses are going to suffer in the immediate future as the brutalities of the free market force individual horse owners to make painful personal, national and cultural choices, all the while horses will increasingly be seen not only as a financial liability but also a potential legal target if charges of animal abuse are brought against the financially-burdened owner.

In addition, Long Riders will be facing other serious problems in the immediate future.

Disconnect with Nature

Horses have accompanied our species for thousands of years. Because of its charisma and beauty mankind has embraced the horse, treating it as a universal totem with iconic power.

On a more practical level, at the dawn of the last century horses were a part of most people's lives, even if they did not work with them directly. Large numbers of people were employed by companies that used horses. Household goods such as coal, milk and ice were delivered by horse-drawn wagons.

As horses were increasingly removed from the modern world, there has been a corresponding severance from the natural world by an increasing portion of humanity. This serves to illustrate how over the span of a century things have changed in terms of everyday interaction with nature and the animal kingdom.

The population of the countryside is decreasing annually. An unforeseen side-effect of this migration to an urbanized commodity culture is the loss of traditional wisdom.

For example, a recent survey revealed that 60% of British adults could not identify an oak tree.

Nor is other evidence lacking. A story reached the Guild of a teacher who had elementary students that did not know the difference between a cow, sheep or a pig. These children have never seen meat that isn't wrapped in plastic. They have lost generations of genetic fear of large hungry predators.

As urbanization increases, and the majority of humans find themselves residing in cities, the numbers of people who ride, for any reason whatsoever, will continue to decline.

Health

This is all the more worrying because humanity's collective health is cause for serious concern.

While physical activity has decreased, calorie intake has dramatically increased. Brazil has moved from hunger to obesity in less than a generation. England reports that more than a fifth of that nation's adults are obese. And worldwide, the number of obese people surpassed the 800 million who are estimated to be malnourished.

Long Rider authors in the 19th century, such as John Codman and Daniel Slade, repeatedly advocated the physical benefits of what was then termed equestrianopathy.

"No exercise can compare with that of horseback riding," Slade wrote.

Horse riding is not merely a unique recreational activity, it is also tremendously healthy. Yet in an age when humans should be seeking the saddle to protect their physical condition, ever greater numbers pass a lifetime without having ever ridden or even interacted with a horse.

Political

Whereas all of the challenges and changes I have mentioned are of grave concern, our most serious apprehension may be the decreasing amount of liberty which Long Riders face around the world.

Throughout history Long Riders have often been social dissidents. They don't like to be controlled. They are highly individualistic. They enjoy the freedom to roam at will. They aren't afraid of speaking their mind. They are a potent symbol of personal independence, resistance to oppression and defiance of the power of the state.

Two examples spring to mind.

In the late 18th century William Cobbett was exiled from England because of his political views. Upon his eventual return in the 1820s Cobbett set out on horseback to make a series of personal tours through the English countryside. His book, *Rural Rides*, was an exposé which enraged the political establishment.

After spending his youth riding across the pampas of Argentine, Robert Cunninghame Graham returned to Great Britain. There he became an outspoken Member of Parliament who supported the civil rights of workers, women and minorities. When the government suppressed the rights of free speech and freedom of assembly in 1887, "Don Roberto" led a protest at Trafalgar Square which resulted in him being badly beaten by the police and incarcerated in Pentonville Prison.

Throughout history totalitarian regimes have realized that horses presented a potent political threat. A tyrannical system is designed to keep people close to home, where they can be kept under tight social, political and geographic control. Horses threaten to undermine this oppression. People who can ride might travel without permission. Riding might encourage the growth of resistance. Rebellion might be spread via the saddle.

Oliver Cromwell certainly understood this. After he conquered Ireland in the 17th century, he quickly passed a law forbidding Irishmen to own a horse valued at more than £5. This instantly destroyed any hope of a mounted opposition or of travel.

Stalin was no friend of horses. After seizing control of all private farmland, his ambitious goal was to create an enormous agricultural collective. The first step was to confiscate every animal larger than a chicken. Horses were no exception. They were forcibly taken from the people and placed into state-controlled farms. In 1928 he passed a law making it illegal for private individuals to own a horse.

Nor were other dictators slow to follow this lesson.

Enver Hoxha made it illegal for Albanians to own and ride horses. More recently, the Iranian government passed a law forbidding Kurds to own and ride horses.

Popular culture reflects painful lessons from our political past, as the film series, *Planet of the Apes*, demonstrates. If a tyrant, be he an ape or a man, wants to subjugate, dominate and control a frightened civilian population, they must be kept unarmed, on foot and under constant surveillance.

Long Riders represent an alternative to the world of urban power. They are a potent symbol of personal liberty, resistance to oppression and defiance of the power of the state.

Unfortunately equestrian emancipation is under various types of attack. In previous chapters I have explained how the nation of Panama has effectively blockaded equestrian travel between North and South America. But there are other types of governmental threats.

The City of Los Angeles is encouraging equestrians to license their animals; whereas the City of Paris has made it illegal to ride a horse within the city limits.

Another case in point is how it is illegal for people to ride on the Appalachian Trail in the United States. Even though this famous American trail was laid out in the 1930s by two horsemen, and was funded by the federal government, it is now illegal for a horseman to ride on the trail.

National and state parks in that nation are also increasingly hostile to equestrian travellers.

One of the most draconian measures occurred in Romania in 2007 when legislators banned horse-drawn carts from the roads. The result was that thousands of horses were thrown out of work. Many were then abandoned and left to starve. Others were sold to abattoirs and eventually made their way illegally into the European food chain.

Certain themes run through mankind's history. One is the on-going struggle between authoritarianism versus individualism.

It was the Italian dictator Mussolini who said, "All within the state, nothing outside the state, and nothing against the state."

More recently the political whistle-blower Edward Snowden warned, "It's going to get worse with the next generation who extend the capabilities of this sort of architecture of oppression."

Despite tyranny, suspicion, intolerance and institutional hostility, there are a few brave souls bred in every generation who will not be suppressed, dismounted or extinguished. Long Riders represent an ancient flame that endures. Yet as politicians and securocrats increase their powers of surveillance, the liberty of future generations of equestrian travellers will be increasingly threatened.

Ancient Questions – Consistent Answers

In the face of such depressing events one might be tempted to conclude that equestrian travel was an activity doomed to extinction. You would be wrong.

While it is true that human destiny is fragile and uncertain; it is equally correct to acknowledge that the union of the horse and human carried our ancestors out of savagery through barbarism into civilization.

Old generations died off and new ones populated the earth. But through the mists of time a consistent message was transmitted through the ages. Nothing could interrupt or even delay its appearance among a chosen few in each generation.

This was not the wisdom of any one sedentary civilisation. This was the practical equestrian knowledge, passed on to us by the people of the past who had mastered the magnificent art of conquering space here on Earth.

In their continual mounted wanderings, they roamed from continent to continent, from one climatic extremity to another. They were not meek and obedient instruments of the state. They were never willing to stand in place, were not paralyzed by belief or left immobile from a lack of personal courage. They were subject to a gnawing restlessness.

Paradoxically, while so much of the past has disappeared, their spirit has survived.

The Dawning of a New Equestrian Era

For centuries horses and humans have upheld each other in this darkening world. Now their mutual courage is called upon again. That is because humankind still yearns to fulfil its ageless longing to explore and the horse is still the answer.

The present problems facing the world of equestrian travel come out of the womb of the past. Yet the story of equestrian travel is not fixed in time or rooted in place. As circumstances change, every generation has created a new version of equestrian travel in its own image. Every Long Rider has been called upon to follow his own quest.

The wise eye of history proves the need to safeguard the heritage of centuries and the future of individualism. As always, equestrian travel will remain a cradle of old values and a nursery of new ideas.

But how do we balance the lessons of the past with the problems of the present? We cannot afford to look back at times of yore for answers. It's not about where we've been. It's about where we are going.

Revelation is an ongoing process and it is the responsibility of the next generation to continue the process of discovery.

One example of this is connected to the most famous Long Rider of all time.

At the conclusion of his ride across England and Scotland in 1932, Aimé Tschiffely wrote in his book, *Bridle Paths*, about the urgent need for the horsemen of Great Britain to "put their heads together" and create maps showing bridle paths and tracks in their respective neighbourhoods. "These rough sketches could later be compiled and made into a general map."

Tschiffely also foresaw the need to form an "Equestrian Touring Club." His idea served as one of the inspirations for the Long Riders' Guild which has now spread via a tremendous groundswell to more than forty countries.

Harmonious Horsemanship

And what of our friend, the horse?

No one can deny that the horse has played a pivotal role in human events.

With the disappearance of the cavalry and the demise of the plough, humanity is faced with a dilemma. What do we do with the horse? Breed it to be admired as an ornament? Exploit it as a disposable piece of sports equipment? Ride it in circles like a goldfish in a bowl? Or continue to explore the world as our ancestors before us did?

For too long the horse has been dominated by the purse not the spirit.

As fewer human beings ride, those that do are increasingly representatives of the world's rich and elite.

Billionaire Bill Gates spent $1 million to encourage his 15-year-old daughter's ambition to participate in equestrian competitions. Among various expenses, Gates leased four elite jumping horses for $50,000 to $75,000 each for the girl to ride.

Likewise dressage is not for the faint of wallet. The daughter of the billionaire New York Mayor Michael Bloomberg competes and the wife of American presidential candidate Mitt Romney has spent a fortune in the sport.

Nor should we overlook how a Thoroughbred colt named Forestry, which had never taken part in any race, recently sold for a record $16 million.

The riders of tomorrow need to be told that the horse is not just for the rich and privileged. It is not a symbol of elitism and wealth.

The horse is for everyone and what is needed is a spirit of healing horsemanship whose essential law must be: thou shalt not hurt the horse. What is needed is a confident horse, one without fear. What is required is obtaining the horse's cooperation rather than dominating him. What is sought is the understanding that you don't control him; he changes you.

Long Riders such as Doug Preston have proved that the ancient practice of "one horse, one human, one journey," is still capable of transforming lives.

Doug wrote, "The horse was not bred for the arena. The true rider and the true horse are created, not in the training ring, but in the mountains, deserts, and forests of our great world. When horse and rider journey thousands of miles together and must trust each other with their very lives – that is when true rapport begins. When horse and rider have to ask from each other more than they can give – that is when they reach a level of understanding and empathy that goes beyond words. Only through long-distance travel can horse and rider find the true measure of their courage and endurance. This is the essence of the horse tradition of our ancestors and one that the Long Riders' Guild has brought back from the brink of extinction."

Difficult Times Require Hope

A wise man once said, "Life is a journey! Complete it."

To complete the journey one must first realise that more than physical challenges will await you.

The remote country of Bhutan has provided a startling example of a fundamental shift in national philosophy. The country has rejected the concept of measuring the nation's wealth on GDP (gross domestic production). Bhutan has instead embraced the idea of encouraging GNH (gross national happiness) as a way to evaluate the spiritual, physical, social and environmental health of its citizens and natural environment.

Thakur Singh Powdyel, Bhutan's minister of education, said, "You cannot have a prosperous nation in the long run that does not conserve its natural environment or take care of the wellbeing of its people."

Though the nation may be small, it is implementing the Buddhist teachings about living in harmony with all sentient beings.

His Highness, Charles, the Prince of Wales is another strong advocate for change.

In his book, *Harmony*, the Prince delved into how modern man had lost touch with the forces of nature, had been deceived into believing that consumerism would provide happiness and needed to alter decades of destructive practices in order to save our endangered planet.

"I sense a growing unease and anxiety in people's souls," he wrote, "an unease that still remains largely unexpressed."

The purpose of his book was "to chart what I believe is a fascinating journey from the ancients' understanding of harmony through to a present time when that wisdom has been blown apart by our rush for modernity."

"Although we stand on the brink of considerable ecological upheaval that may spell catastrophe, there are still opportunities to forge a new way forward. This could be a hugely rich period of opportunity. This renaissance could take place during the twenty-first century – if we draw on the ancient knowledge of Nature and on the timeless wisdom that today survives in isolated pockets. The renaissance that is starting to unfold is a flower that needs nurturing and is still a delicate thing.

Harmony between people and the rest of Nature is not simply a philosophical or ethical matter. It is a fundamental, practical and economic priority, but is not seen this way because of the way we have come to measure progress. The proper aim of man is to live in agreement with Nature. To live in agreement with Nature is to live virtuously and to live virtuously is to live happily."

In a summary which might have been written especially for future Long Riders, Prince Charles warned, "We cannot solve the problems of the twenty-first century with the world view of the twentieth century. What I'm saying is that any meaningful response to the crisis of our time has to begin on the individual level, with changes in our own lives."

As the Prince has pointed out, we live in times of great consequence. That is why, even though political ideologies may come in and out of fashion, what remains consistent is mankind's ongoing search for harmony in our lives and in the saddle.

Summary

To understand the immense emotional power of the horse, let me leave you with a story from Russia. When my wife, Basha, rode across the former Soviet Union in 1995 people were astonished to see a woman in the saddle, as that had been a man's privilege for several generations.

In 2014, after having lived her life under Communist repression, Agrafena Vasilyevna, an 80-year-old Russian woman stole her neighbour's horse so that she could go riding before she died. After riding across country for an hour, she returned to find the police waiting for her.

Yet Agrafena was unrepentant.

"The police told me off but it was worth it," she said. "I've fulfilled a dream I've had since childhood and I was running out of time."

Social psychologists have written at length about what they term "the psychology of previous investment"; i.e. the process by which people convince themselves to remain committed to a belief system even though all available evidence demonstrates that it isn't true and doesn't work.

I am not one of those who believe that the future of the horse is behind us. This wonderful animal is still the best antidote for the fatigues of modern man. It is ready to help us understand the modern world, if not better, then to understand it differently.

Ride well, Long Riders.

In an increasingly urbanized environment, horses became another symbol of the lavish perks and privileges enjoyed by the wealthy elite. This equestrian system was based on the extravagant consumption of energy and raw materials by a minority of individuals. Horses were not used to achieve a sense of personal geographic liberty but to define an owner's characterization of themselves to others, in the same manner as a Hummer four-wheel-drive off road vehicle or a luxurious Mercedes Benz sports car might be. For these people, it is not where you ride, but what you own, that makes the difference.

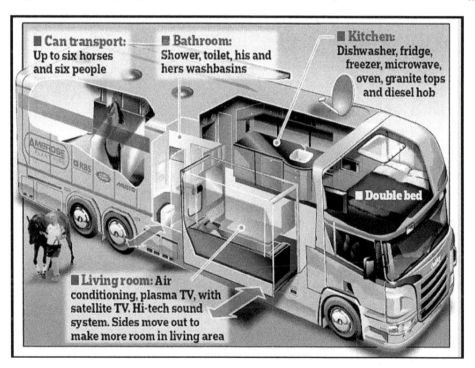

An example of equestrian extravagance is the 39-foot long "temple of power" that costs £500,000 ($700,000). This 26-ton lorry is equipped with an air-conditioned living room, bedroom and fully equipped bathroom. An oven, microwave, dishwasher and freezer are concealed in walnut cabinets. Such ostentatious wealth disguises a hydra with many heads. While exclusivity and elegance are on display, aggression and cruelty are often lurking nearby.

Though it likes to disguise its aims under misleading platitudes, the four corners of equestrian sport are competition, commercialism, ego and patriotism. In such an environment the horse is a disposable commodity whose primary attraction is to enlarge individual reputations, generate corporate profits and enhance national prestige. One notorious example was an endurance race held in Abu Dhabi in 2015, where three horses died and one horse broke both front legs. This mercenary philosophy is a rejection of the horse-human experience which has enriched the history of our species. Photo courtesy the Daily Mail.

Commerce leads to compromise when the only concern is whether the equine investment is performing according to schedule. With its focus on glamour and ceremony, equestrian sports often operate in a moral vacuum that encourages rule-breaking. Geoff Young, publisher of Horse Connection magazine, warned," Money and greed are the biggest threats to the well-being of the horse." One such example occurred in 2013 when Rita Crundwell was sentenced to almost 20 years in federal prison for plundering more than $50 million from the US city where she worked. Among the assets seized by US Marshals were 400 expensive Quarter Horses and 767 trophies. "These trophies symbolize Crundwell's motivation. They were her prized possessions, second only to the horses themselves," said Chief Inspector Jason Wojdylo.

Sceptics may choose to remain loyal to equestrian practices of the past, arguing that a single voice of objection can be ignored. Yet history proves that our collective destiny is uncertain, especially now that climate change has forced horses and humans to confront an altered environment. Russian author Peter Goullart advised that even though civilisations come and go, "The humble horse, man's oldest friend, is ever ready to forge again a link between scattered peoples and nations." Photo courtesy AMC.

Changing times herald a shift in resource management and may result in a re-examination of more traditional means of transportation. John Michael Greer, the author of more than thirty books on the future of industrial society, warned, "The more energy you need to maintain your everyday lifestyle, the more vulnerable you'll be to sudden disruptions when the sprawling infrastructure that supplies you with that energy starts running into serious trouble."

As the 20th century drew to a close, decades of increasing income came to a halt. Then a global financial meltdown and wide-spread political instability further undermined equine practices that were linked to an age based upon cheap petroleum and a wealthy middle-class. Technology has evolved in this new century but human nature has not. Predictability still means control. Authoritarian regimes continue to use horses to enforce conformity, demand obedience, suppress domestic dissent and restrict liberty of movement.

Yet a resistance to authority is a central motif in equestrian travel history. In the centuries since Long Riders first appeared, they have worn many faces including traveller, pilgrim and rebel. There are a few bred in every generation who will not be suppressed or dismounted. Tyrants come and go. This need for liberty cannot be extinguished.

King Arthur bade us, "To improve instead of destroy." The time is overdue to reject the corporate inspired corruption that has polluted the equine world. We should choose instead to defend the horse's inherent dignity and refuse to participate in, or financially endorse, activities which condone cruelty. There needs to be a new reason for riding which is based on individuality instead of competition. The Ebony Horse Club in Brixton, one of Britain's most deprived neighbourhoods, demonstrates that the horse is not just for the rich and privileged. It is for everyone. When HM Queen Elizabeth II visited the club, 13-year-old Cameron Chapman told the British monarch, "I saw them building the centre and came every day to stand at the gates. I had never seen a horse before but offered to do anything to be involved. Now I am here every spare minute. It's really changed my life."

Horses and humans have been suffocated by centuries of conformity, compromise, cruelty and corruption. Shall we remain a set of bickering tribes or evolve into a species of like-minded souls? At a time when millions of urbanized humans are denied a place in nature, the horse continues to evoke a deep emotional response. The time has come for the horse to become an inclusive symbol of all humanity. The elderly, the weak, the young, the unfortunate, the physically challenged, the hopeless, the misunderstood; the horse represents an instrument of change for all of them. Putting the Guild's philosophy of Harmonious Horsemanship into action is as much evolutionary as revolutionary. Photo courtesy of equine inventor Simon Mulholland.

There is no doctrine of equine exclusivity in the Guild. All humans, no matter where they were born, can become Long Riders. That's why equestrian travel will never become extinct because so long as there is one brave human, and one strong horse, some freedom loving team will always ride away from the restrictions of their confining village. Kimberley Delavere was twenty-four when she set off in 2016 to make a 5,330 kilometres (3,311 miles) solo journey along Australia's Bicentennial National Trail. At the conclusion of that ride, Kim wrote, "I think it is a great thing, when ordinary people realise their potential and freedom of choice. As clichéd as it sounds, they are capable of achieving anything they want to do. The hardest bit for many to understand is that the people who undertake these journeys aren't the privileged few – it's just people who work hard, believe and stick at it." As Kimberley proves, anyone can wash away the dust of everyday life by setting off on a journey that simultaneously involves their body, spirit and mind.

The Long Riders represent older values, nomadic traditions, freedom from regulatory village chiefs be they in Scythia or London. We, and our horses, are about freedom. We, and our horses, stand for the right of free movement. We, and our horses, represent a 6,000 year old tradition of inter-species communication and travel. This is not the wisdom of any one sedentary civilisation. This knowledge is free of doctrinarism. It serves life. It is practical. It was passed on to us by the people of the past who had mastered the magnificent and dangerous art of conquering space here on Earth. In their continual mounted wanderings, they roamed from continent to continent, from one climatic extremity to another. They were not meek and obedient instruments of the state. They were never willing to stand in place, paralyzed and immobile. They were subject to gnawing restlessness. Yet it's not about where we've been. It's about where we're going. With the dawning of this new century, the time has come to determine the future course of equestrian events. Shall horses and humans ever travel together beyond the limitations of our planet? This specially commissioned painting, "Aimé and Mancha Ride to the Stars" envisions such a day.

Further Reading

I sat down in the autumn of 2010 thinking that in a few weeks time I would compose a *Horse Travel Handbook* which contained a primer of equestrian travel knowledge. Looking back upon that moment in my life, it is fair to say that my ignorance was only matched by my naiveté. I was one of those would-be equestrian travellers who belong to the 'lost generation', those born in the mid-twentieth century who were too late for the cavalry and too early for the internet.

The more research I did, and the deeper I dug, the more I realized that I had vastly underestimated the subject in question. An apt analogy would be that during the course of many centuries the Great Sphinx of Giza became buried up to its shoulders in sand. It was not until the colossus was finally excavated in 1925 that its true size was understood. Likewise it slowly dawned on me that I had also badly under estimated the true dimensions of equestrian travel.

The *Handbook* kept growing until it became so large that I realized that there was a need for two books - one to be studied at home prior to departure (*The Encyclopaedia of Equestrian Exploration*) and a second to accompany the Long Rider during his journey (*The Horse Travel Handbook*).

After seven years of uninterrupted work, I completed the three-volume *Encyclopaedia of Equestrian Exploration*. Serving as a type of equestrian Rosetta Stone, it chronicles the ancestral story of the Long Riders, revealing their forgotten history and documenting their gallant struggles against inconceivable odds.

The Encyclopaedia's release in 2017 coincides with the 500 year anniversary of the birth of equestrian travel literature, which began in 1617 when Fynes Moryson wrote about his ride through Europe.

The literary journey begins in **Volume 1**.

Section Three – The Equipment

Volume 2 consists of The Challenges, the most extensive examination of difficulties and dangers encountered by Long Riders.

Section Four – The Challenges

Volume 3 concludes the literary equestrian mission by examining the technicalities of living in the saddle. It also contains the first investigation into the emotional repercussions which horse and human endure when the journey is completed. A special Epilogue, inspired by Prince Charles' philosophy of Harmony, explains the on-going importance of equestrian travel.

The Horse Travel Handbook

After studying the information on offer in the Encyclopaedia, the would-be Long Rider is advised to carry a copy of *The Horse Travel Handbook* during the subsequent journey.

The Horse Travel Handbook is a cavalry-style manual drawn from its parent edition *The Encyclopaedia of Equestrian Exploration.* It is small enough to fit into a saddlebag and contains the most critically important information that a Long Rider may need to consult while travelling. The concise, easy-to-use book covers every aspect needed to successfully complete a journey by horse, including how to organize the trip, plan a route, choose the proper equipment and purchase horses.

Traditional challenges such as loading a pack saddle, avoiding dangerous animals, fording rivers and outwitting horse thieves are covered here along with ingenious solutions to modern dilemmas like crossing international borders, surviving vehicle traffic and negotiating with hostile bureaucrats. This handbook covers all aspects of equine welfare including feeding, watering, saddling and health care. Technical details such as daily travel distance, where to locate nightly shelter and ways to avoid cultural conflicts are among the hundreds of specific topics examined.

Equestrian explorers have special linguistic needs. Vital words such as hay and farrier are not found in standard phrase-books. A special appendix contains the Equestionary that provides images of objects and situations most likely to be of use when language is a barrier.

Bibliography

Albright, Verne, *In the Saddle Across the Three Americas*. Bookshelf Press, San Jose, California, USA, 1969.

Anderson, Edward L., *On Horseback in the School and on the Road*. H. Holt & Company, New York, USA, 1882.

Back, Joe, *Horses, Hitches and Rocky Trails*. Swallow Press, Chicago, Illinois, USA, 1959.

Baker, Sir Stanley, *Wild Beasts and Their Ways.* Macmillan Publishers, London, England, 1890.

Ballereau, Jean-François, *Manuel de Randonnée Equestre*. Belin Publishers, Paris, France, 2002.

Baret, Michael*, The Vineyard of Horsemanship,* George Eld Publishers, London, England 1618.

Barnes, Richard, *Eye on the Hill.* The Long Riders Guild Press, Glasgow, Kentucky. USA. 2005.

Beard, John W., *Saddle East.* The Long Riders Guild Press, Glasgow, Kentucky. USA. 2002.

Belasik, Paul, *Riding towards the Light.* J.A. Allen & Co., London, England, 1990.

Blashford-Snell, Colonel John, *Expeditions – The Experts' Way.* The Travel Book Club Publishers, London, England, 1977.

———— *The British Trans-America Expedition Report.* Scientific Exploration Society Publishers, Mildenhall, England, 1973.

Blomstedt, M. *Undervisning För Ryttaren.* Swedish Cavalry Press, Stockholm, Sweden, 1907.

Blyth, Mr., *The Gentleman's Pocket-Farrier, Showing How to use your Horse on a Journey, A New Edition carefully revised by a Veterinary Surgeon.* Thomas Desilver Publishers, Philadelphia, Pennsylvania, USA. 1829.

Bolton, Captain Edward Frederick, *Horse Management in West Africa.* Jarrold & Sons Publishers, Norwich, England, 1931.

Bond Head, Sir Francis, *The Horse and His Rider.* John Murray Publishers, London, England, 1860.

Boniface, Lt. Jonathan J., *The Cavalry Horse and his Pack.* Hudson-Kimberly Publishing, Kansas City, Missouri, USA. 1903.

Bonvalot, Gabriel, *Across Tibet.* Cassell Publishing Company, New York, USA. 1892.

Bosanquet, Mary, *Saddlebags for Suitcases.* The Long Riders Guild Press, Glasgow, Kentucky, USA. 2001.

Borrow, George, *The Romany Rye.* The Long Riders Guild Press, Glasgow, Kentucky, USA. 2007.

———— *The Zincali - An account of the gypsies of Spain.* John Murray Publishers, London, England, 1923.

Brooke, Brigadier Geoffrey, *Horsemanship.* Seeley, Service & Company, London, England, 1929.

Brown, Donald, *Journey from the Arctic.* The Long Riders Guild Press, Glasgow, Kentucky, USA. 2001.

Bull, Bartle, *Around the Sacred Sea.* Canongate Books Ltd., Edinburgh, Scotland. 1999.

Bulliet, Richard, *Hunters, Herders, and Hamburgers: The Past and Future of Human-Animal Relationships.* Columbia University Press, New York, New York, 2007.

Burdon, Captain William, *The Gentleman's Pocket-Farrier, Shewing how to use your horse on a journey and what remedies are proper for common misfortunes that may befall him on the road.* S. Buckley Printers, London, England, 1730.

Büren, Jean-François de, *A Voyage Across the Americas – the Journey of Henri de Büren,* Editions de Penthes, Geneva, Switzerland. 2013

Burnaby, Evelyn, *A Ride from Land's End to John O'Groats.* Sampson Low, Marston & Co., London, England. 1893.

Burnaby, Frederick, *A Ride to Khiva.* The Long Riders Guild Press, Glasgow, Kentucky, USA. 2001.

———— *On Horseback through Asia Minor.* The Long Riders Guild Press, Glasgow, Kentucky, USA. 2001.

Burpee, Lawrence, *Among the Canadian Alps.* John Lane Company, New York, USA. 1914.

Buryn, Ed, *Vagabonding in America - A Guide to Energy.* Book People Press, San Francisco, California, USA. 1973.

———— *Vagabonding in Europe & North Africa.* Random House Publishing, New York, New York, USA, 1976.

Bruce, Major Clarence Dalrymple, *In the Hoofprints of Marco Polo.* The Long Riders Guild Press, Glasgow, Kentucky, USA. 2004.

Carruthers, Douglas, *Unknown Mongolia.* Hutchinson & Company, London, England, 1914.

Cayley, George, *Bridle Roads of Spain.* The Long Riders Guild Press, Glasgow, Kentucky, USA. 2004.

Charvin, Claude, *Le Cheval de Bât.* Editions Crepin LeBlond, Paris, France, 1997.

Clark, Leonard, *The Marching Wind.* The Long Riders Guild Press, Glasgow, Kentucky, USA. 2001.

Cobbett, William, *Rural Rides Volumes 1 and 2.* The Long Riders Guild Press, Glasgow, Kentucky, USA. 2001.

Codman, John, *Winter Sketches from the Saddle.* The Long Riders Guild Press, Glasgow, Kentucky, USA. 2001.

Coquet, Evelyne, *Riding to Jerusalem.* John Murray Publishers, London, England, 1978.

Court Treatt, Stella, *Cape to Cairo.* George Harrap Ltd., London, England, 1927.

Cousineau, Phil, *The Art of Pilgrimage: the Seeker's Guide to Making Travel Sacred.* Conari Press, Berkeley, California, USA. 1998.

Cunliffe Marsh, Hippsley, *A Ride Through Islam.* The Long Riders Guild Press, Glasgow, Kentucky, USA. 2004.

Cunninghame Graham, Robert, *Horses of the Conquest.* The Long Riders Guild Press, Glasgow, Kentucky, USA. 2004.

Daly, Henry W., *Manual of Pack Transportation.* The Long Riders Guild Press, Glasgow, Kentucky, USA. 2000.

Darling, Sir Malcolm Lyall, *At Freedom's Door.* The Long Riders Guild Press, Glasgow, Kentucky, USA. 2008.

Davis, Francis W., *Horse Packing in Pictures.* Charles Scribner's Sons Publishers, New York, USA, 1975.

Denny, J.T., *Horses and Roads: How to keep a horse sound on his legs.* Longmans, Green & Company, London, England, 1881.

Dent, Anthony, *The Horse through Fifty Centuries of Civilization.* Phaidon Press Limited, London, England, 1974.

Denton, Ivan, *Old Brands and Lost Trails.* University of Arkansas Press, Fayetteville, Arkansas. USA, 1991.

Dixie, Lady Florence, *Riding Across Patagonia.* The Long Riders Guild Press, Glasgow, Kentucky, USA. 2001.

Dodwell, Christina, *A Traveller in Horseback in Turkey and Iran.* The Long Riders Guild Press, Glasgow, Kentucky, USA. 2004.

——— *An Explorer's Handbook.* The Long Riders Guild Press, Glasgow, Kentucky, USA. 2005.

Dorondo, David, *Riders of the Apocalypse.* Naval Institute Press, Annapolis, Maryland, USA, 2012.

Dotchin, Jane, *Journey Through England with a Pack Pony.* Wagtail Press, Hexham, England, 1989.

Duberly, Fanny, *Indian Journal.* The Long Riders Guild Press, Glasgow, Kentucky, USA. 2006.

Durant, Dr. Ghislani, *Horseback Riding from a Medical Point of View.* Cassell, Petter & Galpin Publishers, New York, USA, 1878.

Elles, Major-General W.K., *Manual for Bengal and Punjab Cavalry.* Superintendent of Government Printing, Calcutta, India, 1893.

Elser, Smoke and Brown, Bill, *Packin' In On Mules and Horses.* Mountain Press Publishing, Missoula, Montana, USA, 1980.

Farrow, Edward, *Pack Mules and Packing.* Metropolitan Publishing Company, New York, New York, USA. 1881.

Farson, Negley, *Caucasian Journey.* The Long Riders Guild Press, Glasgow, Kentucky, USA. 2002.

Fleming, George FRCVS, *The Physical Condition of Horses for Military Purposes.* Gale & Polden Publishers, Aldershot, England, 1889.

Fox, Ernest, *Travels in Afghanistan.* The Long Riders Guild Press, Glasgow, Kentucky, USA. 2001.

Freeman, Lewis Ransome, *Down the Columbia.* Dodd, Mead and Company, New York, USA, 1921.

Galton, Francis, *The Art of Travel.* John Murray Publishers, London, England, 1855.

Galvayne, Sydney, *The Horse – Its Taming and Training.* Thomas Murray and Sons Publishers, Glasgow, Scotland, 1888.

Galwan, *Ghulam* Rassul, *Servant of Sahibs.* The Long Riders Guild Press, Glasgow, Kentucky, USA. 2001.

Gebhards, Stacy, *When Mules Wear Diamonds.* Wilderness Skills Publishing, McCall, Idaho, 2000.

Gianoli, Luigi, *Horses and Horsemanship through the Ages.* Crown Publishers, New York, New York, USA. 1969.

Gilbey, Sir Walter, *Small Horses in Warfare.* Vinton & Co. Ltd., London, England, 1900.

Glazier, Willard, *Ocean to Ocean on Horseback.* The Long Riders Guild Press, Glasgow, Kentucky, USA. 2001.

Goldschmidt, Lt.-Col. Sidney, *An Eye to Buying a Horse.* Country Life Publishers, London, England. 1944.

Gonne, Captain C.M., *Hints on Horses.* John Murray Publishers, London, England, 1904.

Gordon, William John, *The Horse World of London.* The Religious Tract Society, London, England, 1893.

Goubaux, Armand, *The Exterior of the Horse.* J.B Lippincott Company, Philadelphia, Pennsylvania, USA, 1892.

Gourko, General D., *Wyna: Adventures in Eastern Siberia.* Methuen & Company, London, England, 1938.

Government of India, *The Indian Empire – Hints for Soldiers Proceeding to India.* Central Publication Branch, Calcutta, India, 1927.

Graves, Will, *Wolves in Russia.* Detselig Enterprises Ltd., Calgary, Canada, 2007.

Haker, Ute, *Saddle Up- A Guide to Planning the Perfect Horseback Vacation.* John Muir Publications, Santa Fe, New Mexico, USA. 1997.

Hamilton Smith, Charles, *Equus - The Natural History of the Horse, Ass, Onager, Quagga and Zebra.* W. H. Lizars Publishers, Edinburgh, Scotland, 1841.

Hanbury-Tenison, Robin, *Chinese Adventure.* The Long Riders Guild Press, Glasgow, Kentucky, USA. 2004.

——— *Fragile Eden – A Ride through New Zealand.* The Long Riders Guild Press, Glasgow, Kentucky, USA. 2004.

——— *Land of Eagles.* I.B. Taurus & Co., London, England, 2009.

——— *Spanish Pilgrimage,* The Long Riders Guild Press, Glasgow, Kentucky, USA. 2001.

——— *White Horses Over France.* The Long Riders Guild Press, Glasgow, Kentucky, USA. 2001.

Harlen, General Josiah, *A Memoir of Afghanistan.* J. Dobson Publishers, Philadelphia, USA. 1842.

Harsha, Max, *Mule Skinner's Bible,* Privately published by the author, 1987.

Hart Poe, Rhonda, *Trail Riding.* Storey Publishers, North Adams, Massachusetts, USA, 2005.

Haslund, Henning, *Mongolian Adventure.* The Long Riders Guild Press, Glasgow, Kentucky, USA. 2002.

Hassanein, Sir Ahmed Mohammed, *The Lost Oases.* The Long Riders Guild Press, Glasgow, Kentucky, USA. 2001.

Hatley, George, *Horse Camping.* The Dial Press, New York, USA, 1981.

Hayes, Captain Horace FRCVS, *Among Horses in Russia.* R. A. Everett & Company, London, England. 1900.

——— *Among Men and Horses.* T. Fisher Unwin Publishers, London, England. 1894.

——— *Horse Management in India.* Thacker, Spink & Company, Calcutta, India, 1878.

——— *Horses on board Ship, a guide to their management.* Hurst and Blackett Publishers, London, England, 1902.

Headley , J.T. and Johnson, W.F. , *Stanley's Adventures in the Wilds of Africa.* Edgewood Publishing Co., London, England, 1890.

Heath, Frank, *Forty Million Hoofbeats.* The Long Riders Guild Press, Glasgow, Kentucky, USA. 2001.

Hill, Cherry, *Horse Keeping Almanac.* Storey Publishing, North Adams, Massachusetts, USA, 2007.

Hill, Oliver, *Packing and Outfitting Field Manual.* University of Wyoming Press, Laramie, Wyoming, USA, 1981.

Hilton, Suzanne, *Getting There – Frontier Travel without Power.* The Westminster Press, Philadelphia, USA, 1980.

Hinks, Arthur Robert, *Hints to Travellers.* Royal Geographical Society, London, England, 1938.

His Majesty's War Office, *Animal Management.* T. Fisher Unwin Publishers, London, England. 1908.

———— *Catechism of Animal Management,* Harrison and Sons Publishers, London, England, 1916.

———— *Cavalry Training (Horsed).* Harrison and Sons Publishers, London, England, 1937.

———— *Manual of Horsemastership, Equitation and Animal Transport.* H.M. Stationery Office, London, England, 1937.

Hohenlohe-Ingelfingen, Prince Kraft Karl August Eduard Friedrich, *Letters on Cavalry.* Royal Artillery Institution, Woolwich, England, 1889.

Holt, William, *Ride a White Horse.* The Long Riders Guild Press, Glasgow, Kentucky, USA. 2001.

Howden, Peter, *Horse Warranty – a Plain and Comprehensive Guide to the Various Points to be Noted showing which are essential and which are unimportant.* Robert Hardwicke Publishers, London, England, 1862.

Huc, Evariste, *Travels in Tartary, Tibet and China.* National Illustrated Library, London, England, 1852.

Hunter, J. Kerr, *Pony Trekking for All.* Thomas Nelson & Sons Publishers, London, England, 1962.

Jackson, Frederick George, *A Thousand Days in the Arctic*, Harper & Brothers, London, England. 1899.

James, Jeremy, *Saddle Tramp.* The Long Riders' Guild Press Glasgow, Kentucky, USA, 2001.

———— *The Byerley Turk.* Merlin Unwin Books, Ludlow, England, 2005.

———— *Vagabond,* The Long Riders' Guild Press Glasgow, Kentucky, USA, 2001.

Jankovich, Miklos, *They Rode into Europe.* The Long Riders' Guild Press Glasgow, Kentucky, USA, 2007.

Jebb, Louisa, *By Desert Ways to Baghdad and Damascus.* The Long Riders' Guild Press Glasgow, Kentucky, USA, 2004.

Jervis, John, *The Traveller's Oracle – Volumes One & Two.* Henry Colburn Publishers, London, England, 1827.

Johnson Post, Charles, *Horse Packing – A Manual of Pack Transportation.* The Long Riders Guild Press, Glasgow, Kentucky, USA. 2000.

Johnson, Dusty, *Horse Packing Illustrated.* Saddleman Press, Loveland, Colorado, USA, 2000.

Kellon, Dr. Eleanor VMD, *First Aid for Horses.* Breakthrough Publications, Ossining, New York, USA, 1990.

Kluckhohn, Clyde, *To the Foot of the Rainbow.* The Long Riders Guild Press, Glasgow, Kentucky, USA. 2001.

Koch, Johan Peter, *Through the White Desert.* Verlog von Julius Springer Publishing, Berlin, Germany, 1919.

Kopas, Cliff, *Packhorses to the Pacific.* Touch Wood Editions, Victoria, Canada, 2004.

Labouchere, John. *High Horses.* Labouchere Publishing, North Elmham, England, 1998.

Lambie, Thomas, *Boots and Saddles in Africa.* The Long Riders Guild Press, Glasgow, Kentucky, USA. 2001.

Law, Dr. James, *Special Report on Diseases of the Horse.* U.S. Dept. of Agriculture, Bureau of Animal Industry, Washington DC, USA, 1916.

Lawson, Major E.F., Royal Bucks Hussars, *The Cavalry Journal – "The Reduction of the Weight on the Horse".* Royal United Service Publishers, London, England, 1924.

Leigh, Margaret, *My Kingdom for a Horse.* The Long Riders Guild Press, Glasgow, Kentucky, USA. 2001.

Littauer, Vladimir, *Russian Hussar.* The Long Riders Guild Press, Glasgow, Kentucky, USA. 2007.

MacGahan, Januarius Aloysius, *Campaigning on the Oxus.* Harper Brothers Publishers, New York, USA, 1874.

Maillart, Ella, *Turkestan Solo.* The Long Riders Guild Press, Glasgow, Kentucky, USA. 2001.

Markham, Gervase, *The Perfect Horseman or the Experienced Secrets of Mr. Markham's Fifty Years Practice. Shewing how a Man come to be a General Horseman by the knowledge of the Seven offices: Buyer, Keeper, Feeder, Farrier, Rider, Ambler and Breeder.* Richard Chiswel Publishers, London, England 1680.

Marsden, Kate, *Riding through Siberia.* The Long Riders Guild Press, Glasgow, Kentucky, USA. 2001.

Marshall, Clay, *Ninety Days By Horse.* Create Space Publishing, Seattle, Washington, USA, 2013.

McCullagh, Francis, *With the Cossacks.* Eveleigh Nash Publishers, London, England, 1906.

McGovern, William, *To Lhasa in Disguise.* The Long Riders Guild Press, Glasgow, Kentucky, USA. 2001.

McMullen, Kieran, *Marches and shelter for horse drawn artillery with notes for scouts.* Scholar of Fortune Publishers, USA, 1993.

McShane, Clay and Tarr, Joel, *The Horse in the City.* John Hopkins University Press, Baltimore, Maryland, USA. 2007.

Merrill, Bill, *Vacationing with Saddle and Pack Horse.* Arco Publishing Company, New York, USA, 1976.

Michaux, François André, *Travels in North America.* J. Mawman Publishers, London, England, 1805.

Miller, Everett B., *United States Army Veterinary Service in World War II.* Office of the Surgeon General, Dept. of the Army, Washington, D.C, 1961.

Ministère de la Guerre, *Règlement sur la Conduite des Mulets de Bât.* Paris, France, 1883.

Muir Watson, Sharon, *The Colour of Courage.* The Long Riders Guild Press, Glasgow, Kentucky, USA. 2001.

La Tondre, Richard, *The Golden Kite.* Chez De Press, Santa Clara, California, USA, 2005.

Le Messurier, Colonel A., *A Ride Through Persia.* Richard Bentley & Sons, London, England. 1889.

Meserve, Ruth, *A Historical Perspective of Mongol Horse Training.* Indiana University, Bloomington, USA. 1987.

Miller, Lt. Col. E. D. DSO, *Horse Management in the Field at Home and Abroad.* Gale & Polden Ltd. Aldershot, England, 1919.

Morrison, Frank Barron, *Feeds and Feeding.* Henry Morrison Company, Madison, Wisconsin, USA, 1915.

Moryson, Fynes, *An Itinerary: Containing Ten Years Travel Through Germany, Bohemia, Switzerland, Netherland, Denmark, Poland, Italy, Turkey, France, England, Scotland and Ireland.* The Stationers' Company, London, England. 1617.

Naysmith, Gordon, *The Will to Win.* The Long Riders Guild Press, Glasgow, Kentucky, USA. 2005.

Nicolle, Grant, *Long Trot.* Create Space Publishing, London, England, 2015.

Nolan, Captain Lewis, *The Training of Calvary Remount Horses.* Parker, Furnivall & Parker Publishing, London, England, 1852.

Noyce, Wilfred, *The Springs of Adventure.* John Murray Publishing, London, England, 1958.

Nunn, Captain J.A., *Notes on Stable Management in India and the Colonies.* W. Thacker & Co., Calcutta, India, 1897.

O'Reilly, Basha, *Bandits and Bureaucrats.* The Long Riders Guild Press, Glasgow, Kentucky. USA. 2016.

O'Reilly, CuChullaine, *Deadly Equines: The Shocking True Story of Meat-Eating and Murderous Horses.* The Long Riders Guild Press, Glasgow, Kentucky, USA. 2011.

––––––– *Khyber Knights.* The Long Riders Guild Press, Glasgow, Kentucky, USA. 2001.

Patterson, George N., *Journey with Loshay.* The Long Riders Guild Press, Glasgow, Kentucky, USA. 2001.

––––––– *Patterson of Tibet,* The Long Riders Guild Press, Glasgow, Kentucky, USA. 2001.

Phillips, Mefo, *Horseshoes and Holy Water.* Virgin Books, London, England, 2005

Pigott, Lt. J.P., *A Treatise on the Horses of India.* James White Publishers, Calcutta, India. 1794.

Pocock, Geoffrey, *One Hundred Years of the Legion of Frontiersmen.* Phillimore & Co. Ltd., Chichester, England, 2004.

––––––– *Outrider of Empire: The Life and Adventures of Roger Pocock.* University of Alberta Press, Alberta, Canada, 2008

Pocock, Roger, *Chorus to Adventurers, being the later life of Roger Pocock.* John Lane Publishers, London, England, 1931.

––––––– *Horses.* The Long Riders' Guild Press, Glasgow, Kentucky, USA, 2004.

––––––– *The Frontiersman's Pocket Book.* John Murray Publishers, London, England, 1909.

Reese, Herbert Harshman, *The Road Horse.* Bureau of Animal Industry Publishers, Washington DC, USA, 1912.

Rink, Bjarke, *The Rise of the Centaurs.* Author House LLC, Bloomington, Indiana, USA, 2013.

Robinson, Ian D., *Tea with the Taliban.* David Bateman Publishers, Auckland, New Zealand, 2008.

Runnquist, Åke, *Horses in Fact and Fiction – An Anthology.* Jonathan Cape Publishers, London, England, 1957.

Ruxton, George, *Adventures in Mexico,* The Long Riders Guild Press, Glasgow, Kentucky, USA. 2001.

Saare, Sharon, *Know All about Trail Riding.* Farnam Horse Library, Omaha, Nebraska, USA, 1975.

Salzman, Erich von, *Im Sattel durch die Fürstenhöfe Indiens.* The Long Riders Guild Press, Glasgow, Kentucky, USA. 2004.

Savage Landor, Henry, *Alone with the Hairy Ainu.* Cambridge University Press, Cambridge, England. 1893.

––––––– *In the Forbidden Land.* The Long Riders Guild Press, Glasgow, Kentucky, USA. 2004.

Schoolcraft, Henry Rowe, *Adventures in the Ozark Mountains.* Lippincott, Grambo & Co., Philadelphia, USA. 1853.

Schoomaker, General Peter, *Special Forces Use of Pack Animals.* Department of the Army, Washington, DC, USA. 2004.

Schwartz, Otto, *Reisen mit dem Pferd.* The Long Riders Guild Press, Glasgow, Kentucky, USA. 2002.

Shaw, Robert, *Visits to High Tartary.* John Murray Publishers, London, England, 1871.

Skrede, Wilfred, *Across the Roof of the World.* The Long Riders Guild Press, Glasgow, Kentucky, USA. 2001.

Slade, Major General Daniel Denison, *How to Kill Animals Humanely.* Massachusetts Society for the Prevention of Cruelty to Animals, Boston, Massachusetts, USA. 1899.

––––––– *Twelve days in the saddle; a journey on horseback in New England during the autumn of 1883.* Little & Brown Publishers, Boston, Massachusetts, USA, 1884.

Smeaton Chase, J, *California Coast Trails.* The Long Riders' Guild Press, Glasgow, Kentucky, USA, 2002.

––––––– *California Desert Trails.* The Long Riders' Guild Press, Glasgow, Kentucky, USA, 2002.

Smeeton, Beryl, *The Stars My Blanket.* Horsdal & Schubart Publishers, Victoria, Canada, 1995.

Springfield, Rollo, *The Horse and His Rider.* Chapman and Hall Publishers, London, England, 1847.

Stebbing, Edward Percy, *Cross Country Riding.* Country Life Publishers, London, England, 1938.

Stevens, Thomas, *Through Russia on a Mustang.* The Long Riders Guild Press, Glasgow, Kentucky, USA. 2001.

Stevenson, Robert Louis, *Travels with a Donkey.* The Long Riders Guild Press, Glasgow, Kentucky, USA. 2001.

Stirling, Mrs. Clark J., *The Ladies' Equestrian Guide.* Day & Son Publishers, London, England, 1857.

Strong, Anna Louise, *The Road to the Grey Pamir.* The Long Riders Guild Press, Glasgow, Kentucky, USA. 2001.

Sykes, Ella, *Through Persia on a Sidesaddle.* The Long Riders Guild Press, Glasgow, Kentucky, USA. 2001.

––––––– *Through the Deserts of Central Asia.* MacMillan & Company, London, England, 1920.

Taplan, William, *A Gentleman's Stable Directory.* J. Robinson Company, London, England. 1790.

Taylor, Bayard, *The Cyclopedia of Modern Travel*. Moore, Wilstach & Key Publisher, New York, USA. 1856.

Thompson, Charles, *Hints to Inexpert Travellers*. Sherwood and Company, London, England, 1830.

Trinkler, Emil, *Through the Heart of Afghanistan*. The Long Riders Guild Press, Glasgow, Kentucky, USA. 2001.

Tschiffely, Aimé, *Bohemia Junction*. The Long Riders Guild Press, Glasgow, Kentucky, USA. 2004.

———— *Bridle Paths*. The Long Riders Guild Press, Glasgow, Kentucky, USA. 2004.

———— *Ming and Ping*. The Long Riders Guild Press, Glasgow, Kentucky, USA. 2014

———— *Round and About Spain*. The Long Riders Guild Press, Glasgow, Kentucky, USA. 2008.

———— *Tschiffely's Ride,* The Long Riders Guild Press, Glasgow, Kentucky, USA. 2001.

Thurlow Craig, A.W., *A Rebel for a Horse*. Arthur Barker Publishers, London, England. 1934.

———— *Paraguayan Interlude*. Arthur Barker Publishers, London, England, 1935.

———— *Tackle Pony Trekking This Way*. Stanley Paul Publishers, London, England, 1961.

Ure, John, *Cucumber Sandwiches in the Andes*. The Long Riders Guild Press, Glasgow, Kentucky, USA. 2005.

———— *In Search of Nomads*. Carroll Graf Publishers, New York, New York, USA 2003.

———— *Pilgrimage, the Great Adventure of the Middle Ages*. Constable & Robinson Publishers, London, England, 2006.

US Army Quartermaster General, *The Packer Training Manual*. Government Printing Office, Washington DC, USA, 1927.

———— *The Phillips Pack Saddle*. Government Printing Office, Washington DC, USA, 1924.

US Marine Corps, *United States Marine Corps Animal Transportation Manual*. Government Printing Office, Washington DC, USA, 1940.

US War Department, *Manual for Farriers, Horseshoers, Saddlers and Waggoners*. Government Printing Office, Washington DC, USA, 1915.

———— *Pack Transport*. Government Printing Office, Washington DC, USA, 1944.

Vanderbilt, Tom, *Traffic – Why we drive the way we do*. Penguin Books Ltd., London, England, 2008.

Walchuk, Stan, *Trail Riding, Pack and Training Manual*. Vista Publishers, McBride, British Columbia, Canada, 2003.

Walker, Elaine, *Horse*, Reaktion Books Ltd., London, England, 2008.

Weale, Magdalene, *Through the Highlands of Shropshire on Horseback*. The Long Riders Guild Press, Glasgow, Kentucky, USA. 2001.

Weeks, Edwin Lord, *Artist Explorer*. The Long Riders Guild Press, Glasgow, Kentucky, USA. 2005.

Wells, Spencer, *The Journey of Man*. Princeton University Press, Princeton, New Jersey, USA, 2002.

Weston, W. Val, *The Saddle Horse in India*. Thacker, Spink & Company, Calcutta, India, 1914.

Weygard, Jacques, *Legionnaire – Life with the French Foreign Legion Cavalry*. George Harrap & Company, London, England, 1952.

Wilder, Janine, *Trail Riding*. Western Horseman Publishers, Fort Worth, Texas, USA, 2005.

Wilkins, Messanie, *Last of the Saddle Tramps*. The Long Riders Guild Press, Glasgow, Kentucky, USA. 2002.

Wilson, Andrew, *The Abode of Snow*. The Long Riders Guild Press, Glasgow, Kentucky, USA. 2001.

Windt, Harry de, *From Paris to New York by Land*. The Long Riders Guild Press, Glasgow, Kentucky, USA. 2001.

Wood, Lisa F., *Mustang Journal: 3000 miles across America by Horse*. Lost Coast Press, Fort Bragg, California, USA, 2005.

Wortley Axe, Professor J., *The Horse*. Gresham Publishing Company, London, England, 1905.

Wyman Bury, George, a.k.a. Abdullah Mansur, *The Land of Uz*. MacMillan & Company, London, England, 1911.

Youatt, William, *The Horse*. Baldwin & Cradock, London, England, 1831.

Long Rider Contributors

The following list contains the names of the more than 420 Long Riders who directly contributed to the creation of *The Encyclopaedia of Equestrian Exploration*. Their journeys span 5,000 years and represent millions of miles travelled by horses and humans on every continent.

Abernathy, Bud and Temple – starting at the ages of nine and five they rode from Oklahoma to New Mexico and back in 1909, rode from Oklahoma to New York City in 1910, and in 1911 rode from New York to San Francisco in 62 days, all without adult assistance.
Adshead, Harry and Lisa – rode from Wales to Jordan in 2004.
Aguiar, Jorge de – rode through Brazil in 1991.
Aguiar, Pedro Luis de – rode through Brazil in 1991.
Albright, Verne – starting in 1966, rode from Peru to California.
Alfieri, Vittorio – rode across England and Europe in 1785 .
Amor, Adam del – rode in the United States in 2006.
Anderson, Ed – starting in 2009, made mulitiple journeys along the Pacific Crest Trail.
Armand, Annick - rode across Turkey from the Black Sea to the Mediterranean in 2002.
Asmussen, Conan – in 2004 rode from Canada to the Mexican border when he was ten years old.
Asmussen, Hans – starting in 2004, made multiple journeys in the USA and Canada.
Arsuka, Nirwan Ahmad – starting in 2014, made journeys in Indonesia and Papua New Guinea.
Aspinwall, Two-Gun Nan – was the first woman to ride ocean to ocean across the USA in 1910.
Asseyev, Mikhaïl Vassilievitch – rode from Kiev, Russia to Paris, France in 1889.
Azzam, Adnan – rode from Madrid, Spain to Mecca, Arabia in 1990.
Baaijens, Arita – rode through the Altai Mountains in Kazakhstan, China, Mongolia and Russia in 2013.
Baker, Sir Samuel – rode through Abyssinia in 1865.
Ballereau, Jean François - made a series of rides in Europe and North America, then rode from Argentina to Columbia in 1982.
Barnes, Richard - rode the length and breadth of England, Scotland and Wales in 1977.
Barré, Gérard – rode through the Alps and France in 2000.
Barrett, Elizabeth – starting in 1986, made multiple journeys in Great Britain.
Bartz, Thomas - rode from Osh, Kirghizstan to Panjshir, Afghanistan in 2004.
Bayes, Jeremiah – rode in the United States in 2006.
Beard, John and Lulu – rode the length of the Oregon Trail in 1948.
Beck, Charles – starting in 1912, rode to 48 state capitals in the USA.
Beck, George – led the Overland Westerners Expedtion that rode to 48 state capitals in the USA starting in 1912.
Bedaux, Charles – rode across western Canada in 1934.
Beker, Ana – starting in 1950, rode from Buenos Aires, Argentina to Ottawa, Canada.
Berg, Roland – starting in 2010, made multiple journeys through Europe, Argentina and Patagonia.
Bessac, Frank – starting in 1948, rode through Mongolia, Turkestan and Tibet.
Best, Captain James John – rode through the mountains of Albania in 1838.
Bey, Riza – starting in 1900, rode through Anatolia, Arabia, Mesopotamia, the Middle East and the Balkans.
Bigler, Jessica - rode from Switzerland to the British Isles and back in 2007.
Bigo, Stephane - starting in 1976, rode through Turkey, China, Ethiopia, Brazil, Guatemala and the United States.
Bird, Isabella – starting in 1873, rode in Hawaii, the Rocky Mountains, Japan, Persia, Kurdistan, Korea and Tibet.
Blackburn, Rick - rode from Canada to Texas in 2009.
Blanchard, Augustin – rode in the United States in 2010.
Blashford-Snell, Colonel John – led the British Trans-Americas Expedition through the Darien Gap jungle between Panama and Columbia in 1971.
Blunt, Wilfred – journeyed into northern Arabia and the Nejd Desert in 1878.
Bond Head, Sir Francis - rode through the Argentine pampas, across the Andes Mountains and into Chile in 1825.
Bonneville, Captain Benjamin – rode through the western United States in 1832.
Bonvalot, Gabriel – starting in 1889, rode across the "roof of the world" by crossing the Pamir and Hindu Kush Mountains; then made a second journey across Russia, Siberia, Tibet and the Takla Makan desert before entering China.
Boone, Katherine – rode across Spain in 2001.
Borrow, George – starting in 1862, rode in England and then across Spain.
Bosanquet, Mary – rode from Vancouver, British Columbia to New York city in 1939.
Boshai, Dalaikhan – rode in Mongolia and Kazakhstan in 2010.

Bougault, Laura – rode from South Africa to Malawi in 2001.

Bourboulon, Phillipe and Catherine de – starting in 1859, rode from Shanghai, China to Moscow, Russia.

Bowers, Henry "Birdie" – was a member of the Terra Nova equestrian expedition to Antarctica in 1911.

Boyd, Alistair – rode in Spain in 1966.

Bragge, Michael - rode from Brisbane to Melbourne in Australia in 1982.

Brand, Charles – rode across the Andes Mountains from Chile into Argentina in 1827.

Brenchley, Billy – starting in 2006, rode through Tunisia, Libya, Egypt, Sudan, Uganda and Tanzania.

Brown, Donald – rode across the Arctic Circle and through Lapland, Sweden, Norway and Denmark in 1953.

Brown, Len - rode through New Mexico, Colorado, Utah, Wyoming, Colorado, Kansas and Missouri in 1982.

Bruce, Clarence Dalrymple – starting in 1905, rode from Srinagar, Kashmir to Peking, China.

Bruce, James – rode in Abyssinia in 1770.

Bruhnke, Louis – starting in 1988, rode from the bottom of Patagonia to the top of Alaska, via the Darien Gap jungle.

Bull, Bartle – rode in Mongolia and Siberia in 1998.

Büren, Henri de - rode over the Andes Mountains from Peru into Amazonia in 1853.

Burges Watson, Claire- rode from Ulaan Bator, Mongolia, to Samarkand, Uzbekistan in 1999.

Burnaby, Evelyn – rode in England and Scotland in 1892.

Burnaby, Frederick - rode across all of Central Asia, ending up at the Amir's palace at Khiva in 1875. Then, after having avoided the Czar's spies in Constantinople, Burnaby rode across all of Turkey in 1877.

Burton, Sir Richard – starting in 1867, made extensive equestrian journeys in Brazil, Argentina and Paraguay.

Butler, Samuel – rode in New Zealand in 1862.

Byron, Lord - explored the mountainous regions of Albania in 1809.

Callahan, Charles - rode from Esquel, Patagonia to Rincon de Cholila, Argentina in 1970.

Carmignani, Simone – starting in 2000, rode through the Pamir and Karakorum Mountains in Hunza and Baltistan.

Carpini, Friar Giovanni – starting in 1245, rode from Germany to Mongolia and back.

Carruthers, Douglas – starting in 1910, rode through Dzungaria, an ancient Mongolian kingdom which lay between Siberia and Mongolia.

Carson, Susie – rode through China and Tibet in 1897.

Cashner, Tex – rode from Ohio to Texas in 1951.

Cayley, George – rode through Spain in 1852.

Cazade, Jean-Claude – starting in 1982, rode from France to Arabia and back.

Çelebi, Evliya – starting in 1630, rode from Turkey to England.

Chautard, Edouard – rode across New Caldenonia in 2001 and along Australia's Bicentennial National Trail in 2004.

Chechak, Andy – rode from California to Maine in 1961.

Cherry, Meredith – is the first woman to ride the 48 state route created by the Overland Westerners. She began her journey in 2017.

Cherry-Garrard, Apsley - was a member of the Terra Nova equestrian expedition to Antarctica in 1911.

Child, Theodore – rode across Turkey and Persia in 1892.

Chitty, Jessica – at the age of three, rode from Spain to Greece in 1976 with the aid of her parents.

Claire, Alberta – starting in 1912, rode from from Wyoming to Oregon, south to California, across the deserts of Arizona, and on to New York City.

Clapperton, Hugh – rode across the Sahara Desert, from Tripoli to Sokoto in 1822.

Clark, Keith – rode through Chile in 2003.

Clark, Leonard – rode through Tibet in 1949.

Clifton, John Talbot – died trying to reach Timbukto on horseback in 1928.

Cobbett, William – rode in England in 1830.

Cochrane, John – starting in 1820, rode in Russia and Siberia.

Codman, John – rode through New England in 1888.

Coke, Henry – starting in 1849, rode in the Sandwich Islands, from St. Louis to Oregon Territory and across Spain.

Cooper, Katie - rode across the American Southwest in 2012.

Cooper, Merian C. – rode across the Zagros Mountains and through Persia in 1924.

Cope, Tim – starting in 2004, rode across Mongolia, Kazakhstan, Russia and Hungary.

Coquet, Corinne - rode from Paris to Jerusalem in 1973.

Coquet, Evelyne - rode from Paris to Jerusalem in 1973, then rode in Scotland, through the Amazonian rain forest of Brazil to Peru, and from South Africa to Zimbabwe.

Cunliffe Marsh, Hippisley – starting in 1876, rode across the Ottoman Empire, Persia and India.

Cunningham, Jakki – starting in 2006, made multiple journeys across France and England.

Cunninghame Graham, Robert – starting in 1872, rode across the Argentine pampas, from Texas to Mexico, and through the Atlas Mountains of Morocco.

Cuthbert, Donna and Nic - rode from Bayan-Ulgii aymag, Western Mongolia to Baganuur, Tov aymag, Eastern Mongolia in 2015.

Dalaikhan, Alpamys – rode in Mongolia and Kazakhstan in 2010.

Dalaikhan, Nurbek – rode in Kazakhstan in 2008.

Dalrymple Bruce, Major Clarence – starting in 1905, rode from Srinagar, India to Peking, China.

Danos, Jonathan - rode across the Andes Mountains from Chile into Argentina in 1979.

Darling, Malcolm – rode from Peshawar, North West Frontier Province to Jubbulpore, India in 1947.

Darwin, Charles – starting in 1831, rode in South America, Australia and Africa.

Davenport, Homer – rode in the Ottoman Empire in 1906.

Davies, Garry – rode through England and Wales in 1972.

Delavere, Kimberley – rode across Australia in 2017.

Denton, Ivan - rode from Arkansas to California in 1989.

Digaitis, Vaidotas – starting in 2013, rode from the Baltic Sea in Lithuania to the Black Sea in Ukraine. He next completed a journey around the Baltic Sea to the Arctic Circle and back. He also pioneered a route around his native republic of Lithuania.

Dijkstra, Margriet – rode from the Netherlands to Spain in 2006.

Discoli, Eduardo – starting in 2002, made a journey that took him across South, Central and North America, through all of Europe and Turkey, then on to the Middle East.

Dixie, Lady Florence – rode through Patagonia in 1878.

Dodwell, Christina – starting in 1975, rode in China, Iran, New Guinea, Kenya, Siberia and Turkey.

Dodwell, Edward – rode in Greece 1801.

Dolan, Captain Brooke – starting in 1942, rode from India, across the Himalayas, through Tibet and into China.

Dorman, Sarah – rode from Paris, France to Jerusalem in 1988.

Dotchin, Jane – starting in 1985, rode in the United Kingdom and Ireland.

Duberly, Fanny – rode through India in 1857.

Ducret, Nicholas - rode from Kazakhstan to Afghanistan in 2011.

Dudding, Alina Grace – starting in 2013, rode the length of the Pacific Crest Trail twice.

Dunnam, Roger – rode from Canada to Kentucky in 1988.

Durang, John – rode through New England in 1825.

Dutra, Hetty – rode in the United States in 1994 and 2014.

Dutreuil de Rhins, Jules – was killed in 1894 while riding to find the source of the Mekong River.

Eckleberg, Mary Ellen – rode from Winnipeg, Canada to New Orleans and back in 1975.

Egenes, John – rode ocean to ocean across the United States in 1974.

Ehlers, Otto – rode from Moulmein, Burma to Poofang, French Tonkin in 1896.

Elliott, Arthur – rode from Scotland to Cornwall in 1955.

Ende, Bernice – starting in 2005, made multiple journeys in the USA and Canada.

Endlweber, Sonja – starting in 2013, rode from Texas to Alaska.

Eng, Jeannette van der – rode from the Netherlands to Spain 2006.

Erickson, William – rode in South America, including through the Darien Gap Jungle, in 1990.

Etherton, Lieutenant Percy – starting in 1909, rode from Kashmir, Gilgit, over the Pamir Mountains, through Chinese Turkistan, Mongolia and on into Russian Siberia.

Fairbank, Tom - rode from Washington to Montana in 2011.

Falconer, John – rode across Nigeria in 1911.

Farson, Negley – rode through the Caucasus Mountains in 1929.

Feary, Jayme – rode along the Continental Divide Trail in 2005.

Fields, Fawn – in 1983 at the age of five, rode from Texas to Arizona with the aid of her parents.

Filchner, Wilhelm – rode in Central Asia in 1903 and in Antarctica in 1911.

Fintari, Suellen – rode from Michigan to Alaska in 1995.

Firouz, Louise – starting riding in Iran in 1956.

Fischer, Andre – rode from Patagonia to Bolivia in 2004.

Fissenko, Vladimir – starting in 1988, rode from the bottom of Patagonia to the top of Alaska, via the Darien Gap jungle.

Fleming, Peter – rode from Peking, China to Srinigar, Kashmir in 1935.

Folkins, Bonnie – starting in 2008 made multiple journeys in Mongolia and Kazakhstan.

Fox, Ernest – rode through Afghanistan in 1937.

Franconie, Pascale – starting in 1982, rode from France to Arabia and back.

Frankland, Charles Colville – starting in 1830, rode through the Ottoman Empire and Egypt.

Freeman, Lewis – led an expedition through the Canadian Rocky Mountains in 1920.

Fukushima, Baron Yasumasa – starting in 1892, rode from Berlin, Germany, across Siberia and Manchuria, to Tokyo, Japan.

Knaus, Albert – starting in 1992, made multiple journeys in Europe and rode from Mönchsondheim, Germany to Santiago de Compostela, Spain

Koch, Johan Peter – rode across Greenland in 1912.

Kohmanns, Barbara – Starting in 2002, rode from Ecuador to Mexico.

Kohn, Kareen – starting in 2002, rode in India, Peru and Ecuador.

Kopas, Cliff and Ruth – rode through the Canadian Rocky Mountains in 1933.

Kotwicki, Tadeusz – starting in 1992, rode from Jambyl, Kazakhstan to Moscow, Russia. He also rode from Patagonia to the USA.

Kovačič, Janja – starting in 2002, rode from Uruguay to Bolivia.

Kraus, Orion – rode from Mexico to Costa Rica in 2009.

Krebs, Carl – rode from Irkutsk, Siberia to Peking, China in 1918.

Kudasheva, Alexandra – starting in 1910, twice rode across Siberia. Also rode across Russia and Central Asia.

Labouchere, John – rode in Argentina and Chile in 1991.

Lambie, Thomas – rode in Abyssinia in 1919.

Landerer, Evelyn – rode in Mongolia and Siberia in 2000.

Langford, Pete – rode across New Zealand in 2013.

Langlet, Valdemar – rode in Russia in 1894.

Larssen, Renate – rode from Sweden to Syria in 2007.

Layard, Sir Austen Henry – rode from Montenegro to Persia in 1839.

Leaf, Lucy – starting in 1973, rode across the USA and back.

Leigh, Margaret – rode from Cornwall to Scotland in 1938.

Leite, Filipe – rode from Canada to Brazil in 2012 and from Brazil to Tierra del Fuego in 2017.

Leite, Luis – rode across Mexico in 2013.

Linneaus, Carl – rode through Lapland in 1732.

Liotard, Louis – was killed by bandits while riding through China's Yellow River Gorge in 1940.

Littlechild, Katrina – rode in England and Scotland in 2012.

Lloyd, Lynn – rode from Pennsylvania to California in 2008.

Losey, Linda – rode ocean to ocean across the United States in 2005.

Lucas, Alan – rode in Great Britain in 2008.

MacDermott, Hugh – rode in Argentina and Chile in 2005.

MacGahan, Januarius - rode from Fort Perovsky, Russia, across the Kyzil-Kum Desert to Adam-Kurulgan ("Fatal to Men"), Kyrgyzstan in 1873.

MacKiernan, Douglas - starting in 1948, rode through Mongolia, Turkestan and Tibet.

Maddison, Jamie – rode across Kazakhstan 2013.

Maillart, Ella – rode from Peking, China to Srinigar, Kashmir in 1935.

Mannerheim, Baron Carl Gustaf – starting in 1906, rode from Andizhan in Russian Turkestan to Beijing, China.

Marsden, Kate – rode across Russia and Siberia in 1879.

Marshall, Clay – rode across the American Southwest in 2010.

Masarotti, Dario – starting in 1995, made multiple rides in Europe and Russia.

Matschkus, Sabine – starting in 2010, rode through France, Germany, Lithuania, Poland, Portugal, Russia and Spain.

McCutcheon, John – starting in 1906, rode in Turkestan and Siberia.

McCutcheon, Steve – starting in 2005, rode in India, Pakistan and China.

McGrath, Jeanette and Richard – starting in 2010, rode ocean to ocean across the United States.

Meline, Colonel James – rode from Fort Leavenworth, Kansas to Santa Fe, New Mexico and back in 1866.

Messurier, Colonel Augustus – rode across Persia in 1879.

Meunier, Louis – starting in 2005, rode in Afghanistan and France.

Michaux, André – starting 1789, rode through the eastern portion of the United States.

Mills, Andi – rode across the American Southwest in 2007.

Moryson, Fynes – starting 1517, rode through Germany, Bohemia, Switzerland, Netherlands, Denmark, Poland, Italy, Turkey, France, England, Scotland and Ireland.

Moser, Henri – starting in 1882, rode from St. Petersburg to Tashkent, then rode on to Samarkand, Bukhara and Khiva, made his way to Tehran, crossed the Caucasus Mountains and finally emerged at Istanbul.

Muir Watson, Sharon – rode the length of Australia's Bicentennial National Trail in 1990.

Mullan, Tim – rode in Mongolia in 2013.

Murray, Barry, Barry Jr. Bernadette and Colette – rode the length of the Pacific Crest Trail in 1969.

Nahachewsky, David, Stacia and Teresa – rode across Canada in 2017.

Naysmith, Gordon – starting in 1970, rode across South Africa, Lesotho, Rhodesia, Mozambique, Malawi, Tanzania, Kenya, Ethiopia, Arabia, Jordan, Syria, Greece, Macedonia, Yugoslavia, Hungary and Austria.

Salzmann, Erich von – rode from Tientsin, China to Tashkent, Uzbekistan 1902.
Saupiquet, Isabelle – starting in 2001, rode in France and Europe.
Savage Landor, Henry – starting in 1893, rode in Japan and Tibet.
Schamber, Pat and Linda – rode ocean to ocean across the United States in 1979.
Schoedsack, Ernest – rode across Persia in 1924.
Schoener, Otto – rode from Kashgar, Turkestan to Srinigar, Kashmir in 1938.
Schwarz, Captain Otto – starting in 1946, rode 48,000 kilometres in Europe, North and South America, Iceland, Scotland and Japan.
Schweiger, Robert – rode from Ilinois to Texas in 1976.
Scott, Quincy and Ella – rode from Minnesota to Washington in 1907.
Scott, Robert Falcon – led the Terra Nova equestrian expedition to Antarctica in 1911.
Seney, Robert – starting in 1976, made multiple journeys in the United States.
Shackleton, Sir Ernest – led the Nimrod equestrian expedition in Antarctica in 1907.
Shamsuddin, Hadji – rode across Afghanistan in 2005.
Shaw, Robert – starting in 1868, rode from Ladakh, across the Karakorum Mountains, into Turkestan.
Shoji, Professor Takeshi – rode across Japan in 1984.
Shor, Jean and Frank - rode across the Wakhan Corridor of Afghanistan to Gilgit, Pakistan in 1949.
Sigurdsson, Vigfus – rode across Greenland in 1912.
Singh, Giyan – starting in 1909, rode from Kashmir, north to Gilgit, across the Pamir Mountains, through Turkistan, Mongolia and into Siberia.
Skifter, Gorm - rode across the Arctic Circle and through Lapland, Sweden, Norway and Denmark in 1953.
Skrede, Wilfred – rode across Turkestan and into India in 1941.
Slade, Daniel Denison – rode across New England in 1883.
Smeaton Chase, Joseph – rode from Mexico to Oregon and across the Mojave Desert in 1911.
Smith, Lt. Cornelius – rode from Fort Wingate, Arizona to Fort Sam Houston, Texas in 1895.
Somerset Maugham, William – rode across Spain in 1898.
Southey, Sam – rode in Mongolia in 2013.
Spizzo, Antonietta – starting in 1995, made multiple rides in Europe and Russia.
Spleiss, Chantal – starting in 2003, made multiple rides in Europe.
Stebbing, Edward Percy – rode across Great Britain in 1937.
Stein, Esther – starting in 2003, rode across Lesotho, South Africa, Botswana, Zambia, Tanzania and Kenya.
Stevens, Thomas – rode across Russia in 1890.
Stewart, Lisa - rode through New Mexico, Colorado, Utah, Wyoming, Colorado, Kansas and Missouri in 1982.
Strandberg. Mikael – rode across Patagonia in 2002.
Strong, Anna Louise – rode through the Pamir Mountains and across Tadjikistan in 1928.
Suttle, Gill – rode across Syria in 2005.
Swale Pope, Rosie – rode through Chile in 1984.
Swift, Jonathan – rode across Ireland in 1725.
Sykes, Ella – rode across the Ottoman Empire, Persia and India in 1894.
Szesciorka, Samantha – rode through America's Outback, the desolate desert country of Nevada, in 2016.
Tanner, Diamond Dick – rode from Nebraska to New York and back in 1893.
Thomas, Carine – rode across New Caldenonia in 2001 and along Australia's Bicentennial National Trail in 2004.
Thompson, Catherine – starting in 2008, made multiple journeys across Western Canada.
Thurlow Craig, Charles – starting in 1920, rode across the Gran Chaco Jungle in Paraguay and Brazil.
Tolstoy, Count Ilia - starting in 1942, rode from India, across the Himalayas, through Tibet and into China.
Traver, Matt – rode across Kazakhstan 2013.
Trinkler, Emil – rode across Afghanistan in 1920.
Tschiffely, Aimé – starting in 1925, rode across Argentina, Bolivia, Peru, Ecuador, Columbia, Panama, Costa Rica, Honduras, El Salvador, Guatemala, Mexico and the United States.
Tsutsumi, Hideyo – rode across Japan in 1971.
Tucker, Luke – rode across France and England in 2006.
Tugler, Marie-Emmanuelle – rode across Brazil and Bolivia in 2002.
Turner, Penny – starting in 2004, made multiple rides through Greece.
Ure, Sir John – rode in Chile and Argentina in 1973
Vasconcellos, Raul and Margarita – starting in 1987, rode across the USA, Mexico, Guatemala, Honduras, Nicaragua, Costa Rica, Panama, Peru, Bolivia and Argentina.
Verdaasdonk, Ingrid – rode in Spain and France in 2014.
Vickers, Simon – rode through Brazil in 2001.

Vischer, Sir Hanns – rode across the Sahara Desert, from Tripoli, Tunisia to Lake Chad in 1906.

Vision, DC - starting in 1991, rode from Maine to Florida, across to California, north to Washington and east to Missouri.

Walchuk, Stan - rode from Alberta, Canada into Alaska in 1982.

Wallace, Harold – starting in 1910, rode from Shanghai, China to London, England.

Wamser, Günter – starting in 1994, rode from Patagonia to Alaska.

Waridel, Catherine – rode from the Crimea to Karakorum in Mongolia in 1995.

Watson, Claire Burges – rode from Ulaanbaatar, Mongolia to Samarkand, Uzbekistan in 1999.

Wauters, Robert – made multiple journeys in Europe in the 1990s.

Weale, Magdalene – rode in Great Britain in 1934.

Weeks, Edwin Lord - rode across Turkey and Persia in 1892.

Wegener, Alfred – rode in Greenland in 1912.

Wentworth Day, James – rode in England in 1942.

Westarp, Eberhard von – rode across the Ottoman Empire and Persia in 1913.

White, Iain - rode from Brisbane to Melbourne in Australia in 1982.

Wild, Frank – was a member of the Nimrod equestrian expedition in Antarctica in 1907.

Wilde, Oscar – rode in Greece in 1890.

Wilder, Jim and Janine – made multiple journeys in the United States in the early 2000s.

Wilkins, Mesannie – rode from Maine to California in 1952.

Wilson, Andrew – rode through the Himalaya Mountains from Ladakh to Afghanistan in 1873.

Windt, Harry de – rode across Persia and Baluchistan in 1890.

Winter, Mike – rode in the USA in 2001.

Witz, Marc - rode across Brazil and Bolivia in 2002.

Wonfor, Peter - rode from Chipinge, Zimbabwe to Mbeya, Tanzania in 1990.

Wood , Lisa – rode ocean to ocean across the United States in 1993.

Wood Gee, Vyv and Elsa – rode from John O'Groats, Scotland, to Land's End, Cornwall in 2007.

Wooldridge, Howard – starting in 2002, rode ocean to ocean across the United States, in both directions.

Yamakawa, Kohei – rode across Japan in 2014.

Yavorski, Deb – rode ocean to ocean across the United States in 2011.

Young, Arthur – starting in 1776, rode in Ireland, England and France.

Younghusband, George – rode across Burma in 1887.

Zvansov, Vasili - starting in 1948, rode through Mongolia, Turkestan and Tibet.

Zemuun, Temuujin – rode in Mongolia in 2008.

Index

CuChullaine O'Reilly (left) is an investigative reporter who has spent more than thirty years studying equestrian travel techniques on every continent. After having made lengthy trips by horseback across Pakistan, he was made a Fellow of the Royal Geographical Society and the Explorers' Club.

He wrote *The Horse Travel Handbook*, a field guide that is referred to as "the Long Rider's Bible." O'Reilly is also the author of *Khyber Knights*. This equestrian travel tale has been described as a "masterpiece" and the author as "Jack London in our time".

The author is married to Basha Cornwall-Legh, (right) who rode her Cossack stallion from Volgograd to London. Her book, *Bandits and Bureaucrats*, describes how she became the only person in the twentieth century to ride out of Russia. As director of the Long Riders' Guild Press, Basha has published more than two hundred travel books in five languages. The *Encyclopaedia of Equestrian Exploration* is the most complex project she has ever published.

Because of Basha's skills as a publisher and her knowledge of equestrian travel, Lady Polwarth, heir to the famous Swiss Long Rider Aimé Tschiffely, appointed Basha to be the guardian and executrix of the Tschiffely Literary Estate.

The O'Reillys founded the Long Riders' Guild, the world's first international association of equestrian explorers. Its mission is to protect, preserve and promote the ancient art of equestrian travel. The Guild also reassures the public that they can trust the word of a Long Rider, as being a Member is more than just a matter of miles. It is a question of honour, dignity and behaviour.

There is no fee to become a Member of the LRG: it is an invitation-only organisation, and there are neither advertisements nor cookies on the LRG website.

There are Members in forty-six countries, all of whom have made a qualifying equestrian journey of at least one thousand miles. More than a hundred Long Riders are also Fellows of the Royal Geographical Society, which along with the Guild hosted the first international meeting of equestrian explorers in London.

The Guild, which has supported more than a hundred equestrian expeditions on every continent except Antarctica, also assisted in liberating Long Riders imprisoned in Turkmenistan and India.

The O'Reillys are the webmasters of The Long Riders' Guild website, the repository of the largest collection of equestrian travel information in history. They also maintain the Long Riders' Guild Academic Foundation, an open-source website designed to encourage the growth of an equestrian enlightenment.

As literary archaeologists, the O'Reillys believe there is a need to recognize the human value and historical importance of travel writing, that ancient art which enriches our souls, enlightens our minds and preserves the memory of bygone cultural traditions. This is especially true in terms of equestrian exploration, which has been veiled in mystery and confusion for centuries.

Like all of the books published by the Long Riders' Guild Press, the *Encyclopaedia of Equestrian Exploration* is created using the environmentally friendly "print on demand" system. Unlike traditional publishing methods which print books and then pulp them, causing needless destruction of trees and paper, the LRG Press assures our readers that "not a twig is wasted" and that because every title is printed as and when it is needed, "every Guild book is a wanted book."

The O'Reillys' goal is to create a lasting legacy that will keep equestrian travel alive for posterity and guarantee the transfer of valuable knowledge for generations to come.

9 781590 482940